HIGH CULTURE

SUNY series, Hot Topics: Contemporary Philosophy and Culture

Ron Scapp and Brian Seitz, editors

HIGH CULTURE

Reflections on Addiction and Modernity

edited by

ANNA ALEXANDER
and
MARK S. ROBERTS

STATE UNIVERSITY OF NEW YORK PRESS

Published by
STATE UNIVERSITY OF NEW YORK PRESS, ALBANY

© 2003 State University of New York

For information, address State University of New York Press,
90 State Street, Suite 700, Albany, NY 12207

Production by Marilyn P. Semerad
Marketing by Fran Keneston

Library of Congress Cataloging-in-Publication Data

High culture : reflections on addiction and modernity / edited by Anna Alexander and
Mark S. Roberts.
    p. cm. — (SUNY series, hot topics)
Includes bibliographical references and index.
ISBN 0-7914-5553-X (alk. paper) — ISBN 0-7914-5554-8 (pbk. : alk. paper)
    1. Substance abuse. 2. Creative ability. 3. Inspiration. 4. Civilization, Modern. I.
Alexander, Anna, 1956– II. Roberts, Mark S. III. Series.

HV4998 .H544 2002
394.1'4—dc21

                                                                          2002029181

10   9   8   7   6   5   4   3   2   1

When he wanted to formulate the task of a philosophy yet to come, Friedrich Nietzsche committed this thought to writing: "Who will ever relate the whole history of narcotica?—It is almost the history of 'culture,' of our so called high culture". . . . Our work settles with this Nietzschean "almost"—the place where *narcotics* articulates a quiver between history and ontology.

Addiction will be our question: a certain type of "Being-on-drugs" that has everything to do with the bad conscience of our era.

—Avital Ronell, *Crack Wars*

CONTENTS

Acknowledgments

This collection of essays continues a critical theoretical discussion of addiction that includes a 1993 issue of the journal *differences,* Richard Klein's *Cigarettes are Sublime,* Avital Ronell's *Crack Wars,* a conference on Addiction and Culture held in 1997 at Claremont Graduate School, and numerous essays and interviews by Eve Sedgwick, Jacques Derrida, Félix Guattari, and others. Conceived in a mode of "high" philosophical and ethico-political experimentation, it raises fundamental questions about subjectivity, ontology, and desire, as well as political/ideological issues of representation, identification, and control.

The book has benefited from panel presentations at diverse conferences, many of which have been in the field of Continental Philosophy. Specific pieces, as well as some of the larger themes subtending this collection, have been tried out at a number of panels on addiction and presented at various academic conferences since 1995. These include: The International Association for Philosophy and Literature "Virtual Incorporations: Textual Spaces," Villanova University, PA, May 1995; The Society for Phenomenology and Existential Philosophy, University of Georgetown, Washington, DC, October, 1996, for scheduling our disappearing panel on "Psychotropic Writing: Language, Subjectivity, and Addiction"; Addiction and Culture Conference at the Claremont Graduate Humanities Center, Claremont, CA, February 29-March 2, 1996; The Association for the Psychoanalysis of Culture and Society, The George Washington University, Washington, DC, November 1996; The Canadian Society for Hermeneutics and Postmodern Thought, University of Ottawa, ON, May 1996, The Canadian Society for Hermeneutics and Postmodern Thought, Brock University, St. Catherine's, ON, May 1998; The Radical Philosophy Association, Social Scholars' Conference, Borough of Manhattan Community College, New York, NY, March 1998.

We are especially grateful to Jacques Derrida for his kind permission to reprint his "The Rhetoric of Drugs: An Interview." It has been this central, comprehensive essay by Derrida which, for all intents and purposes, indicates the direction of this volume. This interview with *Autrement* originally appeared as "La rhétorique de la drogue," in a special issue of *Autrement* 106 (1989), "L'Esprit des drogues," edited by Jean-Michel Hervieu. It was translated by Michael Israel for *differences: A Journal of Feminist Cultural Studies: On Addiction,* 5.1 (Spring 1993): 1-25. The interview also appeared in *Points de suspension: Entretiens* (Paris: Galilée, 1992); Michael Israel's translation was first published in *1-800* 2 (1991).

Innovators in the field of rhetoric and addiction, Derrida and Ronell have continued to write about theories of intoxication and dependency. In a recent work presented at New York University in 2001, Derrida offered his interpretation of some of the key aspects of Ronell's work on addiction, linking the fate of the hospital to the addicted body that emerges in Ronell's "pathbreaking reflections" ("Substitution: la drogue, l'hôpital, l'hospitalité"). We wish to acknowledge the lexicon and trajectory of Ronell's 1992 *Crack Wars* reflected in several of the contributions. Ronell has not only facilitated the English translation of Derrida's "Rhétorique," she also extended it to produce an important theoretical site for addiction studies in America.

The editors would also like to acknowledge the permission of the following publishers to reprint material that has appeared elsewhere: Éditions Recherches for their permission to translate and reprint Félix Guattari's "Socially Significant Drugs," in *La révolution moléculaire* (Paris: 1997); originally published by Union Générale, 10/18 (Paris: 1977); Éditions *Autrement* for their permission to reprint Félix Guarrari's "Une révolution moléculaire: An Interview" with *Autrement,* which originally appeared in a special issue of *Autrement* 106, "L'Esprit des drogues," edited by Jean-Michel Hervieu (avril 1989): 18-20; John Hopkins University Press for their permission to reprint Elissa Marder's "Trauma, Addiction, and Temporal Bulimia in *Madame Bovary,*" in *Diacritics* 27.3 (1997): 49-64; and David L. Clark's "Heidegger's Craving: Being-on-Schelling," in *Diacritics* 27.3 (1997): 8-33; Rowman and Littlefield for their permission to reprint Bruce Wilshire's "Possession, Addiction, Fragmentation: Is a Healing Community Possible?" in *Wild Hunger: The Primal Roots of Modern Addiction* (Lanham, MD: 1998); Duke University Press for their permission to reprint Jeffrey Nealon's "'Junk' and the Other: Burroughs and Levinas on Drugs," in *Alterity Politics: Ethics and Performative Subjectivity* (Durham: 1998); Cambridge University Press for their permission to reprint Jon Elster's "Gambling and Addiction," in *Getting Hooked: Rationality and Addiction* (New York: 1999); Fernwood Books for permission to reprint selections from Lorraine Greaves' *Smoke Screen: Women's Smoking and Social Control* (Halifax: 1996).

We personally thank Marc Redfield who organized the Claremont conference on Addiction and Culture. The book owes five of its contributions to the Addiction and Culture conference organized by Marc Redfield, where they were presented as papers. The contributors Alina Clej, David Clark, John Fitzgerald, Elissa Marder, and Gary Shapiro presented their essays as papers at this conference, giving us the opportunity to engage with their contributions and begin organizing the ideas for this book along the lines of culture. We also acknowledge the following authors for their kind permission to publish original material: Anna Alexander, David B. Allison, Alina Clej, John Fitzgerald, Lorraine Greaves, Alphonso Lingis, Zvi Lothane, Mark S. Roberts, Gary Shapiro, Allen S. Weiss.

Very special thanks to Alina Clej without whose early collaboration and support this project would not have been undertaken. Thanks also to David Allison and Gary Shapiro for ongoing contributions, enthusiasm and support; we thank Babette Babich, Tim Murphy, Michael Dorland for their insightful comments and suggestions; John Carvalho and Hugh Silverman for supporting the project at IAPL in its early stages; Debra Bergoffen and Dorothea Olkowski at SPEP; and Jeff Mitscherling for his support at the CSH. We wish to thank Ron Scapp and Brian Seitz for their opening on philosophical perspectives on culture at SUNY and Marilyn Semerad for production. Carol Mitchell and Amy Vincent at the Simone de Beauvoir Institute have provided indispensable research assistance and John Antonopoulos precious proofreading of selected texts. Finally, we express our thanks to the kids—Chris, Iris, and Keif—for their being there.

We acknowledge the following organizations for their financial assistance in exploring and realizing the ideas that formed the backdrop for this project: CUPFA Professional Development Funds, Concordia University; McGill Center for Research and Teaching on Women, McGill University; Fonds de Développement Pédagogique of the Université du Québec à Montréal; Explorations Program of the Canada Council.

Introduction

ANNA ALEXANDER AND MARK S. ROBERTS

Who will ever relate the whole history of narcotica? . . . It is almost the history of "culture," of our so-called high culture.

—Friedrich Nietzsche, *The Gay Science,* §86

HISTORY OF NARCOTICA

Narcotica have always had an intimate connection with human reality. Desires exist that are not confined to the bare necessities of life and whose objects are more than "a palette of substances."[1]

The euphoriant and narcotizing effects of agents of no directly nutritive value have been recorded from the very beginning of our history, in literate and pre-literate cultures, in the East as well as the West. Western culture—the *Bible* and heroic myths, Orphic cults and mysteries, as well as the history of testimonial writing—contains numerous references to these substances taken solely for the purpose of their mind-altering properties. Their potential energy has conquered the earth and established communication between various peoples and races, in spite of dividing mountains and surrounding seas. These substances have filtered pathways between peoples of different worlds, from the tribal to the modern and have, moreover, opened passages that proved of use for many other purposes.

According to Louis Lewin's classic 1931 survey of the use of mind-altering plants—*Phantastica*—the discovery of the properties and uses of narcotic and stimulating drugs marks the beginning of culture in its primeval stage. He writes:

If it can be taken as a *symptom of civilization* when men's desires, hitherto exclusively confined to the bare necessities of life, pass beyond these
limits, and the individual, no longer satisfied with the crude sustenance
afforded by or wrested from nature, finds and delights in stimulants
which mainly affect the central nervous system, then a suitable background for such cravings must form part of the human constitution.[2]

Although the use of narcotica implies in and of itself a certain degree
of observation, it is not until the middle of the nineteenth century that
we begin to isolate the social-scientific problematic of addiction "itself."
Loaded with ethical value, modernity's isolation of the phenomenon of
addiction marks a radical break from the past, "a revolution in consciousness."[3] This occurred when narcotica—cocaine, morphine,
codeine, opium—became increasingly available in the consumer phase
of international capitalism and were introduced into medical science.
The taxonomic pressures of scientific method witnessed the rise of a
newly pathologized, and later criminalized, subject of drugs: "questions
of acts crystalized into questions of identities and the drug-user became
a drug addict."[4]

In this extended paradigm of addiction, the "abstract space where
substances and behaviors become 'addictive' or 'not addictive'"[5] is *the
space of the body* itself. Unlike the space of inert material or biological
existence—a space outside of history, culture, and sociopolitical life—
the nature of the addicted body, under this definition of addiction
"resides only in the *structure* of a will that is always somehow insufficiently free, a choice whose volition is insufficiently pure."[6]

The further extension of "addiction–attribution" to a wide variety
of drugs over the first two-thirds of the twentieth century is a development that quite explicitly brings not only every form of substance ingestion, but also more simply every form of human state and/or behavior
into its orbit. In this high culture of modernity, any substance, any
behavior, even any affect, may be pathologized as addictive.[7]

ADDICTION AND MODERNITY

A few years ago, the U.S. media reported a remarkable breakthrough in
the War on Drugs: a home drug detection kit, fully sanctioned by the
U.S. FDA, that works more efficiently than any other previous kit. This
fantastic little device consists of a selection of litmus tabs that can be
dipped into a child's urine samples and which could, with uncanny accuracy and speed, detect illicit drugs like marijuana, hashish, cocaine,
crack-cocaine, heroin and even an array of exotic "natural" substances.

Only drawbacks: the final results have to be confirmed by an outside laboratory, and you have to get your kid to piss in a flask.

We open this collection of essays on cultural views of addiction and modernity with this "breakthrough" news flash because it symbolizes perfectly the punitive, prescriptive direction that the majority of societal and institutional views of drugs and addiction has taken.

Most of the modern research into addiction and addictive practices has been shaped strictly by the disciplinary rhetorics of medicine, criminology, politics, and social psychology and psychiatry. Hence, the majority of studies and debates on the subject—though in many instances, substantial—has focused largely on the practiced, systematic control of addictive substances and their users. The modern referent of addiction, then, is a necessarily pejorative one: addiction is a socially deviant, unacceptable behavior that must, in virtually all respects, be feared, ferreted out, and contained. And the addict, as the subject of his or her addictions, tends to become largely vilified and eclipsed.

But, as we demonstrate here, the complexity, creative value, and diversity of addiction considerably surpasses this rather limited disciplinary view of its limitations. When seen from a broad cultural perspective, addiction emerges directly alongside modernity, haunting the various discourses of digression, dissent, and the transcendence of the commonplace so often associated with the modern era. Who could even imagine the advent of modern literature without the addictive, visionary excesses of writers like Baudelaire, Rimbaud, De Quincey, Poe, Burroughs, Ginsberg, or Artaud; or, for that matter, modern culture without its perennial outsiders, its incorrigible addicts, its defaced subjects: the smokers, tokers, overeaters, the alcoholics, the insane and "eccentric," and so on?

HIGH CULTURE

High Culture is a collection of chapters on precisely these socially marginalized addictive practices and discourses so central to modernity. It is the first comprehensive text to address addiction with its multiple effects on and extensions into art, literature, philosophy, psychology, and the field of culture in general. Indeed, culture, viewed from this modern perspective, is a remarkably complex process; it can be seen as a way of life, an instrument of expression, and as a literary and artistic tradition. Moreover, culture is always shaped by language and by language's multiple and various discursivities. And these discursive language formations are particularly important with regard to the study of addiction. For, viewed from the discursive perspective, addiction can no longer be treated fully in terms of a concrete substance or system to which the subject is uncontrollably drawn, but rather must also be seen as an aleatory operation akin to that of language production itself.

The culture of addiction is precisely a self-constituting and self-evacuating world that absorbs the complete and complex notion of "culture." It is also a culture whose value for potentially shedding new light on the very notion of modernity is absorbed and reflected by this volume. In the context of addiction and modernity, "culture" emerges as a kind of hinge or *threshold concept*: it is to be found somewhere between a psychic or lived interiority manifested in the subjective experience of the addict's altered states of consciousness and a more medical and sociopolitical exteriority, that is, the context of addiction and addiction attribution, which in turn constitutes the background of the subject's experience of interiority.

If we speak of addiction as though it stood for a clearly defined reality, at the end, a paradox and an enigma. The difficulty in our modern lexicon is that one can adopt neither a nominalist nor a conceptualist view of addiction. Although addiction is traditionally seen as something that happens with the incorporation of a foreign substance, it cannot possibly be confined to a concept or notion of addiction as substance use/abuse itself. Rather it involves an experimental field that is both dependent and independent of the world, the substance, the plant, the chemical, and the prosthesis. It is this field we have named "addiction." Thus, the works collected here belong to a language of (by and about) drugs that ranges from the literary to the scientific, the intimately personal to the generally collective, and that spans more than a century of often scandalous, often electrifying, discourses on the subject of addiction.

Divided into two parts that deal separately with the inner (literature, philosophy, and the arts) and the outer (sociology, psychology, and media) worlds of addiction, the text also challenges the division, by emphasizing the fact that drugs "are animated by an outside already inside."[8] Both parts will therefore utilize the inner and outer worlds. The division is, moreover, useful when following a disciplinary path along this fully interdisciplinary network of pathways through what Derrida terms our "narcotic modernity."

The text, moreover, combines a high level of theoretical competence across both of its parts: Philosophical and Literary Reflections on Addiction and Sociocultural and Psychological Reflections on Addiction. To enhance the value of the collection, these parts can be further broken down. Contributions from several authors in Part II could, therefore, be categorized as philosophical (e.g., Guattari, Alexander, Lingis, Wilshire, and Elster), while contributions listed in Part I profit from a distinction between philosophical reflections (e.g., Derrida, Allison, Shapiro, and Clark) and, because they are so utterly nonidentical, literary reflections (e.g., Weiss, Clej, Marder, and Nealon).

PART I

In the first part of the book, Philosophical and Literary Reflections on Addiction, each one of the chapters points to a body of literature arising in tandem with modernity. Here the subject and act of addiction are addressed through aesthetic, philosophical, and literary universes of discourse. In these diverse reflections, culture, literature, language, art, and critical theory displace the traditional opprobrium and exteriorization so often associated with addiction and its subjects.

The entire work, then, is indebted profoundly to the opening piece by Jacques Derrida, "The Rhetoric of Drugs." Going beyond the recognition of addiction as the disease of modernity, he shows us the birth of a "narcotic modernity" as a cultural formation shaped by drugs, a formation in which the themes of language, culture, and text are intimately bound. He thus takes addiction out of the metaphysics of substance and places it squarely within the prescriptive domain of a high culture that emerged at about the same time as the academic and scholarly institution of "literature." Here, the now famous—or infamous—"il n'y a pas de hors texte" becomes transformed into the equally challenging "il n'y a pas de drogues dans la nature." This journey through the rhetoric of drugs traverses the legal, medical, philosophical, and literary traditions, opening the gateway to the cultural appreciation of the subject of drugs. In the course of the journey, Derrida is particularly careful to "deconstruct" the old "saws" about addiction and its subjects: the plight of the addict (mother, brother, and child), the War on Drugs, and America itself are all exposed to his non-partisan and non-reprobationary point of view.

Without slavishly following Derrida, David B. Allison's "Nietzsche's Dionysian High: Morphin' with Endorphins" focuses on the subject's transitive position in addiction. Reading subjectively induced simulacra through the Dionysian high created by the trances of wine and music, Allison engages addiction as a subject outside itself. His chapter links the postmodern state of the absence of referentiality found in language to the exteriority of the ek-static subject of drugs and trance. Through his careful analysis of this notion of ecstasis as both a surpassing and a coming together, Allison posits addiction as a point at which the subject may transcend his or her limitations, a threshold state that conjures terms other than dependency and abuse. In "Allison's pharmacy," addiction does not devolve into a rhetoric of negative effects or medical implications. Rather, we begin to see it as a subjective force, as an active willing and desire. Working with the notion of a "trigger" instead of a substance, he is able to address addiction as a process, an operation that functions in ways comparable to the operations of language and literature. In the end, a new autonomy of the individual arises, carved out of self-modification and the will to power. Read alongside Derrida, Allison's chapter makes sense of a "high culture" that belongs to the narcotic as much as to the literary tradition of the West.

Unlike the literary tradition, however, this narcotic tradition has remained in the shadows, buried, at the margins of western intellectual practice and respectability. One thus learned about this nether tradition either by stumbling over a peripheral text by Cocteau, Michaux, or, perhaps, Zola on drug use, or, more directly, by using drugs. It is clearly the latter that inspired the noted literary critic and theorist Walter Benjamin, who wandered through the great cities of France in what he himself characterized as a deeply poetic, "experimental," drug-induced state. It is Benjamin's reflections on this experience, collected in his *Über Haschisch* and elsewhere in fragments, that has inspired Gary Shapiro's "Ariadne's Thread: Walter Benjamin's Hashish Passages." Shapiro's work centers on the theme that there is no passage out without an equally forced passage in. The terms "in" and "out," though, are not borrowed from a narcotic vocabulary but from that of the actual act of writing. Benjamin, according to Shapiro, is thus, ultimately, addicted to writing, which for Benjamin becomes a kind of switching metaphor for addictive experience in general. Indeed, the "passages" of Shapiro's title—apart from their metaphoric meanings—refer precisely to those literal passages in Benjamin's writing that posit a deep affinity between all writing and the hashish or psychotropic writing. This sort of writing, Shapiro argues, is mediated by the image of Ariadne's thread. The writer, under the lure of the narcotic state, is able to "unravel" his or her deepest imaginings: "one is unrolling something that is already there, one's own thoughts, one's language, one's style." Moreover, the intensification of artistic vision and perception in the drug-induced state leads one to focus on the very contours, the specific character of spaces, within the architecture of the city. And it is precisely this collection of perceived spaces, of passages, both literal and metaphoric, that, for Shapiro, ultimately carves out the space of writing.

Walter Benjamin also figures prominently in Alina Clej's "Profane Hallucinations: From *The Arcades Project* to the Surrealists." But here we see a somewhat different approach. Rather than centering on his obsessive immersion in writing itself, Clej focuses on Benjamin's fascination with mental imagery, particularly with the imagery associated with surrealism. Benjamin was initially drawn to surrealism because it offered a means of delivering images that carried a "poetic kernel of reality itself." This move corresponded to his intense desire to save the prestige of personal experience, to avoid what the Surrealists termed "the poverty of reality." It allowed him to enter the unconscious domain and to experience an intoxication that offers a chance for the total transformation of the self. And Benjamin understood this transformation in very complex terms—that is, as a fruitful living experience that allowed one to step outside the domain of intoxication. Later in the text, Clej draws parallels between Benjamin's conception of unconscious mental imagery and André Breton's poetics. Breton saw surrealism as an addictive practice, a new vice that he compares to Baudelaire's "artificial paradise." This claim was based on the idea that surrealism works on the mind very much as drugs do; like drugs, it creates a frightful state of need, a longing to free mental expression from the confines of bourgeois life. And, Clej argues, it was precisely these intoxicating powers of the surrealist imagination that drew Benjamin to the movement and "offered him a justification and a space for deploying his own phantasms of identity."

David Clark's interpretation of Heidegger's reading of Schelling, "Heidegger's Craving," turns on the question of understanding an uncanny, age-old propensity for dependence. Effectively, this is an addiction without drugs, a metaphysical craving where dependency meets Dasein and falls into thrown-ness once again. Only now, there is no way back. Constant craving rules in this language of an existential phenomenology of transport—a state in which language is not only the vehicle of meaning but also the subject of meaning itself, a subject that craves, desires, imagines, much like the subject haunting Descartes's cogito. In short, Clark traces meticulously Heidegger's fascination with Schelling's entire concept of the uncanny, what represents "unreason," arguing, in the end, that Heidegger's fascination is itself an instant of uncanny craving, of an addiction to the "arbitrary violence of the human appropriation of language and longing."

The peculiar blend of states evinced in Heidegger's multiple readings of Schelling is also evident in the awesome fluctuation from the high of drugs to the low of drugs expressed in the vertiginous, oscillating world of *Madame Bovary*. Capturing the nonsensical quality of Emma's impossible sense of time, Elissa Marder traces the effects of drugs and addiction on the feminine condition itself. *Madame Bovary* stands supreme as the arch-Madame of feminine boredom, passivity, and that narcissistic withdrawal that belongs so much to our contemporary era. Effectively, Emma's addiction is set alongside her fundamental trauma. Marder argues that both bear similarities, in that the former slips away from the inassimilable event while the latter evades it. Thus Flaubert's Emma, trapped in time but unable to assimilate the past, is, Marder argues, one of the earliest expressions of narcotic modernity: "Flaubert announces a temporal structure of addiction that exceeds the confines of the nineteenth century and seeps into the experience of modern life."

Such avante-garde gains, however, are not made without their pains. In Allen S. Weiss's chapter on Baudelaire and Artaud, we see clearly both the exultation and the anguish and distress that attends the precious narcotic tools offered by modernity. If narcotics can open the gateways of the artistic unconscious and unlock the treasures of creativity, they can also plunge their users into a hideous abyss of pain and misery, death, and shock, both electric and electrifying. Here we see a fascinating apposition between the narcotic positivities of Baudelaire and his tradition and the oppressive, painful effects of "the electric drug" on Artaud. Enmeshed in the Romantic tradition of the nineteenth century, Baudelaire used drugs and stimulants as a kind of stagecraft, as a way of "confusing the senses," so as to interiorize all aesthetic experience. Having accomplished this, he could declare the imagination as the sole source of representation, of inspiration, indeed, even as a kind of autonomous mental perception. In fact, the imagination, sequestered from reason and ordinary perception by the narcotic haze, served to form Baudelaire's "artificial paradise." Not so for Artaud. His voyage inward would not terminate in some crafted "artificial paradise." Instead, the "extreme corporeal desublimation manifested in his writings and his psychopathology" would effectively culminate in an aesthetics of pain and delirium. This would, in turn, Weiss argues, lead to an "implosion of the sublime" that created immense fragmentation and heterogeneity in Artaud's *Gesamtkunswerk*—a condition that revealed "a torment so intense that no intoxication would suffice as a cure."

Jeffrey T. Nealon's "Junk and the Other: Burroughs and Levinas on Drugs" is an extended comparison of two very different types of alterity. He argues that "junk" affects the Other in remarkable ways, giving Levinas's ethics of alterity a new and unexpected twist. The other of junk is not just the other as subject, but the other as a drug that enters *into* the subject, infesting it with an alterity that must be reckoned with differently. As Nealon stresses, "Just Say No!" just doesn't cut it any more. Rather, he urges us to think about how "the logics of intoxication," as well as the kinds of desire one can read in the spaces of addiction, are inexorably tied with current critical vocabularies of alterity and identity. Moving away from thematizing addiction as an "inexorable lack," Nealon borrows from the work of Burroughs and Levinas to come up with a new formula: "Junk," he writes, "opens onto an unrecoverable exteriority beyond need," since intoxication or drug addiction brings to the subject not only "the disappearance of the world," but also the terrifying chaos of what Levinas calls the *il y a* ("there is")—a radical givenness without direction. This absorption by a "depersonalized realm of pure materiality" is precisely the "metaphysical" craving at play in the face-to-face encounter with the other, and, in Nealon's account, "cannot be confused with a simple need." Modernity's revelation of a "total need," a need beyond any possible satisfaction, inaugurates the emergence of something other than "a need that could be serviced by a person, object, or substance addiction." As Burroughs proclaimed: "junk is a way of life."

PART II

The second part of the book, Socio-cultural and Psychological Reflections on Addiction, contains a group of chapters centered largely on the psychosocial extensions of addiction and addictive behavior. It is, however, by no means oriented to what might be considered the standard forms of interpretation and analysis of these sorts of behaviors and discourses. In fact, most of the chapters extend widely and wildly beyond the rather narrow clinical and statistical methods of the more common sorts of psychosocial approaches to addiction—while at the same time revealing the possibility of reflecting constructively on appropriate treatments for and approaches to addiction in general. This extensive and inclusive view corresponds, of course, to the first part of the text, which is designed to provide the reader with a strong sense of the centrality and diversity of addiction and addictive visions within modern philosophy, art, and literature.

This section on the psychosocial dimension of addiction opens, appropriately, with an important set of interviews with the noted psychoanalyst and social theorist Félix Guattari. Published about five years after his collaboration with Gilles Deleuze on *Anti-Oedipus*, "Socially Significant Drugs" first appeared in the collection *La révolution moléculaire* (1977). As is the intent in virtually all his work, Guattari here tries to situate drugs within their social context, that is, in terms of the specific ways in which drugs become subject to socioeconomic forces. He begins by making the distinction between hard and soft drugs. This, in turn, leads to the general claim that hard drugs are treated in a radically different way than other "drug-like" substances, including alcohol. The difference consists in that hard drugs invoke a profound, metaphorical sense of darkness and despair, of catastrophe, and thus constitute the other of traditional cultural drug use, that is, as medicinal remedies or as spiritual guides. Indeed, hard drugs are always associated with exploitation, with the criminalization of certain individuals within society. In fact, Guattari goes so far as to compare hard drug use to psychosis but finds drug use even more susceptible to social opprobrium, in that mad people can be excused as being mad, while drug addicts are seen as having only themselves to blame. The solution, Guattari argues, lies in the broad decriminalization of hard drugs, which, he suspects, will eventually bring them into line with other controlled substances. Guattari further fleshes out this solution in a newly translated interview, appended to the main text.

Reassessing addiction's place within modernist and postmodernist discourse, Anna Alexander's "Freud's Pharmacy: Cocaine and the Corporeal Unconscious" draws upon a variety of heuristic contexts, including those of deconstruction, cultural studies, feminism and early psychopharmacology, with a particular emphasis on Deleuze and Guattari's critique of conventional psychoanalysis. Her general claim is that, due largely to the psychoanalytically derived perspective that divides the individual into inner and outer, addiction has been viewed in a simplistic and reductionist way. It is merely adduced as the result of some hidden, inner dimension. But this view, as Deleuze and Guattari argue, remains singularly unconcerned with some of the most important factors involved in addiction: gender, context, social inscription, and the possibility of social change. To counter this "monistic" view of addiction, the author proposes a much more extensive and inclusive one, which, she argues, is broached in the so-called Cocaine Papers, published by Freud, intermittently, between 1884 and 1895. In these remarkable essays, Freud advances nothing less than a nascent theory of narcotic desire—one that reveals the ontological structures of addiction in ways that are entirely necessary to the understanding of the very meaning of drugs and to adequate treatments that might follow. The remainder of Alexander's chapter delves into the subtle connection between drugs, addiction and the passage into a new kind of "addictive subject," one who, freed from the inner–outer myth, may now explore fully the extremes of personal liberation and autonomy.

In his "Schreber's Ecstacies," Zvi Lothane stresses the until now little-known importance of Daniel Paul Schreber as a visionary. Schreber is often referred to in the psychoanalytic literature as the most famous mental patient of all time. This appellation evolved due to the tremendous influence his *Memoirs of My Nervous Illness* (1903) has exerted on the psychoanalytic tradition. Effectively, there has been a running controversy over his legal status, mental condition, pathologies, influence, etc. since his death in 1911. Lothane, who has added significantly to this debate in his definitive study, *In Defense of Schreber* (1992), now argues that Schreber's so-called hallucinations and delusions were in reality ecstatic visions, comparable to those of the great mystics. He traces the historical development and conditions of these particular visions, arguing that they were rooted in the basic mechanisms of virtually all ecstatic visions: a free sexuality and the direct experience of deity. To this end, Lothane suggests that Schreber may have also anticipated what Aldous Huxley had later referred to as "the doors of perception." Lothane continues to build a general theory of ecstasy, concluding that one might consider ecstasy and intoxication, induced by a number of techniques, including fasting and drugs, as the common denominator of human experience, as a means of encountering "visions, revelations, miracles, prophesies, and the like"—a theory invoking the ghostly presence—a vision, perhaps—of the great psychologist, William James.

Lorraine Greaves's "Smoke Screen: The Cultural Meaning of Women's Smoking" deals with anything but the miraculous and visionary. She takes a hard look at the changes in the social and historical positions of women as expressed in the history of twentieth-century cigarette ad campaigns. Greaves proposes that the ads reflect a slippage from freedom and independence to a discourse of dependency that has left women in tragic and highly contradictory positions. Analyzing the rift between societal expectations of women and their actual needs, Greaves reveals the contradictory messages conveyed to women about their addictions by medical, legal, educational, and therapeutic institutions. In doing so, she also offers a glimpse at the contradictory ways in which women are compelled to counter such messages. The chapter explains the experiences of women within the boundaries of a social control that not only extends to women's practices of smoking (and to their addiction), but also to the vicissitudes of fulfilling their obligations as women to the values of society and culture, that is, values of family and nurturance that run counter to women's need for self-protection, self-medication, and self care.

In a spectacular, physically and emotionally moving literary dialogue, Alphonso Lingis' "Love Junkies" challenges his readers to enter the grim world of two real-life Australian prisoners who, on the surface, seem to exist under the most harsh and demeaning conditions possible. Cheryl, a transvestite, and Wayne, her lover, are both long-time junkies, suffer from HIV/AIDS, and, of course, live within the brutal confines, the "cubicles, partitions, walls and fences" of Long Bay Goal. But despite the physical limitations of their everyday existence, Lingis exposes the deeply moving and poetic nature of their respective characters and their loving, caring relationship. Combining Nietzschean affirmation and Heideggerian being-toward-death (see *Deathbound Subjectivity* [1989]) with his recently developed ideas of cosmic chance, transformation, and reciprocal death, Lingis makes the point that these two junkie lovers are not simply jailhouse deviants, but came together as the result of a remarkable twist of cosmic fate, of the astronomical number of possible combinations of DNA spiraling in their parents' genetic signatures. Within this lovers' dialogue, the easy, simple, child-like faith and desire of two ordinary yet extraordinay people emerges poignantly. Knowing fully their restrictions, their impending suffering and death (Wayne has full-blown AIDS and bowel cancer), they wish only to share their lives and care for one another: "How lucky I have been! How lucky to have met Wayne. How lucky not to die alone, like the other transvestites." This, even to the extent of Cheryl committing a robbery only hours after she was released, so as to return to Wayne's side.

Bruce Wilshire's "Possession, Addiction, Fragmentation: Is a Healing Community Possible?" treats the question of addiction from the perspective of the experiencing (and literary) subject—a position he is eminently familiar with due to his long-time involvement with existential and phenomenological philosophy and the empirical philosophies of John Dewey and William James. The essay opens with a reflection on the author's own experience of the natural world. Then, the questions are asked: what is it precisely that experiences the natural world? Is "I" equal to "I?" Ego, to Ego? The answers involve consideration of the position of the body vis-à-vis the question of self. In this regard, Wilshire argues, the self can be reduced to a body—a personal space of "dark inner cavities," of "fluids," and "subvocal speech." Thus addiction, seen from this perspective, is precisely the inablility to trust the world, to respect the integrity of the inner self, of our body–selves. But how, given this distrust, can the addictive individual become part of the ongoing regenerative world? Precisely through ritual, through the embrace of myth, and the power of myth. While Wilshire seems to depend on binary thinking in his vision of a "healing community," this would be a naive reading of his position. On the contrary, his eco-phenomenological argument challenges, from the ground up, the modern obsession with the cure, the fix, indeed the "end" of addiction. And it is this embrace of myth and ritual that helps to integrate addictions into the "wilderness" of life itself. Wilshire thus argues against purely physiological theories of brain chemistry and addictive behavior, claiming, along with Dewey and

James, that such limited theories overlook the whole reality of human experience, the "brain-in-body-in-enviroment." What the answer to addictive behavior really requires, then, is a study of the whole individual, immersed in the world of his or her total experience.

Jon Elster begins his chapter, "Gambling and Addiction," with some crucial questions: (1) How does one explain gambling addiction? (2) Is compulsive gambling actually an addiction? The first question is initially approached through a critical evaluation of the rather large body of literature on the subject. The subsequent evaluation centers on the ways in which gambling addiction is viewed. Gambling addiction or compulsive gambling should not, Elster argues, be confused with other forms of self-sustaining activity. Alcoholism or overeating, for example, do not have the same causal mechanisms as those involved in gambling in order to earn money to pay off gambling debts. The alcoholic may drink to cover the fact that he or she is an alcoholic, but in the case of gambling, the gambler is actually involved in a process of escape. The nature of the actual process of gambling is further explored in subsequent sections. Of particular interest is the section dealing with "The Phenomenology of Gambling." Here, Elster draws a detailed picture of what it is like to be a gambler. Once again, a contrast between other types of addiction and gambling addiction is drawn. What seems facinating about the gambler is the question of risk. In alcohol, food, and nicotine, there is a pleasurable payback, and these sort of addictions can be understood, at least in part, introspectively. But risk, to most people, is not a pleasant experience. Indeed, most people are fearful of risk. The phenomenology then, is focused largely on the various temporal internal phenomena that contribute to compulsive gambling behaviors: craving, tolerance, withdrawal, and problems of self-control. In sum, Elster proposes that compulsive gambling is not a singular phenomenon, brought on exclusively by some psychological need or quirk. Rather, it is something that evolves over time, playing itself out in four primary stages. Effectively, it is the absorption of the gambler into a gambling environment, one which eggs him or her on, that sets the act into motion. And, according to Elster, the study of compulsive gambling must center on the irrational belief formation effected in this exchange between the gambler and the environment. As for the question of whether compulsive gambling is an addiction, Elster defers to the neurophysiology of addiction, which, he suggests, has not yet developed ways of accurately measuring neuroadaptation in compulsive gamblers.

The question of a totalizing environment and its relation to addiction is addressed in Mark S. Roberts's "Addicts without Drugs: The Media Addiction." But the addiction here is radically different from those expressed anywhere else in this volume. Employing modern media theory, particularly that of Marshall McLuhan, Jean Baudrillard, and Paul Virilio, the author proposes that the information age has created a new brand of addict, one who quite directly "acts out," monitors what he or she experiences in the media, particularly television. This acting out, however, does not follow the standard addictive patterns. It is not primarily the result of childhood trauma, of hatred, frustration, craving, anger, or perverse desire. Nor does it maintain the traditional subject–object relation of most classical poetic and aesthetic theory. Rather, it consists of an irresistible need to directly enter, merge with, and appropriate the hyperreal space created by information technology, to make life conform to the blinding speed of electronic media. And it is precisely this craving, the author suggests, that drove the likes of Luigi Ferri to slaughter eight people in a San Francisco law firm as a failed means of telling his story on a major talk show (after his suicide, a list of major television talk shows was found in his briefcase). Or, which led a recent grisly suicide on a Los Angeles freeway to first unfurl an enormous banner, specifying his grievances, for the television news helicopters.

The final contribution, John Fitzgerald's "The Drug Addict in Absentia: Hidden Populations of Illicit Drug Users and the Gaze of Power," also addresses the question of technology—more precisely, technological strategies—in its relation to drug addiction. What fascinates Fitzgerald in this work is how illicit drug users are made visible by public health organizations. His general approach borrows from a broad range of postmodern, poststructural, and deconstructive methods, particularly Michel Foucault's idea of the "gaze of power" as it relates to scopic technologies. Using a Melbourne youth rave as the model for hidden drug use populations, Fitzgerald lays out a series of questions as to what it is to be seen by the gaze of power (i.e., counted) and, conversely, to be absent from it. In doing so, he reveals the various rhetorical strategies used to make these populations "visible," concluding, in the end, that many of these strategies fail because they do not address the real problems of hidden populations but are merely extensions of the discourse of power that has put them into play. The final portion of the chapter is especially interesting, in that it involves some of the counterstrategies, ways of resisting being seen and counted, employed by the rave population. This resistance even extends to the language and imagery of their posters and advertising materials.

PHILOSOPHY YET TO COME

In the end, addiction will emerge from these chapters as an operation (akin to language production) which is not reducible to substance abuse or compulsiveness per se. We thus hope to document addiction as the ecstatic and psychotropic eruption of the subject of drugs into language and culture, weaving its way through the corridors of modern life, much in the way Benjamin's "hashish passages" meandered through the streets of Marseilles. This work, moreover, is intended to intervene in modernity's insistent drive to medicalize, discipline, rehabilitate, and contain the subject of drugs within explanatory frameworks that disguise deeply rooted moral and religious fears, values and beliefs or prejudices (as in the use of the term "dependency" and "abuse") and that lock this subject into a "metaphysics" of substance that, paradoxically, has no substance. Indeed, we might almost go so far as to say that our task has been to relate Nietzsche's impassioned call for "a history of narcotica" to the making of an era and to a "philosophy yet to come."

NOTES

1. See the lovely passage in Ernst Jünger's *Approaches, drogues et ivresse* (Paris: Gallimard, 1991), p.'56.

2. A fascinating source for further reading in this area is Louis Lewin's *Phantastica* (Rochester, NY: Park Street Press, 1998), p. 2. A contemporary and adversary of Freud, Lewin's was the first book to bring scientific insights to a survey of the world-wide use of drugs. He furthered a classification of psychoactive drugs which was used in the original formulation of U.S. narcotics laws. For a more recent survey, see Richard Rudgley's *Essential Substances: A Cultural History of Intoxicants in Society* (New York: Kodansha, 1993).

3. Richard Klein, *Cigarettes are Sublime* (Durham, NC: Duke University Press, 1993), p. 27.

4. Eve Kosofsky Sedgwick, "The Epidemics of the Will," in *Zone 6: Incorporations,* eds. Jonathan Crary and Stanford Quinter (Cambridge, MA: MIT Press, 1992), p. 582.

5. Ibid., p. 583.

6. Ibid., p. 584.

7. Ibid., p. 583–584.

8. Avital Ronell, *Crack Wars: Literature, Addiction, Mania* (Lincoln: Nebraska University Press, 1992), p. 29.

Part I

PHILOSOPHICAL AND LITERARY REFLECTIONS ON ADDICTION

Chapter One

THE RHETORIC OF DRUGS

JACQUES DERRIDA

Translated by Michael Israel

When the sky of transcendence comes to be emptied, a fatal
rhetoric fills the void, and this is the fetishism of drug addiction.

—Jacques Derrida, *Supra*

AUTREMENT: You are not a specialist in the study of drug addiction, yet
we suppose that as a philosopher you may have something of particular
interest to say on this subject. At the very least, we assume that your
thinking might be pertinent here, if only by way of those concepts common both to philosophy and addictive studies, for example dependency,
liberty, pleasure, *jouissance.*

JACQUES DERRIDA: O.K. Let us speak then from the point of view of the nonspecialist, which indeed I am. But certainly you will agree that in this case
we are dealing with something other than a delimitable domain. The criteria for competence, and especially for professional competence, are very
problematic here. In the end, it is just these criteria that, whether directly or
not, we will be led to discuss. Having identified me as a philosopher, a
nonspecialist in this thing called "drug addiction," you have just named a
number of highly philosophical concepts, concepts that philosophy is

obliged to consider as priorities: "liberty," "dependency," "pleasure," or "jouissance," etc. So be it. But I propose to begin quite simply with "concept," with the concept of concept. "Drugs" is both a word and a concept, even before one adds quotation marks to indicate that one is only mentioning and not using, that one is not buying, selling, or ingesting the "stuff itself" *(la chose même)*.

Such a remark is not neutral, innocently philosophical, logical, or speculative. Nor is it for the same reasons, nor in the same manner that one might note, and quite rightly, that such and such a plant, root, or substance is also for us a concept, a "thing" apprehended through the name of a concept and the device of an interpretation. No, in the case of "drugs," the regime of the concept is different: there are no drugs "in nature." There may be natural poisons and indeed naturally lethal poisons, but they are not as such "drugs." As with addiction, the concept of drugs supposes an instituted and an institutional definition: a history is required, and a culture, conventions, evaluations, norms, an entire network of intertwined discourses, a rhetoric, whether explicit or elliptical. We will surely come back to this rhetorical dimension. There is not in the case of drugs any objective, scientific, physical (physicalistic), or "naturalistic" definition (or rather there is: this definition could be "naturalistic," if by this we understand that it attempts to naturalize that which defies any natural definition or any definition of natural reality). One can claim to define the nature of a toxin; however, not all toxins are drugs, nor are they considered as such. Already one must conclude that the concept of drugs is not a scientific concept, but is rather instituted on the basis of moral or political evaluations: it carries in itself both norm and prohibition, allowing no possibility of description or certification—it is a decree, a buzzword *(mot d'ordre)*. Usually the decree is of a prohibitive nature; occasionally, on the other hand, it is glorified and revered: malediction and benediction always call to and imply one another. As soon as one utters the word "drugs," even before any "addiction," a prescriptive or normative "diction" is already at work, performatively, whether one likes it or not. This "concept" will never be a purely theoretical or theorizable concept. And if there is never a theorem for drugs, there can never be a scientific competence for it either, one attestable as such and which would not be essentially overdetermined by ethicopolitical norms. For this reason, I have seen fit to begin with some reservations about the division "specialist/nonspecialist." No doubt the division may prove difficult for other reasons.

From these premises one may draw different, indeed contradictory, ethicopolitical conclusions. On the one hand, there would be the argument advocating a sort of *naturalism* and a return to nature: "'Drugs' and 'drug addiction,'" one might say, "are nothing but normative concepts, institutional evaluations, or prescriptions. They are artificial and their artificial flavor leaves an unpleasant aftertaste. Let us return to true natural freedom. Natural law dictates that each of us be left the freedom to do as we will with our desire, our soul, and our body, as well as with that stuff known as 'drugs.' Let us then do away with this law which the history of conventions and of ethical norms has so deeply inscribed in the concept of 'drugs'; let's get rid of this suppression or repression; let's return to nature."

In response to this liberal, naturalistic, and indeed permissivist decree *(mot d'ordre)* one may, on the basis of the same premises, oppose an *artificialist* politics and a deliberately repressive position. Occasionally, this may, just like its liberal counterpart, prove to be therapeutic, if you prefer, preventative, inclined to persuasion and pedagogy: "we recognize," such a one might say, "that this concept of drugs is an instituted norm. Its origin and its history are obscure. Such a norm does not follow analytically from any scientific concept of natural toxicity, nor, despite all our best efforts to establish it in this sense, will it ever do so. Nonetheless, entirely accepting the logic of this prescriptive and repressive convention, we believe that *our* society, *our* culture, *our* conventions require this prohibition. Let us rigorously enforce it. We have at stake here the health, security, productivity, and the orderly functioning of these very institutions. By means of this law, at once supplementary and fundamental, these institutions protect the very possibility of the law in general, for by prohibiting drugs we assure the integrity and responsibility of the legal subject, of the citizens, etc.

There can be no law without the conscious, vigilant, and normal subject, master of his or her intentions and desires. This prohibition and this law are thus not simply products of artifice, not artifacts like any other—they are the very condition for the possibility of a respect for the law in our society. A prohibition is not necessarily bad, nor must it necessarily assume brutal forms—its methods may be complex and symbolically overdetermined; however, no one can deny that the survival of our culture presupposes this prohibition. It belongs fundamentally to the very concept of our culture, etc.

From the moment we recognize the institutional character of a certain concept of drugs, drug addiction, narcotics, and poisons, two ethicopolitical axiomatics appear in conflict. Briefly put, I am not sure that this contradiction is more than superficial; nor am I convinced that both of these logics can follow through to their conclusions; and finally I am not sure that the two so radically exclude each other. Let us not forget that both start from the same premises—that is, the opposition of nature and institution. And not simply of nature and the law, but indeed already of two laws, of two decrees. Naturalism is no more natural than conventionalism.

A: The word *toxicomanie* first came into use just before the end of the last century; the kind of behavior which we now understand as the progressive disease of addiction previously was not considered a medical, nosological phenomenon. In England one used the old term *addiction,* which emphasized the subject's dependency on a given product, but there was as yet no question of a drug pathology, of a toxicomania as such. Toxicomania, the notion of drug addiction as a disease, is contemporaneous with modernity and with modern science. Electronic circuitry got hooked up in the argot of drugs and the addict got wired.[1] And at some point, someone, abusively consuming certain products, was for the first time called a toxicomaniac.

JD: Actually, in the eyes of the law, dependency on a toxic product or even on harmful medications is not, in itself, what constitutes drug addiction. But let's try to slow down and take a moment to consider this modernity. As always, drugs are here the effect of an interpretation. Drugs are "bad" but the evil in them is not simply a "harmfulness." Alcohol and tobacco are, as objects of consumption, just as artificial as any drug, and no one will now dispute their harmfulness. One may prescribe—as does the medical community and a certain segment of society—abstinence from drinking (especially while driving—a decisive question for the public/private distinction) and abstinence from smoking (especially in *public* places). Still, even if they are considered as somehow "bad," as driving or health hazards, alcohol and tobacco are never denounced as narcotics, they are never branded with such a moral stigma. The relation to "public safety" thus must lie elsewhere.

One can, of course, refer to alcohol or tobacco as "drugs," but this will necessarily imply a sort of irony, as if in so doing one only marked a sort of rhetorical displacement. Tobacco and alcohol, we tranquilly assume, are not really drugs. Of course, their harmfulness can form the object of dissuasive campaigns and of a whole quasi-moral pedagogy, but the simple consumption of these products, in and of itself, does not form the object of moral reprobation nor certainly of criminal prosecution. One can prosecute a drunkard because he is *also* a dangerous driver, but not because alcohol might have been "classified" as a narcotic (to use the legal terminology of the articles defining the *War on Drugs*). The (secular) prohibition of alcohol, if I'm not mistaken, will be seen as a brief and unique interlude in the history of mankind; and, for well-known reasons, more unthinkable in France than anywhere else.

This should remind us that in France drugs, unlike wine, are supplied mainly by *foreign* productions. And this is also the case in most Western nations. But of course this fact hardly suffices to explain our modern legislation, that of the [French] laws of 1970 in particular.

What, then, is the modernity, if indeed there is one, of the phenomenon of drug addiction, of its definition, which, as we were just saying, always involves a normative or prescriptive interpretation? This is a very difficult question—really rather a swarm of obscure questions. One of these leads back to the entire, intimidatingly intertwined history of the division between public and private. I wouldn't presume to take on the issue here. Let us simply note that the legislation of 1970 also condemns the *use*, whether public or *private*, and not just the dealing of drugs—what article 626 calls "production, conveyance, importation, exportation, holding, tender, transfer, acquisition." One might have thought this would be enough to prosecute anyone who used drugs, for one cannot very well use drugs without having in one way or another "acquired" them. Were such the case, the principle dictating respect for private life and a right to the free disposal of one's person would at least have been formally and hypocritically respected. But no, the law explicitly specifies that the "use" of classified substances will be punished by fine and imprisonment. The word "use" completes the list of acts that I cite above.[2]

And the opening of title VI of the law establishing the *War on Drugs* also speaks of simple *use:* "Any person who illicitly uses plants or substances classified as narcotics is to be placed under the surveillance of the sanitary authorities." The nonillicit use of substances thus classified would be the supervised, medical use, the other version of the same *pharmakon* (an enormous problem, and now more timely than ever before).

Another question is tied up with technical considerations and with any given technological mutation. Drug addiction, as you have made clear, suggests not just a casual use, but rather more a frequent and repeated drug use: thus, not simply an ample supply (numerous techno-economical transformations of the marketplace, transportation, international communication, etc.), but the technical possibility for an individual to reproduce the act, even when alone (the question of the syringe, for example, to which we shall have to return). It is this crossing of a quantitative threshold that allows us to speak of a modern phenomenon of drug addiction: namely, the number of individuals who have easy access to the possibility of repeating the act, alone or otherwise, in private or in public, and throughout that zone where this distinction loses all pertinence or rigor.

I think that now, at this moment, it is no longer possible to dissociate this narcotic "modernity" from what is now one of the major events facing humanity, one of the most revealing and, what amounts to the same thing, one of the most "apocalyptic" in its most essential and "interior" history—that is, AIDS. But we will no doubt have to come back to this . . .

A: Then do you link this modernity to mass production? to repetition? Do we rediscover here a questioning of writing, of the *pharmakon?*

JD: I have indeed attempted to link up, the problematic of the *pharmakon* with the very disconcerting "logic" of what we casually call "repetition." In the *Phaedrus,* writing is presented to the king, before the law, before the political authority of power, as a beneficial *pharmakon* because, as Theuth claims, it enables us to repeat, and thus to remember. This then would be a good repetition, in the service of anamnesis. But the king discredits this repetition. This is not *good* repetition. "You have found a *pharmakon* not for memory *(mneme),* but rather for recollection *(hypomnesis).*" The *pharmakon* "writing" does not serve the good, authentic memory. It is rather the mnemotechnical auxiliary of a bad memory. It has more to do with forgetting, the simulacrum, and *bad* repetition than it does with anamnesis and truth. This *pharmakon* dulls the spirit and rather than aiding, it wastes the memory. Thus in the name of authentic, living memory and in the name of truth, power accuses this bad drug, writing, of being a drug that leads not only to forgetting, but also to irresponsibility. Writing is irresponsibility itself, the orphanage of a wandering and playing sign. Writing is not only a drug, it also is a game, *paidia,* and a bad game if not guided by a concern for philosophical truth. Thus, in the idiom of the familial scene, there is no father to answer for it, and no living, purely living speech can help it. The bad *pharmakon* can always parasitize the good *pharmakon,* bad repetition can always parasitize good repetition. This parasitism is at once accidental and essential. Like any good parasite, it is at once inside and outside—the outside feeding on the inside. And with this model of feeding we are very close to what in the modern sense of the word we call drugs, which are usually to be "consumed." "Deconstruction" is always attentive to this indestructible logic of parasitism. As a discourse, deconstruction is always a discourse about the parasite, itself a device parasitic on the subject of the parasite, a discourse "on parasite" and in the logic of the "superparasite."

Thus, however tempting and instructive it might be, the transposition of this problematic (which for lack of time I have very much simplified) toward what you call "modern drug addiction," together with its theoretical and practical interpretations, requires, as you may well imagine, the greatest prudence.

A: Certain drug users unwittingly tell us that by writing they seek to end their addiction. When they carry out this project, we often witness an intensification of their agony and of their addiction. And yet, some psychoanalysts insist on the function of writing in providing a release from the symptoms of addiction: in writing itself, does drug addiction end?

JD: We cannot trust in the simple opposition of symptom and cause, of repression and the release from repression, no more than we can count on a simple opposition of memory and forgetting, especially considering the paradoxes of repetition and of the rapport to the other. "Good" repetition is always haunted or contaminated by "bad" repetition, so much the better and so much the worse for it. The *pharmakon* will always be understood both as antidote *and* as poison. As you were just saying, the drug addict may seek to forget even as he takes on the job of an anamnesic analysis, may at once seek repression and a release from repression (which may well portend that this is not the important boundary, and that it has other, more twisted forms . . .). To this end the addict uses a "technique," a technical supplement which he also interprets as being "natural.". . . Another way of thinking would bring us to that distrust so common at the site of the artificial, of the instrumentalization of memory, thus at the site of the *pharmakon, both* as poison *and* as antidote, at which point we would also feel that supplementary discomfort inherent in the indecidability between the two. . . .

A: In this regard, we might also consider the consequences of Platonic *mimesis,* itself the product of a technique which at once recalls and opposes itself to an original model.

JD: The question of *mimesis,* or, if I might risk a shortcut, the question of drugs as the question—the grand question—of truth. Neither more nor less. What do we hold against the drug addict? Something we never, at least never to the same degree, hold against the alcoholic or the smoker: that he cuts himself off from the world, in exile from reality, far from objective reality and the real life of the city and the community; that he escapes into a world of simulacrum and fiction. We disapprove of his taste for something like hallucinations. No doubt, we should have to make some distinction between so-called hallucinogens and other drugs, but the distinction is wiped out in the rhetoric of fantasy that is at the root of any prohibition of drugs: drugs make us lose any sense of true reality. In the end, it is always, I think, under this charge that the prohibition is declared. We do not object to the drug user's pleasure per se, but we cannot abide the fact that his or hers is a pleasure taken in an experience without truth. Pleasure and play (now still as with Plato) are not in themselves condemned unless they are inauthentic and void of truth. This then is the system we will have to consider carefully and which we will need to articulate with the political question of fiction or literature. If he does not at least subordinate his poetics to philosophy and to the politics of the philosopher, the man or woman of the simulacrum will find himself or herself driven from the community by Plato (etc.). If in "modernity" we still suppose there to be some affinity between, on the one hand, the experience of fiction (literary or otherwise, whether from the perspective of the "producer," the distributor, or the consumer) and, on the other hand, the world of drug use; and if we imagine this affinity even when the poet does not search for any "artificial paradise," in that case the writer can be acceptable only to the degree that he or she allows himself or herself to be reincorporated in the institution. He or she restores the normal order of intelligible production; he or she produces and his or her production generates value. Such a justification has its roots in the evaluation of a productivity which is at least interpreted as a source of truth, albeit one that comes through the medium of fiction. The drug addict, in our common conception, the drug addict as such produces nothing, nothing true or real. He is legitimate only in certain cases, secretly and inadmissibly, for certain portions of society, and only inasmuch as he participates, at least indirectly, in the production and consumption of goods. . . .

A: With certain writers, those of the "Grand Jeu,"[3] Burroughs currently, Artaud when he was with the surrealists, in his "Letter to the Legislator," drugs are advanced as the object of a political battle, indeed the definitive political battle. With Burroughs, drugs are a "weapon" used in an endless war, as the final form of "world trade." Such a consideration seems rather timely.

JD: Certainly, for Artaud, in any case, there was the project of uncovering a system of norms and prohibitions which themselves constitute European culture and especially European religion. He hoped that Mexican drugs would allow the emancipation of the subject; provide an end to that subjection which from birth had somehow expropriated the subject; and most of all, provide an end to the very concept of the subject. Already at birth, God had stolen his body and his name. Indeed, at stake is this desire to be done with the judgment of God. But speaking thus extemporaneously we oversimplify the matter, and I would rather go back to Artaud's texts, to those written not simply "on drugs" and under the influence, but which moreover, in their very language, call into question and wrestle with systems of interpreting drugs. And then we shall have to distinguish carefully between discourses, practices, and experiences of writing, literary or not, which imply or justify what we call drugs. Abysses often lie between them. There is not any *single* world of drugs. Artaud's text is not Michaux's or Benjamin's (I am thinking in particular of his "Hashish in Marseilles"), neither of which should be confused with Baudelaire's text which in turn is not that of Coleridge nor of De Quincey. To conflate such differences in a homogeneous series would be delirious, indeed narcoticizing. But then, can one ever condemn or prohibit without also somehow confusing?

A: In literature at least, we can date the concept of drug addiction *(toxicomanie)*, in the modern sense of the word, from the publication of De Quincey's *Diaries of an Opium-Eater*. By the same token, alcoholism first appeared in French literature with Zola.

JD: This path deserves to be followed. Pending a more thorough investigation, we might perhaps risk a hypothesis. Let us consider literature, in a fairly strict sense, distinguishing it, at least in Europe, from poetry and belles lettres, as a modern phenomenon (dating from the sixteenth or seventeenth century). Well then, is it not thus contemporaneous with a certain European drug addiction? In fact, one that was tolerated? You've mentioned De Quincey, but we also have Coleridge. We might, just this once, add a word on coffee and tobacco: whole theses, even whole departments of literature (general or comparative) should perhaps be consecrated to the study of coffee and tobacco in our literatures. Consider Balzac or Valéry, two otherwise and obviously very different cases. Would we not be rather hard pressed to find anything analogous, from Homer to Dante, before this literary modernity? We will soon enough come back to Homer. But first consider the figures of dictations, in the dissymmetrical experience of the other (of the being given over to the other, of the being as prey of the other, of quasi-possession) which dictates and compels a certain writing, perhaps all writing, even the most masterful (gods, the demon, the muses, inspiration, etc.). These forms of originary alienation, in the most positive, productive, and irreducible sense of the word, these figures of dictations—are they not implicated in a history in which drugs, following "the flight of the gods," might one day move into a place that has been left vacant, or otherwise play the role of an enfeebled phantom? Rather, it would be a matter of methodical provocation, of a technique for calling the phantom: the spirit, the ghost *(Geist)*, inspiration, dictation. More precisely, and what makes the matter even more convoluted, we would be dealing here with a methodology of the contraphantom. What is a contraphantom? It is the phantom that one plays against another phantom, yet it is also the phantom of the phantom, the alibi phantom, the other phantom. Thus, do we not have a choice between phantoms, or between the simulacra of phantoms?

But let's not act as if we knew just what a phantom or a phantasm was, and as if it would be enough simply to set out the consequences of such a knowledge. Inasmuch as we may not have recognized the full magnitude of this enigma ("What is a phantom?" "What is a phantasm?" "What is the flight of the gods?"), beyond the opposition of presence and absence, of the real and the imaginary, even beyond the properly ontological question, the philosophical, political, and ideological "answers" to what we call "the drug problem" will remain expedients incapable of any radical autojustification. We're back where we began, back to the problem of the criteria for competence and the impossibility of any theorem. The responsibilities which anyone (and first and foremost the "decision maker"—the legislator, educator, citizen in general, etc.) should accept in such an emergency are only all the more serious, difficult, and ineluctable. Depending on the circumstances (tirelessly analyzed, whether macroscopically or microscopically) a discourse of "prohibition" can be justified *just as well or just as badly* as a discourse of liberalization. A repressive practice (in all its brutal or sophisticated, punitive or reeducational forms) can be justified just as well or just as badly as a permissive practice (with all its ruses). As one can never fully explicate neither the one nor the other of these practices, so one can never absolutely condemn either of them. In an emergency this can only lead to equivocations, negotiations, and unstable compromises. And in any given, progressively evolving situation, these will need to be guided by a concern for the singularity of each individual experience and by a sociopolitical analysis that is at once as broadly and as finely tuned as possible, I say this not to avoid the question, no more than I do to argue for relativism or opportunism; rather, I would simply describe the lay of the land on which such decisions ought to be made, though the ultimate extent and boundaries of the problem remain unanalyzed and unthought.

This "lay of the land," this equivocation of discourses incapable of any radical justification, this is just what we observe both in the customs and in the discourses that now dominate our society. The only attitude (the only politics—judicial, medical, pedagogical, etc.) I would absolutely condemn is one which, directly or indirectly, cuts off the possibility of an essentially interminable questioning, that is a critical and thus transforming questioning.

By critical and transforming questioning I mean, of course, a work of analysis (in every sense, from psychoanalysis to the socio-economico-political study of the conditions of drug addiction: unemployment, the geopolitics of the marketplace, the "real" condition of what we call democracy, the police, the state of criminal law and of medical institutions, etc.), but also a thoughtful reflection on the axioms of this problematic and on all those discourses which inform it. We have just spoken of the phantom and of ontology; before that we were talking about the simulacrum, truth, and repetition. Thus, we have at stake here the very genealogy of a vast number of conceptual oppositions: nature/culture or nature/convention, nature/artifice, emancipation/alienation, public/private, etc.

Coming back to the role of the inspired trance in what we habitually call writing, are we not obliged to attempt some sort of a history of dictations, and more precisely, of what we call *inspiration:* if possible, literally, that is to say "physically" (for example, inhalation), or figuratively? What is still "inspired," what "inspires," and who "inspires," in the proper or the figural sense, in the experience of drugs? Where is the boundary between poetry and prose, between poetry and the novel, and between various types of novels and various structures of fictionality, etc.?

There are those who would say, and not without "common sense": when the sky of transcendence comes to be emptied, and not just of Gods, but of any Other, a fatal rhetoric fills the void, and this is the fetishism of drug addiction. Not religion as the opiate of the people, but drugs as the religion of the atheist poets—and of some others, more or less atheists, more or less poets.

We have neither enough time nor enough space to do it, but were we to follow this thread further, we might come back to those questions we have just touched upon, questions of nature and of production. These two concepts themselves belong to a series of oppositions and lead back to their "history." But let us for the moment put this aside for it is not something that lends itself to improvisation (a brief treatise, in parentheses, on the question of drugs and improvisation, in the arts and elsewhere). We imagine that the drug addict–writer seeks to discover a sort of gracious and graceful inspiration, a passivity that welcomes what repression or suppression would otherwise inhibit: "By the grace of the technical or artificial, and ever *interiorizing* violence of an injection, inhalation or ingestion, by taking into my self, inside myself a foreign body, and actually a nutriment, I will excite a state of productive receptivity: the word being at once received and sent forth, in a sort of creative spontaneity or transcendental imagination, I will let it go, and the violence will have put an end to violence. Reappropriation will be induced by the foreign body and production will take place without effort, etc." This transcendental-imaginary discourse (imaginary for anyone who would profess it as well as for anyone who might hope to unmask it), this is what is condemned by a society based on work and on the subject answerable as subject. A poem ought to be the product of *real* work, even if the traces of that work should be washed away. It is always nonwork that is stigmatized. The authentic work *(oeuvre),* as its name suggests, ought to be the result of an effort (with merit and rewards) and of a responsible effort, even up to the point where the effort effaces itself, erasing its traces or erasing itself before that which is given to it. And even if the work *(oeuvre)* comes from an effortless work, a work without work, subordinate to the dictation of the other, still we require that this alterity be authentic and not factitious, neither simulated nor stimulated by artificial projections. It is in the name of this authenticity that drug addiction is condemned or deplored. This authenticity can be *appropriated*—either simultaneously (in confusion) or successively (in denial) to the values of natural or symbolic normality, of truth, of a real rapport to true reality, of free and responsible subjectivity, of productivity, etc. And it *appropriates* such values, makes them *proper* to itself the more so in that it is itself founded on the value of *properness or property,* and of the appropriation or reappropriation of self. It is the making proper of the proper itself *(propriation du propre même),* at least inasmuch as the proper is opposed to the heterogeneity of the improper, and to every mode of foreignness or alienation that might be recognized in someone's resorting to drugs. And this value might just as easily be the mainstay of a right-wing as of a left-wing discourse, and just as easily in the Orient as in the West.

This specularity should not surprise you. It is inexhaustible. Anyway, some form of drug addiction might just as well have this same fantasy of reappropriation. It might do so naively or with a great "cultivation," dreaming of emancipation and of the restoration of an "I," of a self or of the self's own body, and indeed dreaming of the restoration of a subject once and for all taken back to the forces of alienation, to repression and suppression and to the law which speaks in religion, metaphysics, politics, the family, etc.

As convoluted and paradoxical as this "logic" of reappropriation may be, especially when it's mixed up with the simulacrum, still one can never quite get beyond it. Certainly, for example, it is not missing from certain of Artaud's texts. This logic goes together with a thinking or an experience of the proper, which no doubt carries it beyond itself, which carries away and otherwise expropriates itself, which takes itself out of its self. The boundaries here are not between two opposed camps nor between two metaphysics in which one might clearly recognize certain commonalities. They are not the boundaries between "repression" and "release from repression," between suppression and nonsuppression. Rather, even if up to a point they could or should yield to certain more or less refined typologies, these boundaries run between an endless number of experiences.

And I find no better word than *experience,* that is to say the voyage that crosses the boundary. An experience *between* two experiences: on the one hand, the passage, the odyssey, with or without *nostalgia*—you are perhaps familiar with the work of Adorno and Horkheimer on the lotus-eaters and on this Homeric *nostos*[4]—the wandering from which one cannot return, so many possibilities wrapped up in a certain etymology of the word "experience," occasionally associated, like the "trip," with the experience of "drugs," with the rapport to the other and with an opening up to the world in general; and, on the other hand, we have the organized experiment, the *experimental* as an "organized voyage." What does this *between* signify? Perhaps it means that the experience to which I now refer, the thought of this experience or this experience as thought does not as yet yield to a determination within the usual series of oppositions, for example nature/artifice, nonwork/work, natural experience/artificial experimentation, etc. Thus, I do not speak merely of drug experiences or drug-free experiences (which, after all, are no more natural than drugs), but rather of experiences which are qualitatively highly nuanced, occasionally even for the same "individual," and which we cannot mention without multiplying qualifications and points of view. Every name and every concept by which one might hope to define these criteria, these qualifications, and points of view, is already caught up in the most embarrassing discursive sequences. All of them answer to an exceedingly rigidified program, one that is particularly difficult to disentangle. We are here dealing with a metaphysical burden and a history which we must never stop questioning. We have at stake here no less than the self, consciousness, reason, liberty, the responsible subject, alienation, one's own body or the foreign body, sexual difference, the unconscious, repression or suppression, the different "parts" of the body, injection, introjection, incorporation (oral or not), the relationship to death (mourning and interiorization), idealization, sublimation, the real and the law, and I could go on.

A: Do all drug addicts then tell of a lost body or a body they seek to discover, an ideal body, a perfect body?

JD: Here again the opposition between *dominant* or *canonical* is not at the root of the problem. It seems rather secondary to an axiomatic that remains common to the majority of those who speak and act *against* drug addiction as well as to the majority of those who act and argue *for* it—or who would at least redirect the prohibition toward more liberal, softer forms (for example, the legalization of "soft" drugs) or toward more intelligent forms, compromises, mediations, negotiations (after all, in our society one rarely finds anyone who publicly advocates drug use). From the prohibitionist, then, we hear of a need to protect society from everything we associate with drug use: irresponsibility, nonwork, irrationality, unproductivity, delinquency, promiscuity, illness and the social costs it implies, and more generally, the destruction of the social bond. But this protection of the social bond, and thus of a certain symbolicity, indeed of rationality in general—this is almost always presented as the protection of a "natural" normality of the body, of the body politic and the body of the individual member.

In the name of this organic and originary naturalness of the body, we declare and wage the war on drugs, the war against these artificial, pathogenic, and foreign aggressions. Again, we find a desire to reconstitute what you just called the "ideal body," the "perfect body." But you mentioned this speaking from the user's point of view, from the other side of the problem, if we can so call it (for you see how this opposition remains problematic). Those "products" otherwise considered as dangerous and unnatural are often considered fit for the liberation of this same "ideal" or "perfect body" from social oppression, suppression and repression, or from the reactive violence which constricts originary forces or desire, and indeed constricts the "primary processes." And this is the same naturalistic metaphysics that in order to restore a "prior" body—we could almost say prior to the fall—is translated through codes that can occasionally turn out to be quite diverse (of a sort that is vaguely "Nietzschean," "Freudian," "Artaudian," "Marcusian," etc.).

In outlining this false opposition and exaggerating its characteristics, I have spoken of *canonical* or *dominant* discourses. Now, in analyzing, as I intend to do, the common grounds of these two discourses, we must ask ourselves how and why, precisely, they have become "canonical or dominant." Where does their force or their authority come from? What contract binds them together? What do the two together exclude, etc.? What contradictions or tensions are at work even inside the canonical? As I see it, these are the fundamental questions, or rather, and by the same token, the most indispensable philosophical moves. Their necessity cannot, moreover, fail to be felt throughout every "crisis" or "symptom" of "crisis" that our societies are currently undergoing.

Neither of the two opposed "canons" takes into account what we might call the technological condition. The natural, originary body does not exist: technology has not simply added itself, from outside or after the fact, as a foreign body. Certainly, this foreign or dangerous supplement is "originarily" at work and in place in the supposedly ideal interiority of the "body and soul." It is indeed at the heart of the heart. Rushing things a bit, I would say that what, without being absolutely new, now takes on particular and macroscopic forms, is this paradox of a "crisis," as we superficially call it, of naturalness. This alleged "crisis" also comes up, for example, throughout the problems of biotechnology and throughout the new and so-called artificial possibilities for dealing with life, from the womb to the grave, as if a naturalness had never been in circulation and as if the boundary between nature and its other were susceptible to objectification. Let me just quickly add that in certain always unusual circumstances, the recourse to dangerous experimentation with what we call "drugs" may be guided by a desire to consider this alleged boundary from both sides at once, to think this boundary as such, in any case to approach its formation, its simulation, or its simulacrum as it forms (for this boundary does not exist, is never *present* and has no essence). This experience (one to which artists and thinkers occasionally devote themselves, but which is by no means the unique privilege of those who claim or in whom we recognize such a status), this experience may be sought with or without "drugs," at least without any "narcotic" "classified" as such by the law. We will always have unclassifed or unclassifiable supplements of drugs or narcotics. Basically everybody has his own, and I don't just mean stuff that is patently comestible, smokable, or shootable. As you know, the introjection or incorporation of the other has so many other resources, stratagems, and detours. . . . It can always invent new orifices, in addition to and beyond those, for example the mouth, which we think we naturally possess. Besides, orality does not open up only to receive, but also, as they say, to emit, and we should have to wonder whether drug addiction consists simply and essentially in receiving and taking in, rather than in "expressing" and pushing outside, for example, in a certain form of speaking or of chanting, whether or not we drink what we "spit." There is no doubt, at least for orality, for the hearing and the hearing-oneself-speak, a zone of experience where giving and receiving, inspiration and expiration, impression and expression, passivity and activity can only with great difficulty be opposed to one another, or even distinguished. And then, even supposing that we could draw the lines around it, oral consumption is not limited to any particular classified narcotic, but covers all sorts of nonclassified objects of compulsive eating or drinking, things like peanut butter, chocolate, coffee, liquor, and tobacco.

And since I've just mentioned coffee and tobacco you might think of that really very "French," very "Cartesian" writer, one who was also a philosopher of vigilance and freedom, of the will, self-awareness, and self-mastery both in thinking and in writing—I have in mind Valéry, who everyday at dawn organized his trances of writing and lucidity in a secular temple dedicated to the cult of coffee and cigarettes. Another very "French," very "Cartesian" writer, himself also a philosopher of vigilance and freedom, of the will, self-awareness, etc.—I have here in mind Sartre, who was at one time, so they say, a serious user of pharmaceutical drugs, etc., and "abused" these "nonclassified" substances for his writing. . . . Fine, enough of that, but as you see this *coincidentia oppositorum* always takes us back to the question of consciousness, reason and work, truth, the good memory, and of the anamnesis of allegedly primary or natural processes. In the final analysis, or in the very long run (for by definition there will never be any absolutely final analysis) a thinking and a politics of this thing called "drugs" would involve the displacement of these two ideologies at *once* opposed in their common metaphysics.

I would rather you didn't just yet ask whether I am for or against either one of these. Today, here and now, in my private–public life, and in the fixed situation of "our" society, I feel rather more inclined towards an *ethos,* shall we say, that, according to the dominant codes, would be understood as somewhat repressive or prohibitory, at least in the case of the "classified" drugs. (As I have suggested above, one might extend the concept and the experience of drugs far beyond its legal, medical definition, and in a space at once idiosyncratic and public, arrange all sorts of practices, pleasures, and pains that no one could rigorously show to be unrelated and without analogy to drug addiction. The possibilities are innumerable and quasi-idiomatic. Every phantasmatic organization, whether collective or individual, is the invention of a drug, or of a rhetoric of drugs, be it aphrodisiac or not, with production, consumption, semi-secrecy, and a semi-private market. . . .) But to justify the *ethos* that draws me towards an apparently "repressive" attitude (in the case of "classified" drugs) I should not, in the final analysis, rely on any of those discourses or axiomatics which I have here sketched out. This much would be strictly necessary, and yet so hard! Thus, in an unprepared interview, in the space of a few pages I cannot, so to speak, do right by this justification. However, what most matters to me, as you might guess, is precisely the necessity—or the difficulty—of such a justification, and it is this that guides me in all that I say or do, whether in "public" or in "private," and even when there is apparently no question of drugs as such. And if you consider that I believe neither in the infallible pertinence of the distinction between public and private (a distinction threatened by the very structure of language, and even before language, by the iterability of any mark) nor in the simple essence of the aphrodisiac (the economy of pleasure is so very convoluted . . .) so much the more will you understand my reserve. . . .

As we were saying, the logic of *technological supplementarity* is not much tolerated by either of these two sides, by either of these two "canons." The "new" (new thinking, new behavior, new politics) here supposes a formalization powerful enough to allow us to understand *both canons at once,* even as we displace their shared axiomatics. On the subject of this newness, one may have two contradictory feelings. On the one hand, as they say, "you can't get there from here." Such a formalization can never be fully accessible. Granted, but then "fully accessible," plenitude and absolute access, is this not still the language of these two "canons," the shared desire of the drug user and of the one who would "just say no"? On the other hand, and no less obviously, this formalization and displacement are *practically* underway and following a laborious, turbulent, apparently chaotic course; indeed, this is itself the experience of our current "crisis." If today so many socio-ethico-political problems intersect and condense in the problem of drugs, it is not simply because of the modern technology we were just talking about. The indissociability of all these emergencies, the impossibility of isolating a "drug problem" only becomes all the more clear; and, by the same token, so does the necessity of treating as such a "general logic" of discourses on the subject of drugs, and *simultaneously* discourses on the subject of, for instance, artificial insemination, sperm banks, the market for surrogate mothers, organ transplants, euthanasia, sex changes, the use of drugs in sports, *and especially, especially* on the subject of AIDS, which we will finally have to discuss. For isn't it true that henceforth AIDS will offer us an opportune and inevitable entry into all these questions?

A: It is ironic that athletes, the role models of our children, should find themselves, because of steroids, in the front lines of the war on drugs. A bike racer says that he does drugs in order to be the first one at the top of the hill. And yet, doesn't the drug addict also say that he wants to come in, if not in first place, in any case at the top of the hill that is life?

JD: Yes, basically, the farther we go, the more the question of drugs seems inseparable not only from such tremendous questions as "the concept," "reason," "truth," "memory," "work," and so forth, but inseparable also from the emergency rooms where all these things appear to gather symptomatically: for example, what does a society make of literature?

What of birth, death, and AIDS? And, yes, you are quite correct, what of
sports? etc. Right now everything about the politics of sports (discourses,
markets, entertainment) opens up a new main line for the analysis of the
social bond. And in this case we can never get around the problem of athletic drug use: where does it begin? How can we classify and track its
products? And by what authority do we condemn this drug use or
such-and-such a chemical prosthesis? And what about female athletes
who get pregnant for the stimulating, hormonal effects and then have an
abortion after their event? In any case, as the basis of this condemnation,
one still supposes that the athletic hero should treat his or her body *naturally*. As such he or she works out, he or she makes the body work in a
production that is not simply individual. Through the socialization of
sports, whether it be professional or not, this so-called disinterested work
brings into play everything that relates to education: and first and foremost to the education of the will as in itself the overcoming of the self. In
this sense not only should sports avoid drugs, but also as the antidrug
itself, the antidote for drugs, *the pharmakon of the pharmakon*, it is the
very thing which should be kept safe from drugs, far from any possible
contamination. Thus, and nothing could have been easier to foresee, we
have here the zone closest, most analogous, and most exposed to the evil
it excludes. And not merely because, whether as exercise or as entertainment, sports can become literally intoxicating and depoliticizing (if you
prefer, the arena for a certain drunkenness)—and as such, moreover,
sports can be manipulated by the political powers that be—but rather
more because competition seeks to stretch, and precisely by the use of
such things as steroids, the body's "natural" powers (and also the soul's:
there are no sports without soul! I would bet that someone may recognize in sports the essence of man. Man, the rational, political animal,
alone privileged with the possession of language and laughter, with the
experience of death and with other experiences "proper to man"—
among them drugs!—let us not forget that he or she is also an athletic
animal). In seeking to stretch out these "natural powers," it is only natural, indeed I should say inevitable, that one should think of using such
artificially natural methods to go beyond man, toward the hero, the
superman, and other figures of a man who would be (no) more man,
more man than man. The use of drugs in sports is condemned because it
cheats nature, but also because it cheats a certain idea of justice (the
equality of all participants in the contest). One wants to uphold the
integrity not only of the natural body, but also of good will, of conscience, and of the spirit which runs the body in the athletic effort, in this
free work or in this politically healthy game which is, and from Plato on
has been, athletic competition.

And yet those who, under certain prescribed conditions, would defend the use of steroids for example, claim that, after all, such drug use does not corrupt an independent will, and thus cannot constitute drug addiction. And furthermore, steroids do not provide any pleasure as such, none that is individual and desocializing. Anyway, as I think we've made clear, drugs in general are not condemned for the pleasure they bring, but rather because this aphrodisiac is not the right one: it leads to suffering and to the disintegration of the self, in short, it desocializes. It belongs to that diabolical couple, pleasure and suffering, denounced in every indictment of drugs. The hierarchy of pleasures goes together with that metaphysics of work and activity (practical and theoretical, thus occasionally contemplative) which is mixed up in the history of Western reason. Here again, Adorno and Horkheimer correctly point out that drug culture has always been associated with the other of the Occident, with oriental ethics and religion (*Dialectic* 63).

So it cannot be said that the pleasure of drug use *(la jouissance toxicomanique)* is in itself forbidden. Rather we forbid a pleasure that is at once solitary, desocializing, and yet contagious for the *socius*. We pretend to believe that if it were purely private, if the drug user only availed himself or herself of the inalienable right to do as one will with one's own body and soul, then even the most insidious delights would be permissible. But such an hypothesis is ruled out in advance: the consumer is a buyer and so takes part in dealing, which means that he or she participates in the open market, and thereby partakes in public discourse. Besides, you might even say that the act of drug use itself is structured like a language and so could not be purely private. Straightaway, drug use threatens the social bond. Again, and now just when we had only rather obscurely and dogmatically gotten beyond it, we come back to the problematic instability of the boundary between public and private. The luminaries of the Enlightenment *(Aufklärung)*, identified essentially by the motif of publicity and with the public character of every act of reason, are in themselves a declaration of war on drugs.

Apparently, in the case of what we call sexual perversion, the boundary between public and private lies elsewhere. In fact, here again the matter is very twisted, but since you have asked about a certain modernity of the problem, we might just limit ourselves to this fact that I believe to be absolutely unique to our time and which has left an indelible mark on us: AIDS. This is not just an event that will immeasurably affect humanity, both on the world's surface and within the experience of the social bond. The various forms of this deadly contagion, its spatial and temporal dimensions will from now on deprive us of everything that desire and a rapport to the other could invent to protect the integrity, and thus the inalienable identity of anything like a subject: in its "body," of course, but also even in its entire symbolic organization, the ego and the unconscious, the *subject* in its separateness and in its absolute secrecy. The virus (which belongs neither to life nor to death) may *always already* have broken into any "intersubjective" space. And considering its spatial and temporal dimensions, its structure of relays and delays, no human being is ever safe from AIDS. This possibility is thus installed at the heart of the social bond as intersubjectivity. And at the heart of that which would preserve itself as a dual intersubjectivity it inscribes the mortal and indestructible trace of the third—not the third as the condition for the symbolic and the law, but the third as destructuring structuration of the social bond, as social disconnection *(déliaison)* and even as the disconnection of the interruption, of the "without rapport" that can constitute a rapport to the other in its alleged normality. The third itself is no longer a third, and the history of this normality more clearly displays its simulacra, almost as if AIDS painted a picture of its exposed anatomy. You may say this is how it's always been, and I believe it. But now, exactly as if it were a painting or a giant movie screen, AIDS provides an available, daily, massive readability to that which the canonical discourses we mentioned above should deny, which in truth they are designed to deny, founded as they are on this very denial. If I have spoken of an event and of indestructibility, it is because already, at the dawn of this very new and ever so ancient thing, we know that, even should humanity some day come to control the virus (it will take at least a generation), still, even in the most unconscious symbolic zones, the traumatism has irreversibly affected our experience of desire and of what we coolly call intersubjectivity, the rapport to the alter ego, etc.

Enough said; I'll stop my little digression. You may tell me that this is not our subject. Quite right, for if there is no theorem for drugs, it is only because there is no longer any purely identifiable and delimitable subject here. But let's at least remember this: the modern problem of drugs has already been judged to be indissociable, in its genesis and thus in its treatment, from the general problem of delinquency (and not just of delinquency *as* drug addiction). From now on it is indissociably tied up with and subordinate to the problem of AIDS. If we consider the fact that AIDS could not, as some had thought or hoped it would, be confined to the margins of society (delinquency, homosexuality, drug addiction), we are facing something within the social bond that we might still want to consider as a destructuring and depoliticizing poly-perversion: an historic (historial!) knot or dénouement which is no doubt unique. In these circumstances the (restructuring and supposedly repoliticizing) reactions are largely unforeseeable and entirely capable of bringing forth the worst political violence.

In any case, were we to attempt the impossible and limit our discussion to drugs, you know that henceforth, in order to treat all these problems as we should, simultaneously and systematically, we can organize a hierarchy, play the bad against the worse, tolerate the sale of syringes in order to fight the spread of AIDS, liberalize sex education like never before, ever *econdomizing* the full range of social visibility, starting with the schools and the media. AIDS is in the process of redrawing the political front lines and the face of politics, the structures of civil society and of the state, at the very moment when governments thought they could organize against an identifiable enemy, the international counterstate of the drug lord. And this is a result in particular, though not solely, of the fact that, as I recently read in *Libération*, "AIDS Plagues Junkies."

A: We see, for example in Latin America, how the drug lords have organized themselves as a state within the state. We hear the mayors of major American cities talk about a need for "tolerance" in order to control drug-related crime. As we've said, and all this is evoked in terms of war, the major dealers are notoriously allied with the extreme right-wing. A strange paradox with the drug addict seen as a marginal figure. The legalization of crack? The state as dealer?

JD: One very brief remark. People hardly talk about it, but in this case the opposition between different regimes and types of society becomes more paradoxical than ever. In so-called socialist societies, those based on a philosophy of work and the ideal of its reappropriation by the worker, certain forms of unemployment and unproductivity need to be disguised, and the phenomena of drugs need to be dissembled. A book written in Czechoslovakia has recently revealed a considerable drug problem in the Eastern bloc nations, despite the severity of their laws and criminal prosecution. (In Prague on my way back from a forbidden seminar, the authorities planted and pretended to discover a quantity of drugs in my luggage. Once I was charged and in jail, I learned that no one ever gets off without at least two solid years of prison, *for the slightest contact* with anything to do with drugs.) If AIDS will not respect international borders, how are these regimes going to react when, as in the West, they may have to adopt a more liberal attitude toward one problem in order to better cope with the other, for example by relaxing restrictions on the sale of syringes? And what if they should need to work together with the international police to control this double network? If the AIDS virus were spliced onto a computer virus, you may well imagine what might happen to Interpol's computers and the geopolitical unconscious.[5] What then would become of the diplomatic corps? What would become of spies? And let's not even talk about soldiers—we can now no more distinguish between military and civilian than we can between public and private.

We are left with a small and from now on only secondary contradiction: the production and distribution of drugs are, of course, primarily organized by right-wing forces or regimes, by a certain form of capitalism. But in Western Europe drug consumption and a certain drug culture are commonly associated with a vaguely antiestablishment, left-leaning ideology, whereas the brutality of repressive politics generally has the characteristics of the right, and indeed of the extreme right-wing. We can in principle account for all these phenomena: they are not so strange as they first appear. In its particulars and within its boundaries, the code of these paradoxes is destined for an upheaval, and, to tell the truth, it is already undergoing one. But by recording, transcribing, or translating such an upheaval, we can only hope to mitigate its danger. To economize it. This is always possible and it always works: up to a point. As sudden and overwhelming as it may be, this event had broadcast itself even before we could talk about history or memory. The virus has no age.

NOTES

Translator's note: I would like to express my deep appreciation to Avital Ronell for giving me the opportunity to do this translation and for her invaluable advice and comments on the work. Thanks are due as well to Peter T. Connor and Elisabeth Bloomfield for their very generous help. Any inaccuracies or infelicities of expression are, of course, entirely my own responsibility.

1. Translator's note: The interviewer here uses the term *le flash,* which was imported into French drug jargon from the vocabulary of photography. The word is roughly equivalent to the English slang "rush."

2. Article L. 626: "A penalty of two months to two years imprisonment, or of a fine of 2,000FF to 10,000FF, or of both these penalties together is established for any person who will have contravened the provisions of those regulations of public administration concerning the production, conveyance, importation, exportation, holding, tender, transfer, acquisition, and *use* of substances or plants, or the cultivation of plants classified by statutory decree as harmful, *as well as any act relating to these operations*" (emphasis added).

3. Translator's note: *Le Grand Jeu* (the Big Game) was a literary movement in France contemporary with the surrealists that included among its numerous members Georges Gilbert LeComte.

4. "One of the first adventures of the *nostos* proper reaches much further back. The story of the Lotus-eaters goes back well beyond the barbaric age of demonic caricatures and magic deities. Whoever browses on the lotus succumbs, in the same way as anyone who heeds the Sirens' song or is touched by Circe's wand. But the victim does not die: 'Yet the Lotus-eaters did not harm the men of our company.' The only threats are oblivion and the surrender of will. The curse condemns them to no more than the primitive state without work and struggle in the 'fertile land': 'All who ate the lotus, sweeter than honey, thought no more of reporting to us, or of returning. Instead, they wished to stay there in the company of the Lotus-eater, picking the lotus and forgetting their home-land.'" Obliteration of the will, unproductivity (a society of foragers), nonwork, oblivion as the forgetting of the city. Adorno and Horkheimer correctly tie all these motifs tightly together, and, by contrast, tie them to the history of truth or of Western rationality. Moreover, they propose a modern political reading: "This kind of idyll, which recalls the happiness of narcotic drug addicts reduced to the lowest level in obdurate social orders, who use their drugs to help them endure the unendurable, is impermissible for the adherents of the rationale of self-preservation. It is actually the mere illusion of happiness, a dull vegetation, as meager as an animal's bare existence, and at best only the absence of the awareness of misfortune. But happiness holds truth and is of its nature a result, revealing itself with the abrogation of misery. Therefore, the sufferer who can-not bear to stay with the Lotus-eaters is justified. He opposes their illusion with that which is like yet unlike: the realization of utopia through historical labor . . ." (*Dialectic* 62–63). I find this reading compelling, at least within the general perspective of the book. But this would raise other types of questions which I cannot go into here.

5. I propose the word *telerhetoric* or *metatelerhetoric* to designate that gen-eral and more than general space in which these matters would be treated. For example: in the case of computers, is the use of the word "virus" simply a metaphor? And we might pose the same question for the use of the word "par-asite." The preliminary to this sort of problematic should deal with rhetoric itself, as a parasitic or viral structure: in its origins and in general. Whether viewed from up close or from far away, does not everything that comes to affect the proper have the form of a virus (neither alive nor dead, neither human nor "reappropriable by the proper of man," nor generally subjectivable)? And does-n't rhetoric always obey a logic of parasitism? Or rather, doesn't the parasite log-ically and normally disrupt logic? If rhetoric is viral or parasitic (without being the AIDS of language it at least opens up the possibility of such an affection) how should we consider the rhetorical-semantic drift of words like "virus," "parasite," etc.? And furthermore, the computer virus, just like its "literal" counterpart, attacks, in this case telephonically, something like the "genetic code" of the computer (cf. Fabien Gruhier, "Votre Ordinateur a la vérole" ["Your Infected Computer"]. The author notes that computer viruses are "con-tagious" and "travel through telephone lines at the speed of an electron. . . . One need only be equipped with a modem to be contaminated by a virus from Asia,

America, or Timbuktu.") Even now software vaccines" are being developed. Once again we have the question of the *pharmakon* as the familial scene and the question of paternity: last year it was a student at Cornell, the son of an official responsible for electronic security, who sent out the virus "guilty" of spreading this "infection" (and will we put quotation marks everywhere, these speech act condoms, to protect our language from contamination?). This so-called computer infection, spliced onto the AIDS virus itself grafted onto drugs, this is more than a modern, worldwide figure of the plague; we know that it mobilized the entire network of American security forces, including the FBI—and the DST (Direction de la Surveillance du Territoire) and the DGSE (Direction Générale de la Sécurité Extérieure). . . . I bring this up to revive our initial exchange concerning the determination of competence. Who will determine the pertinence of these questions? By what authority? According to what criteria? These questions should in return affect everything that we have up to now said about drug addiction. I might take the liberty of mentioning the many places where I have attempted to treat the alogic of the parasite (for example: *Of Grammatology,* "Plato's Pharmacy" in *Dissemination,* "Signature Event Context" in *Margins of Philosophy, Limited Inc abc* . . . and passim).

WORKS CITED

Adorno, Theodor W., and Max Horkheimer. *Dialectic of Enlightenment,* translated by John Cumming. London: Verso, 1979.

Artaud, Antonin. "Letter to the Legislator of the Drug Act." *Collected Works of Antonin Artaud,* translated by Victor Conti. Vol. 1. London-Calder, 1968, pp. 58–62. 1968–1974.

Baudelaire, Charles. "Les Paradis artificiels." *Oeuvres complèes.* Ed. Claude Pichois. Vol. 2. Paris: Gallimard. 1975.

Benjamin, Walter. "Hashish in Marseilles." *Reflections: Essays, Aphorisms, Autobiographical Writings,* translated by Edmund Jephcott. Ed. and introduction by Peter Demetz. New York: Schocken, 1978, pp. 137–145.

Burroughs, William S. *Naked Lunch.* New York: Grove, 1962.

De Quincey, Thomas. *Diaries of an English Opium-Eater, and Susperia de profundis.* Boston: Ticknor, 1855.

Derrida, Jacques. *Of Grammatology,* translated by Gavatri Chakravorty Spivak. Baltimore: Johns Hopkins University Press, 1976.

——— . *Limited Inc.* Evanston: Northwestern University Press, 1988.

——— . "Plato's Pharmacy." *Dissemination,* translated by and introduction by Barbara Johnson. Chicago: University of Chicago Press, 1981, pp. 61–171.

————— . "Signature Event Context." *Margins of Philosophy,* translated by Alan Bass. Chicago: University of Chicago Press, 1982, pp. 307–330.

Gruhier, Fabien. "Votre Ordinateur à la vèrole." *Nouveau Observateur* 18–24 Nov. 1988.

Plato. *Phaedrus,* translated by C. J. Rowe. Warminster, LJK: Aris, 1988.

Zola, Émile. *L'Assomoir*. Paris: Fasquelle, 1977.

Chapter Two

NIETZSCHE'S DIONYSIAN HIGH

Morphin' with Endorphins

DAVID B. ALLISON

> Every tissue and nerve vibrates in me . . . I have never had
> such a feeling of rapture as when listening to [the Overture to
> *Die Meistersinger*].
>
> —Nietzsche, Letter to Rohde, 27 Oct., 1868

Throughout the entire course of Nietzsche's writings, from the notebooks of the 1860s right up until his final delusional correspondence, one is struck by the transformative, transfigurative agency Nietzsche finds in the notion—and in the experience—of ecstasy. In one way or another, ecstasy will play a principal role in Nietzsche's accounts of art, myth, religion, and politics, and it will resonate in his accounts of a Joyful Wisdom, of the Eternal Return, the Will to Power, and the Overman—lending them an intensity with which the subject, the reader, or audience is inspired to identify.

Ecstatic is, of course, eccentric—to put out of place, to be outside, to be drawn outside oneself, out of one's wits, transported: at once, rapture and dispossession. It has to do with transgression of limits, forms, bound-aries—of oneself, one's own limits, and often enough, of imposed limits, laws, and prohibitions. Generally speaking, the whole issue of ecstasy is marginal enough to be proscribed by authority, normalcy, and traditional orthodoxy. Derrida tells us that philosophy has always had it in for the margins, i.e., that philosophy always wanted to govern its other, such that it could set its own limits.[1] Philosophy, he says, is the only discourse that consistently defines itself. What exceeded those stated limits simply could not be articulated. Perhaps it could only be seen or felt, in some most unusual manner. For Schopenhauer, this inarticulable excess was the metaphysical "World Will"—for Kant, the metaphysical "thing in itself," the *"Ding an sich."* For Lacan, when the margin opens up between need and demand, it is more simply, and quite simply, "the thing," *"das Ding."* Piercing the symbolic order of law and language, desire finds *"das Ding"* as a point, a real place, the earthly delight of desire's own saturation: but, speechless, a place of death for the socially constructed ego. In other words, *jouissance*—a supralapsarian garden, paradisiacal ecstasy.

In the post-Hegelian discourse, there seems to be a renewed interest in ecstasy. Beginning with the emotional intensity of the spiritual subject in Kierkegaard, through the dialectical constitution of the subject in Kojève—from the surrealists (drawing upon Freud) through the work of Bataille, Foucault, and Lacan, followed by Deleuze and Guattari—ecstasy is given a rigorous psychological, i.e., antimetaphysical examination, an analysis which, at the same time, opens up a remarkable social–political dimension to this phenomenon.

What were formerly held to be the objects, or even the causes of ecstatic rapture—the Passion of Jesus, hierarchies of Cherubim and Seraphim, Thrones and Principalities, choruses of Archangels and Plotinian Emanations of the Divine, not to mention the overwhelming waves of the World Will and the ineffable, ungraspable Sublime—redolent of Oscar Wilde's English foxhunters—these objects are now regarded by psychologists as psychologically causative "triggers," i.e., certain occasions or events that seem to be associated with the onset of ecstatic states.[2] Some triggers are termed "inducing triggers" and others are called "inserted triggers," the latter of which are said to be the set of intense qualities that correspond to the lived or experienced sense of ecstasy. Inducing triggers include nature, sexual love, exercise, religion, art, poetic knowledge, recollection, beauty—even "those short, plump little cakes called *petites madelines.*" Inserted triggers include experiences described in what are termed "up-words" and phrases—i.e., experiences associated with sensations of flying, weightlessness, floating, rising up, etc., as well as by what are termed "contact words," namely, experiences that include claims of union, presence, mingling, identification with totality, god, nature, spirits, peace, timelessness, perfection, eternity, knowledge, and bliss. Such feelings include loss of self, of time, of place, of limitation, and language. One likewise feels a gain of eternity, a feeling of release, a new life, another world, joy, satisfaction, salvation, perfection, mystical knowledge and enhanced mental capacity.[3]

Now, it was precisely because Nietzsche could vividly experience and undergo such ecstatic states,[4] that he came to criticize Schopenhauer's metaphysical account of the World Will, the noumenal reality, which purportedly underlied all empirical individuation and sensible representation, i.e., that metaphysically real realm, which subtended and thus precluded, any possibility of its appearance, its actual experience.

Schopenhauer claimed that the World Will can be experienced in one unique way—namely, in music, where he argued, that the object of music is the Will itself. But, since experience itself belongs to the order of representation, of phenomenal reality, of appearances only, this perforce excludes by definition any experience of the noumenal. Now while this Schopenhauerian metaphysical division seems to prefigure the Nietzschean distinction between the Apollonian and Dionysian orders in the *Birth of Tragedy*, Nietzsche will in fact cast this distinction forth, *not* in metaphysical terms, but in exclusively *psychological* terms—indeed, in strikingly modern psychological terms of an entirely naturalistic, empirical order. In order to do this, however, Nietzsche had to explain to himself *how* these ecstatic states were possible, and in what they consisted. The key to his explanation was what served as a "trigger" for his own experience, and he found this in his passionate experience of music—as had Schopenhauer himself. Beginning with his drafts from 1869, he focused on this complex ecstatic experience of music, and this resulted in an unpublished work of 1871, entitled "On Music and Words."[5] The very title suggests his early dependency on Schopenhauer, since its terms are predicated on the opposition between representation, i.e., language, or the language of images, and the purported object or ground of representation, music—i.e., the nonimagistic Will.[6]

What complicates matters for Nietzsche is that he finds himself in the perplexing situation of trying to explain all this by trying to accommodate himself to the prevailing aesthetic models of music, all of which were hopelessly conflicted. The romantic view has music expressing every variety of emotion and feeling. Hanslick's formalist view has music expressing nothing beyond the formal properties of the composition itself—tonality, melody, harmony, rhythm, etc. For Hanslick, music certainly does not express emotion or feeling, since music is nonintentional, and for him, at least, it surely does not express any urgings, strivings, and conflicts of a World Will. Schopenhauer's metaphysical view is championed by Wagner—and, initially, by Nietzsche.[7] Yet at this very time, Wagner himself goes on to develop a view of opera which has music becoming instrumental to the drama and the libretto, thus subverting the primary expressive value of music, and contradicting Schopenhauer's own claims as well.[8]

Nietzsche's resolution to all this—to the competing models of romanticism, Schopenhauer, Hanslick, and Wagner One and Two—is simple and dramatic. By focusing on his own ecstatic experience of music, he undercuts each of these models, yet he leaves the so-called integrity or primacy of music intact. While the immediately preceding tradition had debated the objective status of music, according to one model or another, Nietzsche comes to realize in this early essay of 1871 the very simple truth that it is the subjective states of our experience of music that provokes our ecstatic response. Again, what is now termed its "trigger" effect. And because our ecstatic response is of such a nature that we feel positively transfigured by the experience, an experience characterized by loss of ego and by a suspension of ordinary object-relations, the very distinction between subject and object becomes blurred, attenuated, if not entirely suspended. The distinction that supports ordinary intentional experience, between the objective and subjective genitive, simply does not obtain in the ecstatic state.

In addressing exactly what the object of music is, i.e., the theoretical model of its subject matter, Nietzsche realizes that its object *(Gegenstand)* is given to us as the content *(Inhalt)* of our own intensely undergone aesthetic experience, our ecstatic states of dispossession. This musically charged state of ecstatic disposession is precisely what he terms "The Dionysian State," and such a state is effectively the entire *field of experience,* shorn of simple subject–object relations. Schiller had earlier termed this state one of intense "mood" or "disposition": specifically, it was a "musical mood" *(musikalische Stimmung),* and this had been discussed by Schopenhauer, but it is Nietzsche who really analyzes it in detail—to be followed in a strikingly similar fashion by Heidegger's account of *Stimmung* in *Being and Time.*

To explain the nature of this state, Nietzsche argues against the romantics (and with Hanslick) that this intense, musically ecstatic mood cannot take place on the level of feelings or sensations, since they are still bound with specific object representations. Rather, what occurs in this state of Dionysian-musical enchantment is an emotional dissociation or detachment of affective states from specific object relations. It will be this new distinction—between feelings *(Gefühle)* and emotions or affects *(Affekte)*—that will begin to emerge as an explanation for the broader phenomenon. The former (i.e., feelings) do not have the power to generate the Dionysian state of dispossession because they retain their fixed association with representations. It is on the level of affect or emotion that the dissociation begins to take place. The excitement provoked by musical tonality is experienced as a fluidity of affect, in that intense emotional states lose their conventional associations and tend toward reinvesting their objects of pleasure with more immediate, hallucinatory cathexes—and such states involve an extreme intensification of psychic discharge, resulting in a heightened increase of satisfaction. But to the extent in which further intensification of psychic discharge is provoked and occurs, with its concomitant increase in pleasure, so do the states of affect become progressively freed from their associative connections, their regular accompanying object representations, until the point of frenzy *(Rauch)* is attained, in which case the underlying drives *(Triebe)* become completely free-flowing, anarchic, and unbound. These deeper instinctual drives will ultimately constitute the power *(Kraft)* or force *(Macht)* that drives the emotions themselves—and for the intense, musically aesthetic experience, they will constitute what he calls the very "sanctuary of music."[9]

Nietzsche will often speak of these states of Dionysian excess and frenzy as states of "drunkenness," "the horrible 'witches brew' of sensuality," "intoxication," "wanton abandon," etc., and indeed, by the time he composed *The Birth of Tragedy,* he begins to explain the Dionysian drives themselves by appeal to these most natural—and most extreme—states of intoxication and frenzy. This is, of course, opposed to the other natural term by which he addresses the Apollonian drive—as the state of dreaming. Now, this experienced state of intense emotional intensity and dissociation, when one's drives themselves are no longer bound—what Freud would later describe as the psychic level of primary process formation—this is precisely the Dionysian state of disindividuation or dispossession.[10] Thus, Nietzsche would write in a draft as early as 1869, that music is "through and through symbolic of the drives *(der Triebe),*" and is thus "more general than any particular action." And, since the drives—the instinctual expressions of psychic energy—are themselves unconscious or sublimated, their subjective translation occurs to us as intense emotional states. The musical effect *(musikalische Wirkung)* thus occurs on the deeper level of drives, and is in turn quickly discharged or depotentialized to become an emotional affect *(Affektwirkung).* Or, according to a strikingly similar Freudian vocabulary, all drives are expressed in terms of emotion and representation, and emotion—or affect—is, for Freud, the qualitative expression of

the quantity of instinctual energy, or drive. That these affective states
can be transformed, for example, through conversion, displacement, and
transformation of affect, etc., this will constitute the very dynamics of
tragic drama in *The Birth of Tragedy*.

With Nietzsche's analysis of the psychological dynamics of the ecstatic state brought about by music, in the writings leading up to his "On
Music and Words" essay of 1871, he then turns to consider the origin of
these states in *The Birth of Tragedy*. Specifically, he will turn towards
the musical origins of tragedy—what he, following Aristotle, considered
to be the highest, most developed art form, in classical Greek culture.
Indeed, the original subtitle for *The Birth of Tragedy* was *Out of The
Spirit of Music*.

It is well known that Nietzsche traces out the structural components
of tragic drama according to his understanding of its historical development. Basically, he identified its earliest moments with the emergence of
lyric poetry and primitive folk music, where versification was intensified
by musical accompaniment—specifically, by the intensely rhythmic and
tonal language of flutes, pipes, drums, zithers, sackbuts, heptagons, etc.
The intoxicating effects of these instruments on the Greek populace is
sufficiently witnessed by Aristotle's strenuous rejection of them, in *The
Politics*. Aristotle tells us that such music serves only the "vulgar pleasure" of the audience. "It does not express a state of character, but
rather a mood of religious excitement; and it should therefore be used
on those occasions when the effect to be produced on the audience is the
release of emotion, and not instruction."[11] What Nietzsche finds especially significant in this musical accompaniment is the element of *tonal
dissonance,* which manifests the forcefulness and dynamic character of
the visionary's world—a Dionysian world capable of every tension,
transformation, stress, intensity, and pulsion.

It is with the early Dionysian cults, and with the dithyrambic poetry
of Archilochus, in particular, that the dynamics of music become focused
on provoking the ecstatic states of dispossession, of disindividuation,
among the fellow cult participants. The lyric poet effectively created a
musical mood in his audience, inducing an emotional or affective disposition that was so all-pervasive in its intensity and generality, that the
poet and his audience literally become intoxicated, dispossessed. Effectively, the musical mood was intensified by the addition of Dionysian ritual and erotic imagery—with a little help from one's other friends: narcotics, wine, and stimulants[12]—and, especially, by the addition of the
chorus. Composed of the Dionysian cult participants themselves, the
chorus would chant and sing, lending resonance and harmony to the
musical instrumentation; they would reinforce its melodic progression

and thus contribute a heightened emotionality to the music—all the while, dancing, swaying rhythmically, overcome with passion.

That Nietzsche chose to focus on *dissonance* as "the primordial phenomenon of Dionysian art" was prescient. Dissonance presuposes the entire creative reservoir of musical elements within the tonal system—arguably, within any tonal system: tone, sonority, beat, rhythm, tempo, harmony, measure, melody, polyphony, progression, etc. Modern cognitive science shows that, much like the visual field—which we continually stabilize and model, according to a relatively small number of visual foci—so with the auditory field, we anticipate tonal progression, chord development, and harmonic resolution—according to the cultural norms which govern the tonal scale.[13] On the twelve-tone scale, resolution usually occurs within the diatonic frame, offset by the chromatic or "dissonant" tones above that, as well as by certain minor keys. We know from his early essays that Nietzsche was familiar with Helmholtz' important work on tone sensation, which experimentally demonstrated that pleasure tends to accompany the listener's resolution of musical dissonance into consonnance. Effectively, music sets up anticipations and then satisfies them. As Robert Jourdain has recently described this, the anticipation is of temporally developing patterns in tone, melody, harmony, rhythm, tempo, phrasing, and form. As Jourdain says, music is basically "a construction of a continual temporal flux, orchestrated according to precise proportions in which the listener's anticipation of tonal movement and proportion are gracefully integrated and resolved."[14] To the extent that the musical composition can continually reshape and heighten anticipation, by witholding resolution—by temporarily violating and delaying resolution—and then satisfy the more complex anticipation with a crescendo of resolution, music becomes far more "expressive" and more richly satisfying. In short, it yields great emotional satisfaction—where our experience is heightened to exceed the fulfillment of ordinary satisfaction, i.e., of built-up tension and its satisfying, pleasure-giving release.[15]

Recent work in musical psychoacoustics shows that with the auditory resolution of dissonance, within the neural routings of the primary and secondary auditory cortex, the entire kinesthesic muscular system becomes subsequently engaged to help "score" or "model" or "map" these complex tonal progressions and structures onto the body itself, as a kind of sensory-motor register, so as to supplement the auditory system in attaining resolution, completion, and thereby, satisfaction. And it is with this supplement of kinesthesic modeling (effectively, a somatic encoding)—whereby the body is moved to mimic beat, rhythm, harmony, and melody through muscular flex and contraction, i.e., through bodily gesture, movement, and dance—that the higher order neural networks in the somatosensory and motor cortex areas of the brain begin to produce endorphins. And it is precisely this production of endorphins that transforms what was largely an automatic, relatively homeostatic response to auditory stimuli, into an intensely pleasurable experience: ecstasy.[16] Or, as Nietzsche expressed this in 1869, the power of musical experience operates upon our instinctual drives so as to provoke their discharge into highly excited emotional states, characterized by fluidity of affect and ego loss—that is to say, dispossession, disindividuation.

Reexamining the Dionysian states of frenzy *(Rauch)* some sixteen years later, Nietzsche would devote some four sections in *Twilight of the Idols* to this issue, beginning with Section 8 of the chapter "Skirmishes of an Untimely Man." He says, for example, in Section 10, that

> In the Dionysian state [of frenzy] . . . the whole affective system *(das gesammte Affekt-System)* is excited and enhanced, so that it discharges all its means of expression at once and drives forth simultaneously the power of representation, imitation, transfiguration, transformation, and every kind of mimicking and acting. The essential feature here remains the ease of metamorphosis, the inability *not* to react (similar to certain hysterical types who also, upon any suggestion enter into *any* role). It is impossible for the Dionysian type not to understand any suggestion; he does not overlook any sign of an affect *(Zeichen des Affekts)*. . . . He enters into any skin, into any affect: he constantly transforms himself. Music, as we understand it today, is also a total excitement and a total discharge of the affects, but even so, only the remnant of a much fuller world of expression of the affects, a mere residue of the Dionysian histrionicism.[17]

And it is at this state of charged and fluid affect that Nietzsche claims his distinctive resolution to the question of tragedy. This is the point where the Dionysian dithyramb, or the classical tragic drama, rejoins with the voice of Apollo, to form the celebrated "fraternal union" between Dionysus and Apollo.

Insofar as it is a specific cult ritual, the Dionysian transformation entails a modification of the ecstatic process. One "loses" oneself and becomes an other, but only according to a certain image of deep ritual significance. The follower of Dionysus ritually reenacts a precise mythological role, i.e., he ritually invokes a specific image or vision according to which he becomes other than himself in this emotional reconfiguration, this new affective cathexis, or bond. In the case of the Dionysian ritual, the image extended to the excited participant is that of the Satyr.

Once the ritual dithyramb was brought to the stage as a public spectacle (i.e., during the reign of Pisistratus), the actor intervened and assumed the part of what was until then the visionary state of the satyr chorus. Wearing the ritual mask, the actor became the figure of Dionysus himself, or, that of his surrogate, the tragic hero. Nietzsche explained that "drama in the narrower sense" began here, with the introduction of the actor, since it implied a forceful distinction between the chorus and audience. The chorus itself did not require the real representation of Dionysus, since it already held Dionysus before itself as a visionary state. Representation was required only for the audience, not for the chorus. Accordingly, the function of the chorus changed radically. As Nietzsche would remark in section nine of *The Birth of Tragedy,*

> Now the dithyrambic chorus was assigned the task of exciting the mood *(Stimmung)* of the listeners to such a Dionysian degree that, when the tragic hero appeared on the stage, they did not see the awkwardly masked human being but rather a visionary figure, born as it were from their own rapture.[18]

Nietzsche went on to argue that the representation of the god or hero was made fully convincing to the audience by the double process of transference and condensation. Initially, the audience transferred its own rapturous vision of Dionysus onto the specific representation (the actor), thereby transforming the concrete actor into the god Dionysus (or, into the tragic hero, who was himself one ritual image of Dionysus): "He transferred the whole magical image of the god that was trembling before his soul to that masked figure and, as it were, dissolved its reality into the unreality of spirits."[19] Once the transfer was made, the process of transformation could be completed by a second stage—a kind of image intensification—and this was brought about by the actor himself.

Ecstatically charged by both the chorus and audience to a heightened state of divinity, of divine presence and authority, the actor then took it upon himself to condense this fevered excitement into the most economical form of expression: the epic pronouncement, the precise statement of Dionysian wisdom, which until the moment of his speech had been everywhere only felt. Viewed as this trembling figure and sustained by the intoxicated chorus and the transported audience, "Dionysus no longer speaks through forces but as an epic hero, almost in the language of Homer." He now appeared dream-like, and spoke through the clairvoyant language of images. The forces struggling for expression—the frenzied music and dance, the disindividuated states of excess, joy, suffering, and abandon—all found their voice, but now in the language of Apollo.

It was Sophocles and Aeschylus who intervened and invested the ritual dithyramb with the more extensive mythological content of the epic tradition. And by doing this, Nietzsche maintained, not only did they save these myths from the inevitable fate of becoming mere historical curiosities, but they also gave them their highest achievement: they infused the myths with the profound significance of Dionysian wisdom. The already fading world of Homeric myth henceforth became reanimated by a far deeper and more penetrating world view. As Nietzsche would remark,

> Dionysian truth takes over the entire domain of myth as the symbolism of its knowledge which it makes known partly in the public cult of tragedy and partly in the secret celebrations of dramatic mysteries, but always in the old mythical garb.[20]

Under the hand of Sophocles and Aeschylus, the old myths were retained and became strenghened; they became vehicles of Dionysian wisdom, which taught that all human suffering comes from individuation—whether this be of the individual who confronts the laws of nature, society, the gods, or fate. By the same token, this reinvigorated mythical teaching would reawaken the possibility of a social and political community. And this could only occur when the frenzied disindividuation of the Dionysian celebrant yielded and submitted to modification: when it became transformed, at the urging of the chorus, into a collective embrace, an impassioned identification by the audience with the spectacle of a common mythology, history, and destiny. All this would occur immediately, on the very stage set before them. It was an ecstatic embrace indeed.

NOTES

1. Jacques Derrida, "Tympan" in *Margins of Philosophy,* Eng. tr., Alan Bass (Chicago: University of Chicago Press, 1982), pp. ix–xxix.

2. Marghanita Laski, *Ecstasy: A Study of some Secular and Religious Experiences* (Bloomington: Indiana University Press, 1961), p. 16.

3. Ibid., compare, especially, Appendices A–J, pp. 375–533. Laski gives an interesting analysis of Nietzsche's remarks on musical ecstasy in Section 1 of *The Case of Wagner,* in Appendix A (pp. 405–409).

4. A friend of Nietzsche's, Resa von Schirnhofer, recalled one such experience, from the Spring of 1884: "Nietzsche invited me to accompany him to a bullfight in Nice, where an official regulation prohibited the use of horses or killing of bulls, which agreed with my animal-loving views. Soon, however, this tame skirmish seemed like a caricature of a bullfight and began intensely to stimulate our desire to laugh. The similar behavior of the six bulls, which succeeded one another in the same arena, seemed to betray knowledge of the regulations on their part, and it had an especially comical effect when at the end the bull ran as fast as he could out of the large gates that opened in the background.

"We applauded and hoped he would come back out and bow gratefully like an actor. The music of *Carmen* at prelude and intermezzo was absolutely out of place at this bullfight in the 'Happy Laughter' arena, like sounding battle-trumpets at a rural dance. And suddenly, provoked by the contrast between this ridiculous spectacle and the stimulating rhythms and exciting melodies, I felt, out of unconscious depths, a strong desire to see a genuine Spanish *corrida de toros* with all its breathtaking splendor and *grandezza*, with its stylized wildness and bulls that defended themselves heroically. . . . This music had an electrifying effect on Nietzsche, who listened ecstatically, calling my attention to its pulsating rhythm, its elemental vigor, and picturesqueness. I had not yet seen *Carmen*, only heard fragments from it, knew nothing about Bizet, and so I listened with interest to what Nietzsche told about the composer, who had died at the age of 37 without achieving recognition. Later, when I read somewhere that Nietzsche's enthusiasm for Bizet's music had been contrived, artificial, a pose, a reaction against Wagner, it conflicted with my memory of him from Nice. It seems to me, rather, that Nietzsche may have felt the nerve-stimulating element in this music as a vivifying current, which, penetrating into the depths of his inherently psychopathic nature, confused it and filled his whole interior, producing a feeling of happiness similar to the effect of the rushing mistral" (in Sander Gilman, *Conversations with Nietzsche*, Oxford University Press, 1987, pp. 149–150).

5. The essay is translated into English by Walter Kaufmann, and is to be found as an appendix in Carl Dalhaus' *Between Romanticism and Modernism: Four Studies in the Music of the Later 19th Century*, Eng. tr., Mary Whittall (Berkeley: University of California Press, 1980), pp. 106–119, and in the *Kritische Studienausgabe* (KSA), Vol. 7 (Berlin: de Gruyter, 1980), pp. 359–369, and pp. 185–190. For an extended analysis of this text, see D. Allison, "Some Remarks on Nietzsche's Essay of 1871, 'On Music and Words,'" in *New Nietzsche Studies*, Vol. 1 1/2, Fall/Winter, 1996, pp. 15–41.

6. Interestingly, the title itself was given to the essay by Nietzsche's subsequent editors—perhaps reinforcing their view, the common view, that Nietzsche was indeed a rigorous Schopenhauerian. Nietzsche strongly contests this charge in his later 1886 Preface to *The Birth of Tragedy*.

7. Already by 1868, however, Nietzsche was highly critical of Schopenhauer's general metaphysical claims. See, for example, Vol. III of the Historical-Critical Edition *(HKG)* of Nietzsche's works (5 Vols. Ed. H. J. Mette and K. Schlechta. Munich: Beck, 1934), pp. 352–361.

8. On Wagner's theoretical position at this time, see Carl Dahlhaus, "The Twofold Truth in Wagner's Aesthetics: Nietzsche's Fragment 'On Music and Words,'" in Dahlhaus, op. cit., pp. 19–39.

9. Music is indeed a "sanctuary" in that it is its own world—it is a constructed, artificial world, which is immediately experienced as a completely controlled environment, engaging the emotions and structuring the reception of temporality and movement: it resolves an enormity of elements and anticipations into perfect form, beauty.

10. For an extended account of the contrast between the Apollonian "dream state" and the Dionysian state of "disindividuation," see D. Allison, *Reading the New Nietzsche* (Lantham: Rowman & Littlefield), Ch. I, "On the Birth of Tragedy."

11. *The Politics of Aristotle*, Book VIII, ch. 6, Eng. tr. by E. Barker (New York: Oxford University Press, 1962) pp. 348–349.

12. Due to Nietzsche's recurring bouts of painful illness, it should be recalled that he regularly sought refuge in the use of such drugs as opium, chloral hydrate, potassium bromide, ameline hydrate, sulfonal, and others. In fact, Resa von Schirnhofer recalls that he "had written for himself all kinds of prescriptions signed by Dr. Nietzsche, which had been prepared and filled without question or hesitation." She suspected he frequently smoked hashish, especially after one occasion, when appearing at the doorway of his room, completely disheveled, "he described to me how, when he closed his eyes, he saw an abundance of fantastic flowers, winding and intertwining, constantly growing and changing forms and colors in exotic luxuriance, sprouting one out of the other. 'I never get any rest,' he complained"(Gilman, op. cit., pp. 163–164).

13. In his recent volume, *Music, the Brain, and Ecstasy: How Music Captures Our Imagination* (New York: William Morrow & Co., 1997), Robert Jourdain specifies three kinds of dissonance to be resolved by the listener: auditory critical band frequency interference and synchronicity of sound beat—both of which are complemented by overtone interactions—as well as the more complex structural element, harmonic dissonance, involving chord movement. Compare, especially, pp. 100–105.

14. Ibid., pp. 302–303.

15. Ibid., pp. 312–313.

16. While the auditory cortex is densely connected to the temporal and frontal lobes of the brain, it is not so connected with the motor cortex or the somatosensory cortex (and this would seem to block the automatic engagement of the kinesthetic-motor system by the auditory system). Rather, we seem to use our muscular system to represent musical patterns of tension, anticipation, impetus, movement, trajectory, contour, etc., so as to serve as a system of notation to inscribe and remember musical patterns as they transpire temporally, and

thus to amplify our experience of its complexity and the satisfaction this yields. Thus, musical patterns are replicated in the motor system as well as in the auditory system. In this sense, our kinesthetic system becomes a kind of resonator, our body literally permits itself to become an instrument, to be played by the music. More simply stated, perhaps, this is exactly how we "go with the flow," how we "get into" musical rhythms and harmonic cadences. And it is at this level of *bodily representation* that the neurons within the kinesthetic-motor system are excited and begin to discharge endorphins, further enhancing the sense of pleasure—in this case, delight, ecstasy—in our experience of music. And we become transformed. Ibid., pp. 324–326. As Nietzsche would remark in Section Two of *The Birth of Tragedy*, with "Dionysian *music* . . . the entire symbolism of the body is called into play, not the mere symbolism of the lips, face, and speech but the whole pantomime of dancing, forcing every member into rhythmic movement" (*The Birth of Tragedy* and *The Case of Wagner*, Eng. tr., W. Kaufmann. New York: Vintage, 1967), Sec. 2, p. 40.

17. *Twilight of the Idols*, in W. Kaufmann, *The Portable Nietzsche* (New York: Viking, 1968), pp. 519–520. KSA 6, pp. 117–118.

18. *Birth of Tragedy*, Sec. 9, p. 66.

19. Ibid., Sec. 9, p. 66.

20. Ibid., Sec. 10, p. 74.

Chapter Three

ARIADNE'S THREAD

Walter Benjamin's Hashish Passages

GARY SHAPIRO

In a letter of 1932 to Gershom Scholem, Benjamin outlines his literary ambitions; he plans four major books, one of which would have been on hashish. The others were to include the *Passagenwerk*, his essays on literature, and his letters. It could be said that we now have those three books, if only in the form of sprawling and gigantic ruins. The *Passagenwerk* has been the object of many inspired and yet hopeless projects of reconstruction; the literary essays are available in German and other languages; and letters from throughout his life have been collected and published. All can be supplemented by texts like the *Moscow Diary*, and the complexities of the European city are clearly implicated in Benjamin's work on both Paris and hashish. The city is the site of intoxication, whether provoked by commodities, a drug, or the erratic wanderings of the *flâneur*. It is in the city that we find the fix that we need.

In the case of the proposed hashish book, we ostensibly have only fragments: it is notable that the most substantial is the essay "Hashish in Marseilles," and there is also a short story set in the same city; then there is the four-page "Crocknotizen" and about 80 small pages called "Protocols" by Benjamin and his companions in drug experiences in the

Suhrkamp collection *Walter Benjamin: Über Haschisch;* these are to all appearances a series of dated, miscellaneous, rough, and unedited notes. Yet, when Benjamin writes to Scholem on July 26, 1932, about the four books that will be the fruit of his lifetime's work, he says that one will be "a truly exceptional book about hashish," and he distinguishes it from the other projects by requesting that his friend keep it confidential: "Nobody knows about this last topic," he writes, "and for the time being it should remain between us."[1] Why the warning, the secrecy? In the "Surrealism" essay he says that hash is a dangerous introduction to profane illumination. Dangerous in where it might lead us? Perhaps into a labyrinth from which there is no exit?

Given his statement to Scholem, written when he was immersing himself in the *Passagenwerk* or *Arcades Project,* we have some reason for thinking of Benjamin's hashish experiences as more than a casual, experimental, or episodic use of intoxicants. Some people do drugs and experiment with writing or philosophy. In these cases, psychotropic writing is a record or reflection of, or a meditation upon the experience; the writing is seen as a sign, an indication, of what transpires under the influence of the drug. Benjamin's hashish writing, the passages that he composed in relation to the experiences, ought to be seen as avoiding such an external relation of writing and *Rausch.* The *pharmakon* is both the substance ingested and the writing to which it gives rise. (Benjamin sometimes refers to it as a *Gift* in German, with the senses of both present and poison, and of potion, which offers one link between them.) Benjamin came to see hashish as an avenue of "profane illumination," one whose force coincided to some extent with surrealism and which became important to him at around the same time as the latter.

One of the profane illuminations achieved in reflecting on "Hashish in Marseilles" was that the writer of prose and the hashish eater are engaged in deeply analogous forms of rapture. Writing about hashish, Benjamin discovers the joy and the difference of repetition that are writing and his writing; writing prose he threads his way through a labyrinth like the streets of Marseilles or Naples. The space of writing and the time of the hashish trance (these are Benjamin's words, even if I abbreviate "hashish") are uncanny variations of one another. If Walter Benjamin was addicted to anything, it was to writing. Benjamin's hashish writings are already inscribed in a literary tradition, in which Baudelaire's name is the most obvious.[2] His use of hashish was occasional, and much of it was undertaken in controlled conditions, where protocols of the experience were transcribed; other men of science and letters (Ernst Bloch, Ernst Joel, and Fritz Fränkel) participated in the same spirit.

Benjamin sees it as characteristic of the flux of the modern world that it encourages the "short habits" that Nietzsche endorsed. One of the dangers of this world is the commodification of experience, a threat that Benjamin finds in the thought of eternal recurrence which appears in the nineteenth century in such diverse figures as Baudelaire, Blanqui, and Nietzsche. As he understands this idea, it means that each moment of experience is indefinitely repeatable and replicable, like a mass-produced commodity, or like a photograph; and yet the thought of recurrence is designed to endow each of these moments with an aura, testifying by means of myth to the contradiction between repetition and aura that is analyzed in the essay on the reproduction of the work of art.[3] In such a world, addiction could have the attraction of being a true constant.[4] If there is a reason for rethinking and rereading Benjamin's writings on hashish in our context, it may have to do with what I propose was his deepest and most continuous addiction, the addiction to writing, an addiction that would link Benjamin's hashish use to culture, in the sense of a "high" or literary culture and would reinforce the suggestion in Plato's *Phaedrus* that writing is a drug. Such an exploration will have to touch on the question of how one writes about states of intoxication that many have said are pre- or extra-linguistic.

The connection between trance and writing is made explicit in this passage that reflects on the passages of both by means of the figure of the labyrinth:

> To begin to solve the riddle of the ecstasy of trance, one ought to meditate on Ariadne's thread. What joy in the mere act of unrolling a ball of thread. And this joy is very deeply related to the joy of trance, as to that of creation. We go forward; but in doing so, we not only discover the twists and turns of the cave, but also enjoy this pleasure of discovery against the background of the other, rhythmical bliss of unrolling the thread. The certainty of unrolling an artfully wound skein—is that not the joy of all productivity, at least in prose? And under hashish we are enraptured prose-beings in the highest power (R, 142).[5]

Rather than seeing the experiences as escapes from language or culture, Benjamin thought of them as forms of "profane illumination," consistent with and amplifying a material critique of society by inducing the subject to attend to the neglected underside, the unthought in the surrounding world, and to articulate the illumination (in writing, in his case). There is nothing in Benjamin's writing to suggest the apocalyptic claims (which many of us recall from the 1960s) to the effect that the psychotropics lead us to a realm beyond language, beyond the conceptual, or beyond culture. As he explicitly notes, the illumination achieved is not in the experience itself but in the relection upon it, a reflection that takes a specifically literary or prosaic form. The hashish *Rausch* will "not teach us half as much about thinking (which is eminently narcotic) as the profane illumination of thinking about the hashish trance" (R, 190). The passage through the hashish trance must be supplemented by the passages of prose, and we will find that their twists and turns evoke that complex of passages which Benjamin calls the labyrinth.

Sometimes what Benjamin discovers seems surprisingly familiar, and familiar even within the specifically German and European cultural world in which he lived. In "Crocknotizen," for example, he finds that one of the chief effects of intoxication is to focus our attention on ornament and design, to allow us to linger with it rather than pass it by as we usually do when pressed by our usual concerns (H, 57).[6] Lingering with it and meditating on it, we ponder the many different ways in which shapes, colors, and configurations can be read; we become aware of the fragility of the boundary between figure and ground. But this is just to reproduce Kant's classical analysis of the aesthetic experience in the *Critique of Judgment,* and even to employ Kant's examples drawn from the decorative arts. As the latter declares, "Flowers, free designs, lines aimlessly intertwined and called foliage; these have no significance, depend on no determinate concept, and yet we like them."[7] It might seem that Benjamin did not travel very far in the psychotropic world. Nevertheless, in some of the passages from the "Protocols" of the hash experiences, he develops this meditation on ornament into an analysis of the aura which plays such an important part in his canonical essay on "The Work of Art in the Age of Mechanical Reproducibility." Indeed, even in the passages on ornament Benjamin differs sharply with Kant, insofar as he takes the intensified effect of color to be a major aspect of the aesthetic experience; Kant had generally dismissed color as an adventitious charm in contrast to linear form.

The auratic two-dimensional complexity of design that holds Benjamin's attention under hashish can be taken to be a relatively simple anticipation of the fuller experience of finding oneself in a labyrinthine space. Like the labyrinth as understood by Benjamin, such designs offer many ways into an interior from which it is not easy to escape. In the passage quoted earlier from the published essay "Hashish in Marseilles"—indeed this essay is nothing but a series of passages, in the several senses that word takes when we speak of literature, architecture, and travel—there is the suggestion of a deep affinity between the writing of prose and the hashish trance. The passage suggests that all prose is psychotropic writing, that it leads us through passages that are uncanny in being at once familiar and unfamiliar. Benjamin says something similar about his childhood reading, that it was an initiation into "the labyrinth of stories"; the serial form of publication in the periodical that he read, *New Companion of German Youth,* allowed "the longer stories, interrupted many times to appear as continuations, extended through the whole like subterranean passages" (*R,* 56). So reading is like finding one's way through the labyrinth, constantly being forced to double back, and so to become familiar with the involutions of a structure that are veiled by the linear form and the entryway by which it invites us in. In the passage on Ariadne's thread, Benjamin says that experience unrolls; the unrolling is repetitive yet it takes us through new places, surprising passages. To unroll Ariadne's thread is to find one's way to the heart of the labyrinth and also to prepare an exit for oneself. Writing is different from reading, insofar as the former is governed by an effect of unrolling, while the latter requires an inventive questioning of various possible routes and connections.

Benjamin's taste for the labyrinth is evident, and the ones that he discovers through hashish should be articulated in relation to those he finds in the city. The ancients, he tells us, dreamt of the labyrinth; but the form is actually realized in the European city (*GS* V.2, 1007). Benjamin's materialistic spin on Freud is to see the topography of the city as a realized, concrete dream. If the *flâneur* is the dreamer, then the student of the dialectical image of the lived, contemporary labyrinth is the analyst of the dream. Some of us (and we may speculate that Benjamin was among them) frequently dream of spaces that open up or double back in surprising and uncanny ways; so there are multiple ties between the dream-world and the labyrinthine experience. Hashish plays the role of inducing a waking dream in a setting that can be revisited awake and sober, thus lending itself to analysis.

Benjamin's essay on Naples, written with Asja Lacis (his Ariadne through the convoluted passages of the city that lies in the direction of the mythical Mediterranean?) celebrates an urban architecture that is "anarchical, embroiled, villagelike in the center" (*R,* 166). Hidden doors open onto mysterious courtyards; space is porous, with balconies and courtyards turning into theater, so that the relation of inside and outside is strangely reversible. It could be read as a loving account of postmodern architecture *avant le lettre* (think, for example, of Fredric Jameson's description of the Bonaventure Hotel). Behind, before, and beneath the boulevards of Haussmann's Paris lies a baroque labyrinth of narrow streets, tunnels, and catacombs that require the skills of Ariadne. The *flâneur* is the "flesh and blood" in which the image of the labyrinth has incarnated itself.[8] The boulevards were not enough, however, to prevent the erection of barricades in the time of the Paris Commune, and these cul de sacs reinstated the ancient labyrinth that the modernizers had attempted to suppress. When Benjamin writes at the beginning of "Hashish in Marseilles" that not even the space of Versailles is large enough for the trance, he could very well be thinking of its labyrinths. The labyrinth is one of Benjamin's primal experiences; a labyrinthine walkway near the Tiergarten is one of the very first things that he recalls from his travels beyond his home in the autobiographical "Berlin Chronicle" (R, 3). It is through the labyrinths that he finds himself in foreign cities (Moscow, for example), that Benjamin sees more clearly the labyrinths of Berlin. All of his cities—real, imagined, literary—form a labyrinth of labyrinths, one leading into and out of the others.

Perhaps we can begin to see why Benjamin might have felt that the planned book on hashish should be kept secret. There are so many dangers associated with the labyrinth. There may be a Minotaur or monster at its core. Sometimes the goal of the labyrinth is said to be the market, where the market can be read in either its literal, old world sense, or in a Marxist one, with a sense of the dangerously dehumanizing.[9] At other points, both in the fragmentary essay "Central Park" and in the *Passagenwerk*, the labyrinth is said to lead to prostitution; Benjamin speaks enigmatically of the "prostitution of space under hashish when it serves everything that has been *(Spleen)*."[10] More generally, the Minotaur is the power of death that is secreted in the passages of the city.

This brings to mind another analysis of urban geography, by Freud, who also fancied ruins and older cities, and whose analysis of dreams contributed to Benjamin's understanding of the metropolis. To evoke an experience of the uncanny, Freud recalls going astray in an Italian town:

> Once, as I was walking through the deserted streets of a provincial town in Italy which was strange to me, on a hot summer afternoon, I found myself in a quarter the character of which could not longer remain in doubt. Nothing but painted women were to be seen at the windows of the small houses, and I hastened to leave the narrow street at the next turning. But after having wandered about for a while without being directed, I suddenly found myself back in the same street, where my presence was now beginning to excite attention. I hurried away once more, but only to arrive yet a third time by devious paths in the same place.[11]

In the hashish writings, and elsewhere, there are the germs of an atypical transcendental aesthetic, one in which space resists the attempts of time to assert its hegemony, and in which space is no longer uniform, homogeneous, and Euclidean, but already structured, striated, marked, and twisted back upon itself. Benjamin supplies the hint of a transcendental aesthetic in this contrast between addictive behavior in space and in time: "To the phantasmagorias of space to which the *flâneur* abandons himself, correspond the phantasmagorias of time indulged in by the gambler. Gambling converts time into a narcotic" (*R*, 159). And so it would also follow, in this proportional metaphor, that strolling through the city as a labyrinth converts space into a drug.

Benjamin recalls a diagram he drew of his life one afternoon at a Paris cafe. Although it was lost, he remembers its labyrinthine character; it was "not concerned with what is installed in the chamber at its enigmatic center, ego or fate, but all the more with the many entrances leading into the interior." At this pont Benjamin recalls Nietzsche, that other thinker of the labyrinth and of a self without a center, or perhaps an empty center, and his saying "If a man has character he will have the same experiences over and over again." And it was this that Benjamin read in the labyrinthine diagram of his own life:

> . . . there are perhaps paths that lead one again and again to people
> who have one and the same function for us; passageways that always,
> in the most diverse periods of life, guide us to the friend, the betrayer,
> the beloved, the pupil, or the master. (*R*, 31–32)

Benjamin is thinking of a certain form of the labyrinth here, that in which there are many paths and many entrances; it is to be contrasted with the maze that has only a single entrance (and exit). The description of the "paths" of life here may appear to be somewhat metaphorical, insofar as it is concerned with events and people rather than the space of bodily location and mobility; nevertheless, a more literal spatiality is implicated in this analysis because, for Benjamin, as the context makes clear, these paths and passages are always those of the city or of a network of cities. The approach recalls Heidegger's almost contemporary analysis of the spatiality of *Dasein* in *Being and Time*, which is said to be primordially oriented toward the meaningful paths that we actually live or inhabit, rather than a neutral space of Euclidean coordinates. In that phenomenology of space, human existence is characterized by *Ent-fernung* (dis-stance or de-severance) and *Ausrichtung* (directionality). Both Benjamin and Heidegger have a complex relation to Kant's transcendental aesthetic of space and time; both seem to change position with regard to how these are related and whether one is prior to the other.

Am I digressing in considering the labyrinthine, doubling and redoubling my steps, caught up, like Benjamin, in the memory of something archaic? (The word "labyrinth," like the myth, is from Crete, marking it as one of the oldest European words). Let me retrace my steps to the question of prose and hashish, a relation that is mediated through this figure of Ariadne's thread. The identification may seem puzzling at first; rapture and trance might be associated more easily with the lyrical and poetic rather than with prose. But in the first draft of the Marseilles essay Benjamin says at this point that lyric poetry is not worth a sou (*H*, 101).[12] Yet his assertion that "under hashish we are enraptured prose-beings in the highest power" recalls a long line of German romantic and postromantic apotheoses of artforms as modes of self-transcendence. It could be compared with Nietzsche's declaration in *The Birth of Tragedy* that "Only insofar as the genius in the act of artistic creation coincides with this primordial artist of the world, does he know anything of the eternal essence of art."[13] Nietzsche's own later criticism of his first book faults it for striving after an ecstatic union within the constraints of prose and quasi-Hegelian formulas. Benjamin, whose *Trauerspiel* book must be understood in many ways as an anti-*Birth of Tragedy*, adopted a baroque, labyrinthine style in writing about allegory. It is the writing of prose, the joy of creation *(Schaffenslust)*, that Benjamin has in mind in the figure of Ariadne's thread. This prose writing feels as if one is unrolling something that is already there, one's own thoughts, one's language, one's style; this is the ball of thread with which we begin and in whose rhythmic turning we rejoice. As it is unrolled it takes us, however, into new places, passages that we could hardly have anticipated. Even when prose turns to the apparently banal or everyday, it leads us into strangely new pathways.

Benjamin was already familiar with the neighborhood of Marseilles where he ventured out under the influence. His passage through the neighborhood and his intercourse with its well-known landmarks is transformed by prose and hashish as he threads his way through a labyrinth of his own making. The essayist, unlike the systematic writer, might enter into the subject almost anywhere, for there are many entrances; what becomes important are the passages that he marks out, the structure that emerges. There is something very secure in holding the pen, or sitting at the computer; it is our words that will fill up the page. Yet we could not have said what they would be. We find ourselves amazed as the sentences and paragraphs unroll and as we find ourselves repetitively pushing pen across paper or fingers playing over the same keyboard; we become involved in the essay *(Versuch, essai)*, a true work of prose, perhaps, like Benjamin's *Trauerspiel* book, too labyrinthine to serve as a philosophical calling card at the university, but a provocation to a certain ecstasy.

This seems close to what Roland Barthes describes as the middle voice of writing, where the agent is interior to the action.[14] In Herman

Schweppenhäuser's essay on Benjamin's hashish writing, "Dialectics of Profane Illumination," he explains these reflections as meditations upon the collapse or identification of subject and object. While he is certainly on the right track in emphasizing that Benjamin does not simply accept such an apparent dissolution of boundaries at face value, as so much ecstatic writing about drug experiences does, Schweppenhäuser does not see the possibility that the middle voice of writing may call the subject/object schema itself into question rather than simply questioning the possibility of its resolution in a speculative synthesis.[15] Neither active nor passive, both active and passive, it unrolls: prose happens.

While the philosophical construction projects like the Cartesian demolition and rebuilding or the Kantian architectonic have their own special pleasures and are by no means easy to achieve, the essay that meanders, twists, and occasionally loops around to take us through where we have been in a way that strangely transforms the passage that we thought we already knew is the focus of readerly and writerly ecstasy—think of the writings of Montaigne, Emerson, and Nietzsche. After all, even the reading and writing of philosophy depends on the activity, *is* the activity, of finding our way through the text, to that monstrous thing buried in its heart, and then finding our way out again.

Monsters? In "Hashish in Marseilles" they are the faces of the men in the bar, faces whose ugliness turns into a beauty that Rembrandt would have understood. "Hashish in Marseilles" is the narrative of a labyrinthine passage, in which space and Benjamin's movements are subject to a complex set of constraints. One of the first sensations he records about leaving his hotel is that his walking stick began to give him a "special pleasure." It is not exactly the thread of Ariadne, but it is an accompaniment, a supplement to ordinary walking, one that might promote the impression that one's way is not merely arbitrarily chosen but results from the confluence of a number of cooperative forces. Space becomes tactile, something whose passages we must feel our way through. After announcing that "the hashish eater's demands on time and space . . . are absolutely regal" he records his bemused reaction at the restaurant when he is told that the hot kitchen is closed after he had been anticipating an eternal feast. But before Benjamin gets to the meal he must tell us about finding his seat. This matter of locating himself in a restaurant is no longer a simple thing. Wanting a place by the window, he takes a large table that has just been vacated but, feeling shame at having seized so much space for himself he retreats to a smaller one. This pattern of advance and retreat, of circling round, is repeated on a larger scale in the unfolding or unrolling of the essay itself.

Benjamin gives us a glimpse of his game of musical chairs at the restaurant only to tell us that the full story of his meal there must come later; reversing himself, he says "First, the little bar on the harbor" (R, 139). This is the first, but not the only place in the essay, where we begin to explore a passage of some sort only to be brought up short by the stage direction "first," pointing us to another scene, another passage. Always a doubling back, a repetition with a difference: the square changes constantly with each new arrival. The very material of the passages, the stones and sidewalk seem to be "bred of my imagination," Benjamin says, adding that they could have been in Paris; which is to say, the labyrinthine Paris of his architectural and historical imagination. Hashish intensifies the experience of the *Traumstadt,* as it is called in the *Passagenwerk.* Armed with Ariadne's thread, in his literary or hash-inspired imagination, the structure becomes his own and yet other, like the words he unfolds in his writing. The labyrinth function reinstates itself wherever he is or whenever he writes.

In the essay on "Surrealism" we come across an extended meditation that again links hashish with reading and writing; these passages on hashish themselves form a labyrinthine structure that runs through the assemblage of Benjamin's writing. Perhaps the hashish book does exist in the form of such a labyrinth; perhaps it is the only way that it could or should appear.

> [W]e penetrate the mystery only to the extent that we recognize it in the everyday world, by virtue of a dialectical optic that perceives the everyday as impenetrable, the impenetrable as everyday. The most passionate investigation of telepathic phenomena, for example, will not teach us half as much about reading (which is an eminently telepathic process), as the profane illumination of reading about telepathic phenomena. And the most passionate investigation of the hashish trance will not teach us half as much about thinking (which is eminently narcotic), as the profane illumination of thinking about the hashish trance. The reader, the thinker, the loiterer, the *flâneur,* are types of illuminati just as much as the opium eater, the dreamer, the ecstatic. And more profane. Not to mention that terrible drug—ourselves—which we take in solitude. (R, 190)

Reading may be about as telepathic as we get. Certainly the "messages" reported by researchers into extrasensory perception seem more like the signals of the so-called language of bees, whose deficiencies are remarked by Lacan, than like the most rudimentary examples of human conversation or communication. As Benjamin points out, Baudelaire's exemplary writing on hashish was not composed while under the influence of the drug, but as a later reflection; it is this delayed effect that offers something like a dialectical optic, that is, one that allows for a simultaneous multiplicity of perspectives. In this respect it is instructive to see how Benjamin incorporates some of the notes taken during and just after the hash trances into the prose of the Marseilles essay. In the numbered notes entitled *"Hauptzüge der ersten Haschisch-Impression,"* Benjamin remarks on the transformations of spatiality:

> 4. Both of the coordinates through the dwelling: cellar-floor/horizontal. Great horizontal extension of the dwelling. A suite of rooms, from which music comes. But perhaps also fear of the corridor. (*H, 65*)

Even speaking becomes a spatialized experience, as he feels his words spreading out, and he compares this, even in the protocol, to the *Passagenphänomen*:

> 9. It occurs to one that one is speaking in very long sentences. This is connected with horizontal extension and (even) laughter. The *Passagenphänomen* is also a long horizontal stretching out, perhaps combined with a dissolution into vanishing, narrow perspectives. In such minuteness there is a tie between the idea of the *Passage* and laughter. (*H, 66*)

One's place in the room becomes less determinate (*H, 67*). And yet the literary, the prosaic already enters into the formation of Benjamin's hashish experience, so that the later reflection will be a double one. He observes the *"Kolportage und Unterschrift"* in the trance; that is, that there is a kind of hawking of books, a proliferation of signatures in space, so that far from escaping from the textual, the world presents itself as already and everywhere inscribed.

The incomplete and incompletable *Passagenwerk* is often described as a ruin, the ruin of a life's work by a man who was fascinated by and theorized ruins. We should add that it is the ruin of a labyrinth by a writer who was, by his own testimony, obsessed with that figure from his youth. The Paris of Baudelaire is a labyrinth into which the walker or the writer can stray and wander without end. As Benjamin writes in "Berlin Chronicle":

> Not to find one's way in a city may well be uninteresting and banal. . . .
> But to lose oneself in a city—as one *loses oneself in a forest*—that calls
> for quite a different schooling . . . Paris taught me this art of straying;
> it fulfilled a dream that had shown its first traces in the labyrinths on
> the blotting pages of my school exercise books.[16]

The *Passagenwerk* was to be a vast labyrinth of baroque reason, an intoxicated materialist analysis of a cityscape that was the condition of wandering and writing; it is the nature of such places and of the writing they provoke that there will always be more passages, more corridors and connections. While the main theme of the project has been said to be a "dialectics of seeing," it should be emphasized that the vision Benjamin analyzes is not one detached from space and mobility; it is always, as Heidegger says of vision, an *Umsicht,* a looking around in a space where we are to some degree oriented, even in those relatively disorienting experiences of the labyrinthine.[17] How is such a proliferating structure to be presented? In part through summoning up archaic images of spatiality, as in this account of the uncanniness of the city by night and of the infernal depths of the Paris metro:

> In ancient Greece places were pointed out from which one could descend into the underworld. Our waking existence is also a land in which one can descend from hidden, completely invisible places into the underworld, where dreams lead. Every day we pass them by unsuspectingly; but as soon as sleep comes on we find our way back there with rapid movements and lose ourselves in dark passageways *(Gänge)*. By bright daylight the city's labyrinth of houses is like consciousness; the arcades *[Passagen]* (which are the galleries that lead to a past existence) flow daily and unnoticed into the streets. At night, however, among the dark masses of the houses a more compact darkness rises up in a frightening way and the walker who is out late hurries past them, encouraged perhaps to go through the narrow lanes *(Gasse)*.
>
> The metro, where evenings the lights glow red . . . shows the way down into the Hades of names: Combat, Elysee, Georges V, Etienne Marcel, Solferino, Invalides, Vaugirard have thrown off the tasteful chain of streets and squares, and, here in the whistle-pierced darkness, have become misshapened sewer gods, catacomb fairies. This labyrinth conceals in its innards not just one, but dozens of blind, rushing bulls, into whose jaws not once a year one Theban virgin, but every morning thousands of anemic young cleaning women and still sleepy salesmen are forced to hurl themselves.[18]

This working section of the *Arcades Project* is entitled "Ancient Paris, Catacombs, Demolitions, Ruins of Paris." The excerpted passage aims at demonstrating that the labyrinthine underworld which we enter in our dreams also appears with the coming of night and is always accessible through the stations of the Metro.

Benjamin began his hashish experiments at just about the same time as the *Arcades Project,* perhaps superficially inspired by Baudelaire, but more profoundly by the elective affinity between his writing project and its pretext, or pretextual space. Included in *Über Haschisch* are a number of inscriptions Benjamin made under the influence of mescalin, in which the writing circles around the page, and into the midst of the circle it forms; these are labyrinths of writing and Benjamin seems to have reveled in getting lost in them, as he did in those texts that might be the products of a medical sobriety, even if written under the influence of the narcosis of prose composition.

It is this not finding oneself, this talent for getting lost, for which the architectural theorist and historian Manfredo Tafuri seems to criticize Benjamin and his hashish taking toward the end of *The Sphere and the Labyrinth,* a book that interrogates the discourse of architecture from Piranesi to the 1970s. Tafuri finds a contrast between Benjamin's use of hashish and his asking how the intellectual positions himself with respect to the means, specifically the intellectual means, of production; he finds the contrast to be an emblem (perhaps an allegory?) of the dilemma of the avant-garde:

> "The disenchanted avant-garde," completely absorbed in exploring from the comfort of its charming *boudoirs* the profundities of the philosophy of the unexpected writes down, over and over again, its own reactions under the influence of drugs prudently administered. Its use of hashish is certainly a conscious one: but it makes of this "consciousness" a barrier, a defense.[19]

The question is not simply whether there was a kind of escapism in Benjamin's use of hashish, but whether such an escapism was characteristic of his thought. Benjamin was clearly aware of this as a general possibility, if we can take a comment about those with a taste for the labyrinthine to apply to that species of the labyrinth lover, the hashish eater. In "Central Park" he wrote that the labyrinth "is the home of the hesitant. The path of someone shy of arrival at a goal easily takes the form of a labyrinth." The labyrinth is the place of the sexual drive "in those episodes which precede its satisfaction" and it is the home of "humanity (the social class) which does not wish to know what will become of it."[20] One might find or create labyrinths for oneself by various means: producing a life plan that could only, like Benjamin's, be represented by a labyrinthine diagram; writing, especially the writing of an ambitious, multifaceted work that itself revolves around the question of passageways, a historical book that aims at countering a more linear conception of history by a certain spatialization of time; cultivating a taste for wandering and getting lost in European cities; consuming hashish or mescalin to provoke an experience of the labyrinth in otherwise ordinary surroundings. These are all modes of profane illumination, ways of revealing the impenetrability of the everyday and the everday character of the impenetrable. Many strategies are available to the hesitant; we might think of them as alternative entryways into the labyrinth, as we might think of Benjamin's four projected books as such openings to the thought that possessed him like a narcotic. And the labyrinths are not only of our own devising; we might remember, in connection with Benjamin's comments on the labyrinthine delay of sexual satisfaction, his impression (and Freud's experience) of the site of the red light district in the convoluted streets of an old city.

Tafuri discusses Benjamin's hashish use but not his fascination with the labyrinth; this seems odd, considering that the title of his book suggests that it will be thematized. If we can only continue to wander, to unroll Ariadne's thread, to write in circuitous and meandering fashion, we might avoid the confrontation with the monster at the center of the structure until the very last moment, perhaps escape it altogether. Is this to be seen as nothing but an evasion of moral and political responsibility? Or should it be understood as one of the ways in which time and history are intensified and realized by becoming space?[21] The ecstasy of the labyrinth and of prose, both of which can become thematic in the hashish *Rausch* are consistent responses to the Benjaminian conception of history as catastrophe, in which the production and enjoyment of strategies of ecstatic postponement and deferral may be among the very best things that we can do. This line of thought coexists in Benjamin with his view of surrealism as having "the particular task . . . to win the energies of intoxication for revolution." Benjamin's essay on Marseilles and his labyrinthine cityscapes can be read as transformations of the city into surrealist sites. What seem to be contradictory attitudes toward time—revolutionary metamorphosis or the luxury of deferral, embodied in the figures of the activist and the *flâneur*—are in fact different modalities of the profane illumination achieved in the space of writing and the writing of space.

NOTES

1. *The Correspndence of Walter Benjamin,* Gershom Scholem and Theodor W. Adorno, eds.; translated by Manfred R. Jacobson and Evelyn M. Jacobson (Chicago, 1994), letter of July 26, 1932, pp. 395–396.

2. As early as 1919 Benjamin records that he has read Baudelaire's "Artificial Paradise" and says that it will be necessary to repeat his attempt independently (*Correspondence,* p. 148); the drug is introduced by a book. But what are we to make of the notion of an independent repetition?

3. For Benjamin's thoughts on eternal recurrence see correspondence of Walter Benjamin, op. cit., pp. 156–178.

4. Walter Benjamin, "Central Park," p. 36.

5. Walter Benjamin, *Reflections*, translated by Edmond Jephcott, edited by Peter Demetz, 1978.

6. *Über Haschisch*, p. 57.

7. Immanuel Kant, *Critique of Judgment*, translated by Werner S. Pluhar (Indianapolis, 1987), p. 49.

8. "Central Park," p. 53.

9. "Central Park," p. 40.

10. "Central Park," pp. 53, 35.

11. Sigmund Freud, "The Uncanny," translated by Alix Strachey in Benjamin Nelson, ed. *On Creativity and the Unconscious* (New York: Harper & Brothers, 1958), pp. 143–144.

12. *Über Haschisch*, p. 101.

13. Friedrich Nietzsche, *The Birth of Tragedy*, section 5, translated by Walter Kaufmann (New York: Vintage Books, 1967), p. 52.

14. See Roland Barthes, "To Write: An Intransitive Verb?" in *The Rustle of Language* (New York, 1986); Hayden White, "Writing in the Middle Voice," *Stanford Literature Review* (9:2), fall 1992, pp. 179–187; Martin Jay, "Experience Without a Subject: Walter Benjamin and the Novel," *New Formations* (20), summer 1993, pp. 145–155.

15. Herman Schweppenhäuser, "Dialectics of Profane Illumination," in Gary Smith, ed. *On Walter Benjamin: Critical Essays and Recollections* (Cambridge, MA, 1988), pp. 35–37.

16. Walter Benjamin, "A Berlin Chronicle," in *One Way Street and Other Writings*, translated by Edmund Jephcott and Kingsley Shorter (London, 1979), p. 298.

17. See Susan Buck-Morss, *Dialectics of Seeing: Walter Benjamin and the Arcades Project* (Cambridge, MA, 1989); Martin Heidegger, *Being and Time*, translated by John MacQuarrie and Edward Robinson (New York, 1962), pp. 134–148.

18. Benjamin, V.1, pp. 135–136; partially quoted and translated in Susan Buck-Morss, *Dialectics of Seeing* (Ithaca, 1989), p. 102.

19. Manfredo Tafuri, *The Sphere and the Labyrinth: Avant-Gardes and Architecture from Piranesi to the 1970's*, trans. Pellegrino d'Acierno and Robert Connolly (Cambridge, MA, 1990), pp. 289–290.

20. "Central Park," translated by Lloyd Spencer, *New German Critique* (34), 1985, p. 40, translation modified.

21. I am alluding to Jacques Derrida's characterization of *différance* as the becoming-space of time and the becoming-time of space in "Difference," in *Margins of Philosophy,* translated by Alan Bass (Chicago: University of Chicago Press), pp. 1–27.

Chapter Four

PROFANE HALLUCINATIONS

From *The Arcades Project* to the Surrealists

ALINA CLEJ

Although never affiliated to André Breton's surrealist group, Walter Benjamin may well be considered one of its devotees. This is both on account of the surrealist spirit that imbues his work and of his critical efforts on behalf of the surrealist movement. Oddly enough, however, in spite of this spiritual allegiance, and the opportunity of meeting the terrible children of the new avant-garde during his stay in Paris (1927–1929), Benjamin kept his distance. This chapter is meant to shed a fresh light upon Benjamin's ambiguous ties to surrealism, by focusing on the writer's peculiar understanding of the surrealist movement.[1]

As many critics have recognized, Benjamin's discovery of surrealism was instrumental in his transformation from "language mystic to dialectical materialist."[2] It was a slow transformation that began with the collage techniques or "picture puzzles" of *One-Way Street* (1928)—written under the immediate influence of Louis Aragon's *The Peasant of Paris* (1925)—and continued in a sinuous way with the monumental project of the Parisian *Arcades,* which like so many other things in Benjamin's life remained unfinished.[3] The surrealist influence affected not only Benjamin's writing techniques but also his thinking on esthetics, as evidenced

by his article on "Surrealism" (1929), his theoretical articles on the function of art "in the age of mechanical reproduction," on the role of the
author "as producer," and his experimental papers on hashish.[4] And yet,
I would argue that Benjamin's transformation into a dialectical materialist was never complete; among other things, surrealism offered Benjamin
a convenient disguise for his mystic propensities. The result was a hybrid
philosophy, best exemplified by "Theses on the Philosophy of History,"
written in 1940, the year Benjamin took his life while trying to escape
German-occupied Europe.

Since the task of tracing the various ramifications of the surrealist
influence on Benjamin's mature work exceeds the scope of a chapter, I
will focus on a limited set of issues that concern Benjamin's "elective
affinities" with surrealism and his appropriation of surrealist concepts
for his own creative purposes. From the outset, Benjamin's encounter
with surrealism bears the marks of an extraordinary experience. As the
writer himself acknowledges, the joy (and perhaps anxiety) of discovering a spiritual kin while reading Aragon's *Peasant of Paris* was overwhelming enough to produce panic attacks. This is how Benjamin
describes his first contact with a surrealist text:

> Evenings, lying in bed, I could never read more than two or three pages
> by [Aragon] because my heart started to pound so hard that I had to
> put the book down.[5]

The mere act of reading Aragon's surrealist novel seems to transport
Benjamin to a different zone of existence, as that reading itself becomes
a "dangerous" enterprise.

If we are to take them seriously, the exorbitant effects of Benjamin's
first encounter with surrealism seem to suggest an epiphany, the lived
counterpart of the "profane illumination" that Benjamin was soon to
theorize in his essay, "Surrealism." Strangely enough, however, although
the discovery of Aragon's *Peasant of Paris* clearly gave Benjamin the
idea of the *Arcades* project, it also had an inhibiting effect on the writer's
creative powers.[6] As Benjamin confessed to his friend Gershom Scholem,
the task of writing the *Arcades* had to be delayed. Judging by his own
statements, the articles that Benjamin did write in the years that followed his discovery of surrealism were a means of coming to terms with
the powerful influence of the French avant-garde movement, a tactic
that is most visible in the essay "Surrealism," published in 1929. Benjamin conceived this essay as a foil, "a screen placed in front of the
Parisian Arcades," and which, for reasons he could not disclose, was
meant to "keep secret what [went] on behind it."[7]

What was there to conceal, one might wonder, beyond what Benjamin half revealed in his letter to Scholem, namely the desire to "attain the most extreme concreteness for an era, as it occasionally manifested itself in children's games, a building, or a real-life situation."[8] After all, Benjamin had already explored this venue in *One-Way Street*. Moreover, why should such an enterprise be "perilous" and "breathtaking," as to require considerable precautions and repeated postponements, as was the case with the reading of Aragon's *Peasant of Paris*.

Some of Benjamin's hesitations about embarking on the *Arcades* project may be understood by referring to the historical context of his literary career at the time. Reading Benjamin's correspondence from that period, one discovers the writer's uneasy predicament. As he himself admits, his "profane" interest in surrealism, and in "Parisian arcades" was in "terrible competition with Hebrew," more exactly with the task of learning Hebrew, for which he had been generously financed by Scholem.[9] One may reasonably assume that this conflict of interests must have been quite painful, if not "paralyzing." Reading between the lines of Benjamin's correspondence, one also gathers that the prospect of renouncing a mystical approach to language (largely inspired by Jewish texts), for a thoroughly "profane," materialist view of literature, could not have been an easy matter.

Moreover, in the late 1920s, Benjamin's personal malaise was certainly aggravated by political circumstances. As democracy was coming to a standstill in the frail Weimar Republic, a free spirit was at risk. The Jewish–German intelligentsia was particularly in danger of losing both its livelihood and its identity. Some, like Scholem, chose exile; others stayed but often had to resort to Aryan pseudonyms to continue publishing.[10] In this charged political context, in which Benjamin was faced with intractable dilemmas, surrealism appeared as a fortuitous lifesaver. A rereading of Benjamin's article, "Surrealism," will show the peculiar kind of investment that the Jewish–German writer made in André Breton's movement.

Benjamin published "Surrealism" in *Die literarische Welt*, the Frankfurt journal that, during the Weimar Republic, had become one of the main organs of ideological debate for German intellectuals. As pressures from both right and left were intensifying, Benjamin, like many of his peers, felt compelled to politicize his thought, without surrendering, for that matter, his intellectual freedom. "Surrealism" gave him the opportunity to examine his options. Taking stock of his critical situation—that of a "German observer . . . long acquainted with the crisis of the intelligentsia, or, more precisely, with that of the humanistic concept of freedom," and without mentioning the added difficulties that plagued the

Jewish–German "observer"—Benjamin acknowledged that the moment of decision could no longer be avoided.[11] Having occupied the "highly exposed position between an anarchistic *fronde* and a revolutionary discipline" (R, 177), a situation which previously made him shun both communism and Zionism,[12] Benjamin now hails in Breton's surrealism the providential solution to his existential and political dilemmas.

There are a number of reasons which, from the outset, may explain Benjamin's attraction to surrealism. Firstly, as Benjamin puts it, surrealist art no longer "presents the public with the literary form of existence while withholding that existence itself" (R, 178). In theory, the qualitative difference between art and life is meant to disappear. In their writing "praxis," the Surrealists therefore abandon the artificiality layers of poetic conventions, to offer instead the unsuspected "poetic" kernel of reality itself. With surrealism, a certain experience of life (produced through defamiliarization techniques, oneiric experiments, and the valorization of "the outmoded") becomes as important as its *representation*.

Second, "image and language take precedence" (R, 179) over the message. In the practice of automatic writing (exemplified, for instance, by *The Magnetic Fields,* 1920), Breton made it clear that the writer(s)—in this case, Philippe Soupault and Breton himself—are no longer dependent on their medium—language—for the purpose of communicating a "meaning," but rather use language to probe the untapped resources of the psyche in a process than can involve several practitioners, including the reading public who become privy to the experiment. In Breton's formulation, put forth in the *First Manifesto of Surrealism* (1924), surrealism is defined by this writing technique, and as such it is synonymous with "psychic automatism," practiced "in the absence of all control exercised by reason, and outside any aesthetic or moral preoccupations."[13] By dismissing the Cartesian grounding of the representation in the *Cogito,* as well as the Romantic foundation of the image in a zone of affectivity, Breton's surrealism favors what could be called a "physiology" of writing, in which the body itself (the unconscious) becomes the site of the creative process.

The Surrealists' combined emphasis on experience and language were meant to have a deep resonance with Benjamin. The characteristically surrealist lament over "the poverty of reality,"[14] and the withering of individual experience, which motivates to a large extent the first surrealist experiments, also runs like a thread through Benjamin's writings, connecting his early autobiographical pieces with his theoretical ones. "A blind determination to save the prestige of personal existence," as Benjamin puts it in *One-Way Street* (1928) (R, 74) informs his literary and philosophical activities at the time. Benjamin had already addressed this existential question in "Program of the Coming Philosophy" (1918), an essay in which the historical threats to the individual's existence are discussed through a polemics with neo-Kantian philosophy.

For Benjamin, the modern (Kantian) subject, as heir of the Enlightenment, is faced with "an experience virtually reduced to a nadir, to a minimum of significance."[15] If in Kant's argument, philosophy legitimates the estrangement of the subject from the ground of being, for Benjamin the "coming philosophy" is destined to establish "a higher concept of experience" derived from a "linguistic" understanding of knowledge. Moreover, Benjamin's concept of experience viewed as a "concrete totality" (i.e., *existence*) can only be given in religion. On the (theological) assumption that at its origins (in its Adamic manifestation) language was intimately tied to the materiality of being, from early on, Benjamin set his hopes on the transformational powers of language.

In the 1920s and before his own involvement with surrealism, Benjamin's faith in language expressed itself in his translating activities and in theoretical essays, such as "The Task of the Translator" and "On Language as Such and on the Language of Man."[16] Obliged to "map his way through the barren forest of the real,"[17] the writer could presumably relieve his anguish through translation, in the artificial "birth pangs" induced by "ripening the seed of pure language," which is always at work in any linguistic transfer (I, 73, 77). The profusion of organic metaphors in "The Task of the Translator" (1923) suggests indirectly the desert-like conditions of modern life, which are also directly represented in the work that occasioned Benjamin's prefatory essay, namely Baudelaire's *Tableaux parisiens*.[18]

In Benjamin's earlier essays on language, translation clearly played the saving role that was later assumed by surrealism. The task of the translator was not merely linguistic, but also religious, leading to a complex transfiguration. As Benjamin puts it, the relation between the translation and the original is "a natural one, or, more specifically, a vital connection." The original depends on the translation to come into full bloom, and in the process of facilitating this "abundant," though belated "flowering," "the mother tongue of the translator is transformed as well" (I, 72–73). Although the act of translation may appear "superfluous" from the point of view of the original, and incongruous or ironic from the point of view of the translation, which is said to "envelop the content [of the original] like a royal robe with ample folds" (I, 75), it is clear that Benjamin is speaking of an abstract match, never to be consummated in actual practice. The act of translation can only hint to the ultimate "kinship" of all languages, "which is realized only by the totality of their intentions supplementing each other: pure language" (I, 74). But the "embryonic

attempt" at making visible this "hidden significance" redeems the inade-
quacy of the translation, and saves it, in a sense, from ridicule.

Moreover, a "hidden significance" that was not explicit in Benjamin's "The Task of the Translator," becomes apparent in the later
essay, "Surrealism," and adds a new dimension to Benjamin's spiritual
investment in translation and surrealism. Positing a new relation
between subject and object—the implicit goal of Benjamin's literary and
philosophical writings at the time—entailed not only the transformation
and enrichment of the objects of experience, but also the simultaneous
transformation of the experiencing subject, as well. In this respect, Rimbaud's *"Je est un autre,"* ("I is someone else"), which served to "push
the 'poetic life' to the utmost limits of possibility" (R, 178) was as
important to Surrealists's experiments, as it was to Benjamin's own literary pursuits.

Following Rimbaud's example, the Surrealists proposed not only to
transform reality, but also to change the very nature of subjective experience, by delivering it from its long-worn shackles—reason and morality.[19] And to this effect, it is again language that plays a crucial role, by
miraculously undoing the foundations of the Cartesian subject—in the
process of automatic writing, for instance. According to Benjamin, in
surrealism, language takes precedence not only before "meaning," but
also "before the self" (R, 179). "In the world's structure," as Benjamin
puts it, "dream" or more exactly the linguistic transposition of the
dream, "loosens individuality like a bad tooth" (R, 179). The "loosening of the self by intoxication"—and by "intoxication" Benjamin means
here the "profane" surrealist experience that removes the subject from
its familiar setting—parallels in many ways the process of translation.

In "The Task of the Translator," the original is said to be displaced
by translation into "a higher and purer linguistic air," in a movement
that defamiliarizes and transfigures both original and translation, but
this metamorphosis is never complete. "The transfer can never be total"
("with root and branch"), as Benjamin literally puts it (I, 75).[20] While
translation seems to stop short of uprooting the original "tree," and as
the transposition into a higher sphere is, accordingly, never perfect (leaving the translator himself in limbo, as it were), surrealist intoxication, on
the other hand, seems to offer a chance for a total transformation of the
self. "Loosening" the self like "a bad tooth" pulled up by its roots, surrealist experiments work from within, since it is the language of the
unconscious ("the discourse of the Other," in Lacanian terms) that takes
possession of the subject and awakens its ability to experience itself and
the world in a radically new light. In Benjamin's eyes, surrealist intoxication represented in effect the possibility of "overcoming religious illu-

mination"; it was, as he memorably put it, "a *profane illumination,* a materialistic, anthropological inspiration, to which hashish, opium, or whatever else can give an introductory lesson" (R, 179).

Moreover, for Benjamin, this kind of intoxicating experience also represented "the fruitful, living experience that allowed [the Surrealists] to step outside the domain of intoxication" (R, 179). In other words, "intoxication" takes the subject not just outside itself but also outside what is traditionally understood by "intoxication." This paradox is not surprising, given Benjamin's gnomic style. Hermann Schweppenhäuser, one of Benjamin's main editors, has convincingly argued that for Benjamin surrealist intoxication was a form of "materialist inspiration" which served to demystify the reified world of things, "the fetishism of the object as 'thing' world *(Dinglichkeit)"* that "kept both subject and objects under its spell."[21] One could add that from a "materialist" perspective, surrealist "intoxication" also freed the writers from their narrow professional sphere, giving them access to a larger field of experience. In a paradoxical way, then, it is precisely the "intoxicating" effects of surrealist experiments (which involve performative acts, rather than contemplative states) that in Benjamin's understanding had freed the Surrealists from the narcotic domain of "literature":

> [A]nyone who has perceived that the writings of this circle are not literature but something else—demonstrations, watchwords, documents, bluffs, forgeries if you will, but at any rate not literature—will also know, for the same reason, that the writings are concerned literally with experiences, not with theories and still less with phantasms. (R, 179)

From a more general perspective, surrealism offered Benjamin a chance to evade his social predicament. To become more than a litterateur, or rather to rediscover the value of existence through an alternative writing practice, originating outside of Germany, must have been particularly appealing to Benjamin at a time when the meaning, and even the possibility of a career as a Jewish–German writer were increasingly in doubt. Although the Surrealists's notions of language and experience did "compete" with Benjamin's previously mystic theory of language, the very ambiguity of their definitions of writing as praxis *("activité"),* and their flirtation with the idea of revolution appeared to offer a more congenial solution to Benjamin's existential and political quandaries than the unequivocal embrace of a political cause (be it communism or Zionism).[22]

Judging by Benjamin's statement concerning the potential of "intoxication," it is not clear exactly how opium or hashish were supposed to work as a "propaedeutic" to "profane illumination," and even less clear what kind of equivalent to these drugs was intended by Benjamin's

vague term, "whatever else." What is abundantly clear though is that
surrealist intoxication, like translation before that, involved not only
considerable promise, but also considerable "danger," a possibility that
seemed in itself "intoxicating."

In "The Task of the Translator," "the danger"—assuming it is the
same—is mentioned by Benjamin in relation to Hölderlin's translations.
"[T]he enormous danger inherent in all translations," appears to be the
dissolution of the translating subject, his disappearance in language:
"the gates of a language thus expanded and modified may slam shut and
enclose the translator with silence" (I, 81). If translation, like the *Oral
Torah,* can represent the "gate of the Lord," the portal or passage that
leads to God ("pure language"),[23] it may also represent the final station
to the awaited revelation before which all individual meaning is reduced
to silence. The point of maximum expansion of the self coincides then
with that of its minimum extension. In Baudelaire's "profane" expression, this dangerous paradox could be stated as: "Vaporization and cen-
tralization of the self. All is there."[24] According to Benjamin's implicit
syllogism, if translation can modify the boundaries of language(s), and
if language is an essential dimension of the subject, then any radical
modification of language will also radically modify the subject. Hölderlin's final madness seems to verify this formula.

To play devil's advocate, one could say that as a translator of Baudelaire, Benjamin was not running the same "risk" as Hölderlin was, in
translating Sophocles, but since Benjamin's discourse takes place at an
abstract, metaphysical level, one can reply in Benjamin's defense that the
"danger" was potentially there. In Benjamin's case, moreover, this danger takes a curiously erotic quality, insofar as the translation/tors appear
to surrender to the imperatives of "pure language," by offering themselves to the task of "ripening the seed *(Samen)* of pure language" (I,
77). With all its discreet references to a woman in labor ("birth pangs,"
"embryonic attempt"), in the context of a highly mystical parable on the
theological virtues of language, the translator in Benjamin's essay seems
touched, ever so lightly perhaps, by a psychotic delusion.

Indeed, from an oblique angle, one can discover in Benjamin's essay
a strange analogy between the feminized posture of the translator, or
translation (their semantic equivalence in the text already points to a
case of gender ambiguity: in German *Übersetzer* is masculine and *Über-
setzung* is feminine), and Paul Schreber, the psychotic judge, who
attracted Benjamin's interest during his readings in psychoanalysis.[25] In
his delusions, Schreber imagined himself "transformed into a female
body" and treated like "a whore," by a number of unspeakable characters, including God himself. The sexual aspect of Schreber's fantasies is

supplemented by a desire to procreate like a woman.[26] This fantasy of procreation is related, in Schreber's case, to his role as redeemer of a world destroyed by a momentous catastrophe. In a similar way, and through a parallel pregnancy fantasy, Benjamin's translator appears to participate in the ultimate "reconciliation" of tongues, the cabalistic *tikkun,* which figures the messianic restoration of all things that had been shattered at the moment of original collision of lights that accompanied creation.[27] Through the "birth pangs" of his own mother tongue, the translator can conjure, albeit as "an embryonic attempt," the utopian contours of "pure language" (I, 72–73).

But unlike Schreber's psychotic hallucinations, Benjamin's vision of procreation is highly sublimated. In effect, although the seductive "danger" of being "impregnated" by "the seed of pure language" is there, the purely symbolic relation between translation/tor and the Other makes it comparable to an "immaculate conception."[28] The more immediate danger, however, is that in the process of translation, the translator can lose all interest in his individual voice and become a disembodied "echo." In Benjamin's words, "the original has already *relieved* the translator and his translation of the effort of assembling and expressing what is to be conveyed" (I, 78). Through the subtle desire of giving up the burden of communication, Benjamin's concept of translation comes close to a form of symbolic suicide. "In this pure language," Benjamin tells us, "which no longer means or expresses anything but is, as expressionless and creative Word, that which is meant in all languages—all information, all sense, and all intention finally encounter a stratum in which they are destined to be extinguished" (I, 80). If translation may have initially appeared as a promise of revitalizing the self through the encounter of the other (the language of the original), and of the big Other ("pure language"), it ends up leaving the writer on the brink of the "abyss."

Comparing this apocalyptic view of language to the one expressed in the essay "Surrealism," one can say that although there may have been a "danger" in surrealist experiments, their promise of renewal at least seemed far more tangible than the rarefied utopian vision offered by Benjamin in his essay on translation. With surrealism, language appeared not only as the possibility of transforming individual experience, but also of "revolutionizing" life as a whole, in ways that seemed seductively within reach. In effect, the Surrealists's proposal to "liquidate the sclerotic liberal–moral–humanistic ideal of freedom," which can only be compared to Bakunin's "radical concept of freedom," appeared especially in the mid 1920s and early 1930s as a providential way out of the impasse of liberal political thought.

Following in this upbeat direction, Benjamin views surrealism as an energizing stream, a possibility of salvation that before could only be found in religion ("the opium of the people"), and which promised to fulfill the dream of social transcendence sketched in Marx's *Communist Manifesto*. This revolutionary potential is determined, according to Benjamin, by surrealism's ability to "organize pessimism," that is, to refuse all forms of ideological compromise. "Mistrust in the fate of literature, mistrust in the fate of freedom, mistrust in the fate of European humanity, but three times mistrust in all reconciliation: between classes, between nations, between individuals" (R, 191). As surrealism abandons the cloistered space of high culture and turns to the streets, as writing becomes performance, and poetic imagery a form of "radical" intervention in everyday life, art has for the first time, at least on Benjamin's reading, the chance to enter in close contact with its material base, and transform it from within.

Surrealist experience is simultaneously a form of knowledge and a form of action, as the production of the image in language effectively collapses the difference between the two. "[I]n all cases where an action puts forth its own image," Benjamin states, "and exists, absorbing and consuming it, where nearness looks with its own eyes, the long-sought image sphere is opened . . . the sphere . . . in which political materialism and physical nature share the inner man, the psyche, the individual, or whatever else we wish to throw to them, with dialectical justice, so that no limb remains unrent" (R, 192–93). Benjamin's notion of "dialectical annihilation," which in spite of its Hegelian overtones evokes a scene of sacrificial massacre (more in tune with Antonin Artaud's "theater of cruelty"), is directed primarily to the world of images. On this view, surrealist images can become a political weapon, charged with the purifying energies of the unconscious, and directed against the phantasmagoric (ideological) creations of bourgeois culture. Following Benjamin's argument, one can say that one form of intoxication undoes another; the unconscious energy of surrealist images liberates the subject from the narcotic effects of culture (in Nietzsche's understanding of the term), and even from the mystic residues of surrealism itself.[29] The details of this transformation are not altogether clear, although it is technology that is given the utopian role of bringing the subject back into contact with its material grounds.

Unfortunately, a close look at surrealist practices can reveal something that Benjamin missed in his eagerness to adopt them, namely the extent to which these practices participated in the ideological mystification of bourgeois culture they were supposed to critique. More precisely, I wish to reexamie in my conclusion Breton's conception of surrealism as an addictive practice, a "new vice," as he puts it, and which he compares to Baudelaire's search for an "artificial paradise."[30] Unlike Baudelaire, however, whose petulant moralism is aimed at discouraging readers from indulging into the exquisite, but destructive pleasures offered by drugs, Breton is intent on converting his audience to the intoxicating experience of surrealism. Indeed, if for Breton surrealism is no longer an aesthetic phenomenon that requires a contemplative attitude on the part of the reader, the activity or practice envisaged by Breton is one that often involves the reader as consumer.

Breton's *First Manifesto of Surrealism* (1924) is quite explicit about the potent effects of dependency that surrealism is supposed to induce in its assiduous practitioners. Surrealism "acts on the mind very much as drugs do; like drugs, it creates a certain state of need that can push man to frightful revolts[;] . . . like hashish [surrealism] has the ability to satisfy all manner of tastes" (OC, I, 337). In the preface to the first issue of *La Révolution surréaliste* of December 1924, surrealism is said to be at "the crossroads of the enchantments provided by sleep, alcohol, tobacco, ether, opium." The innovation that surrealism brings is not only that it occurs as a "new vice," modeled, however, on the effects of drug addiction, but also, that unlike some other refined vices, it is not necessarily "restricted to the happy few." In other words, like poetry for Lautréamont, surrealism is supposed to be a democratic, populist pleasure. What were Breton's reasons, one wonders, in posturing as a powerful advertising agent for the surrealist addiction?

For one thing, in 1924, Breton was still facing strong competition from Tristan Tzara's Dada activities in Paris. The dada "microbe" was losing its virulence, but Tzara's self-promoting energies were still formidable. Breton, who not long before had adulated the Romanian Dadaist, suddenly decided to break with his former idol and create a movement of his own. If Tzara had designed the impact of Dada on the public on the model of infection, Breton had to counter with the model of addiction. New advertising techniques in the early 1920s prompted Breton and his followers to find new ways of appealing to the public, and fueled their desire to emulate market strategies.

There is, indeed, a fascination with posters and ads in many surrealist writings and publications—the dazzling Mazda bulb in *Nadja* (1928) being a notorious example. The analogy between mass consumption as an addictive practice and surrealist activities is evident even in a later text by Breton, entitled, *Position politique du surréalisme* (1935) *(The Political Position of Surrealism)*. "Ideally," Breton writes, "the authentic surrealist object should be recognized immediately, through some external distinctive sign, like a designer cachet or a seal, as Man Ray had suggested."[31] The analogy here is with a Paramount film production that the spectator is immediately hooked on, as soon as the logo appears on the screen.

What constitutes, one may ask, the "inimitable" mark that produces not only immediate recognition: "aha, this is a surrealist object," or "this is a surrealist image," but also "creates a state of need," as Breton puts it, "[that] can push man to frightful revolts"? I have already suggested, in an article on Breton's *Nadja*, that surrealist products, including texts, should be interpreted as imaginary objects or dream-objects.[32] In his *Introduction to the Discourse on the Poverty of Reality* (1925), Breton had described a kind of ur-type for this imaginary object. It consisted, according to Breton, of "a rather curious book," whose back "is formed by a wooden gnome" with a long white beard, "clipped in the Assyrian manner," and whose pages are made of "thick black wool" (OC, II, 277). Such dream-objects, Breton says, could be easily "manufactured" and "put into circulation" in real life, for the sake of their "distinctly puzzling and disturbing" effect. The surrealist product as dream-object *("objet de rêve")* may be compared to the surrealist objects described by Dali, especially to an object that operates "symbolically," which is to say, using Dali's definition, an "object which fulfill[s] the necessity of being open to action by our own hands and moved about by our own wishes."[33]

Identifying surrealist products with the dream-object mentioned above, the "curious book" that could be "opened by our own hands and moved about by our own wishes," would explain the teasing obscurity of many surrealist productions as the result of a "necessity" or "wish," which may concern the writer no less than the reader. If we take, for instance, the cutout on the cover of the paperback edition of *Nadja*—the assemblage of the woman's head, Nadja's, and the man's hand—such a hybrid object teases us by its invitation to set the object in motion.[34] The movement of the pendulum hand, with its sexual connotations, acts as an incentive, only to reveal behind it the empty silhouette of a woman, the way the veil stripped from the face would reveal an absent jaw. On the other hand, there is an opacity about the woman's hair that suggests layers of cloth or scrolls of writing, which like the "thick black wool" of the dream-book, seem to forbid the *jouissance* they invite. The triangular shape of the veil matching the heart-shaped drawing enclosed in it evokes, moreover, the pointed cusp of a guillotine, which further leads to the motif of the cut hand—the symbolic token of the revolutionary Terror that haunts Breton's novel.

Trying to interpret these surrealist objects according to a Lacanian reading, and using Žižek as a guide, we may say that they exhibit, at one and the same time, a surplus of meaning—a density that prohibits circulation and *jouissance*—and a lightness and elusiveness that invite desire, including the desire to interpret.[35] This alluring secretiveness is typical of the *objet petit a,* the object of fantasy or the cause of desire, which we cannot examine too closely without discovering the emptiness that lies at the heart of desire itself. It is this double, contradictory appeal of surrealist objects that makes, I think, for their addictive quality. The point is not the satisfaction of desire, which cannot be satisfied anyway, but its frustration, the wish to abide at the level of fantasy.

If surrealist products are addictive, in the sense of promising to fulfill a lack that they cannot or rather would not fulfill, in what way does their production mirror the physiological process of intoxication, as Breton pretends? In the 1924 *Manifesto of Surrealism,* Breton compared the production of surrealist images to that of opium images, and in this respect he quoted Baudelaire's comment on De Quincey's opium nightmares, which the poet translated in *Artificial Paradises:* "man does not evoke the images anymore; rather they come to him spontaneously, despotically. He cannot chase them away; for the will is powerless now and no longer controls the faculties" (Breton, OC, I, 337). Moreau de Tours, the famous psychiatrist who experimented with hashish eating, in order to better understand the nature of mental diseases, had mentioned De Quincey in his book, *On Hashish and Mental Alienation* (1845), under the guise of "an Englishman living in India," and made a similar observation: "It is with *his eyes* that [the opium-eater] thought he saw the phantoms whose presence he dreaded, and which he only evoked with trembling."[36]

Indeed, as Bernard-Paul Robert has shown in his comparative study of Baudelaire, Moreau de Tours, and Breton, this type of opium vision may be described as a phantasmal image formed by submerged memories and present impressions, and which differs sharply from the hallucinations or distortions of vision generated by hashish.[37] In both opium and hashish forms of intoxication, however, the important factor is the automatic quality of the visions produced. In this respect, there seems to be a clear analogy between delirium, as a form of mental illness, and the irresistible visions and hallucinations of the opium or hashish eater. This is how Alfred Maury, a psychiatrist who published a study on mania in the *Annales médico-psychologiques* (1853), analyzed the "two principal phenomena that governed almost single-handedly the causes of delirium": [these are]—"a spontaneous and almost automatic action of the mind, and a vicious and irregular association of ideas."[38] Given Breton's early training as an intern in psychiatry, one can legitimately assume that Breton's definition of surrealism, as a form of "psychic automatism," is inspired by nineteenth-century medical accounts of narcotic imaging and delirium.[39]

It is perhaps useful to remember to what extent this definition of surrealism influenced Lacan's early writings on paranoia. In a collective article, "Ecrits 'inspirés': schizographie," published in *Les Annales médico-psychologiques,* of December, 1931, Lacan and his colleagues, Lévy-Valensi and Pierre Migault, had actually commented favorably on the psychiatric value of the automatic experiments made by Breton and his followers.[40] Later on, in Lacan's description of psychotic discourse, and in his concept of the unconscious being structured as a language, we may find theoretical clues pointing to Breton's surrealist writings. In spite of this early influence, Lacan (not to mention Freud to whom Breton sent a copy of his *Communicating Vases,* 1932), remained skeptical of the liberating vistas that Breton and his followers (including Benjamin, for that matter), ascribed to surrealism.

The same skepticism, although for very different reasons, was also shared by the Communists, with whom the Surrealists sought to ally themselves. Surrealists, like the state of supreme intoxication, the *Kief,* as the Arabs called it, and which Baudelaire described as the state "where all contradiction resolves in unity" (OC, I, 394), represented for Breton a nondialectic reconciliation of the pleasure principle and the reality principle: "I believe in the future resolution of these two states, dream and reality, which are seemingly so contradictory, into a kind of absolute reality, a *surreality*" (*Manifesto of surrealism,* OC I, 319). Breton's phrase here echoes nineteenth-century statements about the "fusion" between reality and dream brought about by intoxication. In Baudelaire's words, for instance, "The hashish eater utterly confuses dream and action . . ." (*Paradis artificiels,* OC, I, 436). It is also typical for the Surrealists to consider dream images as a direct mode of intervention into reality, a pretense that could only exasperate the Communists, but which for Benjamin had a particular salutary resonance.

The fallacy, entertained by both Communists, and in a different sense, by the Surrealists, was that the imaginary was at the opposite pole of reality, and hence, depending on the case, must be repudiated, or co-opted. Yet, as a Lacanian argument that the role of the imaginary in social life (the Symbolic order) has demonstrated, reality is already permeated by the imaginary through the ideological fictions that suffuse it. As Žižek has put it, "the fundamental level of ideology . . . is not of an illusion masking the real state of things but that of an (unconscious) fantasy structuring our social reality itself."[41] Breton's claim to raise the individual dream to the level of "certainty" granted to phenomena in social life can be read as an attempt to influence the "collective unconscious," on the premise that the surrealist poet, the opium eater or why not, the madman, had in their power the ability to single-handedly affect the social imaginary. "Can't the dream also be used in solving the fundamental questions of life?" Breton asks, in rhetorical fashion (*Manifeste du surréalisme*, OC I, 318).

Unlike the drug addict who usually consumes his or her fantasies in utter solitude, Breton is eager to produce and disperse surrealist images through active publications, exhibitions, and instances of happening. The paradox, however, is that in all this "activity," the subjects remains passive. By erasing the distinction between body and mind, Breton's "physiological" understanding of writing also transforms the subject into an object. Writing, which was once conceived as an active act of inscribing, is redefined in terms of a passive experience of inscription (see for instance, the definition of "automatic writing"), to which opium visions or hallucinations serve as a model. Surrealist language functions as a potent drug, which controls the subject with the same relentless power of Lacan's "discourse of the Other."

Why, one wonders, would Breton wish to relinquish conscious control in favor of this tyrannical power, when he so adamantly rejects the constraints of logical reason? There are a number of possible answers that I would like to suggest here. One has to do with the autoerotic or masochistic seduction of being dominated by an imperious Other, which in Breton's case disguises, as I have previously argued, a repressed homosexual fantasy.[42] The other reason has to do with the more general ideological premises of surrealism. The notion of consciousness as a material surface, which can be found in both literary and medical sources describing the nature of visions and hallucinations in a state of intoxication, corresponds to another form of surrealist "addiction," such as cinema.

What these forms of "influence" have in common is the fact that they allow for an almost simultaneous inscription and erasure of signals; messages can be displaced as fast as they are received. The fascination that the Surrealists had for the image of consciousness-as-surface resides precisely in its limits. The screen (like the presumed state of the mind in intoxication) captivates by its tenuous contact with reality, and ultimately by its blankness. On its unstable surface, the movement of consciousness is reduced to a mirage. The surrealist image is in fact this mirage produced, as Breton says, by the fortuitous juxtaposition of two terms, and whose beauty resides in the "spark" that occurs from the "difference of potential between the two conductors." To conclude, I will cite at length the passage describing the dizzying effect of surrealist images that chase and obliterate each other like images on a screen.

And just as the length of the spark increases to the extent that it occurs in rarefied gases, the surrealist atmosphere created by automatic writing, which I have tried to put within everyone's reach, is especially conducive to the production of beautiful images. One can even go as far as to say that in this dizzying race the images appear like the only guideposts of the mind. By slow degrees the mind becomes convinced of the supreme reality of these images. At first limiting itself to submitting to them, the mind soon realizes that these images are flattering to reason, and increase its knowledge accordingly. The mind becomes aware of the limitless expanses wherein its desires are made manifest, where the pros and cons are constantly consumed, where its obscurity does not betray it. (*Manifeste du surréalisme*, OC, I, p. 338)

Surrealism is thus the space where desires are briefly conjured like phantom-like opium visions, and also consumed and concealed, where, as Breton puts it, the "obscurity [of the unconscious] does not betray itself." This concept of "obscurity" is, I believe, inseparable from Breton's practice of "occultation," which represents for him the very essence of surrealism, and has subsequently had a significant impact on the artistic forms and techniques developed by his surrealist followers. And it may be that it is this very obscurity that attracted Benjamin to surrealism, by offering him a justification and a space for deploying his own phantasms of identity.[43] In this imaginary space, the difference between the regenerating potential of the image, and its obfuscating counterpart seems to disappear, as does the difference between its materialist and mystic understanding.

For Benjamin, however, this dream-like space also offered a provisional haven, an island outside the threatening currents of history, where he could rethink the very meaning of history itself. From this perspective, "Surrealism" was also an object of thought, one of the "themes" that Benjamin mentions in his last writing, "Theses on the Philosophy of History" (1940). As the "storm" called "progress" is "blowing from Paradise," "piling wreckage upon wreckage," and tangling the Angel's wings, applied thinking becomes the last resort for all the disenfranchised. As Benjamin puts it, "The themes which monastic discipline assigned to friars for meditation were designed to turn them away from the world and its affairs. The thoughts which we are developing here originate from similar considerations" (I, 257–58).

NOTES

1. For previous significant discussions of Benjamin's relation to surrealism, see, among others, Margaret Cohen, *Profane Illumination: Walter Benjamin and the Paris of Surrealist Revolution* (University of California Press, 1993); Peter

Osborne's essay, "Small-scale Victories, Large-scale Defeats: Walter Benjamin's Politics of Time," in Andrew Benjamin and Peter Osborne, eds., *Walter Benjamin's Philosophy* (Routledge, 1994), and Max Pensky, "Tactics of Remembrance: Proust, Surrealism, and the Origin of the *Passagenwerk*," in Michael Steinberg, ed., *Walter Benjamin and the Demands of History* (Cornell University Press, 1996).

2. Bernd Witte, *Walter Benjamin. An Intellectual Biography*, translated by James Rolleston (Wayne State University Press, 1991), p. 89. See also Hermann Schweppenhäuser, "Propaedeutics of Profane Illumination," in Gary Smith, ed., *On Walter Benjamin* (MIT Press, 1988), p. 37.

3. *The Arcades Project (Das Passagen-Werk)* was Benjamin's darling project, initiated during his first year in Paris (1927) and carried on until the very end of his life (1940). Its topic—the architectural form of the arcades—is emblematic in Benjamin's view of the entire history of the nineteenth century. First published in 1982, *Das Passagen-Werk* was translated into English by Howard Eiland and Kevin McLaughlin, as *The Arcades Project* (Harvard University Press, 1999).

4. Benjamin intended his work *On Hashish (Über Hashish)* to become "a highly significant book," alongside *The Arcades*, and his *Collected Literary Essays*. See Walter Benjamin-Gershom Scholem, *Briefwechsel* 1933–1940, Gershom Scholem, ed. (Frankfurt: Suhrkamp, 1980), pp. 22f.

5. Letter to Theodor W. Adorno, Paris, May 31, 1935, in *The Correspondence of Walter Benjamin (1910–1940)*, Gershom Scholem and Theodor W. Adorno, eds.; translated by Manfred R. Jacobson and Evelyn M. Jacobson (The University of Chicago Press, 1994), p. 488.

6. In *The Arcades Project*, Benjamin declared: "Surrealism was born in an arcade" (*The Arcades Project*, p. 83). If it is true that the Surrealists were fascinated by arcades, which take on a special significance in Aragon's *Peasant of Paris*, it is equally true that the "preliminary sketches" of Benjamin's own *Arcades* project, and its subtitle, *A Dialectical Fairy Play*, "originated at that time." The surrealist notions of dream and intoxication are, in great part, responsible for the conceptual frame of Benjamin's project. As Rolf Tiedemann wrote in his essay, "Dialectics at a Standstill," which serve as a postface to the English translation of *The Arcades Project*, "Benjamin wanted to carry [the] profane illumination [practices by the Surrealists] into history by acting as an interpreter of the dreams of the nineteenth-century world of things."

7. Letter to Gershom Scholem, March 15, 1929, in *Correspondence*, p. 348.

8. Idem.

9. Scholem had been trying to convince Benjamin to join him in teaching literature in Jerusalem, a task for which Benjamin's knowledge of Hebrew was not adequate. See Gershom Scholem, *Walter Benjamin. The Story of a Friendship*, translated by Harry Zohn (Schocken Books: New York, 1981), p. 143f.

10. Before his final exile to Paris, Benjamin had difficulty getting his articles accepted in Germany, but continued to publish in German journals that were published abroad, such as Adorno's *Zeitschrift für Soziale Forschung.*

11. Walter Benjamin, "Surrealism," in *Reflections,* translated by Edmund Jephcott (Schocken Books: New York, 1986), p. 177. Henceforth cited in the text as R.

12. On Benjamin's ambiguous attitude towards political engagement, see my article, "Walter Benjamin's Messianic Politics: Angelus Novus and the End of History," in *Cross Currents,* No. 11 (1992), pp. 23–41.

13. André Breton, *Manifeste du Surréalisme,* in *Oeuvres complètes* (Bibliothèque de la Pléiade, Gallimard, 1988), vol. 1, p. 328. Henceforth cited as OC. Translations are mine.

14. See the title of Breton's text, "Introduction au discours sur le peu de réalité" (1925), ("Introduction to the Discourse on the Poverty of Reality"). The phrase is also mentioned in a different context by Lacan, in "The Mirror Stage," *Écrits. A Selection,* translated by Alan Sheridan (W. W. Norton & Co., 1977), pp. 3–4.

15. Walter Benjamin, "Program of the Coming Philosophy," translated by Mark Ritter, in *The Philosophical Forum,* vol, XV, Nos. 1–2, Fall–Winter 1983–1984, p. 42.

16. "The Task of the Translator" is included in Walter Benjamin, *Illuminations,* translated by Harry Zohn (Schocken Books: New York, 1969), pp. 69–83. Henceforth cited as I.

17. This reference is also to Kant, in Benjamin's "Goethes Wahlverwandtschaften." *Illuminationen* (Frankfurt: Suhrkamp, 1980), p. 64.

18. For an analysis of natural metaphors in Benjamin's essay, see Carol Jacobs, "The Monstrosity of Translation," *MLN,* No. 90, 1975, p. 758. I have discussed Benjamin's interest in translation in a different context, in an article entitled "The Debt of the Translator: An Essay on Translation and Modernism," *Symploke,* Vol. 5, Nos. 1–2 (1997), pp. 7–26.

19. For a cogent illustration of the relation between Rimbaud's esthetics and his life, see Graham Robb's biography, *Rimbaud* (W. W. Norton, New York & London, 2000).

20. "Total" renders the German *"mit Stumpf und Stiel"* in the original, "Die Aufgabe des Ubersetzers," in Walter Benjamin, *Gesammelte Schriften,* Rolf Tiedemann and Hermann Scweppenhäuser, eds., 7 vols., Suhrkamp, 1972, Vol. IV:1, p. 15.

21. Hermann Schweppenhäuser, "Propaedeutics of Profane Illumination," in Gary Smith, ed., *On Walter Benjamin* (Cambridge, MA: MIT Press, 1991), p. 37

22. See my argument in, "Walter Benjamin's Messianic Politics: Angelus Novus and the End of History" cited above.

23. See Gershom Scholem, "Revelation and Tradition as Religious Categories in Judaism," in *The Messianic Idea in Judaism* (Schocken Books: New York, 1971), p. 299.

24. Charles Baudelaire, "Mon coeur mis à nu," in *Journaux intimes, Oeuvres complètes* (Bibliothèque de la Pléiade, Gallimard, 1975), vol. 1, p. 676. Translations are mine.

25. Benjamin was well acquainted with Paul Schreber's case and kept the judge's memoirs of his illness in his library, on a special shelf reserved to the "mentally ill." See Gershom Scholem, *Walter Benjamin. The Story of a Friendship*, p. 57. See also Benjamin's letter to Scholem (Berlin, July 21, 1925) in Walter Benjamin, *Briefe*, ed. Gershom Scholem and Theodor W. Adorno (Frankfurt: Suhrkamp, 1978), I, p. 397, n. 7.

26. References are to Daniel Paul Schreber, *Memoirs of My Nervous Illness*, translated by Ida Macalpine and Richard A. Hunter (Cambridge: Robert Bentley, Inc., 1955). Schreber's case is discussed by Freud in terms of repressed homosexuality ("Psychoanalytic Notes Upon an Autobiographical Account of a Case of Paranoia"), and by Lacan, who uses Schreber as an argument for his theory of the unconscious as "the discourse of the Other" (*Psychoses*, The Seminar III). The translators and commentators of the English translation of Schreber's memoirs emphasize a relatively neglected syndrome, that of the "pregnancy fantasy," and it is this particular complex that interests me here.

27. See "Walter Benjamin and His Angel," in *On Walter Benjamin*, Gary Smith, ed., p. 84. One should also note that in Benjamin's vision, "Agesilaus Santander," commented by Scholem, the angel "accosted" Benjamin in its "feminine form."

28. In his earlier essay on "Socrates" (1916), Benjamin saw this form of procreation as a feminized version of masculine conception: "Just as immaculate conception is for the woman the rapturous notion of purity, so conception without pregnancy is most profoundly the spiritual mark of the male genius" ("Socrates," translated by Thomas Levine, in *The Philosophical Forum*, Vol. XV, Nos. 1–2, Fall–Winter 1983–1984, p. 53). "The existence of the feminine," moreover, is necessary only insofar as it guarantees "the asexuality of the spiritual in the world" (p. 53).

29. See Nietzsche's discussion of the relation between "narcotica" and the "history of 'culture,' of our so-called higher culture," in *The Gay Science*, translated by Walter Kaufmann (New York: Vintage Books, 1974), p. 328.

30. The influence of Baudelaire on Breton and the Surrealists has also been discussed by Bernard-Paul Robert, in his study *Antécédents du surréalisme* (Les Presses de l'Université d'Ottawa, 1988).

31. "Situation surréaliste de l'objet," "Position politique du surréalisme," in André Breton, *Oeuvres complètes* (Bibliothèque de la Pléiade, Gallimard, 1992), Vol. II, pp. 474–475.

32. "Phantoms of the Opera: Notes Towards a Theory of Surrealist Confession—The Case of Breton," in *MLN,* Vol. 104/No. 4, pp. 819–845.

33. Salvador Dali, "Surrealist Objects," in Hershel B. Chipp, ed., *Theories of Modern Art* (Berkeley: University of California Press, 1968), p. 425.

34. See revised edition of Breton's *Nadja* (Paris: Gallimard, 1964).

35. See Slavoj Žižek, *The Sublime Object of Ideology* (London & New York: Verso, 1989), pp. 52–53.

36. J. Moreau de Tours, *Du Hachisch et de l'aliénation mentale* (Paris: Librairie de Fortin, Masson et Co., 1845), p. 226.

37. Bernard-Paul, Robert, op. cit., pp. 14ff.

38. Quoted by Robert, op. cit., p. 16.

39. For further discussion of this point, see my article on Breton, "Phantoms of the Opera," *MLN,* Vol. 104, p. 830.

40. This text has been republished as an appendix to Lacan's doctoral thesis on paranoia, *De la psychose paranoïaque dans ses rapports avec la personnalité,* under the title *Premiers écrits sur la paranoïa,* Paris: Seuil, 1975).

41. Žižek, *The Sublime Object of Ideology,* p. 33.

42. See discussion of Breton's youthful erotic attachment to Jacques Vaché, in my article on Breton cited above.

43. The issue concerning Benjamin's troubled sense of identity, in all its dimensions (sexual, social, ethnic, and religious), would necessitate a separate discussion. It suffices to look back at the erotic overtones of "The Task of the Translator," and Benjamin's attempts to transform (or rather disguise) himself into a surrealist revolutionary in the essay "Surrealism" to gauge the extent of his malaise. His experiments with hashish recorded in the papers *On Hashish,* were similarly used as a way of subjective modification.

Chapter Five

HEIDEGGER'S CRAVING

Being-on-Schelling

DAVID L. CLARK

What we call *spirit* exists by *virtue of itself*, a flame that fuels itself. However, because as something existing, it is opposed by Being, the spirit is consequently nothing but an addiction to such Being, just as the flame is addicted to matter. The most base form of the spirit is therefore an addiction, a desire, a lust.

—Friedrich Schelling, *Stuttgart Private Lectures*

JUST SAY NO

How *not* to speak of addiction? We know from Derrida that in talking this way we are always asking two overlapping questions,[1] both of which remind us that what is still confusedly called "addiction"—and with it, a host of related concepts ranging from "drugs" and "toxicity" to "dependence" and "simulation"—is perhaps best held open *as* a question or, rather, in the strange space *between* two questions, quite possibly more. First, an interrogative: a query that calls for a certain vigilance and responsibility when it comes to thinking about addiction, and that draws attention to the ways in which addiction is figured, the rhetorics or tropologies as well as the knowledges of addiction. Like mourning and longing, Schellingian philosophemes to which it is closely related and to which I will return in this essay, addiction is among other things a *figure of understanding,* to use Tilottama Rajan's evocative phrase.[2] *As* a figure, so the first question goes, "addiction" deserves to be written and to be read slowly, not only for what might be called "political" reasons, which is to say, reasons having to do with the normalizing efficiency that comes of speaking the word too quickly, of claiming to know "who" the addict is as such and "what" it means to be addicted, but also because when it comes to addiction—again, like mourning and longing—we are dealing with a term that is irreducibly allegorical in nature, a term that inevitably says more than it says. One could *almost* say that "how *not* to speak of addiction" means "let us try to speak well or properly of addiction, even and especially if this means speaking properly of addiction's multiple improprieties." One could *almost* say this, if "addiction," understood as a fundamental structure of desire that "holds valid for all possible contents of the world" [Slawney 42], were not precisely that which displaces and disorganizes firm oppositional limits between propriety and impropriety, as it does between responsibility and irresponsibility, voluntary and compulsion, delinquency and productivity, sickness and health, the very limits that the medical, juridical, and criminal discourses of addiction often seem most in the service of inscribing and enforcing.

But of course the inability unequivocally to speak well (or, for that matter, unwell) of "addiction" in no way suggests that we have nothing to say about it—the collection of papers of which this one forms a small part is proof of that—and this goes to the heart of my second question, not interrogative but rhetorical in kind. "How *not* to speak of addiction?" also means that there is no way *not* to speak of it; insofar as addiction names a structure that precedes and exceeds the knowing subject (and is thus "older" than it), that subject is *always* "speaking" of it, as if answering and answerable to an imperious law, the law of addiction that amounts to an addiction to the law. *Addiction there is:* that is the strange, anonymous, and always anterior logic of craving, a craving no longer necessarily in thrall to the thought of self-possession and sobriety that Schelling scandalously evokes and explores, and that Heidegger directly pursues in his lectures on Schelling. More: where the human is, so too is "the deepest self-craving *[der tiefsten Eigensucht]*" [Heidegger, *ST* 140; 42, 244].[3] Under these maximally habituated conditions, "how *not* to speak of addiction?" means that we are not unwilling but incapable of just saying no to a form of radical intoxication. Instead, we find ourselves, *as* ourselves, whether speaking specifically about addiction or not, responding in a kind of passive affirmative to an originary craving, saying yes to addiction even when, in the name of an imagined pure sobriety or abstemiousness or willfulness, we may in fact choose to say no. This "yes" would be of the kind that Derrida describes as an "affirmation that is not addressed first of all to a subject" ["Eating Well" 274]. Before the undeniable aegis of this question, the "not" in "how not to speak of addiction?" marks the trace of a resistance that prevents us from simply saying what we mean and meaning what we say when addiction is the subject; there is no speaking about addiction as such, but for this very reason there is no *not* speaking about it, either. If addiction *is* originary, if it is constitutive of the subject, including, incredibly, the absolute subject of God—as, Schelling argues—then there is no metalanguage *on* addiction that is not itself already fundamentally "addicted."

Although I refer to a range of works in this chapter, the target texts are F. W. J. Schelling's *Philosophical Investigations into the Essence of Human Freedom and Related Matters (Philosophische Untersuchungen über das Wesen der menschlichen Freiheit und die damit zusammenhägenden Gegenstände)* (1809) and Martin Heidegger's *Schelling's Treatise on the Essence of Human Freedom (Schelling: Vom Wesen der Menschlichen Freiheit)* (1936). There is a third text always under consideration, too, and that is the hybrid or perhaps virtual text produced by the close interaction of the other two, a text that is neither Heideggerian nor Schellingian but both at once. What interests me here is not only the differing and complementary ways in which Heidegger and Schelling explicitly employ "addiction" as a figure of understanding. I want also to pursue the "rhetoric of drugs" (Derrida) and the notion of "being-on-drugs" (Ronell) that appears inevitably to accompany the question of addiction. Both Schelling and Heidegger suggest that craving is *infectious* (Heidegger: "a sickness which strives to spread itself" [*ST* 125]); one working premise of this chapter is that philosophical narratives about addiction have a habit of becoming evocatively pharmaceutical, that is, of getting caught up in everything that modernity associates with habituation and drugs. These include, very briefly: the "pleasure taken in an experience without truth"; "the asymmetrical experience of the other (of being-given-over-to-the-other, of the being prey to the other, of quasi-possession)"; the ingestion, idealization, and incorporation of "substances" that obey the logic of the supplement and the *pharmakon* (that is, these "substances" play ambiguous roles in the texts that evoke them and turn out to be both essential and additive, useful and poisonous vis-à-vis the bodies of those texts); the work of mourning (including the work of an impossible mourning) which addiction—never unrelated to the question of loss and renunciation—seems always in some way to incur; the patterns of dependency and parasitization that develop between a powerful commentary and its pretext; and the simulations and fictions, the phenomenon of being-carried-away or carried-across that brings addiction and figurality together.[4] The philosophical narratives that I examine here are often weirdly implicated in their own addictive subject; yet in reading Schelling and Heidegger under such a potentially generalizing rubric as "addiction," I risk the hermeneutical equivalent of looking for contraband and finding it everywhere—of planting drugs. Derrida warns us that "to conflate . . . differences [among texts about being-on-drugs] in a homogeneous series would be delirious, indeed narcoticizing" ["Rhetoric" 237]. But, then, how not to speak of addiction?[5]

HOOKED ON SCHELLING

There may be no master narrative about addiction—and yet there is so much to say where addiction is concerned; like deconstruction, addiction is remarkably text-productive. Nietzsche asks: "Who will ever relate the whole history of narcotica?—It is almost the history of 'culture,' of our so-called higher culture" [§86]. (Derrida responds: "A history is required, and a culture, conventions, evaluations, norms, an entire network of intertwined discourses, a rhetoric, whether explicit or elliptical" ["Rhetoric" 229].) Among the paradigmatic texts and nodal points making up that history would certainly be the sections of *Being and Time* that Avital Ronell has discussed so well. Here Heidegger defines "care" *(Sorge)* as the being of Dasein, the structural totality that gathers together the ways—the "existentials"—in which Dasein always finds itself habituated to and concerned with entities in the world. Oddly enough, Heidegger devotes the greater part of his effort toward describing not care but care's proximate others, the inappropriate propensities that impersonate and threaten to usurp care: *wollen, wünschen, Hang,* and *Drang* (willing, wishing, addiction, and urge). As Ronell demonstrates, Heidegger's interpretation of the relationship between care and these desirous cognates is extremely ambivalent. On the one hand, he insists that the care structure is ontologically primordial, the already-there that is irreducible to the compulsions and hankerings of everyday life. On the other hand, Heidegger recognizes that *Hang* and *Drang* are more than merely "psychological" or "biological" phenomena; they are fundamentally rooted in care, the dangerous supplements that can always threaten to deflect Dasein from its primary way of being, its true course of resolute openness to *Angst*. For Ronell, addiction and urge in particular function like "accelerators" and "artificial additives" [44]—that is, as pharmaceuticals, uppers—that "display the problematic powers of being ontologically constitutive in certain cases" [40], thereby collapsing the oppositional limit that Heidegger compulsively inscribes and reinscribes between being-in-the-world and being-on-drugs. The origins of Heidegger's argument about addiction, including the self-complication that Ronell describes, are in fact clearly evident in *History of the Concept of Time: Prolegomena (Prolegomena zur Geschichte des Zeitbegriffs)*, the lecture course that Heidegger delivered in the summer semester of 1925 at the University of Marburg. Already, Heidegger is insisting on the parasitical nature of *Hang* and *Drang*, their unstable "location" both within and without the boundary dividing the interiority of *Sorge* from the exteriority of its mirror forms: "Care is . . . not a phenomenon composed of addiction *[Hang]* and urge," he argues; yet only a few sentences later he concedes that "along with care[,] addiction as well as urge are constitutive of every Dasein" [HT 297]. As in *Being and Time*, addiction functions suspiciously like a "narcotic," alluring and dangerous, spoiling Heidegger's axiomatic claims that the essence of Dasein's "desires" is nothing vulgarly desirous. For who could tell the difference between being-in-the-world and being-on-drugs? In Ronell's hands, Dasein pretends to designate a drug crisis when it is, in fact, itself the crisis to which it refers.

Ronell's "narcoanalysis" focuses on section 41 of *Being and Time*, but this is not the only place—nor is it the only way—that addiction is discussed in Heidegger's work. Significantly, when he returns to the concept almost a decade later it has undergone a sea-change in his thinking. It goes without saying that a great deal has happened to Heidegger, intellectually, since the mid-1920s, but in terms of his interpretation of the meaning of a general concept of addiction, that change can be summed up quickly here in one word: *Schelling*. In *Being and Time* addiction complexly mimics Dasein, making it a phenomenon to be respected but avoided; under Schelling's influence, however, its status changes dramatically, suddenly becoming *the* philosopheme with which radically to think the essence of human freedom and the origins of evil, and, beyond that, vicariously and supplementally to displace the "doctrine of Being which understands all beings in a thinglike way and takes the merely stufflike object of nature as the decisive being" [ST 94]. That is, Schelling's notion of addiction evokes for Heidegger *die Seynsfrage* (the question of Being) [ST 146; 42, 253]. If addiction is a "prohibited substance" for the Heidegger of the 1920s—as Ronell suggests—then

"Schelling" is the means by which he declassifies (or perhaps more accurately, *re*classifies) that "drug" in the 1930s. Significant though unacknowledged *use* is made of Schelling throughout *An Introduction to Metaphysics* (1935), but it is not until the following year that Heidegger devotes an entire summer semester explicitly to the idealist philosopher's work. Then, as before, the text that principally interests him is Schelling's *Philosophical Investigations into the Essence of Human Freedom and Related Matters,* where Schelling unabashedly argues that the Absolute, and all the creatures that are patterned after it, is primordially structured like craving *(die Sucht)* and like longing *(die Sehnsucht).* To say that Heidegger reads Schelling's text closely is not to say enough, for his appropriation of the freedom essay is *itself* ferociously parasitical, a strange case of dependency, repetition, and "being-given-over-to-the-other" that can be usefully described in Derridean terms as part of "the rhetoric of drugs." "The result of this self-abandonment is curious indeed; as any reader who has set the two texts side by side knows, where Heidegger stops and Schelling begins is often extremely difficult to determine, the former's text is so *consumed* with—by?—the essay on freedom. Jean-Luc Nancy captures the unique nature of Heidegger's appropriation of Schelling's text when he suggests that the 1936 lectures offer "nothing other than a kind of continuous harmonic composition, where Heidegger's own discourse . . . create[s] an incessant counterpoint to Schelling's, without making the matter explicit on its own, and without the latter's discourse being given a clear interpretation by that of the former" [36]. During the course of the lectures, Heidegger *hangs* on to Schelling's every word in an attempt to make legible the traces of a radical thinking that had remained invisible to his contemporaries (Hegel chief amongst them); this, while at the same time subjecting Schelling to a strong reading that is not without "its own peculiar violence" [Sallis 155]. We might say that Heidegger is *using* (Schelling), parasitizing him and ventriloquizing him in a manner that presumably involves all of the ambiguities attendant upon similar acts of incorporation (idealization, internalization, mourning, and so forth) in which the "consumed" object is neither "outside" nor "inside" but both at once. Yet he writes *with* him in such a way that it reads as if he, Heidegger, had fallen prey to a kind of quasi-possession by the German idealist.

Only a year prior to the lectures, in *An Introduction to Metaphysics*—a text that is haunted by the thoughts and words of Schelling's essay—Heidegger had in fact spoken of the task of radical questioning as a form of giving-over-to-the-other, a surrendering at the hands of the exemplary few who, like Schelling, promise "a new beginning" [*IM* 39; *ST* 3]; authentic thinking is equivalent to being-on-philosophy: "granted that *we* cannot do anything with philosophy, might not philosophy, if we concern ourselves with it, do something *with us?*" [*IM* 12]. Yet Heidegger's parasitical dependency upon Schelling's thoughts is troped as a strange form of hermeneutical codependency, for he introduces his lectures by informing his listeners that the true significance of the essay on freedom awaits the touch of the existential analytic; that is, Schelling needs Heidegger as much as Heidegger needs Schelling. Operating as a philosophical supplement, Schelling is foreign and exotic, "the last great representative of anthropomorphic, prescientific theosophy" [Žižek 7], but he is also an uncannily welcome guest in the Heideggerian corpus, not to say deeply familiar to "the German spirit" whose "shape" he is said to have helped form, and is helping still. Schelling's work itself is characterized as the commendable failure whose "questioning thinking" [*ST* 166] ultimately proved toxic to his philosophical project, leaving him, as Heidegger rather melodramatically says, "stranded" within it and "shattered" upon it [*ST* 160]. The essay on freedom is a spectacular instance of blindness and insight: its author represents "the acme of the metaphysics of German idealism" [*ST* 165]—an "idealism preventing him from coming up with the idea of Dasein," as Peter Fenves aptly puts it [xxviii]—this, in a text that "is the sign of the advent of something completely different, the heat lightning of a new beginning" [*ST* 3]. At the precise hour of the "world-darkening" *(Weltverdüsterung),* when the German spirit falters, "debilitated" and held back from *within* by "the demonic" *(das Dämonische)* [*IM* 62; 40, 48, 50], Schelling is there as a kind of antidote, first to be taken in small doses (in 1935) and then all at once (in 1936). Although he goes unnamed, in *An Introduction to Metaphysics* he has given Heidegger the very language with which to think about the radicality of evil and to censure spirit's self-destitution *(Entmachtung des Geistes)* [*IM* 45; 40, 48]; as Derrida notes, "[s]ome of Heidegger's formulations here are literally Schellingian" [*Of Spirit* 63]. (Such literalism calls for analysis, for what is the status of a citation within a text, especially an unacknowledged citation? Particles of "Schelling" that are incorporated or perhaps introjected intact into the tissue of Heidegger's argument, an inoculation of "Schelling" . . . against what?) And in the subsequent lectures on the freedom essay, Heidegger points explicitly to Schelling's "thoughtful life"—a life *full* of thinking—and to the exemplary instance of a philosopher who in his own time was unafraid of "the historical spirit of the Germans as they themselves sought a gestalt" [*ST* 7]. He, Schelling, will be the potent if volatile supplement, a man's drink, so to speak, that will lift and invigorate that spirit once more . . . assuming, of course, that "the age is ready and strong enough for it *[ein Zeitalter dafür bereit und stark genug ist]*" [*ST* 4; 42, 7]. The subject of seminars and lecture courses in 1927–1928, and then again in 1936 and 1941.[6] Schelling proves to be a very hard habit to break, even when Heidegger in effect tells us—as he does, for example, in the 1941 lectures—that he has done precisely that. (In the end it is not the weakened German spirit that fails to have the stomach for Schelling, or at least for a certain Schelling, but Heidegger!) For although during the wartime lectures Heidegger "abandons" Schelling when the philosopheme of "human freedom" no longer proves useful and efficacious to him,[7] the German idealist has an astonishingly persistent afterlife in Heidegger's work. Turns of thought and phrases, some of them drawn word for word from the lectures on the freedom essay, survive in Heidegger's work, like the residue of an unmetabolized drug, through to the late lectures on Trakl (1953), where, as Derrida suggests, they are both "natural and troubling" [*Of Spirit* 127]. Natural *and* troubling: where Heidegger is concerned, Schelling is always such strange "stuff": *familiar* and *native* because he registers the continuity of a certain "metaphysics of evil" in Heidegger, yet *foreign* and *dangerous* to the body of his thinking precisely because this link back to German Idealism, back to the thought of *Geist* that we find there, threatens and disrupts the epochality of Heidegger's history of being [*Of Spirit* 102–03], "Schelling" is for Heidegger the exemplary *pharmakon*.[8]

BEING ADDICTED

What, then, is it about Schelling and specifically his addictive rhetoric that attracts Heidegger's attention, gets him hookcd? It is clear from the lectures that Heidegger is drawn to—among other things—Schelling's daring thesis that finitude and dependency go down to the very ground of God. For human freedom to be more than an abstraction or illusion (and, indeed, for any existing entity to possess the qualities of particularity and individuality), Schelling surmises, it must be rooted primordially in God's agonistic struggle to be free from "himself," or rather, free from that obscure, resistant, and perdurable element within himself against which he can continually posit his independence.

> In order to be divided from God, they [existing entities] must come to be in a ground that is different from him. But since nothing can have being outside God [*außer Gott;* there is no *außer Gott*] this contradiction can be resolved only thus: the things [existing entities] have their ground in whatever in God is not *He Himself,* i.e., in that which is the ground of his existence. [*PI* 33; 4, 359]

Schelling sometimes characterizes this "ground" as an underlying substance awaiting its "transfiguration" into "spirit and understanding" [PI 39]. But more often he speaks of it in most *ungrund*like terms, as a kind of nothingness or absence that has never been (and will never be) fully present, yet whose traces haunt the universe of existing things like so much dark matter or background radiation. "This is the incomprehensible basis of reality in things," Schelling states, "the indivisible remainder, that which with the greatest exertion cannot be resolved in the understanding, but rather remains eternally in the ground" [PI 34]. The ground's nature is to cling to itself and to contract itself (to itself); this "attraction of the ground," which never ceases, "call[s] forth distinctiveness and contrast" [PI 52], thereby constituting the most primitive level of God's positing of himself *as* himself. God's being "is" this "self-seeing" of himself in the obscurity of his ground. Under these conditions, neither the light of understanding nor the darkness of the ground exists as something punctually present, since they are their difference from each other in a "nexus" or reciprocal relation. In Heidegger's terms, the being of Schelling's God is thus precisely *not* "some gigantic, objectively present thing," but a gathering of ground and existence whose topology is closer to a fold or seam: *die Seynsfuge* (the jointure of being) [ST 122, 106; 42, 212, 185].

What words, what figures could one summon to describe the alterity that God himself can neither evade nor comprehend, and that appears always—"eternally"—to have disappeared from the light of understanding precisely because it is the condition of that light's possibility? In the beginning, there is "the first stirring of divine existence *[die erste Regung göttlichen Daseins]*" [PI 35; 4, 252], an anonymous condition of "self"-administered stimulation whose chief effect is to "arouse" the ground to grasp itself (but without an "itself" as such to grasp, this striving and yearning remains unavoidably obscure and chaotic). Because of his inchoate genesis, God is always already *beside himself*, an inexhaustible condition of agitation and ravenousness; he is constitutively a hunger to become himself, an abyss of loss and lack for which a perfectly compensatory act of mourning is, strictly speaking, impossible (and, we shall see, *undesirable*). Unappeasable grief is the mood of the universe; as Schelling says, "the veil of despondency *[der Schleier der Schwermut]* [is] spread over all of nature ["in God, too," Schelling insists, afraid we will flinch from the strangeness and the sadness of his point], the deep, indestructible melancholy of all life *[die tiefe unzerstörliche Melancholie alles Lebens]*" [PI 79; 4, 291]. As Schelling circles warily about this languorous primal bestirring (for *who* or *what* would God be if he is othered by the object of his own hunger and

melancholy? How *not* to speak of this autochthonic event, the very
opening of thought and things?), as Schelling approaches the bizarre
question of a dependency that is older than God, his text is practically
overrun with anthropomorphizing figures—womb, khōra, anagram, billowing sea, gravity *(Schwere)*, feeling, the ruleless *(das Regellose)*, the
glorious mother of knowledge, the darkness of nonunderstanding—in a
manner that recalls a similar rhetorical unfurling in Plato's *Timaeus*.[9]
Schelling twice signals the need to speak anthropomorphically about the
ground of God's existence (I will come back to the question of figurality), but these gestures of accommodation hardly prepare us for the
affectively charged (and theosophically informed) tropes upon which he
finally settles—and which form the rhetorical framework for the
remainder of the essay:

> If we wish to speak of this being in terms more accessible to man, then
> we can say: it is the longing *[die Sehnsucht]* felt by the eternal One to
> give birth to itself. This longing is not the One itself, yet it is co-eternal
> with it. It wants to give birth to God, that is, the ungroundable unity;
> but to that extent unity is not yet in it itself. . . . [W]e must represent
> primal longing *[die ursprüngliche Sehnsucht]* in this manner: it directs
> ifself toward the understanding, which it yet does not know, . . . and it
> moves presentiently like an undulating, surging sea, similar to Plato's
> matter, following a dark, uncertain law, incapable of forming some-
> thing lasting by itself [*PI* 35; 4, 252]

With the deployment of this complex analogy, Schelling's narrative
fills up with a rhetoric of proclivities and searching desires, a rhetoric
that Heidegger immediately diagnoses as infectious (as well he might,
since it spreads throughout his own commentary on the freedom essay):
Sehnsucht, Lust, Wollen, Streben, Hang, Drang. Yearning hungers for
a knowledge about which it knows nothing; before there was the Word
or *Logos*, there was the hunger for the Word, the inarticulate condition
of articulation that Schelling is canny enough to say is structured
"materially" like language.[10] In a modulation of his own rhetoric that
will capture Heidegger's eye, Schelling refers to this unseeing and
incomprehensible striving as "mere craving or desire *[bloß Sucht oder
Begierde]*" [*PI* 38; 4, 255].

No doubt it was writing like this that caused Hegel to wince with
disappointment over what had become of his erstwhile colleague, for
from his eagle-eyed and philosophically sober perspective, Schelling's
thinking seems at moments like these to deteriorate into delirious
Schwärmere. As if he were on drugs, or, at the very least, high (on)
"Romanticism." But Schelling openly concedes that *die Sehnsucht,* like

the Platonic matter to which it is compared, cannot be comprehended or conceptualized *except* through a hallucinatory experience, or what he calls "falsche Imagination" [4, 282] (here citing Plato's very phrase, in *Timaeus,* for the unavoidably *trancelike* and *spurious* way in which the "third nature," or khōra, is to be thought and described). How can he not speak of addiction? Who was it that opened the doors of perception for Schelling? From Jacob Boehme's *Forty Questions Concerning the Soul,* arguably the major theosophical pretext for the treatise on human freedom, Schelling had learned of God's ferocious beginnings in a fiery chaos of introjected and unquenchable yearning, a condition he describes as "the craving to draw into itself *[die Sucht, in sich zu ziehen]*" [qtd. in Beach 72]. Schelling finds historical confirmation of this addictive an-arche in his subsequent study of the mystery cult associated with the deities of Samothrace, a study that in effect gives him an archaeological rhetoric with which to think the habituated ground of creation. Because these obscure deities, known collectively as "the Cabiri," form the most ancient mythological strata underlying the beliefs of ancient Greece, they constitute a matrix in which to glimpse the fundamental structures of reality. Among "the Cabiri," Schelling argues, the "first being, commencing all," is the potency known as Axieros, whose name is derived from Phoenician roots meaning "'hunger,' 'poverty,' and in consequence 'yearning,' [and] 'addiction' *[die Sucht]*" [DS 18; 4, 727]. "Before" anything *is,* "beneath which there is nothing further," Schelling surmises, there is "a nature which is not insofar as it merely strives to be" [DS 19]. That "first nature, whose whole essence is desire and addiction, appears in the consuming fire which so to speak is itself nothing, is in essence only a hunger drawing everything into itself *[ein alles in sich ziehender Hunger]*" [Deities 18; 4, 728].[11]

From these obscure prehistorical and theosophical texts, Schelling adapts a phenomenological rhetoric of embodiment with which to reread and revise the violently idealistic and derealizing impulse he believed governed modern European philosophy. For Schelling, this philosophy was little better than a cult of *Geist*—"a dreary and fanatic enthusiasm which breaks forth in self-mutilation" [PI 31], he calls it—that had violently *cut itself* off from the vital if chaotic origins of thought and being.[12] Primal craving is an important part of a more extensive rhetoric of affective states and borderline conditions (including melancholy)—in other words, a body language of "flesh and blood *[Fleisch und Blut]*" [PI 30; 4, 248]—that Schelling mobilizes against the repressive effects of what he eventually calls "negative philosophy." Hegel will come to stand paradigmatically for this philosophy, whose masterful and disembodying system transforms actuality into essence, form, category, and idea. In ways that I can only touch on in this essay, Schelling takes up the overlapping figures of *die Sehnsucht* and *die Sucht* as part of a more extensive attempt to describe and to insist upon the irreducible reality of humankind's exposure to an array of irrational and other-than-rational forces: to irreducible loss and radical evil (that is, evil that is not simply the absence of good but something possessing a "positive" presence), to the uncanny and the accidental, and, finally, to the future, to what *happens* (and to the happening of what happens). "What we call the world, which is so *completely contingent* both as a whole and in its parts," Schelling will argue in his old age, "cannot possibly be the impression of something which has arisen by the *necessity of reason*. It contains a *preponderant* mass of *unreason*" [qtd. in Bowie, *Schelling* 35]. The essay on freedom, written almost thirty years earlier, makes a similar case: "Order and form nowhere appear to have been original; [instead] it seems as though what had initially been unruly had been brought to order" [*PI* 34].

Primal craving not only gives a name and a desirous face to this mysterious unlawfulness; it also constitutes a nascent psychoanalysis of the work of spirit, a grounding of its labors in what Žižek calls "the drive whose true aim is the endless reproduction of its own circular movement" [87]. Spirit is the displacement of the energies of addiction into the ever more refined rays of the light of understanding; in Heidegger's words, "The ground thus wants to be more and more ground, and at the same time it can only will this by willing what is clearer and thus striving *against itself* as what is dark. Thus, it strives for the opposite of itself and produces a separation in itself" [*ST* 136]. Schelling points to the dynamic process by which the ground's addictive self-seeking differentiates (and thus distances) itself from itself; the distinction that obtains is as sharp as that between the darkest night and the brightest day. Yet the very force of this process's segregating strenuousness remembers the impossibility of complete separation. There is a great deal in Schelling's argument to suggest that this process of deflection and scission is inherently open-ended. In Heidegger's terms, the Absolute, precisely because it "exists," "has eternally taken over the ground and thus affirmed longing as eternal. Thus, it is and remains the continual consumption of itself which never devours itself, but precisely burns toward what is inextinguishable in order to maintain the light placed in it in its innermost darkness" [*ST* 127]. As the craving *for* the ground, primal longing is "itself" abyssal, *groundless,* and thus not an archaic "past" of an existing entity (whether divine, human, or animal) but more accurately its *un*known future, the opening of that future as that which is always about-to-be extinguished. The existent cannot burn this dark ground "off," as it were, in a final blaze of light; this "inextinguishability" comes about not because of the "depth" or "breadth" of the dark ground, but rather because of its abyssal character. As "eternal," the addiction to the ground knows no absolute satiation; yet there is everywhere the *desire* for this imagined end, for becoming clean and sober, as it were, through the expenditure or consumption (without reserve) of the ground's impulsive self-seeking. About this closure, Schelling's text points in two contradictory directions. On the one hand, in the essay's concluding pages, Schelling does imagine a "final, total decision *[endlichen gänzlichen Scheidung]*" [*PI* 89; 4, 300] in which the ground's energies "finally" exhaust themselves and become so distanced from themselves that they sunder the bond altogether. Heidegger suggests that it is here that we see "the keenness of [Schelling's] metaphysical questioning diminish[ing]" [*ST* 159], succumbing as the thinker does to the residue of Christian theodicy in his philosophy [*ST* 146]. On the other hand, the weight of Schelling's argument contradicts or at least disrupts this apocalyptic fantasy of the end of "man." Indeed, the attempt totally to incorporate the ground is for Schelling the paradigmatic structure of the "evil" act. Schelling (and Heidegger after him) is scrupulous in his insistence that primal craving is not in itself malevolent, and therefore that its darkness bears no morally negative connotations. *Die Sucht* does not poison the light of existence; it is the light of existence, in its rageful attempt to dissolve the dark ground and become its own basis, that contaminates *die Sucht,* transforming the urge for particularity and individuality into a parody of itself—the urge for absolute domination over *all* particulars and *all* individuals. For this reason, Schelling argues that evil, properly understood, is *of spirit.* As Heidegger remarks, citing Schelling's Stuttgart seminars, "For evil itself is spiritual, yes, 'in a certain regard the most pure spiritual thing, for it wages the most violent war against all *Being,* yes, it would like to incorporate the ground of creation'" [*ST* 118]. Inasmuch as thinkers as diverse as Spinoza, Fichte, and Hegel are committed, in Schelling's eyes, to spiriting away the radical precedence and exorbitance of primal craving, they have transformed modern European philosophy into a gigantic war-on-drugs.

As "the essence of longing regarded in and of itself" [*PI* 34], irresistible and inexhaustible hankering has no object but itself, and, as such, resembles what Ronell has called a "pure instance of Being-on-drugs: it is only about producing a need for itself" [25]. In lectures designed to clarify the details of the freedom essay, Schelling is explicit and indeed almost compulsive in his insistence that *Geist's* (sub)version lies in a self-sustaining vortex of habituated desire—"a flame that fuels itself":

> The spirit is consequently nothing but an addiction to Being *[die Sucht zum Sehn]*. . . . The base form of the spirit is therefore an addiction, a desire, a lust *[Sucht, Begierde, Lust]*. Whoever wishes to grasp the concept of spirit at its most profound roots must therefore become fully acquainted with the nature of desire . . . for [desire] is a hunger for Being, and being satiated only gives it renewed strength, i.e., a more vehement hunger. [*SS* 230; 4, 358]

For Schelling, "man" and "animals" each come into their own, albeit in radically different ways, because of this self-contracting hunger. "The will of the ground is to particularize everything or to make it creaturely," Schelling argues; "It wants differentiation alone *[Er will die Ungliechheit allein]*" [*PI* 58; 4, 273]. (By translating *Er* as "it"rather than as "he," as Gutmann recommends, we retain something of the anonymous precedence of primal longing, its sheer alterity vis-à-vis both God and "man.") Existing life *as* life is neediness; more sharply and more melancholically, it is craving that recoils upon itself and, in recoiling upon itself, compounds and concentrates itself, forming the basis for the egoity, individuality, and particularity of all existing creatures. Out of a certain squeamishness, perhaps, Schelling tends to say that where God *longs,* the creatures *crave;* but this ontotheological distinction is hardly established before it becomes clear that the creatures come by their addictive creatureliness honestly, and that for God to be alive, he too is *at heart* anchored in *die Sucht.* (For his part, Heidegger finds no meaningful distinction between the yearnings of God or "man"; *"Eigensucht"*—or self-craving—subjects the Absolute, just as it does all the creatures in whose habituated wake they stir into life.)

God's addiction arouses in "man" and "animal" an irresistible hankering to be particular and, paradoxically, independent: it "awakens in the creature a lust for the creaturely *[erwacht in ihr die Lust zum Creatürlichen],* just as a mysterious voice seemingly calls a man seized by dizziness on a high and precipitous pinnacle to plunge down, or as in the ancient myth the irresistible song of the sirens rang out from the depths [not unlike the "billowing ocean" named elsewhere] in order to draw mariners sailing through down into the whirlpool" [*PI* 59; 4, 273). Much could be made of the philosopher's delirious rhetoric of an originary abandonment to the voice of the other, evoking as it does a host of questions concerning the fundamental nature of response, co-respondence, and responsibility (for Schelling mobilizes these figures in the midst of a discussion of the origins of evil). Moreover, we might note how the tenor of Schelling's comparison, primal craving's reviving influence on the life of the creatures, is perfectly at odds with the compelling and fatal violence of its vehicle, which is all about dying. Suffice it to say that Schelling—a voyager on strange seas of thought who knew something about peering into the abyss—resorts here to two curiously elaborate analogies, as if momentarily carried away by figures of the being-transported of being. In this small dilatory gesture, I would argue, Schelling finds himself in the strange position of *calling out*, through his anthropomorphizing figures, to the absolute alterity to which, *as* a creature, he has invariably pledged his allegiance; better, he *listens* for the abyssal summons that his own tropes put always before him and beyond him. Addiction—described, precisely, as a "mysterious" and overpoweringly seductive *language* (a *geheime Stimme* and a *Sirenengesang*)—is *already* speaking to us and creatures like us (divine, human, animal), in advance of whatever figures we conjure up to simulate its radical anteriority [4, 273]. Like an arche-stimulant or growth hormone (for who can say that glandular "instructions" are not a language?), originary appetite in-forms (Schelling: *"Ein-bildung"* [4, 254]) the creature, commanding it with a deeply ambiguous imperative to come into its own: Live life (as an addict)! The command, *as* a command from elsewhere—elsewhere even than God—dispossesses the creature in the same gesture that "awakens" it into life. Or rather, as Schelling says, this craving arouses in the creature the lust for being-creaturely. Which comes "first," then, the lust for creatureliness or the creature, the declaration of independence or the independence "itself"? A fantastic logic—to which I want to return in my concluding remarks—structures desirous life: primal longing excites in "man" and "animal" a craving for that which they already need to be in order to respond to its call: namely, creatures. "It"—primal longing—somehow triggers in the creature a desire to become what it in fact *is*. The creature surges up, stirs into life, but this upsurgence and stirring must always, in some minimal way, have *already* happened and thus is *always* happening—an originary event that beckons from the "future" because it recedes into a "past" that could never be present as such.

Under these inaugural conditions, creaturely life (which includes God's life, even if Schelling often prefers to shift the scene to humans and animals) founds itself in a radically unfounded manner, grasping *at* and referring *to* an always prior genesis. Schelling's notion of an addictive craving that is its own object, "a flame that fuels itself," captures the structure of this paradox exactly. "Life" is not simply the object of primal lust's command; it is its essence to be a command, a declaration of individuated life that is always in excess of that individuation and that makes that independence (im)possible. After Derrida, we could say that *die Lust zum Creatürlichen* evokes "the indispensable confusion" between performative and constative utterances that is created when a speech act—a declaration of independence, for example—claims to bring into existence the very thing that it requires to be brought into existence ["Declarations" 11]. Whence comes this confusion? What are the conditions of its occurrence? As we have seen, a strange compulsion, always from *elsewhere,* propels life into its queer relationship with itself. Again, Schelling's anthropomorphizing rhetoric tells us a great deal, for what is benignly called a mere "awakening," a reviving of life, is figured forth in precisely opposite terms, as violent and impulsive death: drowning in a whirlpool, falling into an abyss. The fact that tropes of *dying* so handily replace tropes of *living,* drowning for rousing, points to the sheer substitutive violence of life's primal scene, where what is only lusted after, namely, *life,* summarily replaces the lust "itself"—this, so that there might always be more longing for life. "Creatureliness," "autonomy," "particularity": these and other, related words are figures and simulations that cover for the twist in thinking that Schelling's primal craving demands of us, figures and simulations that fill in the space or breach in logic that this twist opens up. The originary craving (the "outside" that is "inside" God) that triggers this process remains permanently *elsewhere;* the voice to which Schelling twice compares this craving is abyssal because *radically un*locatable, "the irreducible remainder"or excess in which the performative and constative utterances of life gather into their vexed nexus. The creatures' relationship to the commanding voice of the law of life thus ensures that their autonomy is never absolute; their dependency is not only an addiction to what comes logically or temporally "before" their existence; more subtly, life remembers—it is in the memory *of*—the trace of an anteriority *within itself,* that, strictly speaking, can be called neither dead nor alive. Creatures in and as their lust for life are always caught *possessing,* but what that "substance" is and where it comes from is "mysterious" indeed.

HEIDEGGER'S CRAVING

Reproducing and parasitizing Schelling's argument in ways that I can only briefly evoke here, Heidegger paints a remarkably dynamic, not to say compulsive and agonistic, picture of life on earth, in which each creature, human and nonhuman, hungers principally for itself and, in hungering for itself, simultaneously posits and produces its individuality and particularity. In the lectures on theoretical biology delivered in 1929–1930, Heidegger had cited Paul's remark (in 8 Romans 19) about "the creatures' and all creation's longing gaze" [qtd. in Krell, *Daimon Life* 130–31], but it is not until he has read Schelling closely that he grasps the radical pervasiveness of this yearning, its unique manifestations in the creature called "man." From Schelling (who was no doubt remembering Paul, and reading him through Boehme), Heidegger learns that *Eigensucht*—self-craving—forms the charged basis for corporeal existence as such, for *standing out* "as an individual this" [*ST* 140] through a redoubled, languorous, and infectious motion he describes as a "striving away from itself to spread itself, and yet precisely back to itself" [*ST* 125]. In God, this urging is epidemic; longing stirs divinity into a certain minimal visibility, which in turn triggers a ravenous hunger for more and more of himself: "longing becomes clearer in the self-seeing of God in his ground, but that means precisely all the more aroused and addicted [*so wird im Sich-erblicken des Gottes in seinem Grunde die Sehnsucht lichter, aber das heißt gerade, um so erregter und süchtiger]*" [*ST* 136; 42, 236]. (God's appetite for voyeurism is always bigger than his eyes.) Heidegger deems the coils and recoils of this addicted life to be worthy of a substantial visual representation [see *ST* 136; 42, 236]. The ever-expanding coils of the mesmerizing arabesque that makes up this curious illustration (an illustration that is not without its own counterpart in the footnotes of Schelling's treatise [see *PI* 42–43n1; 4, 258–59n1]) in effect gives us a glimpse of what this escalating "self-seeing" *looks* like from the "inside"—the image is dizzying and oddly clarifying at the same time—even if it also spatializes the fundamentally temporal and temporalizing nature of the rhythms of *Hang und Drang*.

"Man" and "animal" share a desirous origin in addiction, an irresolvable dependency on themselves—or rather, *as* themselves—which uncannily repeats an always prior dependency on the craving that originarily dispossesses God. Heidegger: "The heightened particular will in nature's beings is a return, eternally craving [*süchtige]* but never attainable by nature itself, to the deepest ground—a searching [*ein Suchen]* of God [*ST* 141; 42, 244]. (Although he has told us earlier that *die Sucht* "has nothing etymologically to do with searching [*Suchen]*" [*ST* 125; 42, 216], Heidegger remains beguiled by the euphony of the terms, and to the accidental semantic connections—the momentary, if illusory "fix"—that such euphony provides.) Both thinkers agree that in the midst of this universe of desire, loss, and *Schwermut*, "man," properly grasped, stands alone. Only "man" attains complete particularity and

individuality because in him—*as* spirit—there is at once the most ferocious addiction—"the deepest self-craving of the longing of the ground
[der tiefsten Eigensucht der Sehnsucht des Grundes]" [*ST* 141; 42,
244]—*and* the free opportunity to elevate that craving "to the broad-
est clearing of pure understanding" [*ST* 141]. "Man" occupies the infinitely fragile point of decision *(Scheidung),* not between the ground's
longing and the light of existence, but between differing configurations
of spirit that gather the darkness and the light into an irremediably
unstable whole. Shall I preserve primal craving as the always absten-
tial ground against which the light of understanding clarifies itself? Or
shall I attempt to break the addiction to the ground (what Heidegger
calls "the addiction of longing *[die Sucht des Sehnens]*" [*ST* 125; 42,
217]), and transfigure dependency, the inclination toward self-hood
and particularity, into a selfish dominating will that is its own ground?
Shall I co-respond with the "mysterious voice" that calls me into creatureliness, or shall I appropriate that voice as my own? "Man" *is* decisiveness; "he" is the one for whom these fundamental questions *are*
questions. Heidegger treats Schelling's essay as an opportunity to think
beyond good and evil *as* ontic choices made by individuals, and
argues instead that true decisiveness comes from a still more archaic
decision *for good and evil;* that is, *for* a beginning that remains resolutely open to a redoubled structure of possibilities. This arch-deci-
sion has always already been made; as Schelling says, it "cannot occur
in consciousness, since this act precedes it as it precedes being and
indeed produces it" [*PI* 64]. How or "when" it happens, Schelling
will not even surmise: this, even though he has spent the better part
of his essay talking in detail about the ontological structures of the
origin. Schelling prefers instead to describe its occurrence in hyperbolically fantastic terms—"in One magic stroke *[alles in Einem
magischen Schlage]*" [*PI* 35; 4. 279]—terms that deliberately efface
the question of agency (this is not "God's stroke") in order to bring
out its radical precipitousness, anteriority, anonymity, groundlessness, and irrationality. The striking but always prior decision for decisiveness that sets human life on its perilous way is not strictly speaking, human, but we could be forgiven at this point for describing the
ensuing melancholy project as one in which the human goes from one
"fix"to the next, each ontic act a renewed negotiation with the
antecedent decision *for* primal addiction (which is to say, *for* the
groundlessness of the *Seynsfuge, for* the churning instability of impulsive self-seeking continually distanced from itself, and *for* the sustained divisibility of spirit). Heidegger: "We find such a becoming in
creatures only in man, better yet: as man" [*ST* 141].

"Where [then] does the inclination to evil in man come from?" [*ST* 149]. Schelling argues, as we have seen, that "the general possibility of evil . . . consists in the fact that, instead of keeping his self-hood as the ground or the instrument, man can strive to elevate it to be the ruling or universal will, and, on the contrary, try to make what is spiritual in him into a means" [*PI* 68]. This malignant striving leads to an alarming escalation of indigence that ends, predictably enough, given the rhetoric of addiction with which Schelling works, in violent intoxication:

> For the feeling remains in the man who has moved out of the center that he has been all things, that he was in and with God. For this reason he strives to return there. Hence the hunger of selfishness *[der Hunger der Selbstsucht]* arises, which, to the extent that it dissociates itself from the whole and from unity, becomes ever needier and poorer, and for this very reason increasingly desirous, hungry, and poisonous *[begieriger, hungriger, giftiger]*. [PI 69; 4, 282]

The being-wicked of wickedness is an overdose. The drug? The yearning to come into one's own. Whether or to what degree one could ever determine the precise point at which primal craving, which is the basis of life, finds itself transformed into its over-going, which is death, is never clear in Schelling's work. It is the constitutive exposure to the danger and the possibility of that indeterminacy (which is the indeterminacy of the *pharmakon*) that matters, and is but one way in which Schelling marks his distance from the pieties of Enlightenment humanism. Heidegger is of course largely sympathetic: "Man is not to be understood as that familiar being gifted with reason who hangs around on a planet and can be dissected into his components, but as that being who is himself the 'deepest abyss' of Being *and at the same time* 'the highest heaven'" [*ST* 135].

The familiar beings who *do* "hang around" the planet are the ones who *hang on* to it, hankering and hungering obsessively *after* it in a manner that empties them of true freedom. These creatures do not "have" an addiction; rather, the addiction "has" the creature. In *Being and Time*, Dasein was susceptible to precisely this radical form of passivity, to being "'lived' by the world in which it actually is" [182]. In the Schelling lectures, "animals" occupy the same habituated space. What is revealing is that both Heidegger and Schelling find it impossible to speak of a generalized self-craving without quickly establishing an oppositional limit dividing "man's" way of being-addicted from the craving that fundamentally characterizes all other life-forms, summarily herded together under the rubric "animals." As Krell has fully demonstrated (in *Daimon Life*), Heidegger's desire to retrieve Dasein from human being is often expressed in an axiomatic attempt to isolate what is imagined to be the essence of the human from the essence of animality. In *Being and Time* Heidegger had labored to distinguish care from its proximates—addiction and compulsion. In the Schellingian context of the lectures, having conceded that addiction is fundamental to "the movement of becoming . . . of created beings" [*ST* 133] *in general,* he shifts his efforts toward distinguishing between human and animal, not between Dasein and "psychological" and "biological" phenomena that are merely human.

What distinguishes human beings from all other creatures—"so far as we know" [142], Heidegger adds, as if quickly looking over his shoulder at all the animals looking longingly at him—is that only for "man" does being-on-drugs matter. Unlike human beings, animals lack the *logos* with which to speak, know, and modify themselves as the addicted jointure of ground and existence; in Schelling's terms, terms which Heidegger endorses and reproduces, animals are without *spirit.* (It could be argued that Heidegger opportunistically uses "Schelling," exploits the unique theosophical-idealistic space opened up by the treatise on freedom, in order to continue to speak at length and with a certain freedom about spirit—a philosopheme, as Derrida argues,[13] that Heidegger had otherwise ambivalently renounced after the *Rectorship Address* [1933] and *An Introduction to Metaphysics* [1935]: that is, "Schelling" lets Heidegger experiment with "spirit," without running the risk of inclining toward its merely subjective determinations, its associations with a philosophical tradition that lacks the rigor and sobriety of the existential analytic. In the company of Schelling, Heidegger gets to smoke spirit, but not inhale it. Without the know-how of concernful Dasein, the animal unthinkingly dedicates its self-seeking impulses to "the species" rather than the individual.) For this reason, pronounced with an authority that is nothing if not panicked, animals are most themselves when they are most like others like themselves; "the animal never comes to itself, in spite of its craving" [*ST* 140]. In effect, animals are junkies who are radically *un*conscious of their addictive constitution. (Schelling's cows, as Hegel had said, really are in the dark. We might also recall Nietzsche's cows, who forget their "happiness," and then forget that they have forgotten.) Here, as at so many other places, Heidegger faithfully reproduces Schelling's anthropocentric move *against* animals, moves that Derrida would say are "all the more peremptory and authoritarian for having to hide a discomfiture" [*Of Spirit* 11]. In this case, the anxious difficulty driving Schelling's and Heidegger's polemical claims is presumably that all this talk about craving and desiring inadvertently closes the gap between the animal's urge to live and Dasein's more refined compulsions: this, when the express purpose of Schelling's

treatise, and the single subject that interests Heidegger most, is, precisely, "the *essence* of *human* freedom" (an "essence," it is worth
emphasizing, that is never merely "human" for Heidegger).

This "discomfiture" is especially evident when Heidegger attempts
to distinguish between the origin of evil in animalistic urges and evil
itself, which for Schelling is properly and essentially human. Evil is a
possibility for human beings precisely because only human beings live in
a world of "possibility." Žižek's account of this *Möglichkeit* is useful:
"an unfree entity simply is, it coincides with its positive actuality,
whereas (as Schelling asserts, announcing thereby the existentialist problematic) a free being can never be reduced to what it is, to its actual positive presence—its 'project,' the undecidable opening of what it might do
or become, its 'want-to-be,' is the kernel of its very existence" [20].
Where the animals are immured in their creatureliness, locked within the
bond of their own species, the human uniquely possesses the "faculty"
or "capability" *(Vermögen)* of "being able to relate itself to a possibility
of itself" [*ST* 148; 42, 257]. But Heidegger is quick to ward off the opinion that this "possibility-potentiality of being *[sein können]*" [42, 256]
means that freedom is "a mere explosion of an act out of emptiness into
emptiness, pure chance" [*ST* 149]: "The possibilities of faculty are not
arbitrary for it, but they are nothing compulsive *[nicht Zwingendes]*"
[*ST* 149; 42, 257]. Nothing compulsive because, of course, that would
be to reduce human freedom to the "choices" that animals appear to
make, "choices" which remain in essence the self-protective behaviors
that are impelled by the "urge to live"—and thus not choices at all.
Human possibilities are not compulsive but not arbitrary, either; operating with this double negative and, so to speak, hemmed in by animals,
Heidegger attempts to isolate a space or "faculty" for Dasein that is radically free without being accidental, and habitual without being
addicted. "In order to be itself," a faculty "must cling *[hängen]* to its
possibilities. Oriented in its attraction to these possibilities, it must
incline toward them. An inclination to its possibilities always belongs to
a faculty. Inclination *[der Hang]* is a certain anticipatory aptitude for
striving for what can be done" [*ST* 148; 42, 257]. A great deal could be
said here about Heidegger's rhetoric: the sudden flurry of synonyms for
"tendency"—striving, anticipating, clinging, inclining, and orienting;
the imperatives—*must [muß]*—that amplify some of these tendencies,
almost without seeming to, into something more irresistible; the rhetoric
of *leaning-toward* that inclines Dasein toward its inclinations even while
Heidegger insists that its resoluteness is not compulsive. I might only
remark how, in naming whatever it is that Dasein is doing when it faces
its possibilities, Heidegger resorts to the very term—*der Hang*—that

elsewhere in his work is unambiguously associated with addiction and compulsion. (An addiction that is without compulsiveness? That would mean that the psychological equivalent to Dasein's tendencies is the addict who says: "I can quit anytime.")

Heidegger's highly generalized maneuvering around the question of proclivity and noncompelling compulsion sets the stage for a discussion of the more pressing question, namely the human "faculty" specifically for evil. And again, Heidegger's logic is curious; he borrows the language of inclination, of *leaning-toward,* but modifies and qualifies it in such a way that it both *is* and *is not* compulsive in nature. Evil acts, like the acts of any free creature, cannot simply happen; but also like any act, they cannot be fully predetermined and remain a free act. *Eigensucht* is not inherently evil; yet its addictive energies form the mysterious opening out of which evil can emerge. What the nature of that opening is, Heidegger describes in a way that has the curious effect of bringing primal craving and evil into the closest proximity while making the actual "contact" between the two things more and more subtle. "The ground does not arouse evil itself. It also does not arouse to evil, it only arouses the possible principle to evil" [*ST* 151; 42, 262–63]. As Heidegger states, there must be a pre-existing "inclination to evil *[der Hang zum Bösen],*" a hunger *for* evil that is not itself evil, in order that evil might take place at all. Looking out across the sea and air and land of the planet, Heidegger sees evidence of this *Hang* at every turn; "evil in general" is "evil's ubiquitous wanting   to   become   real   urging   everywhere   in   creatures *[durchgängiges, überall im Geschaffenen drängendes Wirklichwerden-wolletn des Bösen]*" [*ST* 149; 42, 258].The inclination to evil, the urging, innocent as such, that urges evil, once again evokes the logic of the *pharmakon:* for what is the difference, exactly, between urging and the supplementally malevolent urging that comes from this urging? Is inclination *almost* made simultaneously to bear opposed valuations here, evil and nonevil? That the "creatures" that Heidegger evokes are by implication *animals* seems perfectly appropriate, since they must play the role of *pharmakeus* for him. The animal is the scapegoat that most vividly embodies the urge to live, and so provides him with an instance of the irreducibility of a certain inclination; but precisely *because* these creatures are animals, they cannot commit evil acts or think evil thoughts, and so also prove useful for forcefully inscribing the line between an inclination and another inclination that is exemplarily human. "The inclination to evil is not a compulsion," Heidegger insists, "but has its own necessity *[Der Hang zum Bösen ist aber kein Zwang, sondern von eigener Notwendigkeit]*" [*ST* 152; 42, 263].

The *Hang* is not a *Zwang*, yet remains, in a manner that Heidegger leaves unexplained, *irresistible* in a way that he describes (citing Schelling) as "'the attraction of the ground *[Anziehen des Grundes]*'" [*ST* 151; 42, 261]. About this "attraction" (a term whose polyvalence in Schelling Heidegger briefly discusses), Heidegger's language is very odd. In the presence of this *Anziehen*—but not directly solicited by it—the faculty for evil reacts as if it were a kind of body into which had been injected a strange preparatory stimulant: "The faculty contracts, stiffens, becomes tense, and the tension toward . . . still at rest is the inclination to evil" [*ST* 151]. The ellipsis here is Heidegger's, a means by which he evades altogether an attempt to describe the infinitesimally subtle point of transition that divides the solicitation of the ground from the inclination to evil, the contraction-condensation of the self to itself from the egotism of wickedness. By repeatedly bringing addiction, compulsion, and solicitation into such conflicted proximity (all of this deserves much more discussion here), Heidegger manages a duplicity that is fundamental to his attempt to retrieve Dasein from Schelling's "man": he must separate the inclination to evil from the compulsive self-seeking of the creatures in such a manner that does not put the human out of reach of that compulsiveness.[14] Another way of saying this would be that "the attraction of the ground" must be both irresistible and negotiable, so that "the human" becomes what it already is, namely the vexed site where that attraction is interpreted for good or ill.

FIGURING ADDICTION

For Schelling, Heidegger maintains, addiction is the figure par excellence for *"the movement of any living being in general"* [*ST* 137]. But the "urge to life *[Lebensdrang]*" [*ST* 137; 42, 237] that this "movement" embodies is for Heidegger in essence nothing merely "biological." For what *appears* as life is a form of delusion, one that confuses "what has been ascertained as objectively present" with "what is real" [*ST* 137–38]. Natural scientists, as well as those who succumb to their views, are hallucinating the object of their analyses—that is, "life"—as long as they fail to grasp "that there is something inexplicable in living beings." This "inexplicability" does not await a more accurate or penetrating investigation, but remains irreducibly out of mind. All of "living nature" "is only what has become rigidified of a past stirring of that becoming viewed metaphysically, a rest *[eine Ruhe]* behind which lies the unruliness of the ground; just as if it could erupt again, unruliness not just being the lack and indeterminacy of the rule" [*ST* 139; 42, 240].

This radical lawlessness we have of course met before; it is, as Heidegger is careful to point out, not a disorder-about-to-be-ordered, but irreducibly chaotic, the "real" that is "beyond" or "before" *both* the law and the lack of the law. As the groundless ground, the "real" can itself only be glimpsed transversally through the anthropomorphizing figures with which we populate the "objectively" known universe and that grant it—and presumably *us*—some measure of peace *(eine Ruhe)*. Seething beyond that repose is a lawlessness of *die Sehnsucht* and *die Sucht,* themselves, of course, figures, too, that humanize the "real." But these are not two figures among many, for there is an underlying affinity between the Absolute (or "God" in Schelling) and its languorous and languishing human representations. Just thinking of this affinity, Heidegger gets excited:

> The essence of ground in God is longing? We can scarcely restrain the objection that this statement projects a human condition onto God—. Ah, yes! But it could also be otherwise. For who has ever verified the supposition that longing is something merely human? And who has ever refuted thoroughly and with sufficient reason the possibility that what we call longing, which is where we are, in the end is something other than we ourselves? Does not longing conceal something that denies us any grounds for limiting it to humankind, something that would sooner give us cause to grasp it as that in which we human beings are unfettered *out beyond ourselves* [über uns weg *entschränkt*]? Is it not precisely longing that proves the human being to be Other, other than a mere human being? [*ST* 124; 42, 216; trans. modified]

Heidegger's questions form an important part of his response to "the anthropomorphic objection" [*ST* 125], and I want to return to it in a moment. For now, though, what bears emphasis is that Heidegger himself appears to ask them only to move on to more pressing matters, telling us that he must postpone a more extensive discussion until a later point—a promise he will make several times in the lectures, and one that he fulfills only in their last paragraphs. That the concluding pages of the analysis of Schelling's treatise are taken up with the meaning of Schelling's decision to describe the Absolute in such human, all-too-human terms, is itself a measure of both how worrisome and how engrossing the charge—ventriloquized, we should remember, by Heidegger against "Schelling"—is to Heidegger. For now, however, other pressures abruptly urge the narrative of his lectures on; he commands his readers "to put aside all sentimentality," and to face primal *Sehnsucht,* and thus "the essence of the [Absolute's] ruling metaphysical animatedness," for what it "truly" is: namely, *"Die 'Sucht'"* [*ST* 125;

42, 217]. Not *Hang,* whose connotations of "inclination" and "propensity" and "hankering" somewhat neutralize the meaning of Dasein's addiction in his account of the care structure in *Being and Time;* neither *Hang* nor *Drang,* although both terms are of course crucially part of the general "atmospherics" of compulsion that characterize Schelling's text and Heidegger's interpretation of it; not *Hang,* but *Sucht:* in essence, to long is to be a "junkie," with all the morbidly craven connotations that the term inevitably evokes, connotations that Heidegger both embraces—*Sucht,* he says right away, "primordially means sickness which strives to spread itself; sickly, disease" [*ST* 125]—and repels, finally appropriating the term in the same way that he does other ethically charged concepts, that is, as terms that claim neutrally to describe the ontology of Dasein's dilemma.[15]

Heidegger's move faithfully reproduces a similar strategy in Schelling's text, where longing is often troped in more compulsive and compelling terms, as "craving." But there is also a certain brinksmanship going on here. Heidegger's lectures "culminate," as Krell argues, at the point where "he considers Schelling's daring thesis that the essence of ground in God is longing" ["Crisis" 133]; but then, as if *stirred* by his own rhetorical questions—Heidegger will go on to describe longing as a motion of *Regung*—he dares his readers to consider not only *die Sehnsucht,* but also *die Sucht. Die Sucht:* there, I've said it, Heidegger in effect says, abruptly beginning a new paragraph with these words, and isolating that word from the rest of the sentence with an elaborate parenthesis.[16] The fact that *die Sucht* only substitutes one conspicuously affective anthropomorphism for another *(die Sehnsucht)* of course escapes no one's eye, and puts to us in the boldest possible way that for Heidegger's purposes answering "the anthropomorphic objection" is never a question naively of adopting a nonanthropomorphic language— one of the last things that Heidegger says in his lectures is that this is not possible [see *ST* 163]—but rather of speaking anthropomorphically *in a certain fashion* and with a certain vigilance. How not to speak of addiction? The figures of addiction are complexly symptomatic of an "addiction" to figures. This chiasmus may well inform Heidegger's faintly paranoid remark, made at the conclusion of his lectures, informing us how being-on-Schelling had all along meant that "we were constantly pursued *[verfolgte]* [by whom, exactly?] by that reservation which can be called 'anthropomorphic'" [*ST* 163; 42, 282]. As if unconsciously embarrassed to be found with Schelling, or rather, with the sorts of materials Schelling is handling, Heidegger is always looking over his shoulder for the police. Heidegger's scare quotes delicately hold the object of this "reservation" away at the same time that he concedes its nagging proximity. Because Schelling resorts to human analogies of longing and craving, he claims, it would be all too easy to mistake his treatise for a kind of rarefied amusement that borders on self-hallucination, that is, "a genial game of thought which . . . is unproductive for 'objective' cognition, and is only seductive" [ST 163]. Intoxicating, pleasurable, artificial, and *unergiebiges:* improperly used anthropomorphisms would appear to be little better than (recreational) drugs. But Schelling does not talk about God's addiction as if he were on drugs, Heidegger assures us, irresponsibly indulging in theosophically-induced simulations when he should be working productively like a clear-headed philosopher. On Schelling's behalf, then, Heidegger just says No to *that* kind of anthropomorphism, summoning his readers instead to remain resolutely sober and without *Sentimentalität* in their response to the "stimulus" *[Anregung]* [ST 163; 42, 282] that Schelling's analogies of primordial stirring can provide—that is, if taken correctly, and under Doktor Heidegger's care.

When Heidegger lectures on Schelling again in 1941, as Bowie points out, he is dispensing quite different advice, having determined that his "anthropomorphisms . . . are merely anthropomorphisms, and are consequently evidence of Schelling as, in the last analysis, merely another part of the process of subjectification, which is Western metaphysics" [*Schelling* 93]. But in 1936, Schelling's figural language means something altogether different. In bringing the Absolute "'humanly closer to us'" through his figures, Schelling

> only expresses what we have probably already had on the tip of our tongue *[das Wort . . . auf der Zunge liegt]* for a long time with regard to the procedure of thought accomplished here: the whole project of divine Being and Being in general is accomplished by man. God is an elevated form of man. The *morphe* of the *anthropos* is transformed, and what is transformed is asserted to be something else. In scholarly terms, this is called "anthropomorphism." [ST 117; 42, 204. Greek is untransliterated in original text.]

Schelling *spits out* what Heidegger claims he has all along been holding back (but what is a thought, what is *this* thought, such that it has for so long gone unspoken or rather *almost* spoken?). Those who criticize Schelling for sentimentally anthropomorphizing the unruly origin in his addictive figures do so under the mistaken assumption that they already know *what* the human is. "What is insidious about anthropomorphism is not that it gauges according to the form of man, but that it thinks this criterion is self-evident and believes its closer determination and formulation to be superfluous" [ST 163]. Schelling's notion of pri-

mal addiction explodes the smugness of the scholars who have not set
the humanitas of the human high enough. (But Heidegger's Greek is presumably there partly to prompt them into thinking more primordially
about what being human "is.") Who are we to know what we do or
what we are when we long and crave? "Is it not precisely longing that
proves the human being to be Other, other than a mere human being?"
[*ST* 124].[17] These are the sorts of questions that the "scholars" who have
policed Schelling's work for its figural excess have failed to ask, and
have failed to notice that Schelling is asking. "How not to speak of longing and addiction?" is in Heidegger's terms indistinguishable from
another question: "How not to speak of Dasein?" The only way in
which primal addiction can be dismissed as a pathetic, anthropomorphizing figure is if one has an impoverished conception of both figurality and humanity to begin with. Schelling's tropes urge us to think more
essentially about the *anthropos;* they do not obscure and sentimentalize
but disclose and clarify. For Heidegger, this means that Schelling's figures are in the service of "the analysis of a *Dasein* that is not yet determined as human . . . as subject, ego, conscience, person, soul, body"
[Derrida, *Aporias* 44]. Far from humanizing God, Schelling "divinizes"
the human, raising it to the importance that it properly and uniquely
possesses: as the *there* of the occurrence of being, as the place where the
human stands in being and reveals the decision in being. Schelling's
tropological accommodation of God's alterity to "man" is therefore a
trope for "man's" concernful accommodation to and convocation with
being. And it is more than a trope; rather than committing an indignity
to the metaphysical status of God, Schelling's anthropomorphisms
return thinking to finitude, to being resolved to the question of being.
On Heidegger's reading, these tropes *perform* the turn or inclination to
the Other that is the essential *morphe* of the *anthropos.*

PERFORMING ADDICTION

There may be another way to consider Schelling's anthropomorphisms
and it is to this alternative reading of his humanizing figures that I
would like briefly to turn by way of concluding my remarks. Taking
addictive longing as human, Schelling's anthropomorphisms take the
human as given. It is this compulsive *taking* that interests me about his
figures, which is to say, the positing force of the human that takes itself
as human. According to Schelling, the essence of being human is decision, by which he means not the ontic choices that humans make every
day, but the originary choice to be human. "Man" has always already

chosen himself; he is essentially *his own deed* [*PI* 63]. In Heidegger's reading, "[e]very man's own essence is each time his own eternal deed. Thence comes that uncanny and at the same time friendly feeling that we have always been what we are, that we are nothing other than the unveiling of things long ago decided" [*ST* 154–55]. What does this mean? How could "man" decide *for* "man" . . . and not in some basic sense *already be* "man"? The "attraction of the ground *[Anziehens des Grundes]*" as primal craving forms the condition of possibility for this decision; the human "contracts" and "condenses" itself to itself out of this impulsive self-seeking, in precisely the same way that God in the beginning emerges precipitously and without reason out of his own dark ground of longing. But the leap from inarticulate craving to articulate "man," or, in the case of God, from *Sehnsucht* to *Logos,* remains radically inexplicable and unlocatable. In both instances, human and divine, we might recall that among *Anziehen*'s several connotations (contraction, condensation, coming down with) is the sense of *putting on something,* that is, of assuming the face or image or appearance that is not, strictly speaking, its own. The human, I would argue, is just such a prosopopoeia in Schelling, projecting itself as the image of its own projection, coming into itself through the impulsive force of its own positing. Craving posits itself as human, meaning that all the anthropomorphisms that follow—including *die Sehnsucht* and *die Sucht*—are marked in advance by this originary and arbitrary "anthropomorphism," the deed by which the *anthropos* declares itself to be the *anthropos.* (It goes without saying that, like Heidegger, we must at this point put "anthropomorphism" in scare quotes, as a way of registering our suspicion of the naturalness with which "man" is assumed to be "man.") Žižek describes "this primordial act of free self-positing" in psychoanalytic terms as part of "the structure of fantasy: prior to his very being, the subject is miraculously present as a pure gaze observing his own nonexistence" [19]. But the strange "temporal loop" involved here, in which the human is always behind (or ahead) of itself, might just as usefully be described as another instance of the necessary undecidability between the constative and performative aspects of language.[18] It cannot be accidental that Heidegger describes "man's" fundamental decision to choose himself in terms of language's positing power. Only "in man is the word completely uttered. Man utters himself and becomes present in language" [*ST* 141; 42, 244]. For Heidegger, this self-utterance is a figure for the way in which the "human" simultaneously craves itself *and* comes into its own in that craving. (Yet being both the object and subject of *Eigensucht* presumably destroys all notions of "ownness." The "human" can never punctually come into its "own," Schelling repeatedly says, not while it trails behind its positing. To come into its "own," the human would need to establish an illegitimate rapport between the attraction of the ground and the "face" it puts on.) Like other, more familiar kinds of performatives, this originary speech-act is fundamentally preemptory and authoritative in nature, enacting and consolidating humanity, but doing so in a way that involves a certain (rhetorical, that is, *substitutive*) violence. In a proleptic structure that is homologous to the one we encountered earlier with the creatures and the craving for creatureliness, humankind's declaration of itself presupposes the very entity that its declaration inaugurates: namely, *humanity*. The human performance thereby involves a tacit description of the condition it produces. But since there can never be a simultaneous, full coincidence between the performance and the knowledge that it makes possible, what one understands in and through the performance can only be a retrospective "glimpse" at a deed that remains, finally, unfathomable. Schelling's account of this act in *The Ages of the World* (1813) is worth citing at length, not least for the way in which it demonstrates the sheer reversibility of the anthropomorphic gesture that we saw in the essay on freedom. Here, in the slightly later text, Schelling proceeds not by bringing the Absolute "humanly closer to us" but by bringing *the human*—which is now the entity characterized by an alterity that demands the accommodation of figures—closer to us through a comparison with the Absolute.

> For just as it is the law in man that the primordial act *[Ur-tat]*, which precedes all individual actions and never ceases, by which he is really himself, recedes into unfathomable depths in comparison to the consciousness that rises above it, in order that there may be a beginning which is never to be annulled, a root of reality unattainable by anything, *so, too* [my emphasis], in its determination, that primordial act of divine life extinguishes consciousness of itself, so that what was posited in that act as ground can in the sequel be again disclosed only by a higher revelation. Only thus is there a true beginning, a beginning which does not cease being beginning. The decision which is in any way the true beginning should not appear before consciousness, it should not be recalled to mind, since this, precisely, would amount to its recall. He who . . . reserves for himself the right to drag it again to light will never accomplish the beginning. [AW 204; 4, 690; trans. modified]

Humanity is perpetually in arrears vis-à-vis the languorous act of its inauguration, suffering as its instantiating circumstance an irreducible loss for which no work of mourning could ever "succeed" through a stupendous act of interiorization or incorporation. The "human" is rather a trace-effect, an after-image of the "irreducible precedence" of the alterity that sets "man" on his perilous path precisely by withdrawing from the light of consciousness. "This is the sadness which adheres to all finite life, and, inasmuch as there is even in God himself an independent condition, there is in him too, a source of sadness [ein Quell der Traurigkeit]" [PI 79; 4, 291]. With the human—as with God—then, the work of mourning has always already begun, a mourning before the human and before God, both of which are entities in memory of their "own" genesis, a beginning that is always elsewhere and at some other time. "Man's" "beginning," as Schelling describes it, begins compulsively, uncontrollably, as a remembering of its irremediably absent origin, a remembering that is "man," rather than something he actively does, and therefore not a thought, one among many, that could be "re-called" into consciousness as such. The human is unable to recall its beginning; but because the morphe of the anthropos fills in the space, as it were, left by this originary loss, and thus appears to itself as its own substitution, the human is also unable to renounce its beginning. (We might here recall Ronell's definition of addiction "as the inability to mourn"; the addict, she says, is "a nonrenouncer par excellence" [9].) Under these deeply melancholic conditions, as Derrida argues in another context, "the relation to the other (in itself outside myself, outside myself in myself) will never be distinguishable from a bereaved apprehension" [Memoires 33]. "The self appears to itself only in this bereaved allegory, in this hallucinatory prosopopoeia—and even before the death of the other actually happens, as we say, in 'reality'" [Memoires 28–29]. Die Sucht puts on a human face, "anthropomorphizes" itself, but what comes of this substitution is a death mask that mourns its own lively invention out of that which is faceless, inhuman, and, as Heidegger remarks, "nameless" [ST 125]. As Schelling will subsequently argue, citing the freedom essay's characterization of the universe as inherently melancholic, "the subject can never possess itself as what it is, for precisely as it addresses itself [sich Anziehen; which also means, as Bowie points out, "putting on what one is"] it becomes another; this is the basic contradiction, the misfortune in all being."[19]

In considering "man's" decision for itself, Heidegger warns, "[w]e must not slip back into the attitude of naive curiosity which would like at this opportunity to take a look behind the secret of the workshop. This 'back then' does not exist at all, because the occurrence is eternal and that means also a now-moment [ein jetzt augenblickliches]" [ST 131; 42, 226]. Because this "now moment" is never an object of thought, it is narrativized, after the fact, in various fictions about the "origin" of man: for example, the fabulous stories and phenomenologies of spirit in which humankind transforms itself "politically" from a state of amoral nature to moral culture; or ontologically from the dumb animal to articulate, questioning Dasein; or sexually from anarchic pleasures that are only about producing a need for themselves to pleasures that are normalized in their object choice. "Man utters himself and becomes present in language" [ST 141]. But the moment during which "man" comes into himself remains enigmatic, for in order to speak there must already have been language, the very phenomenon that Schelling attributes to the becoming human of humanity. Uttering itself *as* itself, "the human" at best gives a name and a face to an undecidability between the performative and constative functions of language, an undecidability in which, as Geoffrey Bennington observes, the performative "unavoidably . . . must take itself as constative" [237]. It is as if part of the performance must circle around behind or before "man" and take him as given for the performance to "work" and for "'man' [to] become present in language." We could then say that human language is anterior to itself, in excess of the constitutive work that humanity takes it to perform—and thus, arguably, not entirely human, and not in the possession of the human, at all. This inhuman excess of the *saying* of the human over the human that gets *said,* this otherness of the longing in whose cravings the *Logos* miraculously emerges (like a word out of an anagram, as Schelling so revealingly says), this exorbitance that haunts the work of spirit (but does not necessarily lead to spirit's destitution [*Entmachtung*], as Heidegger would claim), throws into relief the arbitrary violence of the human appropriation of language and longing, and the concomitant violence of the human *taking* itself as given. As Schelling's anthropomorphisms disfigure and delegitimate themselves into so many hallucinatory prosopopoeias, and as the "friendly feeling that we have always been what we are" gives way to a certain uncanniness, we recall Heidegger's challenge: "Who has ever refuted thoroughly and with sufficient reason the possibility that what we call *longing,* which is where we are, in the end is something other than we ourselves?" If not Heidegger's answer—which finally legitimates Dasein as the privileged site where this alterity is accommodated—then at least the essence of his question bears repeating: How can we not speak of addiction? Who, *we?*

NOTES

I am grateful for the assistance of Stephen Barber, Marshall Brown, George Grinnell, David Krell, Marc Redfield, and Martin Wallen in the composition of this essay. Partial funding for the project was provided by the Arts Research Board of McMaster University, with funds provided by the Social Sciences and Humanities Council of Canada.

1. Derrida asks, for example, "Today, how can we not speak of the university?" ["Principle of Reason," 3]. As he makes clear in another context, to pose the question in this fashion means, generally, "how if one speaks of it, to avoid speaking of it? How not to speak of it? How is it necessary to speak of it? How to avoid speaking of it without rhyme or reason? What precautions must be taken to avoid errors, that is inadequate, insufficient, simplistic assertions?" ["How to Avoid Speaking," 83].

2. I am thinking here of Rajan's *The Supplement of Reading: Figures of Understanding in Romantic Theory and Practice.*

3. All parenthetical references to Heidegger and Schelling are keyed to the English translation and the German original, respectively, separated by a semicolon. For abbreviations for individual works, see "Works Cited." Unless indicated otherwise, for Schelling and Heidegger I cite the *Sämmtliche Werke* and the *Gesamtausgabe,* respectively (volume number, followed by page number). Although for the most part I have used Gutmann's translation of Schelling's *Philosophical Investigations into the Essence of Human Freedom* (entitled *Of Human Freedom*), I have in some cases adopted elements from two additional sources: Priscilla Hayden-Roy's more recent translation and passages translated in David Farrell Krell's groundbreaking essay on Schelling's treatise ["Crisis"].

4. Derrida discusses these and other aspects of the rhetoric of drugs (which he describes as "a metaphysical burden and a history which we must never stop questioning") throughout "Rhetoric." For the specific references cited above, see 236, 238, and 234, respectively.

5. Eve Sedgwick argues that the nineteenth-century invention of a "pathologized addict identity" is part of a larger historical process in which concepts of "will" and "compulsion" simultaneously emerge as each other's other [135]. We have witnessed "the supervention in this century," she argues, "of addiction and the other glamorizing paradigms oriented around absolutes of compulsion/voluntarity" [139]. Where did this absolutization begin? Sedgwick points to Nietzsche, but we might recall how, at the start of the nineteenth century, it was Schelling who scandalously announced that "Will is original being *[Wollen ist Ursehn]*, and to it alone all predicates of being apply: groundlessness, eternality, independence of time, self-affirmation *[PI* 24; 4, 242]. What makes this claim more extraordinary is that Schelling instantly complicates his own position by arguing that "will" is not, strictly speaking, "original," but shares its primordiality with a primal dependency or addiction. This peculiar divisibility of spirit into volition and dependency marks Schelling as one of the first philosophers of finitude. If modernity suffers from an "epidemic of will" that is indissociable from an "epidemic of addiction and addiction-attribution" [135], as Sedgwick cogently argues, then patient zero is Friedrich Schelling.

6. A record of the 1927–1928 seminar on Schelling can be found in the "Verzeichnis der Vorlesungen und Übungen von Marlin Heidegger" in Richardson. The 1941 lectures appear as *Die Metaphysik des deutschen Idealismus* (vol. 49 of the *Gesamtausgabe*).

7. Nancy makes this point in *The Experience of Freedom* [40].

8. And, apparently, one to which it is hard to say no, for Derrida dedicates *Of Spirit*—his book, of course, on Heidegger—precisely to the "memory of 'Schelling'" [*Of Spirit* 117n3]. But what does it mean to mourn Schelling through Heidegger? What is the nature of the "Schelling" (which Derrida isolates within quotation marks) that survives, lives on, *after* Heidegger? What does it mean for "Heidegger" to deliver "Schelling" over to Derrida? (We could say that according to the rhetoric of drugs, Heidegger is sharing "Schelling").

9. For an analysis of Schelling's figures (including those figures that allude to *Timaeus*), see my "'The Necessary Heritage of Darkness': Tropics of Negativity in Schelling, Derrida, and de Man."

10. As Schelling says, the *Logos* appears mysteriously and precipitously out of this longing like a word out of the random lettering of an anagram, the latter a figure for the meaningless, differential markings that form the condition of the possibility of language. (It is as if God were always already hooked on phonics.) For a discussion of this materiality of language in the essay on freedom, see Clark.

11. Schelling: "But what is the essence of night, if not lack, need, and longing? For the night is not darkness, not the enemy of light, but it is the nature looking forward to the light, the night longing for it, eager to receive it" [*DS* 18]. Is Schelling not here responding to Hegel's infamous criticism of the obscurity of Schelling's Absolute, as "the night in which all cows are black"?

12. Schelling's dominant figure for the philosophers of spirit (i.e., the philosophers who negate the negative) is the cult of Cybele, a cult whose (male) members castrate themselves in frenzied homage to the goddess. Ironically, Hegel will compare German philosophy's task of protecting "spirit" with the cult of Samothrace, which, as we have seen, Schelling evokes in order to critique the derealizing tendencies of German philosophy [see Hegel, *Lectures on the History of Philosophy* 1–2].

13. See especially chapter 5 in *Of Spirit*.

14. I borrow and modify Krell's insight into Heidegger's vexed view of animal life: "Unfortunately, the clear division of ontic from ontological, and biological from existential, depends upon a scission in being that ostensibly would divide Dasein from just-plain-life without making such life absolutely inaccessible to it" [*Daimon Life* 94].

15. As Žižek argues, "Heidegger is in the habit of taking a category whose 'ethical' connotation in our common language is indelible (guilt [*Shuld*], the opposition of 'authentic' and 'unauthentic' existence) and then depriving it of this connotation, i.e., offering it as a neutral description of man's ontological predicament" [88–89n76].

16. Heidegger's sentence reads thus: "Die 'Sucht'—was dem Wortstamm nach nichts zu tun hat mit Suchen—meint ursprünglich und heute noch die Krankheit, die sich auszubreiten strebt; siech—Seuche" [42, 217].

17. But what are we to make of Heidegger's stone-cold phrase, "a mere human being [nur so ein Mensch]"? Under what conditions is human being ever insignificantly human? What are the possible politics—this, in 1936—that spring from speaking for the "Other" whose nearness shrinks and trivializes human being into such mereness? As Ned Lukacher argues, with reference to Derrida, "Heidegger's sacrifice to the Other lends itself too readily to a calculated sacrifice of the others [i.e., the 'merely human'] who do not appear to share the experience of essential thinking" [18].

18. My discussion here has profited from several valuable discussions of the question of the performative. In addition to Derrida ["Declarations"], these include Balfour, Bennington, and Keenan.

19. Bowie cites this passage from Schelling's lectures in Munich (circa 1833–1834) in *Aesthetics and Subjectivity* [87]. (Bowie also notes Schelling's play with *sich Anziehen*.) The phrase, the "basic misfortune in all life," directly recalls "die tiefe unzerstörliche Melancholie alles Lebens" [4, 291].

WORKS CITED

Balfour, Ian. "Promises, Promises: Social and Other Contracts in English Jacobins (Godwin/Inchbald)." *New Romanticisms: Theory and Critical Practice*. David L. Clark and Donald Goellnicht, eds., Toronto: University of Toronto Press, 1994, pp. 225–259.

Beach, Edward Allen. *The Potencies of God(s): Schelling's Philosophy of Mythology*. Albany: State University of New York Press, 1994.

Bennington, Geoffrey. *Jacques Derrida*. Chicago: University of Chicago Press, 1994.

Bowie, Andrew. *Aesthetics and Subjectivity: From Kant to Nietzsche*. Manchester: Manchester University Press, 1990.

——. *Schelling and Modern European Philosophy*. New York: Routledge, 1993.

Clark, David L. "'The Necessary Heritage of Darkness': Tropics of Negativity in Schelling, Derrida, and de Man." *Intersections: Nineteenth-Century Philosophy and Contemporary Theory*. Tilottama Rajan and David L Clark, eds., Albany: State University of New York Press, 1995, pp. 79–146.

Derrida, Jacques. *Aporias,* translated by Thomas Dutoit. Stanford: Stanford University Press, 1993.

———. "Declarations of Independence," translated by Tom Keenan and Tom Pepper. *New Political Science*. 15 (Summer 1986): 7–15.

———. "How to Avoid Speaking: Denials," translated by Ken Frieden. *Derrida and Negative Theology*. Harold Coward and Toby Foshay, eds., Albany: State University of New York Press, 1992, pp. 73–142.

———. *Memoires for Paul de Man*, Rev. ed., translated by Cecile Lindsay, Jonathan Culler, Eduardo Cadava, and Peggy Kamuf. New York: Columbia University Press, 1989.

———. *Of Spirit: Heidegger and the Question*, translated by Geoffrey Bennington and Rachel Bowlby. Chicago: University of Chicago Press, 1989.

———. "The Principle of Reason: The University in the Eyes of Its Pupils." *Diacritics* 13.3 (1983): 3–20.

———. "The Rhetoric of Drugs," translated by Michael Israel. *Points . . . Interviews, 1974–1994*. Elisabeth Weber, ed. Stanford: Stanford University Press, 1992.

Fenves, Peter. "Foreword: From Empiricism to the Experience of Freedom." Nancy xiii–xxi.

Hegel, G. W. F. *Lectures on the History of Philosophy*. Oxford: Clarendon, 1985.

Heidegger, Martin. *Being and Time*, translated by Joan Stambaugh. Albany: State University of New York Press, 1996.

———. *Einführung in die Metaphysik. Gesamtausgabe,* Vol. 40. Frankfurt am Main: Vittorio Klostermann, 1983.

———. *History of the Concept of Time: Prolegomena*, translated by Theodore Kisiel. Bloomington: Indiana University Press, 1985.

———. *An Introduction to Metaphysics*, translated by Ralph Manheim. New Haven: Yale University Press, 1959.

———. *Die Metaphysik des deutschen Idealismus. Gesamtausgabe,* Vol. 49. Frankfurt am Main: Vittorio Klostermann, 1991.

———. *Schelling's Treatise on the Essence of Human Freedom*, translated by Joan Stambaugh. Athens. OH: Ohio University Press, 1985. Translation of *Schelling: Vom Wesen der Menschlichen Freiheit (1809). Gesamtausgabe,* Vol. 42. Frankfurt am Main: Vittorio Klostermann, 1988.

Keenan, Thomas. "Deconstruction and the Impossibility of Justice." *Cardozo Law Review* 11.5–6 (1990): 1675–1686.

Krell, David Farrell. "The Crisis of Reason in the Nineteenth Century: Schelling's Treatise on Human Freedom (1809)." John Sallis, Giuseppina Moneta, and Jacques Taminiaux, eds., *The Collegium Phaenomenologicum: The First Ten Years*. Dordrecht: Kluwer, 1988, pp. 13–32.

————. *Daimon Life: Heidegger and Life-Philosophy*. Bloomington: Indiana University Press, 1992.

Lukacher, Ned. "Introduction: Mourning Becomes Telepathy." *Cinders*, by Jacques Derrida, translated by Ned Lukacher, ed., Lincoln: University of Nebraska Press, 1991, pp. 1–18.

Nancy, Jean-Luc. *The Experience of Freedom*, translated by Bridget McDonald. Stanford: Stanford University Press, 1993.

Nietzsche, Friedrich. *The Gay Science, with a Prelude in Rhymes and an Appendix of Songs*, translated by Walter Kaufmann. New York: Vintage, 1974.

Rajan, Tilottama. *The Supplement of Reading: Figures of Understanding in Romantic Theory and Practice*. Ithaca: Cornell University Press, 1990.

Richardson, William. *Through Phenomenology to Thought*. The Hague: Martinus Nijhoff, 1963.

Ronell, Avital. *Crack Wars: Literature Addiction Mania*. Lincoln: University of Nebraska Press, 1992.

Sallis, John. "Schelling's System of Freedom." Rev. of *Schellings Abhandlung über das Wesen der Menschlichen Freiheit (1809)*, by Martin Heidegger. *Research in Phenomenology* 2 (1972):155–165.

Sedgwick, Eve Kosofsky. "Epidemics of Will." *Tendencies*. Durham, NC: Duke University Press, 1993, pp. 130–142.

Schelling, Friedrich Wilhelm Joseph von. *The Ages of the World*, translated by Frederick de Wolfe Bolman, Jr., ed., New York: Columbia University Press, 1966. *[AW]* Trans. of *Die Weltalter. Sämmtliche Werke* 4:571–720.

————. *The Deities of Samothrace*, translated by Robert Brown. Missoula, MT: Scholars Press for the American Academy of Religion, 1976. *[DS]* Trans. of *Über die Gottheiten von Samothrake. Sämmtliche Werke* 4:721–745.

————. *Of Human Freedom*, translated by J. Gutmann. Chicago: Open Court, 1936. Trans. of *Philosophische Untersuchungen über das Wesen der menschlichen Freiheit und die damit zusammenhängenden Gegenstände. Sammiliche Werke* 4:223–308.

————. *Philosophical Investigations into the Essence of Human Freedom and Related Matters*, translated by Priscilla Hayden-Roy. *Philosophy of German Idealism*. Ernst Behler, ed., New York: Continuum, 1987, 23:217–284.

————. *Sämmiliche Werke. Nach der Original Ausgabe in neuer Anordnung [in a new arrangement]*. Manfred Schroter, ed., 6 vols. and 6 supplementary vols. Munich: Beck and Oldenbourg, 1927–1959.

————. *Stuttgart Seminars*, translated by Thomas Pfau. *Idealism and the Endgame of Theory: Three Essays by F. W. J. Schelling*, translated by

Thomas Pfau, ed., Albany: State University of New York Press, 1994, pp. 195–268. Trans. of *Stuttgarter Privatvorlesungen*. *Sämmiliche Werke* 4:309–394.

Slawney, James. "Hallucinogeneric Literature: Avital Ronell's Narcoanalysis." *Diacritics* 24.4 (1994):41–49.

Žižek, Slavoj. *The Indivisible Remainder: An Essay on Schelling and Related Matters*. London: Verso, 1996.

Chapter Six

TRAUMA, ADDICTION, AND TEMPORAL BULIMIA IN *MADAME BOVARY*

ELISSA MARDER

Lisez, et ne rêvez pas. Plongez-vous dans de longues études. Il n'y a de continuellement bon que l'habitude d'un travail entêté. Il s'en dégage un opium qui engourdit l'âme [Read and do not dream. The only thing that is continually good is the habit of stubborn work. It emits an opium that numbs the soul].

—Gustave Flaubert to Louise Colet

Madame Bovary *I daresay is about bad drugs.*

—Avital Ronell, *Crack Wars*

If Flaubert's *Madame Bovary* remains so timely, it is because its heroine, Emma, suffers from the quintessential malady of modernity, the inability to incorporate time into experience. Emma's missed encounter with her own life, her inability to "get a life," as we say now in America, renders her our contemporary in the strangest sense of the word. She is our contemporary not because we live in the same time but because her failure to live in time has come to define our own. Paradoxically, Emma Bovary has been so well preserved (she is, in some sense, "more alive" now than ever) because she incarnates and inaugurates a modernity that can be defined by the erosion of the possibility of living in time. In Flaubert's minute and meticulous descriptions of the particular temporal disorders that afflict Emma (as we shall see, she can neither bear witness to an event nor remember one, she can neither live in the present nor project a future, she is incessantly subject to bouts of involuntary forgetting even as she is preoccupied by obsessive rites of recollection, she attempts simultaneously to conjure up time and to stop it), we can read the prophetic traces of a depiction of the temporal structure of the many forms of trauma and addiction that have come to define contemporary American culture.

But before turning to Flaubert's prescient and powerful analysis of how Emma Bovary suffers from a "temporal disorder," let us take a brief look at how the notions of trauma and addiction have been described in a contemporary analysis of modern culture. In his recent book *On Flirtation,* the British child psychoanalyst Adam Phillips redescribes ordinary neurosis as a traumatic response to an inability to live in time. He writes:

> People come to psychoanalysis when there is something they cannot forget, something they cannot stop telling themselves, often by their actions, about their lives. And these dismaying repetitions—this unconscious limiting or coercion of the repertoire of life stories—create the illusion of time having stopped (or rather, people believe—behave as if they have stopped time). In our repetitions we seem to be staying away from the future, keeping it at bay.[1]

Philips goes on to explain that "[f]or Freud these repetitions are the consequence of a failure to remember. . . . Whatever cannot be transformed, psychically processed, reiterates iself. A trauma is whatever there is in a person's experience that resists useful redescription. Traumas, like beliefs, are ways of stopping time."[2] Phillips's argument rings with a seductive simplicity: neurosis is defined as a temporal disorder, and the contemporary psychoanalytic "cure" does nothing less than promise time. It presumably offers the subject the option of accepting the contingencies of living in time over the pleasure and pain that attend the attempt to stop it.

Nonetheless, Phillips's claim, that contemporary neurosis can be expressed as an attempt to stop time, should perhaps make us pause. Stopping time, in the time of Balzac, Gautier, Baudelaire, and Flaubert, was once conceived of as part of the privileged domain reserved for art and the artist. We might have naively assumed that in the realm of the "real world," for "real people" time remains an implacable fact of life.

The task of falling out of time, after all, would seem to necessitate either an accident of enormous magnitude (a trauma in the traditional sense) or the reliance upon an external substance—hashish, opium, alcohol, or cocaine—one of those mind-altering substances that so preoccupied the nineteenth-century advocates of *paradis artificiels*. So what is surprising and particularly suggestive about Phillips's observations is not that the ordinary neurotic *fails* to stop time, but rather that he or she *succeeds* so well. This dubious "success" is incontestably well documented in the realm of American popular culture, where—in television talk shows, sitcoms, tabloids, self-help books, and twelve-step programs as well as on the dwindling couches of analysts, who have, for the most part, been replaced by millions of prescriptions for Prozac and Zoloft—trauma and its uncanny other, addiction, are visibly the most emblematic and paradocically *popular* illnesses of our time.

Phillips's invocation of the notion of "trauma" in the context of everyday pathologies only further complicates the problem. When he writes, rather casually, that "traumas, like beliefs, are ways of stopping time," what has happened to our implicit understanding of what trauma is and how it occurs? Trauma is more or less classically understood as a response to an event so extraordinary that, in the language of the American Psychiatric Institute (cited by Cathy Caruth in her introduction to *Trauma: Explorations in Memory*), it is "outside the range of usual human experience."[3] Because the event is so threatening (it often occurs in the case of near-death encounters) and because the experience cannot be assimilated, the event is mechcanically reproduced as recollection bereft of memory. As Caruth writes, "[t]he pathology consists, rather, solely in the *structure of experience* or reception: the event is not assimilated or experienced fully at the time, but only belatedly, in its repeated *possession* of the one who experiences it. To be traumatized is precisely to be possessed by an image or event."[4] Because this atemporal "possession" prevents the traumatized subject from experiencing (in the sense of assimilating) the precipitating event, that nonevent comes to organize a systematic disruption of many, if not all, other life experiences. We could argue that in the uncontrollable and often unmanageable repetitions of the traumatic event, the subject's inability both to forget and to remember the event is lived as if time itself had become a persecutory enemy, an overwhelming other.

But if the subject of "trauma" is, as we have said, "possessed" by time, what is the temporal status of the addicted subject? How and why can trauma and addiction be read as uncanny inversions of a similar temporal disorder? In both cases, certainly, the subject appears to be "possessed" and is apparently condemned to acts of compulsive repetition unto death in either literal or symbolic ways. But where the traumatic subject is seemingly dominated by an inability to forget, the addicted subject seems driven by a strange, compulsive *need* to forget. If trauma can be understood as the attempt to survive an inassimilable encounter with "near-death," the structure of addiction emerges as a strange kind of "near-life" experience. Where the traumatized subject cannot get away from the voice of time, the addicted subject seemingly cannot find a place *in* it. Time, for the addict, is not figured as an anthropomorphized persecutory other—but rather appears almost like something that happens elsewhere, to other people. The time of addiction is a time, like trauma, "outside the range of usual human experience," but in the case of addiction, the subject appears to be exiled from time rather than possessed by it.

The temporal coincidence of the appearance of *Madame Bovary* with that of *Les fleurs du mal* leads one to ask about the historical status of this failure of experience. The traumatized voice of a subject "possessed" by time echoes through many of Baudelaire's poems, but the most explicit example of traumatic paranoid possession can be found in "L'horloge." In "L'horloge," the poet conjures up a demonic figure of time in the opening first line. "Horloge, Dieu Sinistre" ("Clock, Sinister God"), and immediately loses control over his own voice. The voice of the clock usurps that of the poet and then repeats the command "souviens-toi" ("remember") again and again in increasingly mechanized tones until it condemns the poet to death in the last line. But where Baudelaire's work might be dominated by the figure of trauma (even though it is he and not Flaubert who put addiction at the center of his concerns), it is in Flaubert's novel that we find—in place of the drug-like flowers of evil, with their lure of opiate aroma—the fullblown structure of an addiction with no point of return. By insisting upon the effects of his addicted temporality, I hope to explain why, as any reader of *Madame Bovary* knows, Emma never had a life to lose.[5]

Flaubert's *Madame Bovary* is perhaps one of the most eloquent analyses of the temporal pathology of the language of everyday life available to us. Long before Marcel Proust dramatized the problem of time through the figures of *memoire volontaire* and *involontaire,* Emma Bovary struggled against the demon of involuntary forgetting. If Proust must be seen as the indelible archivist of the telling of the modern subject's narration of his relationship to lost time, Flaubert can be read as the scribe, the copyist, of the modern subject's non-narratable relation to wasted time. But unlike Proust's narrator, Flaubert's Emma Bovary cannot seek lost time; instead, as the novel explicitly demonstrates, she is in search of time itself, in the form of an event. Unable to isolate anything in her "daily life" that she can grasp in the form of an "event," she turns to fiction. While virtually all readers and critics of *Madame Bovary* (beginning, of course, with the legal, political, and cultural institutions that saw fit to put the book on trial) would agree with Michael Riffaterre's observation that "*Madame Bovary* is a fiction about the dangers of fiction," critics have widely divergent ways of interpreting the causes and consequences of Emma's reading habit.[6] Reading Emma's reading habits is a favorite activity of *Bovary's* critics, many of whom seem to be vaguely reassured by the notion that Emma's misfortunes and suffering can in large part be attributed to her unhealthy and ultimately misguided dependency on works of fiction. This tendency is exemplified by Victor Brombert's claim that "Emma's flaw is that she uses art to feed her dreams, instead of placing her dreams in the service of art."[7] Such a reading implies that Emma's suffering stems from the fact that she is a bad reader of the relationship between art and life.[8] By turning briefly to the first passage in the text that introduces *Madame Bovary's* readers to Emma as reader, I would like to suggest that if one too quickly concludes that Emma is simply a bad reader, Flaubert's reader risks glossing over the complexity of his idiomatic and highly disturbing articulation of how time and experience can become unhinged in both life and art. In the concluding paragraph of chapter 5, part 1, Flaubert writes:

> Avant qu'elle se mariât, elle avait cru avoir de l'amour; mais le bonheur qui aurait dû résulter de cet amour n'étant pas venu, il fallut qu'elle se fût trompée, songeait-elle. Et Emma cherchait à savoir ce que l'on entendait au juste dans la vie par des mots de *félicité*, de *passion*, et *d'ivresse*, qui lui avaient paru si beaux dans les livres.[9]

> Before marriage she thought herself in love; but since the happiness that should have followed failed to come, she must, she thought, have been mistaken. And Emma tried to find out what one meant exactly in life by the word *bliss, passion, ecstasy*, that had seemed to her so beautiful in books.[10]

The obvious irony of this passage derives from the fact that Emma resolves the discrepancy between her lived experience of love and her reading knowledge of love by concluding that the error lies not in her books but in her life. Such a reading only confirms two common characterizations of Emma Bovary: at worst, she is a foolish, provincial woman who deludes herself with romantic fantasies, and at best she is a pathetic travesty of an artist because she tragically misrecognizes the proper hierarchy between "Art" and "Life." Both of these interpretations are certainly textually justified and are supported and seemingly solicited by Flaubert's explicitly contemptuous descriptions of Emma in the correspondence as well as his implicit critique of Emma throughout the text of *Madame Bovary*. Furthermore, in the passage itself Flaubert seemingly establishes a distance between the voice of narrative authority and Emma's faulty reasoning by adding the telltale attribution "songeait-elle" to Emma's conclusion that she has been mistaken about life: "il fallut qu'elle se fût trompée, songeait-elle." The phrase "songeait-elle" underscores the notion that even when engaging in the act of facing the barren reality of her life, Emma can do nothing other than dream.

Presumably bereft of any form of experience other than those received from books, Emma can only perceive that she has not yet had an event by comparing the lexicon of her life with that of the novels she has read. The word that trips her up is, not surprisingly, "amour." What is surprising is that Emma's difficulty reconciling the difference between book-love and her lived experience emerges not in relation to the word's meaning or definition, but rather in relation to its temporal effects and narrative function. Novel reading has taught Emma that "amour" ought to announce an inaugural event that propels a life into a durable and continued state of "bonheur" ("happiness"). Hence, one knows that one has "possessed love" ("avoir de l'amour") only when that love produces an event that guarantees temporal continuity in the form of "bonheur." The disappointing revelations occasioned by Emma's marriage are consequently multiple: in the first place, the marriage cannot function as an event in itself because it does not occur at the properly eventful hour of midnight: "Emma eût, au contraire, désiré se marier à minuit"[11] ("Emma would, on the contrary, have preferred to have a midnight wedding"[12]). Next, the marriage fails to produce the anticipated state of happiness, and finally, and perhaps most important, these first two failures force her to acknowledge that she has been jilted by an "event" at the altar of time. The temporal finality and precision of the words "le bonheur qui aurait dû résulter de cet amour n'étant pas venu" almost anthropomorphizes "bonheur" into the missing bridegroom, whose absence at the wedding necessarily obliterates the meaning and the function of the event. Instead of enabling her to begin an eventful life by establishing a bridge between the world of fiction and the language of life, the word "love" opens up an irrevocable abyss between the formlessness of lived time and the experience of narrative meaning provided by fiction. The fissure between the fictional temporality of the word "love" and its seemingly absent corresponding referent in the real world functions rhetorically like catachresis, a figural term that has no literal meaning. As we shall see in greater depth later on, the appearance of the word "amour" in *Madame Bovary* is always hyperinvested in strange ways and almost always signals the presence of a temporal disorder.[13] In this passage, once Emma recognizes the disconnection between the word "amour" and its fictional referent, she learns that any and all words could potentially become meaningless in the language of life: "Et Emma cherchait à savoir ce que l'on entendait au juste *dans* la vie par des mots de *félicité*, de *passion* et d'*ivreesse* . . ." [my emphasis].

When, however, this passage is read in the context of Flaubert's presentation of Emma's so-called life, it takes on additional resonances. Let us begin by recalling that according to the narrative structure of the novel, Emma, unlike Charles, never had any "real life experiences" onto which fantasy or fictional events were grafted. Whereas the narrative of *Madame Bovary* begins with the fabulous scene of Charles Bovary's primal traumatic schoolroom humiliation through "decapitation" (the loss of his beloved and monstrous "casquette") and traces the subsequent vicissitudes of his daily life (ranging from Charles's mediocre study habits to the events that culminate in his first marriage), the narrative of Emma's "life" prior to her encounter with Charles emerges only after it becomes clear in the above passage that her marriage has failed to constitute the inaugural events of her life. Immediately after this discovery, chapter 6 begins with the recitation of Emma's reading history ("Elle avait lu *Paul et Virginie* et elle avait rêvé la maisonette de bambous . . ."[14] / "She has read 'Paul and Virginia,' and she had dreamed of the little bamboo-house . . ."), which introduces, supplements, and ultimately supplants the subsequent narration of her past lived life story: "lorsqu'elle eut treize ans, son père l'amena lui-même à la ville pour la mettre au couvent"[15] ("When she was 13, her father himself took her to the convent"[16]). In other words, Emma's substitution of literature for life cannot merely be read as a character flaw since, at the level of the novel's narrative, Flaubert presents her life as if it were actually produced by her readings rather than as a series of lived experiences. Like Emma herself, who apparently has no access to her life that has not been mediated by a prior fictional referent, *Bovary's* reader is given no access to Emma's "life" that has not already been presented as a fictional production. Paradoxically, however, in the very moment in the text when Emma discovers that her marriage has failed to inaugurate her life, at the level of the novel, Emma's disappointment in her marriage initiates the moment when the fictional life of the character known as Emma Bovary is truly born. Prior to this moment, as critics have often observed, the narrative voice displays Emma as a spectacular object of Charles's gaze, seen almost entirely through his eyes.[17] It is only after Emma literally becomes "Madame Bovary" and realizes that her newly acquired identity has nonetheless failed to provide her with a life that her thoughts and feelings begin to permeate the *style indirect libre* of the authorial voice.

Thus, from the outset of the novel, the subjective presence of the character "Madame Bovary" is animated by and depends upon her alienation from her experience of life. For this reason, rather than reading Emma's recourse to fiction as a cause of her future misfortunes, I prefer to read Emma's reading as the first significant manifestation of her temporal disorder—the fact that her life seemingly unfolds in a temporal void.[18] "Therefore, while it is indisputable that Emma displays a naive belief that literature can be directly transformed into life, it is nonetheless quite possible that through her very inability to read her life, Emma provides Flaubert's reader with the novel's most rigorous and lucid embodiment of how time can be severed from experience in modern life. By starting from the assumption that Flaubert's oft-cited utterance "Madame Bovary, c'est moi" should be read quite literally, I hope to resist the temptation to read Emma's plight as either pathetic or tragic in order to uncover critical traces of the history of the modern subject.

Emma's gradual discovery that her life consists of a monotonous temporal vacuum motivates her growing dependency on fictional models of temporal structures. Her most significant early abuse of fiction occurs in the wake of her mother's death. Because the temporal void in which she exists prevents her from being able to sustain the experience in time or to secure its meaning by placing it within a meaningful temporal context, she attempts to compensate for the temporal insufficiency of the literal death by using literary devices to enhance and prolong the experience. Although the actual death fails to constitute a "natural" event for Emma, she welcomes the very idea of death as a potentially fortuitous cure for her timelessness. By applying the basic tenets of romantic aesthetic ideology onto the material fact of her mother's death, she fabricates the following fiction of the future: she anticipates an experience of durable, melancholic inconsolability that culminates in the productive projection of her own future death so that she might ultimately experience a dramatic, spiritual literary rebirth.

> Quand sa mère mourut, elle pleura beaucoup les premiers jours. Elle se fit faire un tableau funèbre avec les cheveux de la défunte, et, dans une lettre qu'elle envoyait aux Bertaux, toute pleine de réflexions tristes sur la vie, elle demandait qu'on l'ensevelît plus tard dans le même tombeau. Le bonhomme la crut malade et vint la voir. Emma fut intérieurement satisfaite de se sentir arrivée du premier coup à ce rare idéal des existences pâles, où ne parviennent jamais les coeurs médiocres. Elle se laissa donc glisser dans les méandres lamartiniens, écouta les harpes sur les lacs, tous les chants des cygnes mourants. . . .[19]

When her mother died she cried much the first few days. She had a funeral picture made with hair of the deceased, and, in a letter sent to the Bertaux full of sad reflections on life, she asked to be buried later in the same grave. The old man thought she must be ill, and came to see her. Emma was secretly pleased that she had reached at a first attempt the rare ideal of delicate lives, never attained by mediocre hearts. She let herself meander along with Lamartine, listened to harps on lakes, to all the songs of dying swans. . . .[20]

However, as the conclusion of the passage demonstrates, Emma never achieves the state of anticipated inconsolability that she had hoped would serve as incontestable proof of an indelible memory. Despite all the excessive gestures that she performs in order to preserve it, her mother's memory quickly evaporates. And even Emma is disillusioned by how her romantic theories of death fail to endure the test of practical application and hence cannot be considered particularly useful. Much to her dismay and confusion, she discoveres that Death offers no greater chance of a future than life does. Her fantasy of a new life, a life renewed by literary tropes of rebirth, is reduced to the vapidity of received ideas. Emma's factory of literary cliches not only fails to supply her with an experience of a lived event that endures, but also hastens the demise of this experience through empty repetition:

> Elle s'en ennuya, n'en voulut point convenir, continua par habitude, ensuite par vanité, et fut enfin surprise de se sentir apaisée, et sans plus de tristesse au coeur que de rides sur son front.[21]

> She soon grew bored but wouldn't admit it, continued from habit first, then out of vanity, and at last was surprised to feel herself consoled, and with no more sadness at heart than wrinkles on her brow.[22]

But in order to appreciate the gravity of this passage and to understand the textual ramifications of its twisted logic, we must take a closer look at the mother/daughter relationship depicted in it. In the first place, we are compelled to observe that this is virtually the only moment in *Madame Bovary* where Emma makes any reference to the mother.[23] Moreover, the missing mother becomes the site of a disruption of moral, psychological, and temporal categories. It appears that this mother exists only through her death: by dying she offers Emma a pretext for the activity of mourning and a promise of rebirth. In a perverse reversal of the natural tropes of maternity, when Emma asks to be buried with her mother in the same grave, the figure of the womb is replaced by that of the tomb in her fantasy of rebirth. But although Flaubert's transvaluation of the maternal function is announced through the substitution of figures of death for figures of life, what is at stake is not simply a confusion of life and death.

This death mother appears as the first unmistakable annunciation of the activities of involuntary forgetting, mechanical repetition, and failed mourning that pervade the text of *Madame Bovary*. Unlike Charles's mother or Emma's father, the figure of Emma's mother never attains the status of a psychological character; she appears only to disappear, and this disappearance becomes remarkable precisely because it leaves no mark. The only "surprise" that this terminal nonevent can elicit is the surprise of nothingness itself. Flaubert circumscribes the surprising emptiness of this voided experience through an analogy between two unwritten texts: the absence of sadness in Emma's heart is strikingly compared to the absence of wrinkles on her forehead. The missing wrinkles prove that time remains unwritten there: "Elle . . . fut enfin surprise de se sentir apaisée, et sans plus de tristesse au coeur que de rides sur son front." The ironic analogy between Emma's absent affect and her unmarked forehead reiterates that the mother's death fails as an event because it cannot mark the passage of time. It comes as no surprise, therefore, that even in her death, Emma's mother cannot give her life because she cannot give her time.

Although she never reappears in the novel, Emma's dead mother is perhaps the most opaque and unreadable figure in the entire text of *Madame Bovary*.[24] This figure becomes unreadable in part because she is barely written—existing only as the void that serves as the apparent origin of all future nonevents, including, of course, Emma's warped nonmaternal relation to her own daughter, Berthe. But if one is tempted (as I am partially suggesting here) to read the failed mourning of the dead mother as the first and most extreme example of the many temporal dysfunctions that permeate this novel, it is no less important to insist that the textual meaning and function of this dead mother cannot simply be read through classical psychological or psychoanalytic paradigms. Flaubert hardly seems to be suggesting that Emma's problems can in any way be attributed to a lack of maternal care. He does, however, seem to place Emma, and the entire world of *Madame Bovary,* in a realm where mothers no longer guarantee the existence of a state of nature. Flaubert's maternal function connotes neither an inviolable, preverbal natural bond between mother and child nor a natural temporal frame in which birth and death constitute events and childbearing insures that generations progress forward naturally through time.

Emma's attempts to mourn the mother's death are doomed to repeat the very formlessness of this maternal nonevent. Although she anticipates that the death will be accompanied by feelings of "sadness,"

Emma soon finds herself in a state of disconnected boredom ("elle s'en-nuya"). In *Crack Wars,* Avital Ronell reminds us that nineteenth-century boredom, like melancholia, is mourning's dysfunctional evil twin. She goes on to argue that when failed mourning passes as boredom, the cultural site formerly assigned to death becomes occupied by addictive structures that often manifest themselves through drug dependency. Ronell writes:

> As symptom, boredom is co-originary with melancholia. It pervades everything, and cannot be simply said to erupt. Nor does it desist of its own. It is prior to signification, yet it appears to be a commentary on life; it is, at least for Emma, the place of her deepest struggle. . . . *Boredom,* with its temporal slowdown and edge of anguish, is also an authentic mode of being-in-the-world. . . . Emma's boredom appears to exhaust a certain reserve before it has been tapped. It is a companion to loss, but raised on tranquilizers. In *Madame Bovary,* boredom opens up a listening to disappearance, fabricating a society's holding pattern over the death that traverses us. . . . This forms the threshold through which the existence of Emma Bovary is made to pass, a zone of experience that conspires with "nothing at all," the extenuation of the subject. Something like an ontology of boredom announces its necessity here. We are reminded that for Baudelaire and Gautier, Flaubert's contemporaries and acquaintances, this experience of nothing is at times laced with drugs.[25]

The link that Ronell suggests between boredom, failed mourning, and the structure of addiction is borne out by the conclusion of the passage: Emma's boredom transforms subjective mourning rituals into an empty habit ("habitude"). This alienated mechanical repetition ultimately degenerates into an eviscerated narcissism, "vanité," before fading away completely.

Although the legacy of the mother's death lies precisely in the fact that she passes away outside the passage of time and without leaving a trace, the aftermath of this maternal disappearance seemingly produces a temporal void in Emma which she attempts to counteract by searching for an event. Having no access to the experience of an event in her life, she turns to fiction in order to learn how to manufacture one. Her readings dispense fictive highs, which she confuses with lived events. The passions she feels when reading stimulate her desire to reproduce in life the excitations simulated by fiction. Because Emma's literary taste for the generic tropes of Romantic fiction teaches her that events (like the "coup de foundre" that heralds love) occur both instantaneously and by chance, she attempts to apply the laws of fiction to life by waiting for an eventful surprise in the form of love or adventure. But since the laws of fiction, unlike life, systematically guarantee the arrival of unanticipated events, Emma's readings place her in a peculiar historical and philosophical predicament: how can one anticipate the arrival of an event which must be, by definition, both surprising and instantaneous?

In the following passage, which comes from the last chapter of part 1, as Emma waits impatiently for the arrival of a hypothetical event that presumably would transform her empty existence into the experience of a real life, she begins to realize, with increasing desperation, that she has not been invited to the dance of Life. Flaubert writes:

> Au fond de son âme, cependant, elle attendait un événement . . . chaque matin, à son réveil, elle l'espérait pour la journée et elle écoutait tous les bruits, se levait en sursaut, s'étonnait qu'il ne vînt pas; puis, au coucher du soleil, toujours plus triste, désirait être au lendemain. . . . Dès le commencement de juillet, elle compta sur ses doigts combien de semaines lui restaient pour arriver au mois d'octobre, pensant que le marquis d'Andervilliers, peut-être, donnerait encore un bal à la Vaubyessard. Mais tout septembre s'écoula sans lettres ni visites. Après l'ennui de cette déception, son coeur, de nouveau, resta vide, et alors la série des mêmes journées recommença.
>
> Elles allaient donc maintenant se suivre ainsi à la file, toujour pareille, innombrables, et n'apportant rien! Les autres existences, si plates qu'elles fussent, avaient du moins la chance d'un événement. Une aventure amenait parfois des péripéties à l'infini, et le décor changeait. Mais pour elle, rien n'arrivait. Dieu l'avait voulu! L'avenir était un corridor tout noir, et qui avait au fond sa porte bien fermée.[26]

> All the while, however, she was waiting in her heart for an event. Each morning, as she awoke, she hoped it would come that day; she listened to every sound, sprang up with a start, was surprised that it did not come; then at sunset, always more saddened, she wished that it would already be tomorrow. . . . From the beginning of July she counted off on her fingers how many weeks there were to get to October, thinking that perhaps the Marquis d' Andervilliers would give another ball at Vaubyessard. But all September passed without letters or visits. After the shock of this disappointment her heart once again remained empty, and then the same series of identical days started all over again. So now they would keep following one another, always the same, innumberably, and bringing nothing. Other existences, however flat, had at least the chance of an event. One adventure sometimes brought with it infinite consequences and the scenery changed. But for her, nothing happened. God had willed it so! The future was a dark corridor, with its door at the end well locked up.[27]

In the opening lines of this passage, it appears to Emma (and the reader) almost as if it is an "accident"—an event of some sort—that has interfered with the arrival of *her* anticipated event" "chaque matin, à son réveil, elle l'espérait pour la journée et elle écoutait tous les bruits, se levait en sursaut, s'étonnait qu'il ne vînt pas. . . ." The text begins by suggesting that it is the absence of an event that impedes Emma's ability to live life daily and concludes with the more disturbing notion that it is her inability to gain access to that temporal unit "day" that renders any potential future even impossible. For Emma, time cannot be measured; it flows away in smaller and smaller doses. Initially week by week, then day by day, and ultimately drop by drop, it becomes clear that the problem here is not with an event that has stopped time, but rather with a figure of time that cannot assimilate an event.

At first, Emma counts *on* time by attempting to count it, literally, in the weeks that she counts off on her fingers. But in order even to be able to count time—to represent time in meaningful units—Emma must be able to rely on the hope that the only event that has ever had any lasting meaning for her, the ball at Vaubyessard, could be repeatable. The ironic futility of this hope is extremely complex and ultimately fatal; the event of the ball cannot be repeated as lived experience for Emma in part because her presence at it was entirely determined by chance. The invitation to the ball depends on the convergence of an inimitable series of chance occurrences: the marquis happened to develop an abscess in his mouth just prior to the ball; the cherries happened to be bad at Vaubyessard and good at the Bovary's farm that year, and when the marquis wants some cherries, he catches sight of Emma and whimsically decides to invite the couple to the ball. It is only by accident, therefore, that Emma goes to the ball in the first place, and once she gets there she is more an alienated and dizzied spectator at the event than a participant in it.

Perhaps because the ball at Vaubyessard appears to correspond, almost uncannily, to the expectations she receives from fiction, it is virtually the only incident in the text of *Madame Bovary* that even remotely functions like a life event for Emma. Moreover, unlike the failed event of her mother's death, which loses all reality, provides neither continuity nor consistency, and evaporates from her memory without leaving a trace, the ball remains the only occurrence in her life that she doesn't inadvertently forget. Everything and everyone else, all other presences and absences are subject to erosion and are effaced.

Functioning as the singular and traumatic temporal point of reference for Emma, the ball tantalizes her into temporary hopefulness by providing her with a powerful, if illusory, repository into which she tries to insert her own experiences. Upon leaving the ball, Emma seizes the viscount's lost cigar-case (which Charles had picked up) in order to sustain and preserve her memory of the event. Emma treats the cigar-case as if this thing could somehow objectify lost time—as if this object were uniquely endowed with the capacity to conserve time by giving it a physical form. As receptacle, this object seems to incarnate formally the very thing missing from her life: a temporal lost object, a representational container capable of incorporating time. After the scene at the ball until the end of part 1, the cigar-case functions as a kind of sacred relic that promises that the life she witnessed at the ball will be hers in an imaginary afterlife. But in the pages directly preceding her discovery that she will never again be invited to the ball, the cigar-case no longer functions as a reliable container for memories of an imaginary future. Bereft of an external temporal object that could contain time for her, Emma now attempts to incorporate time with her body, by counting it on her fingers. But we understand that this attempt has failed when Flaubert writes, in the middle of the passage of "lost days" quoted above, that "tout septembre s'écoula sans lettres ni visites." The verb "s'écoula" reiterates the notion everywhere present in the text of *Madame Bovary* that time is made of fluids (water, sweat, blood, saliva) that flow away drop by drop. Thus, when the month of September "drips away," time dissolves and, like drops of rain, slips through Emma's fingers instead of being counted on them. After this line, time becomes irrevocably detached from both her experience and her body.

Emma's fall out of time is depicted as a fall from grace. When she is not invited to return to the ball, Emma's faith in the redemptive temporality of an event is shattered. And, as Flaubert rather rigorously demonstrates, to lose faith in time's capacity to contain an event is tantamount to losing faith in God, life, and the future. The future becomes lost, and the past is unattainable. From the moment (which is not a moment) when days lose their numerability, Emma's days are effectively numbered. At first she encounters her days as if they are traumatic "shocks" ("elle écoutait tous les bruits, se levait en sursaut, s'étonnait qu'il ne vînt pas") and then falls out of them before they are over: "puis, au coucher du soleil, toujours plus triste, désirait être au lendemain." By the end of the passage, the unit of time normally called "day" has become entirely meaningless. In this context, the Alcoholics Anonymous refrain "one day at a time" rings like a perverse inverted echo of Emma's malady and reminds us, once again, how addiction can be read through its temporal disorders. For the alcoholic, the phrase "one day at a time" functions in a dual fashion—it both reminds the addict that time *exists* and attempts to allow him or her a way of breaking time down into meaningful units.

But unlike the alcoholic, not only is there no twelve-step program to address Emma's predicament, but also the fluid substance that she abuses is not alcohol but time itself. Through the representations of time as well as the verbal time (tenses) of representation in the above passage, we can already read Emma's free-fall into the addictive temporality that leads inevitably to her death and dissolution.

Emma's exposure to the corrosive fluidity of time in the passage of "lost days" reminds us that Flaubert uses the rhythmic sound of water dripping "goutte par goutte" ("drop by drop") as the novel's temporal measure from the famous moment that melting snow first falls on Emma's umbrella during her early courtship with Charles:

> L'ombrelle, de soie gorge-de-pigeon, que traversait le soleil, éclairait de reflets mobiles la peau blanche de sa figure. Elle souriait là-dessous à la chaleur tiède; et on entendait les gouttes d'eau, une à une, tomber sur la moire tendue.[28]

> The parasol, made of an iridescent silk that let the sunlight sift through, colored the white skin of her face with shifting reflections. Beneath it, she smiled at the gentle warmth; and one heard the drops of water, one by one, fall on the taut silk.[29]

But by the time we reach the passage of lost days, Emma's body is no longer granted the symbolic protection implied by the presence of a parasol. From this point on, when water falls, drop by drop, it gradually eats away at Emma's capacity either to conserve time or to be protected from its erosion.[30] Although I do not have the time to develop this point here, I would like to point out that this liquefied time seeps into the very foundations of the novel. At every structural and metaphorical level, *Madame Bovary* relies heavily upon architectural figures. The novel's narrative is constructed on a foundation of literal or metaphorical edifices (from the bizarre "pièces monées" of Charles's hat and the infamous wedding cake to the elaborate structural blueprints that accompany most of the descriptions of houses, churches, statuettes, and factories) that become inundated by the increasingly corrosive presence of watery time.

But the beginning of Emma's ultimate dissolution can be traced in her inability to metabolize time through her body. In the verbal vertigos of the passage of lost days, we can already read the first unmistakable signs of what will later blossom into a full-blown addiction—an addiction that I am choosing to call "temoral bulimia." There is a direct correlation between Emma's anorectic refusal to eat and her numerous bulimic attempts to devour time. Unlike Charles, who consumes time as effectively as he eats dinner ("[il]s'en allait, ruminant son bonheur, comme ceux qui mâchent encore, après diner, le goût des truffes qu'ils digèrent"[31] / "[he] . . . went on, re-chewing his happiness, like those who after dinner taste again the truffles which they are digesting"[32]), Emma rejects food and tries to eat time instead. At the moment when she is planning to run away with Rodolphe, for example, Flaubert writes: "elle vivait comme perdue dans la dégustation anticipée de son bonheur prochain"[33] ("she was living as if lost in the anticipated taste of her future happiness" [my trans.]). But Emma never manages to digest the taste of the "future happiness" that tantalizes her. She vacillates between failed attempts to preserve time, bitter attempts to consume it, and falls into despairing acts of abjecting it.

In the context of this discussion, one might even go so far as to say that Emma is as unable to digest her own death as she is to swallow her future happiness or to assimilate her experiences into the corpus of a "life."[34] As *Bovary's* readers know well, Emma tries to kill herself by literally stuffing her face with poison: "[Elle] . . . saisit le bocal bleu, en arracha le bouchon, y fourra sa main, et la retirant pleine d'une poudre blanche, elle se mit à manger à même" ("[She] . . . seized the blue jar, tore out the cork, plunged in her hand, and withdrawing it full of white powder, she ate it greedily"[35]). As several critics have observed, Emma's attempt to swallow her own death constitutes the final term in a long series of attempted auto-ingestions and self-incorporations [see Tanner; Richard; Ronell]. Philippe Bonnefis has pointed out that while the curious expression "elle se mit à manger à même" is almost grammatically meaningless, the words "à même" function as a homophonic reversal of Emma's name and thus indicate that in the act of eating the poison, she effectively eats her own name.[36] As such, Emma feeds herself with herself in a final attempt to provide herself with a body capable of containing and retaining her experience. It is not clear whether to read this ultimate auto-cannibalistic act as Emma's attempt to feed her death with her life or as an attempt to feed her life with her death. The terrible irony of the gesture is, of course, that both acts are indistinguishable and that they both fail. Emma's death is not more containable than her life was; the suicide scene (if it actually deserves the name) is flooded with vomit. Although Emma's agony consists of constant vomiting, she manages to retain just enough poison in order to live and not quite enough in order to die convincingly.

Let us recall that Emma's vomit continues to flow even after she is dead. Although Emma presumably "dies" at the end of part 3, chapter 8, the most infamous instance of her suicidal vomit occurs posthumously. In chapter 9, Emma's body spews streams of black liquid: "il fallut soulever un peu la tête, et alors un flot de liquides noirs sortit, comme un vomissement, de sa bouche"[37] ("They had to raise the head a little, and a rush of black liquid poured from her mouth, as if she were vomiting"[38]). This powerful and strange image raises several questions concering the fate of Emma Bovary and the text in which she is written. In the first place, it would seem that Emma's body refuses to acknowledge the moment of her own death; paradoxically, her body vomits her death instead of "living" it. The temporal disjunction between the fact of her subjective death and her body's sustained mechanical expulsive activity only repeats in death the many prior instances of failed events Emma experiences in her life. Furthermore, the black liquid that oozes out of Emma's lifeless body seems to transform the death scene into a parodic inversion of a birth scene. But instead of the formless "afterbirth" that accompanies the birth of a child, Emma's posthumous peristalsis appears almost as a figure of a kind of "after-death." Here, if we recall Emma's attempts to give herself a life by confusing her own rebirth with her mother's death, we discover that Emma has no greater access to her own death than she had to her own life.

Although critics have interpreted the black liquid that flows from Emma's mouth as a figure for a writer's ink, the association between posthumous vomit and ink renders the figure even more difficult to read.[39] In other words, who is writing this scene and whose failure to live, die, or write is being expressed in it? If we follow the path indicated by feminist readings by Naomi Schor and Janet Beizer, we might conclude that Flaubert needs to abject his feminine identification with Emma by perversely transforming the formless, ineffectual vomit of her lifeless body into the formal ink of his style [see Schor: Beizer]. And although such a reading is both possible and plausible, I would like to suggest that in this monstrous moment, which couples a disgusting image of lifeless bodily expulsion with a distorted image of literary production, the corrosive liquid temporality of Emma Bovary's "life" seeps into Flaubert's narrative voice through his *style indirect libre*.

For in much the same way as Emma Bovary fails to transform her life or death into an event, the narrative voice of *Madame Bovary* displays the same strange temporal uncertainty about whether a life can be lived, whether a death constitutes an event, and whether the act of writing is an addictive response to a temporal disorder that manifests itself through failed mourning. Throughout the corpus of *Madame Bovary*, we find that the bodies that cannot digest time end up by being consumed by it. As we have seen, although Emma's life was eaten by the time she couldn't contain, her body suffers an even more horrifying fate. It vomits its own death and corrodes the lives of the surviving characters. Emma's death leaks into Charles's life; he attempts to contain her death by ordaining that she be buried in three coffins; he attempts to mourn Emma by liquidating his remaining funds in order to adorn his own body with the clothes that might have pleased her. In short, as the narrative voice makes clear, "elle le corrompait par dela la tombeau"[40] ("She corrupted him from beyond the grave"[41]). But Charles's memory, in spite of his all-consuming efforts to commemorate Emma, is ultimately subjected to the corrosive force of involuntary forgetting: "une chose étrange, c'est que Bovary, tout en pensant à Emma continuellement, l'oubliait; et il se désespérait à sentir cette image lui échapper de la mémoire au milieu des efforts qu'il faisait pour la retenir"[42] ("A strange thing was happening to Bovary; while continually thinking of Emma, he was nevertheless forgetting her. He grew desperate as he felt this image fading from his memory in spite of all efforts to retain it"[43]). Thus, Emma's posthumous existence produces in Charles the same strange combination of simultaneous preservation and erosion that permeated her living existence. Flaubert describes this uncanny temporal dysfunction in one of the most significant and signatory abject images in the entire novel. In part 2, chapter 1, Flaubert's narrative voice shifts abruptly to the present tense:

> Depuis les événements que l'on va raconter, rien, en effet, n'a changé à Yonville . . . les foetus du pharmacien, comme des paquets d'amadou blanc, se pourrissent de plus en plus dans leur alcool bourbeux, et, au-dessus de la grande porte de l'auberge, le vieux lion d'or, déteint pas les pluies, montre toujours aux passants sa frisure de caniche.[44]

> Since the events about to be narrated, nothing in fact has changed at Yonville . . . the spongy white lumps, the pharmacist's foetuses, rot more and more in their cloudy alcohol, and above the big door of the inn the golden lion, faded by rain, still shows passers-by its poodle mane.[45]

This is one of the rare moments (perhaps unique) in *Madame Bovary* where Flaubert links a future tense ("que l'on va raconter") to a past tense ("n'a changé") through a present tense ("se pourrissent"). But the temporal perversity of this passage undermines the apparent normality of its verbal structure: all of these verb tenses depict actions that take place outside of time and that refer to the monstrous nonactivities of aborted nonsubjects. Paradoxically, the very action described is one of a stasis (preservation) that is nonetheless engaged in a nonending process of erosion and decomposition. Moreover, this description of the impact of time on the fetuses in the bottles encapsulates, in miniature, the temporal structure of Emma Bovary's "life." Emma's access to "life" is as stillborn and continuously eroded as that of the bottled babies.

And, just as Homais's fetuses go on marinating in their bottles long after the events recounted in the text of *Madame Bovary* have occurred, Emma's body floats in that fluid, bitter, viscous narrative substance that has been aptly called Flaubert's *free indirect style*. But that name is far too proper, too antiseptic, for the phenomenon it purports to describe. One must not forget that when Flaubert described Homais's fetuses in their bizarre state of suspended petrification and erosion, he addresses us—his readers—directly in the narrative voice of our own time. In the strange reflexive present of the verb "se pourrissent," Flaubert announces a temporal structure of addiction that exceeds the confines of the literature of the nineteenth century and seeps into the experience of modern life. Like Emma Bovary and Homais's fetuses, addicted culture is fermented by a corrosive past that is strangely preserved without being remembered. Whether or not Flaubert ever actually said, "Madame Bovary, c'est moi," we should recall that from the novel's enigmatic first word, "nous," it is certain that Flaubert was always already writing to and about us.

NOTES

I would like to thank Claire Nouvet and Philippe Bonnefis for helping me develop the ideas presented here.

1. Adam Phillips, *On Flirtation: Essays on the Uncommitted Life*. Cambridge: Harvard University Press, 1994, p. 153.

2. Ibid., 153–154.

3. Cathy Caruth. Introduction, *Trauma: Explorations in Memory*. Baltimore: Johns Hopkins University Press, 1995, p. 3.

4. Ibid., p. 4.

5. The problem of drugs and addiction in *Madame Bovary* was first raised by Avital Ronell in *Crack Wars*. My analysis supports most of her conclusions, but is more focused on the relationship between time and addiction.

6. Riffaterre's actual argument is far more complicated. He shows that the act of reading functions as a metaphorical hinge between Romantic definitions of women and the overdetermined presuppositions of the word "adultery." He writes:

Nothing could be clearer: one word's ultimate presupposition, its etymology, entails the whole fictional text. . . . The adulteress either commits suicide or sinks into prostitution. As for the first metaphorical step, I might call it fictional without any play on words, since the errant wife is stepping out of bounds when she secretly indulges in the reading of scandalous novels and in a daydreaming identification with the women who slink about the never-neverland of wish fulfillment.

7. Victor Brombert, "Flaubert and the Status of the Subject," *Flaubert and Postmodernism*, Naomi Schor and Henry Majewski, eds., Omaha: University of Nebraska Press, 1984, p. 113.

8. The implications of this claim should be that Emma is Flaubert's mirror image—where he understands that Life should be put in the service of Art, she, by contrast, is unable to convert her life into Art. It is interesting to observe that in this context, feminist critics such as Naomi Schor and Janet Beizer establish a dichotomy between Flaubert and Emmy Bovary similar to that espoused by more traditional critics like Victor Brombert. Of course, the feminist critics diverge with traditional readings about the cause of the inverted identification between Emma and Flaubert. I am deeply indebted to both Naomi Schor's "For a Restricted Thematics: Writing, Speech and Difference in *Madame Bovary*" and Janet Beizer's chapters on Flaubert and Louise Colet in her recent book *Ventriloquized Bodies: Narratives of Hysteria in Nineteenth-Century France*. Beizer offers a brilliant and persuasive account of how Flaubert hystericizes Emma Bovary in an attempt to purge himself and his text of femininity.

9. Gustave Flaubert, *Madame Bovary*, Jacques Suffel, ed., Paris: Garnier-Flammarion, 1981, p. 69.

10. Ibid., p. 24.

11. Ibid., p. 59.

12. Ibid., p. 18.

13. I am planning to show that love becomes the privileged figure of temporal erosion in *Madame Bovary* in a forthcoming book chapter entitled "Eros, Erosion: Sentimental Liquidations in *Madame Bovary*." Both Jean-Pierre Richard and Tony Tanner pursue the implications of liquidating love.

14. *Madame Bovary*, op. cit., p. 70.

15. Ibid., p. 15.

16. Ibid., p. 251.

17. See Jean Rousset, "Madame Bovary." More recently, Peter Brooks discusses how Emma Bovary's body is systematically inserted into a visual field in "The Body in the Field of Vision."

18. Here I diverge from Jonathan Culler's oft-cited remark in *Flaubert: The Uses of Uncertainty:* "If there is anything that justifies our finding the novel limited and tendentious it is the seriousness with which Emma's corruption is attributed to novels and romances."

19. *Madame Bovary*, op. cit., p. 73.

20. *Madame Bovary,* translated by Paul De Man, ed., New York: Norton, 1965, pp. 27–28.

21. *Madame Bovary,* op. cit., p. 74

22. *Madame Bovary* (translation), op. cit., p. 28 (modified).

23. Emma does evoke her dead mother fleetingly twice: while courting Charles and in the early days of her affair with Rodolphe.

24. Curiously, the absence of this figure has rarely been addressed in the critical literature. One notable exception is Dominick LaCapra's suggestive remarks in *Madame Bovary on Trial.* LaCapra observes that "[e]qually significant for the rupture of the generational cycle is the fact that Emma's mother is dead as the story opens, and she does not seem to play a significant part in Emma's life." It is surprising to note in this context that although Avital Ronell brilliantly identifies the presence of a "toxic maternal" in *Madame Bovary,* she focuses more on Emma's toxic effect on her daughter rather than on the toxic effect of her own mother's absence [see *Crack Wars*]. Likewise, Janet Beizer stresses the importance of the repression of motherhood in the novel from the perspective of Emma as mother rather than as daughter. I think LaCapra is correct in seeing the mother's death as a temporal, generational rupture. As he puts it, "[e]conomically as well as socially, Emma has no productive or reproductive function."

25. Avital Ronell, *Crack Wars: Literature, Addiction, Mania,* Lincoln: University of Nebraska Press, 1992, pp. 119–120.

26. *Madame Bovary,* op. cit., p. 96.

27. *Madame Bovary* (translation), pp. 44–45 (trans. modified).

28. *Madame Bovary,* op. cit., p. 51.

29. *Madame Bovary* (translation), p. 13 (trans. modified).

30. For extremely useful discussions of the importance of fluids in *Madame Bovary* see Jean-Pierre Richard and Janet Beizer. I particularly admire Beizer's conclusion to her chapter "Writing with a Vengeance" : "He chose his poison: it was water. Playing with madness like Mithridates with poison, he volatized the water, the emotional effusion, the rush of ink, the romantic flow. Poisoning himself gently in measured doses, he turned liquid to vapor and cured his style; he vaporized hysteria and hysterized the text."

31. *Madame Bovary,* op. cit., p. 68.

32. *Madame Bovary* (translation), p. 24.

33. *Madame Bovary,* op. cit., p. 22.

34. As Jean-Pierre Richard puts it: ". . . c'est l'un des aspects de la maladie bovaryste que ce manque fondamentale de retenue. . . . Emma se jetta goulûment

sur toutes les proies: en voulant tout immédiatement consommer, elle ne peut rien retenir. Tout l'abandonne, et ses expériences l'appauvrissent au lieu de l'enrichir" ("This fundamental lack of reserve is one of the traits of the Bovary illness. . . . Emma pounces greedily on her prey: but by wanting to consume everything immediately, she can retain nothing. Everything abandons her, and her experiences impoverish her instead of enriching her" [my trans.]).

35. *Madame Bovary,* op. cit., p. 229.

36. Phillipe Bonnefis made this observation in a conversation with me.

37. *Madame Bovary,* op. cit., p. 349.

38. *Madame Bovary* (translation), p. 242.

39. See, for example, Nathaniel Wing, who writes: "Throughout the novel desire, narrative and writing in general produce corrosive effects. These are figured most directly and powerfully, perhaps, during Emma's agony, with the likening of the taste of poison to the taste of ink, and later in the same sequence when the narrator describes a certain black fluid oozing from Emma's mouth."

40. *Madame Bovary,* op. cit., p. 360.

41. *Madame Bovary* (translation), p. 250.

42. *Madame Bovary,* op. cit., p. 363.

43. *Madame Bovary* (translation), p. 252.

44. *Madame Bovary,* op. cit., p. 108.

45. *Madame Bovary* (translation), pp. 51–52.

WORKS CITED

Baudelaire, Charles. "L'horloge." *Les fleurs du mal. Oeuvres complètes.* Claude Pichois, ed., Paris: Gallimard, 1975, 1:81.

Beizer, Janet. *Ventriloquized Bodies: Narratives of Hysteria in Nineteenth-Century France.* Ithaca: Cornell University Press, 1994.

Brombert, Victor. "Flaubert and the Status of the Subject," *Flaubert and Postmodernism.* Naomi Schor and Henry Majewski, eds., Omaha: University of Nebraska Press, 1984, pp. 100–115.

Brooks, Peter. "The Body in the Field of Vision." *Body Work: Objects of Desire in Modern Narrative.* Cambridge: Harvard University Press, 1993, pp. 88–122.

Caruth, Cathy. Introduction. *Trauma: Explorations in Memory.* Baltimore: Johns Hopkins University Press, 1995, pp. 3–12.

Culler, Jonathan. *Flaubert: The Uses of Uncertainty.* Ithaca: Cornell University Press, 1974.

Flaubert, Gustave. *Madame Bovary.* Ed. Jacques Suffel. Paris: Garnier-Flammarion, 1979. Trans of *Madame Bovary,* translated by Paul De Man, ed., New York: Norton, 1965.

LaCapra, Dominick. *Madame Bovary on Trial.* Ithaca: Cornell University Press, 1982.

Phillips, Adam. *On Flirtation: Essays on the Uncommitted Life.* Cambridge: Harvard University Press, 1994.

Richard, Jean-Pierre. *Littérature et sensation: Stendhal, Flaubert.* Paris: Seuil, 1954, pp. 135–252.

Riffaterre, Michael. "Flaubert's Presuppositions." *Flaubert and Postmodernism.* Naomi Schor and Henry Majewski, eds., Omaha: University of Nebraska Press, 1984, pp. 177–191.

Ronell, Avital. *Crack Wars: Literature, Addiction, Mania.* Lincoln: University of Nebraska Press, 1992.

Rousset, Jean. "Madame Bovary ou le livre sur rien." *Forme et signification: Essais sur les structures littéraires de Corneille à Claudel.* Paris: José Corti, 1984, pp. 109–133.

Schor, Naomi. "For a Restricted Thematics: Writing, Speech and Difference in *Madame Bovary.*" *Breaking the Chain: Women, Theory, and French Realist Fiction.* New York: Columbia University Press, 1985, pp. 3–28.

Tanner, Tony. *Adultery in the Novel: Contract and Transgression.* Baltimore: Johns Hopkins University Press, 1979.

Wing, Nathaniel. "Emma's Stories: Narrative, Repetition and Desire in *Madame Bovary.*" *Emma Bovary.* Harold Bloom, ed., New York: Chelsea House, 1994, pp. 133–164.

Chapter Seven

BAUDELAIRE, ARTAUD, AND THE AESTHETICS OF INTOXICATION

ALLEN S. WEISS

It is time to get intoxicated! So as not to be the martyrized slaves of Time, ceaselessly intoxicate yourselves! With wine, with poetry, or with virtue, as you wish.

—Charles Baudelaire, *Petits poèmes en prose*

IN VINO VERITAS

In *The Physiology of Taste,* one of the foundational texts of modern French gastronomy, Jean-Anthelme Brillat-Savarin paradoxically proclaims both that, "cuisine is the most ancient art," and "Gasterea is the tenth muse: she presides over the joys of taste."[1] Whether this apparent contradiction reveals an ambiguity in Carême's mind regarding the aesthetic status of cuisine, or a verity about its newfound status, it occurs at an historic juncture that was to mark the origins of modern French haute cuisine. It should be noted that one of the first references (simile aside) in France to cuisine as art is to be found in the 1793 preface, written by two Jesuits, Guillaume-Hyacinthe Bougeant and Pierre Brumoy, to a reprint of the classic cookbook, *Dons de Comus:* "Cuisine, like all the other Arts invented out of need or pleasure, was perfected through the Genius of the people, and it has become more delicate to the extent that is has been refined. In the civilized Nations, the progress of cuisine followed that of all the other arts."² It is not by chance that these words were penned at the moment that the Terror, despite itself, created the preconditions for a new cuisine, as the great chefs of the Ancien Régime, dispossessed by the Revolution, began to find new sources of income and creativity. The restaurant was born, and it is here that the history of modem French cuisine begins. Simultaneously, a new literary genre emerged, that of gastronomic writing, inaugurated by Grimod de la Reynière's *Almanach des gourmands* (1803) and Manuel des Amphitryons (1808). As Jean-Claude Bonnet explains, "More than providing culinary information, Grimod applied himself to creating a culinary style that associated gastronomy and writing. This gourmet literature comprises a literary genre, perverse writing, and a staging of the artist, for according to Grimod, the gourmet is simultaneously a scholar, a libertine, and an aesthete."³ This mélange of scholarship, libertinage, and culinary aestheticism established a gastronomic imperative, for even if, as Bonnet rightly suggests, "the sexual metaphor is a semantic operative" in Grimod, and even if "Grimod realizes all the possible commutations between the erotic and the gastronomic,"⁴ a certain psychological equilibrium is necessary for all three aspects of the gastronomic art to function properly. Drunken debauchery is excluded, for it would obviate the scholarly, literary, and aesthetic aspects of the experience. All possible sexual hypocrisy aside (something certainly shared by Grimod and his friend and eating companion, the journalist and author Restif de la Bretonne, among many other writers of the epoch). Grimod was to codify, in the *Manuel des Amphitryons,* the "elements of politesse" that would guide the emerging bourgeoisie in its table manners and culinary experiences. Note the "eight qualities indispensable in the formation of a fine Amphitryon: fortune, taste, an inner sense of good food, a penchant for munificence, love of order, gracious manners, amenity of heart, and attractiveness of spirit."⁵ From these qualities would be derived a specific code of civility at table, one that would regulate very specific means of serving and tasting wine. Needless to say, this was not a discourse of drunkenness, excess, and transgression, but of appreciation, moderation, and conviviality.

Brillat-Savarin's *Physiology of Taste* the most influential book in the French gastronomic tradition, prolongs this praise of civility and politesse. One of the aphorisms that opens the book sums up his position: "Whoever causes himself indigestion or drunkenness does not know how to eat or drink."⁶ Indeed, Brillat-Savarin distinguishes the pleasures of eating as such from the pleasures of the table: while the former entail the satiety of the sensual, animal part of man, the latter constitute a civilized experience, that of "considered sensation" [sensation réfléchie].[7] In his introduction to Physiology of Taste, Roland Barthes explains how for Brillat-Savarin gastronomic pleasure (a new form of hedonism) is overdetermined, stemming from several causes organized according to a system of conviviality (a new form of reunion), at the core of which exists, "communication as a pleasure [jouissance]—and not as a function."[8] Culinary pleasure is not mere excitation, but, as Grimod insisted, taste reflected and shaped by culture and ensconced in conversation and writing. As such, for Brillat-Savarin wine has no particular gastronomic privilege, much less an intoxicating role; it is an integral part of the meal, yet should in no way lead to ecstasy or paroxysm. Rather, it has the function of rendering the body "brilliant," an amplification of the conviviality and sociability that establishes the coherence of the group dining at table, consequently ameliorating conversation, the very basis of the gastronomic genre. Barthes continues his analysis by explaining that "Conversation (among several) is, as it were, the law that saves culinary pleasure from all psychotic risk and keeps the gourmet in a 'healthy' rationality: by speaking, by chatting while he eats, the guest confirms his ego and protects himself from all subjective dispersion, through the imaginary discourse."[9] Wine, in this scenario, is a conductor of reasoned conversation; its role is not that of an intoxicant, but of an "antidrug."

It is no wonder that Baudelaire begins Artificial Paradises with a scathing critique of Brillat-Savarin—whom he characterizes, following the pastry named after him, as an "insipid brioche"[10]—noting that other than the meager information that Noah is known as the inventor of wine and that wine is a liqueur, nothing else whatsoever is to be found on the topic in Physiology of Taste. For Baudelaire, to the contrary, as Barthes states, "wine is remembrance and forgetting, joy and melancholy; it is what permits the subject to be transported outside of himself, to make the consistency of his ego cede in favor of strange, foreign and uprooted states; it is the path of deviance; in short, it is a drug."[11] As was already apparent in "Le vin," a section of Les fleurs du mal, intoxication through wine is acknowledged as a savior of modern man, as is evident in this citation from Artificial Paradises: "The profound joys of wine, who amongst you has not known them? Whosoever has had a remorse to appease, a memory to evoke, a pain to drown, a chateau in Spain to build, you have all finally invoked it, mysterious god hidden in the fibers of the vine. How great are the spectacles of wine, illuminated by the inner sun! How true and burning is that second youth that man draws from it! But also how formidable are its overwhelming delights and its enervating enchantments."[12] Indeed, for Baudelaire, intoxication entailed a corporeal sublime, where "we flutter towards infinity";[13] drunkenness leads to the "hypersublime."[14]

And yet Baudelaire's was not an unconditional valorization of intoxication: to the salutary effects of wine he opposed the destructive effects of hashish and opium; though the latter two also permit the indulgence for the "taste for infinity," he argues that, "Wine exalts the will, hashish annihilates it. Wine is a psychic support, hashish is a weapon for suicide. Wine renders one pleasant and sociable. Hashish isolates.[. . .] What use is it, in fact, to work, labor, write, produce anything whatsoever, when one can find paradise in an instant? [. . .] Wine is useful, it produces fruitful results. Hashish is useless and dangerous."[15] Both hashish and opium create an "artificial ideal," a dream-like state, subjugating the will and diminishing freedom, in a joy that is none other than a solipsistic aggrandizement of the self, a vain "enlarging mirror"[16] that creates the illusion of the self as a "man-god."[17] Such intoxication is a fruitless, suicidal addiction in which the subject "rushes, from day to day, towards the luminous abyss where he admires his face of Narcissus."[18]

In all these states of intoxication, whether inspiring or stultifying, spectacle is reduced to illusion or delusion, in what is not quite a conceptual theater, but rather a purely sensual stagecraft. Such ironic, modernist events create the immediate yet ephemeral inscription of sensation directly on the "inner theater" of the body, an iconoclastic technique of theaterless theater which effects a countermemory, counterspectacle, and countersymbolic. This technique is coherent with physiological experimentation and theorization of the nineteenth century, which understood perception to be possible in a nonreferential manner. Such was demonstrated by experiments proving that impressions of light and sound may be produced without any visual stimuli whatsoever, by mechanical, electrical, or chemical means.[19] To seek the aesthetic limits of such techniques would be to theorize not the sublime but the countersublime, where temporality is constituted by a reflexively closed in upon physiological rhythm and thresholds; where consciousness, subsumed by pure presence, eschews all transcendence; where the imagination exists in direct proportion to somatization; and where, purged of language, the symbolic code is abolished. Narration is obliterated, time nullified, and the psychic mechanism thrust into a solipsism rivaling that of the mystics, inaugurating the oxymoron of an innate apocalyptic sublime. In Baudelaire's utopia of an "artificial paradise," the Romantic sensibility merges with a nascent scientific positivism to indicate a major trajectory of modernist aesthetics.

This interiorization of perception, the Romantic implosion of the senses into a unified source of creative intuition (aided by sundry modes of intoxication), was exemplified by the contemporary disintegration of the division between senses, genres, and arts: Wagner's operatic *Gesamtkunstwerk* was the culmination of the genre of the total work, of art, Baudelaire's notion of "correspondences," inspired by Wagner, offered a new aesthetic paradigm: ". . . the *imagination* is the most *scientific* of the faculties, because it alone understands *universal analogy,* or what a mystical religion terms the correspondence";[20] investigations of synaesthesia abounded in the scientific literature; and the ancient encyclopedic literary genre, that literary form that includes all forrns already reconceived by Romantic theorization, found new life.

This aesthetic celebration of intoxication and the subsequent inmixing of the senses would find its major poetic statement, after Baudelaire, in Rimbaud's famed statement that in order to be a poet, one must, "arrive at the unknown through the disordering of *all the senses.*"[21] Parallely, the ultimate metaphysical justification of intoxication was expressed in Nietzsche's theory of the psychology of the artist in the comparison between the form giving Apollonian and the energy providing Dionysian aspects of the soul: "If there is to be art, if there is to be any aesthetic doing and seeing, one physiological condition is indispensable: frenzy. Frenzy must first have enhanced the excitability of the whole machine."[22] Though sexual frenzy is given ontological preference, all sorts of frenzy are appropriate to this end, including that of feasts and narcotics. The goal is the enrichment of the world out of one's own fullness, the idealization and perfection of existence, the transformation of the self into a work, of art, and the overcoming of Time and its inexorable restrictions.

But this aesthetic utopia had its dystopic side, one which was soon to appear at the core of modernist aesthetics, in the writings and life of Antonin Artaud. For Artaud, in the extreme corporeal desublimation manifested in his writings and his psychopathology, would effect the inversion and demonization of infinity in an aesthetics of pain and delirium. This implosion of the sublime would entail a stylistic fragmentation and heterogeneity that made the *Gesamtkunswerk* obsolete, and create a torment so intense that no intoxication would suffice as a cure.

MANIFESTO AGAINST THE ELECTRIC DRUG

State of nerves, states of mind, state of the world. There are moments when the universe seems to resemble most closely a scalp quivering with electric jolts.

—Antonin Artaud, *Lettres à Génica Athanasiou*

"... the liver is the filter of the unconscious, while the spleen is the physical guarantor of the infinite."[23] Flesh has never been as tormented, a soul has never been as bewitched, a voice has never been so threatened. Addicted to opiates early in life, Artaud's liver and spleen were both saturated with an artificial paradise, much more so than his spirit was enamoured of Baudelaire. The unconscious was skewed, infinity foreshortened, nerves frayed. "Imagine that I now physically feel the passage of this volition, imagine that it jolts me with a sudden and unexpected electric shock, a repeated electric shock" (I*, 43). Only by overcoming the difference between force and form—the very rupture at the base of metaphysics—can the essence of life be attained, that "fragile and fluctuating core untouched by forms (IV, 18). Here the myth of force takes on a twentieth-century dimension: the dynamo and the virgin vie for contact with a nervous system that constitutes the soul.

The soul is something of the body; God is the manifestation of organic secretions; grammatical reflexivity returns speech to its corporeal origins; thought is shaken to its core by a foreign volition, by "sudden and unforeseen electricity" (1*, 43). Theater, the theater of cruelty, will touch the marrow, or it shall no longer exist. Theater as surgery (II, 22). "The theater is an exorcism, a summoning of energy [. . .] it must abandon individual psychology, enter into mass passions, into the conditions of the collective spirit, grasp the collective wavelengths . . ." (V, 153). Theater as paroxysm. Indeed, a lifetime of opiates (and their moralistic pharmacological inversion, bismuth cures) hardly sufficed; a certain homeopathy, a curative magic, was necessary. Perhaps the theater would reach deeper, "like a bath of psychic electricity in which the intellect would be periodically reimmersed" (IV, 321).

Obsessed by the idea of Mexico, a Baroque Mexico, volcanic earth, Indian blood, magical realities, chimerical visions, a culture of fire, of the sun. An ancient solar culture founded on the supremacy of death, where destruction is a precondition of rebirth and transformation (VIII, 269). Everything already Weratic, already cruel. Such is the immemorial Indian culture that burns organisms, boils the blood, irrigates the nerves: "The civilization of Mexico lives on a nightmare of organs" (VIII, 159), writes Artaud, echoing "the limbo of a nightmare of bones and muscles" (I*, 117), which characterized his own existence in *Fragments of a Diary From Hell* (1926). Even before his departure, Artaud's Mexico was bound by the clichés of his own partially ecstatic, partially pathological, partially visionary phantasms. This inner Mexico was a fertile nervous illumination or stimulation, strangely resembling Artaud's impossible theater of cruelty. It was in the land of the Tarahumaras that Artaud discovered, or intuited, a scenario that coincided with his desires: the rite of Tutuguri. To reach this land, Artaud—having discarded the last of his opiates, thus being without narcotics for the first time in 17 years—traversed a forest of signs, bewitched. The mountains revealed hallucinated figures of men tortured by gods, amongst which nature capriciously disclosed the image of a nude man nailed to the rocks and tortured under a volatilized sun: Artaud crucified at Golgotha (IX, 219), Artaud burnt at the stake (IX, 62). Beside every road sprouted a burnt tree in the form of a cross or of strange beings, signs that he was approaching his goal (IX, 44–47).

Artaud habitualiy inscribed his name, emblem of his life, into his works: in *The Theater and Its Double* the ship that bore the plague to Marseille was named the "Grand-Saint-Antoine" (IV, 20): in *Suppôts et Suppliciations* the nomination is disarticulated: "AR-TAU, where they always wanted to see the designation of a dark force, but never that of an individual" (XIV**, 147). Artaud's autobiography is an account of various transpositions of the personal into the sacred, across time and space: God is transformed into paranoid torments and psychic catastrophes, where God and the Devil are one, and where Tutuguri is confused with Christ (LX, 103ff); here, the ultimate desire is to void the unconscious of the God that perpetually and monomaniacally tormented him.

Tarahumaras. Tutuguri. Ciguri. Were these names, for Artaud, any less rich than the glossolalia that punctuated his years of madness and his last writings (XII, 13)?

> o dedi
> a dada orzoura
> o dou zoura
> a dada sIdzi
>
> o kaya
> o kaya pontoura
> o ponoura
> o pena
> poni

In *The Theater and Its Double,* Artaud insisted that the theater of cruelty must function as a sort of curative magic, where language would be manifested in the form of incantation (IV, 56). In Mexico he sought one of the last places on earth where the curative peyote dance still existed, a festival that would liberate his body and illuminate his inner landscape. To reach the land of the Tarahumaras, Artaud experienced 28 days of arduous and hallucinatory journey, symptoms of drug withdrawal, psychic turbulence, vast expectations: he was reduced to "a heap of poorly assembled organs" (IX, 50).

His trajectory led him through a Tarahumara village dominated by giant decorated phalli (IX, 125), which could not but cause him to recollect his own tale of that other solar God, Heliogabalus, and of the colossal 10-ton stone phallus that preceded this emperor's triumphal march into Rome. The sun is the most generalized manifestation of energy, of force contra form, a sign of eternity, of God. Artaud would write in *Heliogabalus* of this Emperor-God as, ". . . son of the summits, false Antonin, Sardanapalus, and finally Heliogabalus, a name that seems to be the auspicious grammatical contraction of the highest denominations of the sun" (VII, 14). Antonin Artaud would inscribe his name in this solar theology, celebrating the false Antonin as a Sun-God who is the very principal of anarchy, the breath of chaos itself, a breath which would pierce the body and excite the nerves. "The erectile member is the sun, the cone of reproduction on earth, as Heliogabalus, sun of the earth, is the cone of reproduction in the heavens" (VII, 81). *Heliogabalus* begins: "Just as there was an intense circulation of blood and excrement around Heliogabalus's corpse, dead without a tomb, his throat cut by his own police in the latrines of his palace, there was around his cradle an intense circulation of sperm" (VII, 13). This scatological characterization is later echoed in *The Tarahumaras,* where the sorcerer speaking of the Ciguri explains that the realm of appearances presents itself as, "the obscene mask of he who sneers between sperm and caca" (IX, 31).

Artaud finally participated in the Rite of Ciguri, the Rite of Tutuguri, lead by the Priests of the Sun acting as manifestations of the Word of God. (This heretical, abject Catholicism existed in both the Tarahumara–Catholic syncretism and the inner schismatism of Artaud's phantasms.) Ciguri isn't simply peyote, but rather the god himself who enters one's nerves; Ciguri is infinity (IX, 24). The therapeutic action of this remedy depends on the total pillaging of our organism: Ciguri is man himself assassinated by God (IX, 27). This devastating metaphysical homeopathy is desublimated by Artaud into anticultural poetics (VIII, 267).

The ritual dance takes place on sacred ground: a pyre surrounded by a circle traced on the ground, upon which are ranged 10 crosses of unequal height, each bearing a mirror. As the sun sets, the sorcerers enter the circle and dance, possessed, as if epileptic, chanting, whirling, their heads deformed by the mirrors, swelling and disappearing in the flames of the pyre (IX, 60), as in *The Theater and Its Double,* where, to counter the aesthetic fascination with forms, actors must become as "victims burnt at the stake, signalling through the flames" (IV, 18). But the truth of the rite is not expressed by external forms; rather, an inner transformation, aided by the psychopharmaceutical effects of peyote, changes consciousness, activating the Marvelous, the Fantastic, and producing visions of God. "What emerged from my spleen or from my liver had the form of the letters of a very ancient and mysterious alphabet masticated by an enormous mouth, yet horrendously choked, proud, illegible, jealous of its invisibility . . ." (IX, 32–33). The incantations of the Tarahumaras and the glossolalia of Artaud's madness merged and were hypostatized (IX, 117).

> rai da kanka da kum
> a kum da na kum vönoh

But this vision was followed by another, in which the spleen was transformed into an immense emptiness, an oceanic void upon which a fire-sprouting root was stranded. This was the root of the peyote plant, the root of Ciguri, made one with self and world. The unconscious is a language; the cosmos is nothingness. As things returned to normal, Artaud didn't know whether it was he himself or the world that had fainted. Regardless, he had seen the spirit of Tutuguri.

His written reflexions on these visions end proleptically with the admission of yet other, false and excruciating perceptions and sensations which he suffered while incarcerated in the psychiatric hospital of Rodez during the summer of 1943, the very year in which this chapter of *The Tarahumaras* was written. They bespeak the electroshock treatment that he endured there. He saw himself encircled by demons, which he tried to fend off by making the sign of the cross, or by written and chanted incantations. "I also wrote, on any available scrap of paper or on the books I had in my possession, conjurations which had little value either from a literary or a magical point of view, since things written in this state are no more than the residue, the deformation or rather the counterfeiting of the lofty lights of LIFE" (IX, 35–36). Insisting that Lewis Carroll's poem "Jabberwocky" was in fact a plagiarism of one of his own long-lost works entitled *Letura dEprahi Falli Tetar Fendi Photia o Fotre Indi,* he offered his publisher (in a letter from Rodez, 1945) the following sample of how a translation of the former should appear (IX, 188):

> ratara ratara ratara
> atara tatara rana
>
> otara otara katara
> otara ratara kana

ortura ortura konara
kokona kokona koma

kurbura kurbura k-urbura
kurbata kurbata keyna

pesti anti pestantum putara
pest anti pestantum putra

A curse upon the rotten plague, a curse upon medically inflicted comas, a curse upon his wretched, shocked body. As with the Rite of Ciguri, religious mania manifested itself as a struggle, one now magnified by paranoid deliria, a paranoia based in part on what he suffered at the hands of his doctors.

In a postscript, we are informed that he wrote "The Rite of Peyote" in a state of religious conversion, after having swallowed between 150 and 200 hosts. No longer a theological homeopathy, this eucharistic overdose was part of a christological delirium, now syncretized, briefly, with Tarahumara theology. Yet Artaud seems to have ultimately won his struggle with God at Rodez: his vehement imprecations against his baptism bespeak, a break with God and his angelic, diabolic and priestly minions. He also informs us in this postscript that, "there is nothing more erotically pornographic than the christ, ignoble sexual concretisation of all false psychic enigmas," concluding that his "basest acts of masturbatory magic engage the electric prison release" (IX, 40).

Laudenum, bismuth, peyote, eucharistic wafers: at Rodez a new drug was utilized, the electric drug. Electroshock therapy—which in the then current form passes a 200-volt current of between 5 and 250 milliamperes through the body for between a tenth and a half second—often caused violent epileptoid seizures and a consequent coma, occasionally resulting in loss of memory of the shock itself. This procedure was conceived by Hugo Cerletti in 1938, after having visited the abattoirs of Rome, where the animals were put in a state of shock before being slaughtered. Artaud suffered this avant-garde cure which caused both real and symbolic wounds, resulting in what he protested as being an "artificial death" (XII, 60). As Artaud declaims in "Alienation and Black Magic" (broadcast over French radio in July 1946, just after his release from Rodez), psychiatric hospitals are repositories of black magic, a magic based on modern therapeutic techniques such as insulin shock and electroshock, which he renames BARDO. "Bardo is the death throes that reduce the self to a puddle" (XII, 58). Such "electrical introspection," he explains, is akin to "the spitting of the stalk" *(le crachat de la râpe)*, part of the Tarahumara rituals. Like the Rite of Ciguri, there are theological consequences: electroshock "kills Artaud and makes God return" (XX, 53). Thus it is appropriate that "The Rite of Peyote" ends with a discussion of electroshock, and conversely that his last works evoke Mexico. "Alienation and Black Magic" concludes (XII, 60):

> farfadi
> ta azor
> tau ela
> auela
> a
> tara
> ila

It, too, is followed by a postscript, written just a month before his death, indicating that a blank page should be placed between the text and all the squirmings of Bardo which appear in the limbo of electroshock. In this purgatory, this borderland of lost souls, a special typography should be used to heighten certain verbal effects, specifically in order "to abject god" (XII, 61).

One of the texts that was to have been part of Artaud's radiophonic broadcast *To Have Done With the Judgement of God* (1948) was entitled "The Theater of Cruelty." It opens with the greatest scatological abjecting of God: "Do you know of anything more outrageously fecal than the history of god and of his being: SATAN . . ." (XIII, 107). Earlier in this work, in the section entitled "In Search of Fecality," he insists that man has sacrificed his blood because he desires shit (XIII, 84):

> o reche modo
> to edire
> di za
> tau dari
> do padera coco

In yet another section of this work, "Tutuguri: Rite of the Black Sun," the earlier Christian–Tarahumara syncretism is reversed and abolished, in the desire to have done with the judgment of god. Writing anew of the Rite of Ciguri, Artaud exclaims: "The major tone of the Rite is precisely THE ABOLITION OF THE CROSS" (XIII, 79). This first version of Artaud's "Tutuguri" was followed by a second, completed two weeks before his death. It begins: "Created for the external glory of the sun, *Tutuguri* is a black rite. The rite of the black night and of the *eternal* death of the sun. No, the sun shall no longer return . . ." (IX, 70). This apocalyptic text was a return to Mexico, now and always the phantasmatic projection of an inner conflict. In "The Theater of Cruelty," the guiding metaphor is no longer the sun: "The human body is an electric battery whose discharges have been castrated and repressed, whose capacities and emphases have been oriented toward sexual life, while in fact it was created precisely in order to absorb, by its voltaic displacements, all the stray reserves of the infinite void . . ." (XIII, 108).

To Have Done With the Judgement of God was to have been Artaud's major radiophonic work, if its broadcast had not been suppressed at the last moment, due to its scandalous, blasphemous nature. Artaud (who apparently played Fantômas on the radio earlier in his life) risked his final work on the transmitting capabilities of modern media. Radio, like the plague, would directly attack the nervous system of the socius. Yet there were also inner psychic risks. Perhaps he realized the futility, or at least the unwieldlyness, of the thousands upon thousands of pages of diaries he wrote at Rodez and Paris; perhaps he thought that their essence could be condensed into a single recording, which could then be played back at will, even during sleep, so that his deliria would then reenter consciousness, transformed into the crystalline Apollonian coldness of dreams. . . .

The spoken words of one's own voice resonate through the entire body before ever reentering through the ears. One lives one's own voice as a simultaneous density of bodily overtones, with the tonal center consisting of a vibratory resonance between the pitch of the body and the echos of speech recircuited and returned by the world. The recorded voice, the phonographic voice, the radiophonic voice, the played back voice of one's own enunciations creates a certain disquietude, for this voice arrives from without minus its usual corporeal thickness. The enunciatory mechanism entails a structural solipsism, a sort of psychosis, regulated by the corporeal parallax between speech and audition. In sound recording, the organic rhythms of the body are reified and ultimately destroyed by electromechanical reproduction, only to be returned by artificial means. Thus, sound recording produces a theft and transformation of the voice, an alienation of the self in a mind/body split, with its consequent quotient of anguish. Is such a split the hypostatization of Cartesian metaphysics or the manifestation of psychopathology? The mind is no longer neatly attached to the body by means of the pineal gland, as Descartes insisted; thought is now pandemonium (literally, the abode of all demons).

The psychiatric asylum may be deemed a representational, theatrical system, one which is particularly closed, as closed as the psychoses that breed within its confines. The asylum is thus a prosthesis of that other scene, the unconscious, always suppressed from public view. Compare the recording studio. The ontological risk of recording is evident: one's own voice is returned as the hallucinatory presence of another, or of a god, as in paranoid and religious experiences. Yet while the radio broadcasts and thus externalizes the voice, the asylum interiorizes it, causing an impacting, an agression of the voice within the body, within consciousness, within the unconscious.

Might it be supposed that, in revenge for the massive electroshock treatments he suffered, Artaud created *To Have Done With the Judgement of God* as a countershock? In electroshock therapy, the subject is wired; in radiophonic art, the subject is wireless. The dynamo replaces the virgin, electricity replaces the sun, schizophonica replaces schizophrenia, and potentially paranoid machines are directed outward to shock others, the listeners. Telephone, cinema, radio, television: parallel communication and representational systems exist as alternative prosthetic devices, lures, and prisons for our fears and passions.

We see here the paradox, and the tragedy, of *To Have Done With the Judgement of God*: this unbroadcast broadcast this antirepresentational representation, this fixed spontaneity was repressed and transfigured according to the political, historical, and technical exigencies of the radiophonic art. Did Artaud ultimately have done with the judgment of God, or did God finally prevail in the end, stealing Artaud's voice yet again, this time not to have the spirit descend into a body wracked with pain and speaking in tongues, but rather to sever voice from body, transforming the voice into an object and casting it into the world, where it was doomed to be lost on the airwaves, or in the archives? In a letter to Paule Thévenin written just before his death, Artaud explains that henceforth he will create only, for the theater, never again for the radio: "Where there is the *machine* there is always nothingness and the abyss; there exists a technical intervention that deforms and annihilates all that one has done" (XIII, 146).

Electricity had always plagued Antonin Artaud. In 1901, a year after Nietzsche's death, the 5-year-old Artaud began to suffer those terribly debilitating headaches that were to plague him for the rest of his life. He had contracted meningitis and risked imminent death. In desperation, his father attempted a therapy quite in vogue at the time: he purchased a huge machine that produced static electricity. As the air filled with ozone, electric sparks arched from its wires to an electrode attached to the young patient's head. . . .

NOTES

[Earlier versions of the second part of this text appeared as "Artaud in Mexico," *Lusitania* #4 (1993): *The Abject, America;* reprinted in Allen S. Weiss, *Perverse Desire and the Ambiguous Icon* (Albany: State University of New York Press, 1994). All translations are by the author, unless otherwise stated.]

1. Jean-Anthelme Brillat-Savarin, *Physiologie du goût* (1825; Paris: Flammarion, 1982), 251; p. 297.

2. Cited in Jean-Louis Flandrin and Massimo Montanari, eds., *Histoire de l'alimentation* (Paris: Fayard, 1996), p. 700.

3. Jean-Clause Bonnet, "Introduction" to Grimod de la Reynière, *Écrits gastronomiques* (Paris: Union Générale d'Éditions, 1978), p. 30.

4. Ibid., p. 46.

5. Grimod de la Reynière, *Manuel des Amphitryons,* in *Écrits gastronomiques,* Ibid., p. 382.

6. *Physiologie du goût,* p. 19.

7. Ibid., p. 170.

8. Roland Barthes, "Lecture de Brillat-Savarin" (1975), in *Oeuvres complètes* Vol. 3 (Paris: Le Seuil, 1995), p. 293.

9. Ibid., p. 283.

10. Charles Baudelaire, "Du vin et du hachisch" (1851), in *Paradis artificiels* (1860), in *Oeuvres complètes* (Paris: Gallimard/Pléiade, 1975), p. 378.

11. "Lecture de Brillat-Savarin," pp. 282–283.

12. Paradis artificiels, 379.

13. Ibid., p. 381.

14. Ibid., p. 383.

15. Ibid., p. 397.

16. Ibid., p. 409.

17. Ibid., p. 426.

18. Ibid., p. 440.

19. See Jonathan Crary, *Techniques of the Observer* (Cambridge, MA: MIT Press, 1992), pp. 89–92.

20. Charles Baudelaire, letter of 21 January 1856 to Toussenel, in *Oeuvres complètes,* p. 841.

21. Arthur Rimbaud, letter of 13 May 1871 to Georges Izambard, in *Poésies, Une saison en enfer, Illuminations* (Paris: Gallimard/Poésies, 1984), p. 200.

22. Friedrich Nietzsche, *Twilight of the Idols* (1888), in *The Portable Nietzsche,* translated by Walter Kaufmann (New York: Penguin, 1980), p. 518.

23. All references to Artaud are from the *Oeuvres complètes* (Paris: Gallimard, 1961–1994). References follow the citations in parenthesis, with the volume number in Roman numerals and the page number in Arabic numerals. Note that *Les Tarahumaras* consists of a heterogeneous collection of writings begun in 1936 ("La Montagne des Signes"), with several texts written during his incarceration at Rodez (notably the 1943 "Le Rite du Peyotl chez les Tarahumaras"), the last text having been written just before his death in February 1948 ("Tutuguri"). The version of "Tutuguri" that appears in *Les Tarahumaras* is the second of two, the first being part of *Pour en finir avec le jugement de dieu.* For further considerations, the best biography of Artaud to date is Camille Dumoulié, *Antonin Artaud* (Paris: Le Seuil, 1996). On Artaud's glossolalia, see Allen S. Weiss, "Psychopompomania," in *The Aesthetics of Excess* (Albany: State University of New York Press, 1989), pp. 113–134; on his radiophony, see Allen S. Weiss, "From Schizophrenia to Schizophonica," in *Phantasmic Radio* (Durham: Duke University Press, 1995), pp. 9–34.

Chapter Eight

"Junk" and the Other

Burroughs and Levinas on Drugs

JEFFREY T. NEALON

The metaphysical desire . . . desires beyond everything that can simply complete it. It is like goodness—the Desired does not fulfill it, but deepens it. . . . [Desire] nourishes itself, one might say, with its hunger.

—Emmanuel Levinas, *Totality and Infinity*

Junk yields a basic formula of "evil" virus: *The Algebra of Need*. The face of "evil" is always the face of total need. A dope fiend is a man in total need of dope. Beyond a certain frequency need knows absolutely no limit or control. . . . I never had enough junk. No one ever does.

—William Burroughs, *Naked Lunch*

"Just say no!" An odd response indeed. Say no to what or to whom? Say no to a threat, to something that will draw you too far outside yourself. Say no because you want to say yes. Say no because, somewhere outside yourself, you know that this "you" owes a debt to the yes, the openness to alterity that is foreclosed in the proper construction of subjectivity. of course, "just say no" never says no solely to a person—to a dealer or a user; rather, you "just say no" to the yes itself—a yes that is not human but is perhaps the ground of human response. This constant reminder to "just say no," then, is always haunted by a trace of the yes. As William Burroughs asks in *Naked Lunch,* "In the words of total need, '*Wouldn't you?*' Yes you would" (xi).

In *Crack Wars: Literature, Addiction, Mania,* Avital Ronell argues that the logics of drug addiction can hardly be separated from the discourse of alterity. As she writes, in the exterior or alterior space of addiction, "You find yourself incontrovertibly obligated: something occurs prior to owing, and more fundamental still than that of which any trace of empirical guilt can give an account. This relation—to whom? to what?—is no more and no less than your liability—what you owe before you think, understand, or give; that is, what you owe from the very fact that you exist" (57). Ronell is, of course, no simple apologist for a Romantic celebration of drug use; as she maintains, "it is as preposterous to be 'for' drugs as it is to take up a position 'against' drugs" (50), but it is the case that the logics of intoxication, as well as the kinds of desire that one can read in spaces of addiction, are inexorably tied up with current critical vocabularies of alterity and identity: postmodern thinkers have increasingly come to understand alterity as a debt that can never be repaid, a difference that constitutes sameness, the incontovertiblity of a continuing obligation to someone or something "other."

Of course, the leisurely space of recreational drug use most often can and does serve to produce isolated reveries that cut the subject off from alterity, and we should be careful not to conflate drug *use* with *addiction.* However, the serial iteration of episodes of intoxication—what one might clinically or etymologically call "addiction," literally being delivered over to an other—brings on another set of considerations.[1] For example, as William Burroughs characterizes the junk equation in the second epigraph, it necessarily begins in an economy of simple need over which the subject exercises a kind of determinative imperialism: junkies want to be inside, to protect and extend the privilege of the same; they want the pure, interior subjectivity of the junk stupor—with "metabolism approaching absolute ZERO" (xvii)—to keep at bay the outside, the other.

But that economy of finite need and subjective imperialism quickly shows an economy of desire, an infinite economy of "total need," which breaks the interiority of mere need. In *Naked Lunch,* Burroughs writes, in the voice of the smug, bourgeois "Opium 'Smoker,'"

How low the other junkies "whereas We—WE have this this lamp and this tent and this lamp and this tent and warm in here nice and warm nice and IN HERE and OUTSIDE ITS COLD. . . . ITS COLD OUT-SIDE where the eaters and the needle boys won't last two years not months hardly won't stumble bum around and there is no class in them. . . . But WE SIT HERE and never increase the DOSE . . . never—never increase the dose never except TONIGHT is a SPECIAL OCCASION with all the dross eaters and needle boys out there in the cold." (xlvii, ellipses in original)

Here, the junkies' increasing need for junk shows a finite economy of subjective determination turning into an infinite economy of inexorable exposure to the outside: "But WE SIT HERE and never increase the DOSE . . . never—never increase the dose never except TONIGHT." The junkies' need draws the junkies outside, despite themselves, from their warm tent to the place of "all the dross eaters and needle boys out there in the cold." According to Burroughs, the junk user, as he or she neces-sarily increases dosage, is drawn inexorably from the warm protective interior (the fulfilled need) of use to the cold exterior of addiction—the revelation of "total need" beyond any possible satisfaction. As Bur-roughs writes about his addiction, "suddenly, my habit began to jump and jump. Forty, sixty grains a day. And still it was not enough" (xiii). Addiction, it seems, inexorably mutates from a question of fulfilling need to something else: something other, finally, than a question with an answer; something other than a need that could be serviced by a person, object, or substance.

In other words, addiction takes need to the point where it is no longer thematizable as subjective lack; as need becomes addiction, the junkie is no longer within the horizon of subjective control or intention. As Burroughs contends in *Junky*, "You don't decide to be an addict. . . . Junk is not, like alcohol or weed, a means to an increased enjoyment of life. Junk is not a kick. It is a way of life" (xv–xvi). "Junk" opens onto an unrecoverable exteriority beyond need, an economy that we might call infinite or "metaphysical" desire, following Emmanuel Levinas's use of the term in the first epigraph.[2] For Levinas, the desire at play in the face-to-face encounter with the other cannot be confused with a simple need; rather, it is a *"sens unique,"* an unrecoverable movement outward, a one-way direction: a movement of the Same toward the other which never returns to the Same" ("Meaning and Sense" 91). And, as Burroughs's Sailor reminds us in *Naked Lunch*, there may be no better description of addiction: "Junk is a one-way street. No U-turn. You can't go back no more" (186). However, within Bur-roughs's exterior movement, we will have to encounter an Other other than the Levinasian widow, stranger or orphan—an other, finally, that is other to the human and the privileges of the human that the philosophical discourse of ethics, including Levinasian ethics, all too often takes for granted. An inhuman other—an other that is other even to the irreducible alterity that one encounters in the Levinasian face-to-face encounter. This chapter will try to track what happens when Levinas's humanism of the other person comes face-to-face with junk, the other of *anthropos* traced in Burroughs's "the face of 'evil' [that] is always the face of total need"?

LEVINAS IN REHAB

For Levinas, to be sure, drug intoxication is far from an experience of alterity. In fact, he maintains that "the strange place of illusion, intoxication, [and] artificial paradises" can best be understood as an attempt to withdraw from contact with and responsibility for the other: "The relaxation in intoxication is a semblance of distance and irresponsibility. it is a suppression of fraternity, or a murder of the brother" (*Otherwise* 192n/110n). According to Levinas, such intoxication brings only a greater intensification of the subject's interiority, a refusal of "fraternity" as exterior substitution for the other.

In fact, intoxication or junk addiction brings to the subject only the disappearance of the world and the concomitant submersion in the terrifying chaos of what Levinas calls the *il y a* ["there is"]—a radical givenness without direction that is similar in some ways to Sartre's experience of "nausea."[3] As Levinas describes the *il y a,* "the Being which we become aware of when the world disappears is not a person or a thing, nor the sum total of persons and things; it is the fact that one is, the fact that *there is*" (*Existence* 21/26). For Levinas, the *there is* is the indeterminate, anonymous rustling of being qua being. As Adriaan Peperzak comments in *To the Other,* the *il y a* is "an indeterminate, shapeless, colorless, chaotic, and dangerous 'rumbling and rustling.' The confrontation with its anonymous forces generates neither light nor freedom but rather terror as a loss of self-hood. Immersion in the lawless chaos of 'there is, would be equivalent to the absorption by a depersonalized realm of pure materiality" (18).

A phenomenological–methodological link between his earliest and latest texts, the *il y a* is an unsettling fellow traveler for the entirety of Levinas's career. Curiously, the *il y a* performs a kind of dual function in his texts: as Peperzak's summary makes clear, the first function is the ruining or interruption of a self that would think itself in tune with the harmonious gift of being. In the expropriating experience of the *il y a* (a "depersonalized realm of pure materiality"), being is indifferent to the subject. The *il y a* is the anonymous murmur that precedes and outlasts any particular subject. As Levinas writes, "Being is essentially alien *[étranger]* and strikes against us. We undergo its suffocating embrace like the night, but it does not respond to us" (*Existence* 23/28). So for an ethical subject to come into being at all, such a subject must not only undergo the experience of being as the *il y a*, but he or she must also go a step further and *escape* from it. As Peperzak continues, "With regard to this being, the first task and desire (of the ethical subject] is to escape or 'evade' it. The source of true light, meaning, and truth can~only be found in something 'other' than (this) Being" (18). The horror of the *il y a* finally turns the subject toward the other.

Against the Heideggerian injunction in *Being and Time* to live up to the challenge of being's gift of possibility, Levinas offers a thematization of being as radical *impossibility:* for Levinas, existence or being is the terrifying absurdity named by the *il y a,* and this indolent anonymity functions to disrupt the generosity and possibility named by Heidegger's *es gibt* ["there is" or "it gives"]. For Levinas, existence is a burden to be overcome rather than a fate to be resolutely carried out; the existent is "fatigued by the future" (*Existence* 29/39) rather than invigorated by a Heideggerian ecstacy *toward the end*" (Existence 19/20).[4] To be an ethical Heideggerian *Dasein,* one must live one's life authentically in the generous light of being's possibility, an ontological multiplicity revealed by the ownmost possibility of one's own death.[5] According to Levinas's reading of Heidegger, at its ethical best any particular *Dasein* can live *with* or *alongside* other *Dasein,* each authentically related to his or her own ownmost possibility. Ethics, if it exists at all, rests not in *Dasein*'s relation to others but in the authenticity and resoluteness of its relation to its own death as possibility—and by synecdoche, the relation to being's generosity. In Levinas's version of Heidegger, then, the relation with others is necessarily inauthentic, always subordinated to *Dasein*'s authentic relation with neutral, anonymous Being-as-possibility.[6]

For Levinas, on the other hand, if one is to be an ethical subject, he or she must *escape* the dark, anonymous rumbling of being; in order for there to be a subjectivity responsive to the other, there must be a hypostasis that lifts the subject out of its wallowing in the solipsistic raw materiality of the *il y a* out of the *there is* of anonymous being, there must rise a *here I am [me voici]* that nonetheless retains the trace of the hesitation and debt—what Levinas will call the "passivity"—

characteristic of the *il y a*'s impossibility. As he maintains, hypostasis is subject–production, the introduction of space or place into the anonymous murmur of being: "to be conscious is to be torn away from the *there is*" (*Existence* 60/98).

Subjectivity is torn away from the anonymity of the *there is* by a responding to the other that is not reducible to any simple rule-governed or universalizing code; the ethical subject is, in other words, a responding, site-specific performative that is irreducible to an ontological or transhistorical substantive. As Levinas writes,

> the body is the very advent of consciousness. It is nowise a thing—not only because a soul inhabits it, but because its being belongs to the order of events and not to that of substantives. It is not posited; it is a position. It is not situated in space given beforehand; it is the irruption in anonymous being of localization itself. . . . [The body as subjectivity] does not express an event; it is itself this event. (*E&E*, pp. 71, 72/122, 124)

This is perhaps the most concise statement of Levinas's understanding of a subjectivity that rises out of the *il y a* through hypostasis: the subject comes about through a performative response to the call of the other, through the bodily taking up of a "position," "the irruption in anonymous being of localization itself." Here the subject is brought into being through a radically specific performative event or saying; but it will be a strange "being" indeed, insofar as being is generally understood to be synonymous with a generalizable, substantive said.

Of course, the Levinasian subject is a kind of substantive; it has to have a body—a place and a voice—in order to respond concretely to the other. It cannot merely languish in and among a network of possible responses. Rather, the subject is an active, responding substantiation: ". . . it is a pure verb. . . . The function of a verb does not consist in naming, but in producing language" (*E&E*, p. 82/140). He goes on to explain:

> We are looking for the very apparition of the substantive. To designate this apparition we have taken up the term *hypostasis* which, in the history of philosophy, designated the event by which the act expressed by a verb became designated by a substantive. Hypostasis . . . signifies the suspension of the anonymous *there is*, the apparition of a private domain, of a noun [or name, *nom*]. . . . Consciousness, position, the present, the "I," are not initially—although they are finally—existents. They are events by which the unnameable verb *to be* turns into substantives. They are hypostasis. (*E&E*, pp. 82–83/140–42)

The performative hypostasis is the birth of subjectivity, but the ethical network of substitution or signification that a subject arises from—this network of performative responses that must precede, even if it is finally inadequate to, any particular response—also necessarily makes that hypostatic subject a noncoincident one, open to alterity. The subject that arises in the hypostasis is not a simple substantive or noun, even though it necessarily becomes one through a trick of syntax. As Levinas writes, "One can then not define a subject by identity, since identity covers over the event of the identification of the subject" (*E&E*, p. 87/149–50). Identity, even when all is said and done, is not something that the subject *has;* identity is, rather, the "event of the identification" that I *am,* and this "originary" hypostatic "event" is [re]enacted or traced in the subject's continuing performative responses to the call of alterity.

Hence, it is the preoriginary debt that any subject owes to this prior network of substitution-for-the-other that keeps subjectivity open, keeps the saying of performative ethical subjectivity irreducible to the simple said of ontology. Levinas will call this a network of "fraternity" or "responsibility, that is, of sociality, an order to which finite truth—being and consciousness—is subordinate" (*QTB,* p. 26/33). Sociality, as substitution of potential identities in a serial network of performative subjectivity, both makes identity and response possible and at the same time makes it impossible for any identity to remain monadic, static, and unresponsive. The subject always already responds in the movement from the anonymous "one" to the hypostatic "me"; the subject responds in the very subjection of identity, the very act of speaking.

However, this hypostasis is *not* simply or primarily the intentional act of a subject; it is, rather, subjection in and through the face-to-face encounter with the other person. As Levinas insists, "the localization of consciousness is not subjective; it is the subjectivization of the subject" (*E&E,* p. 69/118). Thus, "here I am" rises out of the *there is* as an accusative, where I am the object rather than the subject of the statement, where I am responding to a call from the face of the other. As Jan de Greef explains, "for Levinas the movement (of subjectivity] does not go from me to the other but from the other to me. . . . *Here I am (me voici)*—the unconditional of the hostage—can only be said in response to an 'appeal' or a 'preliminary citation.' Convocation precedes invocation" (166). It is to-the-other that one responds in the hypostasis that lifts the subject out of the *il y a;* the face of the other, and its call for response-as-subjection is the only thing that can break the subject's imprisonment in the anonymous *il y a* and open the space of continuing response to alterity. As Levinas sums up the project of his *Existence and Existents,* "it sets out to approach the idea of Being in general in its impersonality so as to then be able to analyze the notion of the present and of position, in which a being, a subject, an existent, arises in impersonal Being, through a hypostasis" (19/18). As the evasion of the "impersonal being" that is the *il y a*, hypostasis (as the concrete performative response to the face or voice of the other person) is the birth of the ethical Levinasian subject.

Such a subjection before the other makes or produces a subject at the same time that it unmakes any chance for that subject to remain an alienated or free monad. As Levinas argues, "The subject is inseparable from this appeal or this election, which cannot be declined" (*Otherwise* 53/68), so the subject cannot be thematized in terms of alienation from some prior state of wholeness. In Levinasian subjectivity, there is an originary interpellating appeal of expropriation, not an originary loss of the ability to appropriate. Identity and alterity, rethought as performative response, are fueled by the infinity of substitution, not by the lack and desire for reappropriation that characterizes the evacuated Lacanian subject. And this Levinasian responding signification or substitution leaves the subject inexorably responsive to the founding debt of alterity: "Signification is the one-for-the-other which characterizes an identity that does not coincide with itself" (*Otherwise* 70/89). There is, in other words, no subject unbound from other because the process of subject formation (the production of a subject) takes place in and through this common social network of iterable substitution. In the terms Levinas uses most insistently in *Otherwise than Being,* identity is a performative "saying" that is irreducible to a constantive "said." Insofar as substitution or signification literally makes and unmakes the subject in the performative project of saying "here I am," such an ethical entity—both subject of and subject to alterity—is literally otherwise than being, otherwise than an ontological, synchronic, or substantive identity.[7] The "saying" is *beyond* essence because it makes the "said" of essence possible without ever being merely reducible to it; just as infininte metaphysical desire subtends and traverses mere subjective need, the performative ethical saying is before and beyond the said.[8]

THE JUNK CON

If we return to Burroughs and the question of drugs, then, it seems fairly clear why intoxication or addiction is not akin to ethical subjectivity for Levinas: because intoxication is a wallowing in the terrifying materiality of the *il y a*'s "impersonal being," a state where the call or face of the other counts for nothing. Strictly speaking, there can be no response to alterity—no saying, substititution, or signification—from an entity immersed in anonymous being: in the *il y a,* an ethical subject has yet to arise through a hypostasis. Perhaps we could take, as a concrete example of such anonymous immersion without ethical response, Burroughs's narration of his last year of addiction in North Africa:[9]

> I lived in one room in the native quarter of Tangier. I had not taken a bath in a year nor changed my clothes or removed them except to stick a needle every hour in the fibrous grey wooden flesh of terminal addiction. . . . I did absolutely nothing. I could look at the end of my shoe for eight hours. I was only roused to action when the hourglass of junk ran out. If a friend came to visit—and they rarely did since who or what was left to visit—I sat there not caring that he had entered my field of vision—a grey screen always blanker and fainter—and not caring when he walked out of it. If he died on the spot I would have sat there looking at my shoe waiting to go through his pockets. Wouldn't you? (*Naked Lunch* xiii)

Surely this is a portrait of drug use beyond the production of pleasure or nostalgia for it; rather, this is a portrait of addiction as the horror of immersion in the *il y a,* where the addict does "absolutely nothing," save an interminable staring at anonymous objects, wallowing in a state of sheer materiality.[10]

From a Levinasian point of view, however, more disturbing than Burroughs's portrait of the "bare fact of presence" (*E&E,* p. 65/109) in the interminability of addiction is the accompanying renunciation of a relation with the other: "If a friend came to visit . . . I sat there not caring that he had entered my field of vision . . . and not caring when he walked out of it." And even more horrific than the mere ignoring of the other is the callous disregard shown by the addict for the other's very being: "If he died on the spot I would have sat there looking at my shoe waiting to go through his pockets. Wouldn't you?" There is little for any ethical system to admire in these lines, and they seem particularly to bear upon Levinas's concerns about a subjectivity for-the-other: here Burroughs's junkie is inexorably and completely for-himself; even the death of the other would not disrupt the interiority of the same. In fact, the death of the other would have meaning only insofar as it could feed the privilege of sameness—as long as the other had some cash in his or her pockets to feed the junkie's habit.

However, the approval or condemnation of such behavior is not the location of the ethical in this scene, for Levinas as well as Burroughs. That which calls for response here is, rather, Burroughs's insistent and strategically placed question, "Wouldn't you?" I would suggest that the callous disregard shown here is, on another reading, a kind of absolute exposure—an exposure more absolute and limitless than the Levinasian relations "welcoming" that it would seem one owes to the neighbor or the friend. "Wouldn't you?" calls me to nonreciprocal substitution-for-the-other, interpellates me through a saying that is irreducible to a said. Such a saying calls not for moral judgment, but for ethical response to my irreducible exposure to the other.

It is crucial, I think, to forestall any reading of Burroughs's "Wouldn't you?" that would endorse a kind of perspectival notion of alterity—where "Wouldn't you?" would be read as asking or demanding each reasonable participant in a community to see issues through the eyes of the other.[11] For Burroughs as well as Levinas, that kind of subjective imperialism is not the solution but rather the problem of control itself, what Burroughs calls "sending" as "one-way telepathic control,' (148) projected from "I" to "you." If, as Burroughs writes, "*Naked Lunch* is a blueprint, a How-To Book" (203), perhaps it calls for a kind of hesitation before the other, a responding other-wise: "How-To extend levels of experience by opening the door at the end of a long hall. . . . Doors that open only in *Silence*. . . . *Naked Lunch* demands Silence from The Reader. Otherwise he is taking his own pulse" (203, ellipses in original). Such a Burroughsian "Silence" is not a simple *lack* of response (how can one read without responding, without attention?); rather, it is the hesitation before response—an attention that does not merely project itself as the theme and center of any encounter, does not merely take its own pulse. There is, in other words, a gap or "Silence" between the other and myself, and that gap is precisely my inexorable exposure to the other—that which comes before what "I" think or IIIII do.

Indeed, in Levinasian terms the "welcoming" of the face of the other is precisely this inexorable exposure before a decision: the yes before a no (or a known), saying before a said, the openness or "sensibility" of the body-as-face that precedes any experience of knowing. These are all what Levinas calls "my preoriginary *susceptiveness*" (*Otherwise* 122/157).[12] As he elaborates, "Sensibility, all the passivity of saying, cannot be reduced to an experience that a subject would have of it, even if it makes possible such an experience. An exposure to the other, it is signification, is signification itself, the one-for-the-other to the point of substitution, but a substitution in separation, that is, responsibility" (*Otherwise* 54/70). According to Levinas, the openness to the other—sensibility, saying, signification—cannot finally be reduced to an "experience" of the other; that would be to suture a subjective void, to reduce the saying of the other to the said of the same, and to collapse the subjective "separation" necessary for Levinasian "responsibility."

The other, then, must be attended to not in terms of my experience but in terms of my substitution and separation—not in terms of my project but in terms of my subjection.

That being the case, it seems that one can frown on Burroughs's portrait of addiction as "unethical" only by reducing it to an "experience" of addiction that leads to an utter disregard for the ethics of response. But Burroughs's Levinasian insistence on the consequences of total need as absolute exposure would seem to oblige us to attend to this episode differently—not in terms of the obviously unacceptable ethical behavior represented by Burroughs's junkie, but rather in terms of the condition of absolute exposure that is prior to any ethical action: the question of substitution for-the-other. In other words, the instructive moment here is not the one in which the junkie might rummage through the dead friend's pockets, but the moment where that relation is thematized in terms of an absolute exposure that makes such an action possible, if not inexorable: "Wouldn't you?"

The desiring junkie-subject is never a "said," never a complete or alienated synchronic monad. He or she is constantly in performative process; the junkie-subject "nourishes itself, one might say, with its hunger" (*Totality* 34). The "I" that is the junkie is characterized by a "saying" that constantly keeps the junk-addled subject in touch with its subjection to the other: if the Reagan–Bush drug slogan "Just say no!" seems to put forth a certain faith in intentionality and the choosing monadic subject (when it clearly evidences the opposite), Burroughs's insistence on the junkie's question, "Wouldn't you?," inexorably directs us outside ourselves, to that somewhere between, before or beyond the same and the other. Finally, and perhaps to the chagrin of Levinas, I'd like to suggest that the radically exterior Levinasian ethical subject is always a junkie, moving constantly outside itself in the diachronic movement of desire, a responding, substitutable hostage to and for the other.

Perhaps this opens a certain moral question, but moralizing about junk can begin only when one reads the junkie's inability to "just say no" as a subjective weakness. Levinas, who clearly has no interest in such a moralizing ethics, offers us a way to read Burroughs's episode in wholly other terms. On a Levinasian reading, the problem with junk—as with the *il y a* so closely related to it—is not the absence or evasion of self or destiny; the problem is, rather, the absence or evasion of the other or response. As Levinas claims, the concept of "evasion"—so precious to those who would moralize about drugs sapping the subject's will— already presupposes an unrestrained freedom of the will: "Every idea of evasion, as every idea of malediction weighing on a destiny, already presupposes the ego constituted on the basis of the self and already free"

(*Otherwise* 195n/142n). While the antidrug crusader sees addiction as a fall from or evasion of will, Levinas asks us to read addiction as the continuation or logical extension of an almost pure imperialist will, an extension perhaps of the Nietzschean will-to-power that would rather will nothingness than not will at all.[13]

For the "just say no" moralistic version of drug rehabilitation, the dependency of the addict needs to be exposed and broken so the subject can be free again. If there were a Levinasian rehab, it might proceed in exactly the opposite way—by exposing the dream of subjective freedom as a symptom of addiction rather than a cure for it; such a "cure" might hope to produce not a sutured subject, free again to shape its own destiny, but rather "an ego awakened from its imperialist dream, its transcendental imperialism, awakened to itself, a patience as a subjection to everything" (*Otherwise* 164/209). For a Levinasian ethical subject to come into being, it is clear that "the *there is* is needed" (*Otherwise* 164/209). However, in Levinas the *there is* functions not as the drug counselor's negative portrait of an unfree self but as a kind of deliverance of the self from its dreams of subjective imperialism. Such a deliverance calls for a hypostasis that lifts the subject out of the *il y a* into responsibility, out of the interiority of self into the face-to-face as "the impossibility of slipping away, absolute susceptibility, gravity without any frivolity" (*Otherwise* 128/165).

CAN I TUG ON YOUR COAT FOR A MINUTE?

Finally, though, this leaves us with any number of unanswered questions and potentially unhappy resonances between Levinas's discourse and the moralizing ethics that he rejects. First, there is the question of will. Levinas offers an interesting rejoinder to those who would read the junkie as will-less, but when he argues that intoxication is evasion—"slipping away" from responsibility, away from a "gravity without any frivolity"—and as such is in fact an act of will, he returns full circle to a very traditional discourse on drugs, a discourse perhaps more sinister than the discourse of subjective weakness. For Levinas, it seems that intoxication is a brand of turpitude, a willful renunciation of citizenship and responsibility—"murder of the brother." Certainly, a thematization of the drug user as a passive dupe is inadequate, but Levinas's portrait of the willful druggie may prove to be even more troubling. Both thematizations seem to avoid the question of desire as it is embodied in intoxicants, in something other to or other than the human subject and its will.

This problem of the will is related to Levinas's insistence on "overcoming" or evading the *il y a*. It seems that the overcoming of the *il y a* in ethical face-to-face subjectivity is an avoidance of the very thing that interrupts and keeps open this relation without relation. In other words, Levinas's analysis seems to beg the question of how we can protect the face-to-face's authentic ethical disruption (calling the subject to respond) from the *il y a*'s seemingly inauthentic disruption (sinking the subject into anonymous fascination).

This doubling of disruptions is especially puzzling since the *il y a*—as unethical disruption—seems to be in a position of almost absolute proximity to the material network of ethical substitution out of which arises a specific "passive" ethical subjectification. As Levinas writes, "The oneself cannot form itself; it is already formed with absolute passivity. . . . The recurrence of the oneself refers to the hither side of the present in which every identity identified in the said is constituted" (*Otherwise* 104–05/132–33). This "hither side of the present" *[en deçà du présent]* is the debt that ontology owes to the undeniable proximity or approach of the other, the inexorable upshot of something on *this* side of the transcendental hinter world.[14] This transcendent (but not *transcendental*)[15] "something" on the hither side—the legacy of phenomenology in Levinas's thought—has various names in various Levinasian contexts: desire, the other, substitution, the face, the body, signification, sensibility, recurrence, saying, passivity, the one-for-the-other. This is not, as it would seem at first, a confusion on Levinas's part—an inability to keep his terminology straight. It is, rather, central to his project: signification, as substitution for the other, calls for a specific substitution or response in each situation. Just as, for example, in Derrida's work the economy of *pharmakon* is not the same as the problem of *supplément* (each is a radically specific response to a paticular textual situation), the constant shifting of terminology in Levinas is crucial to the larger "logic" of his thinking.

There remains, however, something of a "good cop, bad cop" scenario in Levinas's thematization of such a preoriginary discourse.[16] Fraternity and responsibility are the preoriginary good cop: holding me accountable to the other and the others, they function as a debt that must be returned to time and again. The *il y a*, on the other hand, is the preoriginary bad cop: exiling me to a solipsistic prison without visitors, it is a horror that must be overcome if I am to be an ethical subject. Certainly, either way there would have to be a hypostasis to bring the subject from the preoriginary network into a specific position in or at a particular site: whether thematized as benign or menacing, the preoriginary network of fraternity or the *il y a* is not itself response, even though (or more precisely *because*) it makes response possible. The response that is "saying" in Levinas is an act, first and foremost; as Jean-François Lyotard puts it in his essay on "Levinas's Logic," it is a doing before understanding (125, 152).

Levinas posits a preoriginary network—a prescriptive call before denotative understanding—to keep open the [im]possibility of further or other responses. Such a network is structurally necessary in his text to account for the subject's not coinciding with itself, but in terms other than alienation, loss or lack: Levinas's discourse can separate itself from the existentialist or psychoanalytic thematization of the other as my enemy only if there is a preoriginary expropriation, such that there can be no simple alienation as a separation or fall from wholeness. Certainly both the revelation of the trace of "fraternity" and immersion in the *il y a* perform this preoriginary function of ruining and opening out the interiority of a monadic subject. A question remains, however, concerning whether Levinas can protect his discourse of fraternity from the *il y a,* and what the consequences of such a protection might be.

Levinas's reasons for insisting on the primacy of human fraternity and contact are easy enough to understand: as we have seen, in an attempt to save something like *Mitsein* in Heidegger from the monadic interiority of *Dasein*'s fascination with "anonymous" death and being as possibility, Levinas introduces the ethical as the exterior irreducibility of human contact in the face-to-face (in *QTB,* the animated ethical "saying" that is irreducible to the neutrality of the ontological "said"). But the ethical in Levinas, we should note, also remains thematized strictly in humanist terms—the *face* and the *voice.*

Burroughs allows us to pose an essential question to Levinas: What happens when one encounters, within the world rather than in the realm of being, the "face" of the inhuman (as junk) and the "voice" that makes voice [im]possible (as an anonymous serial network of subjective substitutions)? If Levinas's problem with Heidegger is that *Dasein*'s relation with being and the other is posed in terms of *possibility* rather than *impossibility,* one has to wonder then about Levinas's own evasion of the radical impossibility named by the *il y a*—about the work done in his own discourse by the face and the voice. In other words, Levinas's posing of the other in terms of the face and the voice may surreptitiously work to evade the "experience" of the impossible that is alterity measured on other-than-human terms.

To unpack this question, we could perhaps turn back to Burroughs—specifically, his "Christ and the Museum of Extinct Species," a story that, among other things, points to the ways in which extinction haunts existents. The domination of "man" has brought about the extinction of its other—animals—but this extinction haunts "man" as "man" experiences its closure; and "man" is constantly kept in touch with the extinction of animals (with its others) by the virus of language: "What does a virus do with enemies? It turns enemies into itself. . . . Consider the history of disease: it is as old as life. Soon as something gets alive, there is something waiting to disease it. Put yourself in the virus's shoes, and wouldn't you?" (272, 268). Of course, "Wouldn't you?" is the junkie's question from *Naked Lunch,* the question of the "inhuman" junkie posed to the human society, the question which should merely reveal the need of the junkie—who seemingly justifies himself or herself with this response—but which also reveals the structure of infinite desire, which grounds all mere need.

This, finally, returns us to the quotation marks around the "'evil' virus" in the quotation from Burroughs that serves as one of this essay's epigraphs: junk is an "evil" to human culture—to thinking and action—because it is quite literally inhuman, that which carries the other of *anthropos:* "junk" brings the denial of logos, the sapping of the will, the introduction of impossibility, and the ruining of community. Given his constant emphasis on demystification, we should be suspicious of any place in Burroughs's text where he seems to be moralizing; it seems that the liminal states that "junk" gestures toward make its ham-fisted identification as merely "evil" impossible, insofar as these states quite literally name the exterior fields of alterity in which any particular opposition must configure itself.

"Junk" forces us to confront the face of that which is wholly other—other even to the other person. And it is also here that one can call attention to Burroughs's continuing fascination with the "virus"; as Benway introduces the concept to the Burroughs *oeuvre* in *Naked Lunch,* "'It is thought that the virus is a degeneration from more complex life form. It may at one time have been capable of independent life. Now it has fallen to the *borderline between living and dead matter.* It can exhibit living qualities only in a host, by using the life of another—the renunciation of life itself, a *falling* towards inorganic, inflexible machine, toward dead matter'" (134). The virus, famously related to language in Burroughs, carries or introduces the alterity-based temporality of the postmodern subject, which "may at one time have been capable of independent life. Now it has fallen to the borderline between living and dead matter": between the individual and the "parasitic" network of iterable performative substitution from which it arises.

Insofar as Levinas teaches us that the individual is nothing other—but nothing less—than a hypostasis within the shifting categories of substitution for-the-other, his own account of subjectivity as such an iterable substitution would seem to create problems for the privileging of the category "human." Levinas himself warns us "not to make a drama out of a tautology" (*Existence* 87/150), not to mistake the hypostasis of subjectivity for an originary category of supposed discovery or self-revelation. Both Levinas and Burroughs force us to acknowledge that the parasitic network of substitution, which seems merely to feed on the plenitude of human identity, in fact makes the plenitude of that identity [im]possible in the first place.[17] But this very logic of the iterable network of performative identity would seem to pose essential questions to Levinas's thematization of identity and alterity by questioning his insistence on what he calls the "priority" of the "human face"[18] and voice (and concomitant evasion of "junk" as radical material iterability). Despite Levinas's well-taken criticisms concerning ontology's fetishizing of "anonymous" being, it may be that the wholly other is traced in other than human beings. That [im]possibility, at least, needs to be taken into account; and the attempt to analyze such an [im]possibility in terms of Burroughs's thematization of "junk" helps to draw Levinasian ethical desire outside the human, where it is not supposed to travel.

In the end, it seems to me that Levinas attempts to exile the very thing that makes his discourse so unique and compelling: the irreducibility of the confrontation with the wholly other. In his insistence that the subject must overcome the crippling hesitation of the *il y a* to respond to the other, Levinas offers us an important rejoinder to those ethical systems that would be content to rest in generalizations and pieties. Levinas insists instead on an ethics of response to the neighboring other in the light of justice for the others. But when Levinas argues that one is subjected solely by other humans in the face-to-face encounter, he elides any number of important ethical considerations. First is the role of inhuman systems, substances, economies, drives, and practices in shaping the hypostatic response that is both the self and the other. Certainly Levinas teaches us that the subject is never a monad: it is always beholden to the other in its subjection; it is always a hostage. But if subjective response is a "saying," the material networks of languages and practices available to the subject in and through its subjection need to be taken into account. The subject's daily confrontation with interpellating inhuman systems is, it would seem, just as formative as his or her daily confrontation with the humans that people these systems.

As Levinas insists, contact with something anonymous like "work" is not of the same order as contact with coworkers. People overflow the roles they are assigned within such systems; Larry in Accounting is *more* than Larry in Accounting. What we do at work or have for lunch today sinks into anonymity, while in our face-to-face meetings—on break from our tasks, over cigarettes and coffee—Larry somehow isn't simply consumed or forgotten. If we attend to his difference as difference, Larry can't sink into anonymity. Burroughs, however, teaches us also to ask after the lunch, cigarettes and coffee, which may not disappear into anonymity quite so quickly. Neither, he might add, should the spaces in which we work and the systems that parse out such space, and therefore frame many of our daily face-to-face encounters. These "inhuman" considerations likewise call for response.

Certainly, Levinas recognizes this when he brings the third into the drama of the face-to-face. As he writes of social justice, "If proximity ordered to me only the other alone, there would not have been any problem" (in Peperzak 180). But the others confront me also in the face-to-face with the other, and demand that the "self-suffcent 'I-Thou'" relation be extended to the others in a relation of justice. Here Levinas—responding, always, to Heidegger—is careful not to pose the relation of social justice with the others as a falling away from some state of authenticity: "It is not that there first would be the facel and then the being that it manifests or expresses would concern himself with justice; the epiphany of the face qua face opens humanity" (*Totality* 213). While the face-to-face has a certain quasi-phenomenological priority in Levinas—there has to be the specificity of bodily *contact* and response if one is to avoid mere pious generalizations—the face-to-face in turn opens more than the closed loop of my repsonsibility for you: insofar as "the face qua face opens humanity," my responsibility for the others is inscribed in my very responsibility for you. The specific other and the social–historical realm of others cannot be separated in the revelation of the face-to-face.[19]

But even in his thematization of justice, there nevertheless remains the trace of Levinas's most pervasive ethical exclusion, an absolute privilege of the same that lives on in this discourse of the other: "justice" in Levinas—infinite response in the here and now—remains synonomous with "humanity"; justice is owed to the others who are as human as the other. The face-to-face extends my responsibility to all that possess a face; the saying of my response to the other human's voice extends to all other humans' voices. I must respond to—and am the "brother" of—only that which has a voice and a face. But what about the face of systems, the face of total need confronted in intoxicants, or the face of animals? As Levinas responds,

> I cannot say at what moment you have the right to be called "face." The
> human face is completely different and only afterwards do we discover

the face of an animal. I don't know if a snake has a face. . . . I do not know at what moment the human appears, but what I want to emphasize is that the human breaks with pure being, which is always a persistence in being. . . . [W]ith the appearance of the human—and this is my entire philosophy—there is something more important than my life, and that is the life of the other.[20] ("Paradox" 171–72)

In thematizing response solely in terms of the human face and voice, it would seem that Levinas leaves untouched the oldest and perhaps most sinister unexamined privilege of the same: *anthropos,* and only *anthropos,* has *logos;* and as such *anthropos* responds not to the barbarous or the dumb or the inanimate, but only to those who qualify for the privileges of "humanity," only to those deemed to possess a face, only to those recognized to be living in the *logos.*[21] Certainly, as the history of anticolonial and feminist movements has taught us, those who we now believe unproblematically to possess a "face" and a "voice" weren't always granted such privilege, and present struggles continue to remind us that the racist's or homophobe's first refuge is a distinction between a privileged humanity and its supposed others.

In addition, we might ask about those ethical calls of the future from "beings" that we cannot now even imagine, ethical calls that Donna Haraway categorizes under the heading of the "cyborg [which] appears in myth precisely where the boundary between human and animal is transgressed" (*Simians* 152). Certainly, the historical and theoretical similarities that Haraway draws among the discourses surrounding her title subjects, *Simians, Cyborgs, and Women,* should force us to ask after and hold open categories that have not been yet recognized as ethically compelling. The "human," in other words, may name the latest—if certainly not the last—attempt to circumscribe a constitutive boundary around ethical response. Of course, the permeability of this boundary is traced in nearly all the crucial socioethical questions of today. From abortion to cryogenics to cybernetics, from animal research to gene therapy to cloning, we see the ethical necessity surrounding the disruption and rearticulation of any stable sense or site we might offer to define (human) life itself. And any strong or useful sense of ethics would seem to entail that ethical response is not limited from before the fact.

In the end, Levinas's insistence on the "human" as sole category of ethical response further protects and extends the imperialism of western subjectivity—what Judith Butler calls, in another context, an "imperialist humanism that works through unmarked privilege" (*Bodies* 118). Despite the Levinasian advances toward a nonontological ethics of response as substitution for the other, Levinas nevertheless also extends the privilege of "man," which, as Haraway reminds us, is quite literally "the one who is not animal, barbarian or woman" (156).[22] And to quote selectively from Levinas's citation of Pascal, "*That* is how the usurpation of the whole world began": with the protection of the category "human" from its others.[23]

NOTES

1. Addiction is from the Latin *addictus, "given over,"* one *awarded to* another as a slave.

2. While they share similar concerns, Levinas's conception of desire and alterity remains in sharp contradistinction to Lacan's, insofar as the Lacanian horizon of desire for the "great other" is tied to a conception of lack. For both Lacan and Levinas, desire is animated by its object, but the Hegelian conception of desire as lack or insufficiency (failure to complete itself) remains characteristic of desire in Lacan: upshot of the Oedipal drama is the lamentable expropriation the self from the real into my locus of ethics in Lacan, the Other in fact remains my enemy, marker for that which constantly frustrates the animating ontological desire of returning to "essence," returning to myself. As Lacan writes in book II of the *Seminar,* desire is "a relation of being to lack. This lack is the lack of being properly speaking. It isn't the lack of this or that, but the lack of being whereby the being exists" (223). Compare Levinas, where desire is "an aspiration that is conditioned by no prior lack" ("Meaning and Sense" 94). As he writes., "Responsibility for another is not an accident that happens to a subject, but precedes essence. . . . I exist through the other and for the other, *but without this being alienation*" (*Otherwise* 114/145–46, my emphasis). In Levinas, being for-the-other—which he will call "substitution"—exists *before essence,* before the real; hence, for Levinas there can be no alienation from and or nostalgia for the return to self: "Substitution frees the subject from ennui, that is, from the enchainment to itself" (*Otherwise* 124/160). For Lacan, need (as loss of the real) subtends and traverses desire. For Levinas, the opposite is the case—any conception of loss or lack is subtended by the infinity of substitution, which exists before the distinction between lack and plenitude.

3. For his engagement with Sartre, see Levinas's "Reality and Its Shadow." Certainly more could be said on this topic, insofar as Sartre's *Nausea* likewise owes a tremendous debt to Heidegger's 1929 lecture on the nothing, "What is Metaphysics?" Suffice it to say, Levinas is interested in an *other than* the distinction between being and nothingness. See *Otherwise:* "Not *to be otherwise,* but *otherwise than being.* And not to not-be. . . . Being and not-being illuminate one another, and unfold a speculative dialectic which is a determination of being. Or else the negativity which attempts to repel being is immediately submerged

by being. . . . The statement of being's *other*, of the otherwise than being, claims to state a difference over'and beyond that which separates being from nothingness—the very difference of the beyond, the difference of transcendence" (3/3).

4. The horror of the *il y a* is, in Levinas's concise words, "fear *of* being and not [Heideggerian] fear *for* being" (*Existence*, p. 62/102, my emphases).

5. For more on this point, see Llewelyn's "The 'Possibility, of Heidegger's Death": "The distinction between a possibility which something *has* and a possibility which something *is* compels us to take notice that Heidegger writes not only of death as a possibility of being, a *Seinsmöglichkeit*, but also of death as a *Seinkönnen*. A *Können* is a capacity, power, or potentiality. Ontic potentialities are qualities that things have and may develop, as a child may develop its potentiality to reason. But being towards death is an ontological potentiality, a potentiality of and for being. Dasein ja its death itself" (137).

6. See Heidegger's *Being and Time*: "Dasein is authentically itself only to the extent that, as concernful Being-alongside and solicitous Being-with, it projects itself upon its ownmost potentiality-for-Being rather than upon the possibility of the they-self" (308). For more on this question, consult Manning, *Interpreting Otherwise than Heidegger* (38–53).

7. Here Levinas seems to have much in common with Butler's work on performative identity in *Gender Trouble*. For Butler, like Levinas, to say that subjective agency is "performative" is *not* to say that agency doesn't exist or that all agency is merely an ironic performance; but rather it is to say that such agency is necessarily a matter of *response* to already-given codes. Certainly, focusing on the question of gender would open up a considerable gulf between their projects, but there is at least some traffic between Butler and Levinas on the question of identity and performativity.

8. See *Otherwise*: "In its *being*, subjectivity undoes *essence* by substituting itself for another. Qua one-for-the-other, it is absorbed in signification, in saying or the verb form of the infinite. Signification precedes essence. . . . Substitution is signification. Not a reference of one term to another, as it appears thematized in the said, but substitution as the very subjectivity of a subject, interruption of the irreversible identity of the essence" (13/16).

9. Levinas specifically points his reader to Blanchot's *Thomas the Obscure* for the experience of the *il y a* (*Existence* 63n/103n). See also Levinas's *Sur Maurice Blanchot* (especially pp. 9–26), and his interview on the *il y a* in *Ethics and Infinity* (45–52). For more specifically on Blanchot, Levinas and the *il y a*, see Critchley, *"Il y a"* (especially pp. 114–119); Libertson (201–11); Wyschogrod; and Davies.

10. As Levinas writes in a similar context, "One watches on when there is nothing to watch and despite the absence of any reason for remaining watchful. The bare fact of presence is oppressive; one is held by being, held to be. one is detached from any object, any content, yet there is presence, . . . the universal fact of the *there is*" (*Existence* 65/109).

11. See, for example, J. Habermas *Theory of Communicative Action II* (Cambridge, MA: MIT Press, 1987, pp. 296–298).

12. Compare Levinas's *Totality and Infinity*: "The idea of infinity, the overflowing of finite thought by its content., effectuates the relation of thought with what exceeds its capacity. . . . This is the situation we call welcome of the face" (197).

13. See Nietzsche's *On the Genealogy of Morals,* essay III, §28.

14. See Levinas's "Reality and its Shadow" (p. 131).

15. Levinas wishes to rescue a notion of transcendence as phenomenological self-overcoming, but shorn of its ontological intentionality. Davies defines "transcendent" as follows: "that is to say, for Levinas, [the transcendent subject] can approach the other *as* other in its 'approach,' in 'proximity'" ("A Fine Risk" 201).

16. This may be more accruately—or at least philosophically-posed as a "good infinite, bad infinite" situation, which would bring us to a consideration of Hegel, for whom Levinas's alterity would be precisely a kind of bad (unrecuperable) infinite. It seems clear what Hegel protects in his exiling of the bad infinite: it keeps the dialectical system safe from infinite specular regression. Here, however, I would like to fold Levinas's skepticism concerning Hegel back onto Levinas's own text: why the exiling of the *il y a* as a bad infinite, and what privilege is—however surrepticiously—protected by or in such a move? See Gasche's "Structural Infinity," in his *Inventions of Difference,* for more on the Hegelian bad infinite.

17. Compare Derrida's discussion of AIDS in "The Rhetoric of Drugs": "The virus (which belongs neither to life nor to death) may *always already* have broken into any lintersubjectivel space. . . . [A]t the heart of that which would preserve itself as a dual intersubjectivity it inscribes the mortal and indestructible trace of the third—not the third as the condition of the symbolic and the law, but the third as destructuring structuration of the social bond" (20).

18. This is Levinas's wording in the interview "The Paradox of Morality" (169).

19. This is contra Peperzak's *To the Other,* which casts Levinas as a metaphysician profoundly disdainful of the social or material world: "The secret of all philosophy that considers society and history to be the supreme perspective is war and exploitation. . . . As based on the products of human activities, the judgment of history is an unjust outcome, and if the social totality is constituted by violence and corruption, there seems to be no hope for a just society unless justice can be brought into it from the outside. This is possible only if society and world history do not constitute the dimension of the ultimate. The power of nonviolence and justice lies in the dimension of speech and the face-to-face, the dimension of straightforward intersubjectivity and fundamental ethics, which opens the closed totality of anonymous productivity and historicity" (178–79).

20. For more on the question of animality in Levinas, see Llewelyn's *The Middle Voice of Ecological Conscience* (pp. 49–67). See also Critchley's treatment of this topic in *The Ethics of Deconstruction* (pp. 180–82).

21. Compare Heidegger's translation of this Aristotelian privilege in "The Origin of the Work of Art": "Language alone brings what is, as something that is, into the Open for the first time. Where there is no language, as in the being of stone, plant and animal, there is also no openness of what is. . . . The primitive . . . is always futureless" (pp. 73, 76).

22. For a critique of Levinas's thematization of the feminine, see Irigaray's "The Fecundity of the Caress" and her "Questions to Emmanuel Levinas: On the Divinity of Love." For an outline of the debate and something of a defense of Levinas, see Chanter "Feminism and the Other."

23. The third epigraph to *Otherwise, Pensées* 112, reads: "'. . . That is my place in the sun.' That is how the usurpation of the whole world began."

WORKS CITED

Burroughs, William. "Christ and the Museum of Extinct Species." *Conjunctions* 13 (1989): 264–73.

———. *Junky*. New York: Penguin, 1977.

———. *Naked Lunch*. New York: Grove P, 1992.

Butler, Judith. *Gender Trouble*. New York: Routledge, 1990.

Chanter, Tina. "Antigone's Dilemma." *Re-Reading Levinas*, eds. Robert Bernasconi and Simon Critchely. Bloomington: Indiana UP, 1991: 130–48.

Critchley, Simon. *The Ethics of Deconstruction: Derrida and Levinas*. Cambridge, MA: Blackwell, 1992.

———. "Il y a—A Dying Stronger Than Death (Blanchot with Levinas)." *Oxford Literary Review* 15.1–2 (1993): 81–131.

Davies, Paul. "A Fine Risk: Reading Blanchot Reading Levinas." *Re-Reading Levinas*, eds. Robert Bernasconi and Simon Critchely. Bloomington: Indiana UP, 1991: 201–28.

Derrida, Jacques. "The Rhetoric of Drugs," trans. Michael Israel. *differences* 5.1 (1993): 1–24.

Gasche, Rodolphe. "Non-totalization without Spuriousness: Derrida and Hegel on the Infinite." *Journal of the British Society for Phenomenology* 17 (1986): 289–307.

Haraway, Donna J. *Simians, Cyborgs, and Women: The Reinvention of Nature.* New York: Routledge, 1991.

Heidegger, Martin. *Being and Time,* trans. John Macquarrie and Edward Robinson. New York: Harper and Row, 1962.

——. "The Origin of the Work of Art," trans. Albert Hofstadter. *Poetry, Language, Thought,* ed. Albert Hofstadter. New York: Harper and Row, 1971: 15–89.

——. "What is Metaphysics?" trans. David Krell. *Basic Writings,* ed. David Krell. New York: Harper and Row, 1977: 91–112.

Irigaray, Luce. "The Fecundity of the Caress," trans. Carolyn Burke. *Face to Face with Levinas,* ed. Richard A. Cohen. Albany: SUNY P, 1986: 231–56.

Lacan, Jacques. *The Seminar of Jacques Lacan, Book II,* trans. Sylvana Tomaselli, ed. J-A Miller. Cambridge UP, 1988: 223.

Levinas, Emmanuel. *Existence and Existents,* trans. Alphonso Lingis. The Hague: Martinus Nijhoff, 1978.

——. "Meaning and Sense," trans. Alphonso Lingis. *Collected Philosophical Papers,* ed. Alphonso Lingis. The Hague: Martinus Nijhoff, 1987: 75–108.

——. *Otherwise than Being, or Beyond Essence,* trans. Alphonso Lingis. The Hague: Martinus Nijhoff, 1981.

——. "Reality and Its Shadow," trans. Alphonso Lingis. *The Levinas Reader,* ed. Sean Hand. Cambridge, MA: Basil Blackwell, 1989: 129–43.

——. *Sur Maurice Blanchot.* Montpellier: Fata Morgana, 1975.

——. *Totality and Infinity,* trans. Alphonso Lingis. Pittsburgh: Dusquene UP, 1969.

Llewelyn, John. *The Middle Voice of Ecological Conscience: A Chiasmic Reading of Responsibility in the Neighbourhood of Levinas, Heidegger, and Others.* London: Macmillan, 1991.

——. "The 'Possibility' of Heidegger's Death." *Journal of the British Society for Phenomenology* 14.2 (1983): 127–38.

Lyotard, Jean François. "Levinas' Logic," trans. Ian McLeod. *Face to Face with Levinas,* ed. Richard A. Cohen. Albany: SUNY P, 1986: 117–58.

Manning, R. J. S. *Interpreting Otherwise than Heidegger: Emmanuel Levinas's Ethics as First Philosophy.* Pittsburgh, Duquesne UP, 1993.

Nietzsche, Friedrich. *On the Genealogy of Morals and Ecce Homo,* trans. Walter Kaufmann. New York: Vintage, 1967.

Peperzak, Adriaan. *To the Other: An Introduction to the Philosophy of Emmanuel Levinas*. West Lafayette: Purdue UP, 1993.

Ronell, Avital. *Crack Wars: Literature, Addiction, Mania*. Lincoln and London: U of Nebraska P, 1992.

Sartre, Jean-Paul. *Nausea,* trans. Lloyd Alexander. New York: New Directions, 1964.

Part II

SOCIO-CULTURAL AND PSYCHOLOGICAL REFLECTIONS ON ADDICTION

Chapter Nine

SOCIALLY SIGNIFICANT DRUGS

FÉLIX GUATTARI
Translated by Mark S. Roberts

The most important thing is to subvert the simplistic attitudes taken toward the phenomenon of drugs—whether in terms of a medicalized view or in terms of psychological, sociological, or criminological ones. These simplistic attitudes are deeply rooted in all of these "specializations."

One cannot separate the mechanisms of delinquency and criminalization from the mechanism of the drug in itself. The drugs are so costly; they involve such a lifestyle, that they imprison the addict in a sort of ghetto. There is an infernal economic machine at work here, that no one can escape—unless *a free distribution of drugs* were to come about. Perhaps this could take place under medical supervision. But the question is inconceivable unless a new nonrepressive approach, and therefore a new relation of power between the people involved and political power, were to be established. By and large, the results would certainly be far less disastrous than the present situation, which drives addicts to live in a state of constant panic and anguish. A situation, moreover, that imbues drug use with a highly developed mythological—proselytizing—atmosphere that enables the pushers to come out on top. That is the problem. It is not the alleged escalation from soft to hard drugs that is at issue. Rather, it is a question of defusing the systems that lead to the proselytizing of drugs. Could one possibly imagine a syphilitic being forced to spread syphilis in order to survive? It seems essential to me that hard drugs have to be freely distributed for there to be a possibility of offering the addict a choice among a range of alternative products. The ways of organizing this kind of therapeutically motivated distribution would be defined by the addicts themselves, with the help of social workers, physicians, and others. But the first principle would be to proscribe any repressive intrusion into this area by the police or the judiciary.

The "scientific" methodology that defines the mechanism of hard drugs as stemming from biochemical processes, which are said to be radically different from other drugs, parallels the mythology conveyed by the addicts themselves. Alcohol is an extremely dangerous drug, and it is not because it is freely sold that there are many chronic alcoholics or cirrhosis of the liver. The same kind of regulation should apply to hard drugs. A regime of free distribution would doubtless lead to a decrease in the volume of drug use, due to the fact that it would lessen the intensity of the drug mythology, and lead to the disappearance of its principal advocates.

Before considering such an orientation, it would be helpful to closely examine an experiment in England based on these principles. It is true that a great number of addicts refused to be registered in the program, and many just equated the use of legally distributed drugs with illicit ones; but the resulting analyses must be given priority over the institutional context of this experiment, which, doubtless, was unable to discount the economic dependence and the criminalization associated with drug use. To repeat myself, the fundamental prerequisite is an unequivocal decriminalization of drugs. If this cannot be obtained from the political authorities—at the level of personal consumption and petty dealing—it may be necessary for a number of militant groups and associations to take responsibility and organize alternative forms of distribution. This has been tried in France (at Vincennes) under difficult conditions, and it at least succeeded in allowing some kind of collective control over the quality of the drug product.

In my opinion, the most general form of the problem stems from the fact that the old modes of subjective territorialization have collapsed. There now exist phenomena of the type I call "echoes of the black hole," which compel people to grab hold of territorialities, objects, rituals, altered behaviors, at any cost, rendering them ridiculous or disastrous. In this respect, one can place the love of a teenager for his motorcycle or for rock music, or the love of a child for her dolls in the same series— much less, the reterritorialization of the gang of four on its emblems, that of a household on goods consumed, or that of a ranking system used for promotions. The question of drugs, then, moves along the passages between the different social, material, and psychological drugs. Why is there a reterritorialization focused on one drug rather than on another, on one "socialized" route, or on something that will be disastrous for the individual or his or her group?

The common characteristic of hard drugs that leads us to place them on levels as disparate as the faked "suicides" of bikers at the Rungis wholesale market, and a generalized audiovisual intoxication appears to me to be the existence of a kind of subjective "black hole," which I would characterize as microfascist. These black holes continue to multiply, proliferating in the social field. It is a question of knowing if subjectivity echoes them in such a way that the entire life of an individual, all his modes of semiotization, depend upon a central point of anguish and guilt. I propose this image of a black hole to illustrate the phenomenon of the complete inhibition of the semiotic constituents of an individual or group, which then finds itself cut off from any possibility of an exterior life. By the expression "echo of the black hole," I wish to resonate several systems of blockage. (Example: You have a stomach cramp and you can no longer think about it; you "embody" it; you invest an erogenous zone on your pain, you torment your wife, your children, and all these domains at once resonate.)

Very few people successfully leave the world of hard drugs unscathed, apart from some rock groups that make it a form of public expression, their license to "theatricalize" their condition. The others, if I might say so, are in deep shit. It would be a mystification to seek support from those few types who are able to articulate something of their drug experience just to sustain the mythology of hard drugs.

The distinction between hard and soft drugs is, in the final analysis, rather artificial. It appears poorly grounded on a clinical level. There is a hard use of soft drugs and a soft use of hard drugs. It is always the same nervous system that is afflicted by "what happened," and there is a replacement of thought by what, in the end, involves the density, intensity, the forms of administration, the material, subjective, and social assemblage (agencement) of drugs.

In other words, what counts are not only the physiochemical characteristics of drugs, but also the style of buying, the atmosphere, the context, and the myths. And the whole question is of knowing if such complex agencies (agencements) do or do not lead to a reinforced individuation of subjectivity, usually in the sense of an inescapable solitude (solitude en impasse), or of a social and addictive entrapment.

The social grid and control imprisons most individuals between extreme situations:

- a solitude without recourse
- a complete inability to accept any type of solitude, and thereby one is constantly draw to all modes of dependence, all the "hang-ups": sports, television, married life, the pecking-order, and others.

Hard drugs seem to heighten the first situation and soft drugs the second, insofar as they sometimes lead to an overcoming.

Soft drugs are consumed by people who build a microeconomy of desire, that is, more or less collective assemblages *(agencements collectifs)* at the center of which drugs intervene only as a lesser constituent.

A drug can be said to be soft from the moment it ceases to work in the sense of the above subjective individuation, of an entrapment, of a break with external realities. Those who use them effect collective assemblages of enunciation *(agencements collectifs d'énonciation),* allowing certain individuals to remove their inhibitions, to question their lifestyles, their moral and political preferences, their social and material environment.

One of the formative elements of the myth of hard drugs lies in the idea that they inspire a specific and novel kind of production. There would thus be a culture linked to drugs—a theme exploited particularly by the "Beat Generation." This mystification appears to me to run parallel to that established with regard to the art of the insane. Consider, for example, the two short films Henri Michaux has devoted to hallucinogenic drugs. In point of fact, they don't have very much to do with the experience of drugs! Certain images are extremely beautiful, but what the film really illustrates is Henri Michaux's *literature,* and not at all the modes of semiotization proper to drugs. It is aberrant to even imagine the existence of an art specific to the insane, children, addicts, etc. That a child or madman produces these artworks only implies that its production is essentially infantile or mad! Certain drug environments develop certain cultures, but one cannot infer from this that drugs create a specific mode of expression.

Perhaps anthropological and linguistic studies will one day demonstrate that far from belonging to a marginal world, drugs have played a foundational role in all societies, in all cultural and religious areas. One might think that it was the use of drugs, beginning in the Paleolithic era, that contributed to producing the earliest "ascent" of human language (which I have called, in another connection, "paradigmatic perversion"). But the solitary drugs of capitalism very rarely function in the collective mode, which was, for example, the case with shamanism. It is our entire society that is drugged, that "hardens" its drugs, and that connects them increasingly to a taste for disaster, to a drive for the end of the world.

There is no longer anything to say, nor anything to do. The only thing left is to follow the movement. Fascism and Stalinism, were collective hard drugs. Consumer society shortens the road to passivity and death. All the less need to build death camps; one can design one on one's own.

In essence, the break between hard and soft drugs occurs between a new lifestyle—I prefer here to call it a "molecular revolution" rather than a new culture—and the microfascist elements of industrial capitalist and bureaucratic socialist societies. I will always stand by, be in solidarity with, the addicts, such as they are, against their repression. But this doesn't imply a defense for hard drugs, which I consider to be essentially microfascist in nature. Not insofar as they are chemical molecules, but to the extent that they are molecular assemblages of desire *(agencements moléculaires de désirs)* crystallizing subjectivity in a vortex of abrogation.

The way in which drugs and psychosis are assimilated or, rather, subtly differentiated, appears to me to be seductive but dangerous. In the case of psychosis, one would experience an attempt to overcome the disabling semiotics of the body, whereas drugs present a micropolitics of the will, an urge to perform this disabling by oneself. I do not believe this idea is tenable. I would always depart from the idea of an assemblage *(agencement)*, of the importance of the assemblage over its components. The design, I believe, is not the delusion, symptom, or the hallucination. Rather, it is something that implies much more and much less than the particular; it includes parts of the socius, economic structures, organic functions, and an ecological environment. Addicts don't have access to a great deal more initiative than psychotics. I am here pushing a process of responsibility and accountability that I myself often challenge. A psychotic is a psychotic. It's not his or her fault. But an addict is a filthy bum; he or she is just a good con artist. Anything that even provides pseudoscientific support for this genre of collective fantasy should, it seems to me, be examined under a magnifying glass and disassembled.

We must end with the idea of collective responsibility and accountability. There are some types who are situated in a field of micropolitical possibility, leaving a way out, and others who find themselves at a complete impasse. This depends both on objective and micropolitical factors at the level of the most intimate and immediate assemblage of enunciation *(agencement d'énonciation)*. There are those who, in a flood, reach out to hang on to a plank, and those who are swept away. It is necessary to arrive at a kind of logic, not dualistic, but triplistic, multiplistic, polyvocal, that gives both *a full responsibility* and *a full irresponsibility* to individuals, according to the micropolitical arrangement through which one considers them.

ON THE ESCALATION OF DRUGS

In a brief statement that lends itself to misunderstanding, Jean Balt-hazar asserts that I extol "the free use of dope and its full-scale circulation." In my polemic with Olivenstein, I simply said that the free distribution of hard drugs—through a pharmacy, by prescription, in dispensaries, or by any other process—would lessen the ravages of the current underground system that frequently forces addicts to become dealers or proselytes. Moreover, there is no other way of controlling—what is indispensable—the quality of the products in circulation! (No one can ignore the ravages brought on by drug trafficking or the lack of prevention.)

Despite the fact that "happy addicts" do exist, it is necessary to admit that the addict's condition is more often wretched, indeed, tragic. Does this suffering justify repression and police control? In fact, it is exactly the opposite, and it is the "specialists" who bring their so-called scientific caution to maintian that repression, purely and simply causing the ongoing play of social controls, the imposition of a totalizing grid on which various mechanisms spread continuously.

In the same sense, every addict must have the freedom to care for himself or herself, or to refuse to care for himself or herself, or to refuse such and such a method of treatment. For my part, I am, furthermore, not convinced that any specific form of treatment will ever be effective if it doesn't take into account the addict's own answers to the questions. (See, for example, the experiment of the "Detox Service" in the South Bronx of New York City). But this obviously involves a complete cessation or a neutralization of all forms of repression directed at the addicts in general!

Many people pretend that repression is justified by the need to contain contamination, to prevent an extension of "being hooked" on hard drugs. This argument is misleading for various reasons. First, even the police admit that the current repression in no way limits the spread of the drug phenomenon. Second, various worldwide experiments have established that normalization of the distribution of drugs does not increase the number of addicts. Everyone knows that cirrhosis of the liver and *delirium tremens* did not increase in the United States after the end of prohibition! And the problem of alcohol addiction—regardless of what some experts might say—is not fundamentally different than that of addiction to hard drugs.

As for the so-called escalation of drug use, that moves necessarily from the joint to the fix, no one even bothers mentioning that such an argument is in bad faith any more!

ON A MOLECULAR REVOLUTION: AN INTERVIEW[1]

Q: How did you arrive at the proposition for your entire approach to the problem of drug addiction?

A: This proposition was somewhat crudely formed on the occasion when I was first asked to intervene on the topic. I am a little split between the different angles from which one can approach drug addiction, because I relate them to everything that counts as addiction: tele-addiction, sports-addiction, leadership-addiction—to all the modes of the crystallization of subjectivity such as they are fabricated today by the various media. How can one fail to reflect upon the Pavlovian behavior of people watching television? Thus a whole dimension of existential territories imposes itself on the problematic of drug addiction from something which functions a little like a transitional object, or, if you prefer, like an institutional object. This is the first pole around which my reflection turns.

The second is that I am very interested in endorphins. For example, it seems to me characteristic that certain anorexic, sado-masochistic syndromes function by auto-addiction: the body secretes its own endorphins, which, as we know, are 50 times more psychoactive than morphines. One can thus say that there is an enterprise of addiction that is generated from the biological, psychogenetic, and psychological point of view. Take the example Kafka presents in *The Diaries*.[2] He is not a drug addict per se. But through the insomnia, anorexia, or through a type of second degree of solitude *(état second de solitude)* he is plunged into during the night, he, in effect, lives out an experience similar to that of the drug addict. One can be drugged by jogging. And this is not a metaphor. It is effectively a question of stimulating the production of endorphins. There is an entire scientific field here to study.

Q: In the 1970s you made the distinction between hard drugs and soft drugs?

A: Yes, but I get the impression that people of good faith have accepted the idea that it is not necessary to establish a continuum between marijuana and hard drugs. I don't know if we have to return to this debate that appears to no longer exist.

Q: But you introduced the framework of this concept not at the level of the chemical characteristics of products, but on that of the effect produced in the individual, directing him or her towards a collective enunciation, or, conversely, further alienation. This distinction is less classic . . .

A: Yes, there is a function of closure that can be exceptionally synonymous with creativity. I stress exceptionally. I know certain intellectuals who smoke a lot of marijuana, and this stimulates them in their work. Conversely, this is not true of other drugs where there is a rapid degradation of the mental faculties (cocaine, for example). The result of all this is that one fabricates a subjectivity disconnected from the microsocial point of view, an *ersatz* of subjectivity.

Today one carries oneself like a celebrity, a bit like those seen on television. I tend to stress this mediatistic dimension of subjectivity, the roles that one plays, like a child. Television has become a presence more important than the traditional father. Given that we're dealing with television, however, it is a strange little person of whom we speak.

Q: To continue, it appears that drugs mainly have the effect of extinguishing the individual; and the political discourse, which dosen't have much of a reputation for altruism, tends to seize upon this process. There seems to be something important at work here.

A: There is a kind of criminalization, a stigmatization of certain segments of society induced by that kind of absurd perspective—a perspective that consists of assuming it is order, law, discipline, or constraint that will change the state of this malaise. The remaining foundation, then, is enormous. We will have to reconstruct a society on the ravages, on the debris of a society that might be called both capitalist and classed. What is involved here, although in an embryonic and confused way, is the entrance into a postmediatistic era, the possibility of arriving at a reappropriation of the means of the production of subjectivity.

Q: Would this reconstructed society extend to drugs?

A: This is another problem. I don't think much about it, particularly given the ambiguity of the term "drug." Drugs are being consumed in enormous amounts, and it is the family practitioner who is prescribing most of them. I don't believe that we can avoid the impact of chemicals on life, in that they appear in the food supply, the production of vitamins, and disinfectants.

Q: But do you think that this evolution is marked by the appearance of new products, like ecstasy?

A: Discovering new molecules doesn't change the problem. The problem does not lie uniquely in the chemotherapeutic response one brings to a state of anguish. It lies, I repeat, in the destruction of social and individual practices. Then what purpose do these molecules serve? What is the setting of chemistry? An immense majority of individuals are placed in a situation in which their personalities fall apart, their intentions become unstable, and the quality of their relations with others is dulled.

Q: Perhaps we've underestimated what you're trying to advance, or conceal, here; but doesn't it place an inordinate stress on the image of the encounter between the innocent drug victim and the "dirty dealer" who produces the drugs?

A: The relation to the dealer is not effectively an element. There are microcultures that also mythologize the use of drugs. I am not immediately convinced that it is necessarily better to short-circuit the dealers by using pharmacists. Rather, one must consider addicts as both free people who have a choice and as sick people who should be treated as such and accepted. Addicts are also depressed people who develop anxiety neuroses, and who are incapable of disposing of the minimum of social layering in order to sustain and stabilize their subjectivity. Consequently, to get things in order, we wind up persecuting them!

Q: Why this persecution? Don't we have to take into account the relation of pleasure when we are examining the drug addict?

A: I think that the collective judgment on the drug addict is an exterior one. It does not take into account the order of either pleasure or desire. It is a reification, and the addicts are groups of scapegoats. The addicts also have to fear an entire generation of psychiatrists. I would be interested in analyzing this sort of phobia. . . . To my thinking, a normal sick person tends to manifest a submissive behavior (of a quasi-ethnological kind) within the doctor–patient relation. The addict, however, rarely effects this sort of behavior. There is a kind of arrogance toward the person who wishes to help them. Thus there is a relation of forces that often discourages the "traditional white-coats."

Q: You don't think that political intervention has made progress toward understanding drug addiction?

A: Absolutely. I think that it is only on the level of a political reconfiguration that would take social, individual, and aesthetic objectives into account that we will be able to alter the situation of drug addicts; otherwise, everything will just get worse.

Q: What do you mean by aesthetic objectives?

A: Aesthetic objectives, yes. This means that it is necessary to give up the scientist's models in order to connect aesthetic models to all the registers by which we judge the human sciences and treatments. This move will help us to understand that life is a performance, that one constructs one's life, that one works it, makes it a piece of work, singularizes it. This is a veritable politics that I have called a molecular revolution. Its purpose is to completely change our objectives. Otherwise, what will we see? A tiny minority of highly sophisticated technical specialists beside a mass of whole populations being treated like cattle.

NOTES

Felix Guattari's "Les drogues signifiantes" is based on a discussion with Claude Olivenstein, François Châtelet, Numa Murard, Jean Balthazar, and others. See the chapter in "La révolution moléculaire" (Paris: Union Générale D'Éditions, 1977), pp. 335–45.

1. This interview with Guattari appeared originally in *L'Esprit des drogues* (Paris: Autrement Review, 1989) pp. 18–20. For considerations of readability and accessibility Guattari's specialized English nomenclature is used in this translation although the original French appears in brackets within the text. The most important case is the term *"agencement"* generally translated "assemblage." Guattari's exquisite phrase *"état second de solitude"* has no exact translation; we have followed Avital Ronell's *Crack Wars* in rendering it as "a second degree of solitude."

2. Franz Kafka, *The Diaries*. Max Brod, ed. (New York: Schocken, 1989).

Chapter Ten

FREUD'S PHARMACY

Cocaine and the Corporeal Unconscious

ANNA ALEXANDER

> Contradictions and pairs of opposites are lifted from the bottom of this diacritical, differing, deferring reserve. . . . It is from this fund that dialectics draws its philosophemes. The *pharmakon,* without being anything in itself, always exceeds them in constituting their bottomless fund *(fonds sans fond).* It keeps itself forever in reserve even though it has no fundamental profundity nor ultimate locality. We will watch it infinitely promise itself and endlessly vanish through concealed doorways that shine like mirrors and open onto a labyrinth. It is also this store of deep background *(réserve d'arrière-fond)* that we are calling the *pharmacy.*
>
> —Jacques Derrida, "Plato's Pharmacy," *Dissemination*

THE PHARMACY

Freud's writings on cocaine conceal a historical, biographical, and analytical reserve that stores the philosophemes of an *other* Freud: a Freud for whom it is the enigma of drugs that opens onto "the enigma of woman." His documented reports on the subject of addiction, in particular cocaine addiction, constitute the deep background from which is lifted the psychoanalytic theory of drives, sexuality, and the feminine.

Traced out of a tradition of drug-writing—what I might call "psychotropic writing"—Freud's cocaine corpus historically produces, dramatizes, medicalizes, and treats (in that order) a subject—the subject of drugs—a disappearing post-analytic subject that curiously but fundamentally has no substance.

I will explore this subject under the sign of "the corporeal unconscious": a fugitive, aleatory, and hallucinatory space, across which one can think through, with, and about drugs. My argument will be that Freud's cocaine studies not only shed light on the relationship between his use of cocaine and the theory of the unconscious that subtends psychoanalysis, but they also drive psychoanalytic theory forward: that is, into a full-blown, post-Cartesian, and thoroughly modern (if not postmodern) theory of addiction.[1]

A DISAPPEARING SUBJECT

"The first time I took 0.05g of *cocaïnum* in a 1% water solution," writes Freud in his first paper on cocaine ("On Coca," 1963*), "was when I was feeling slightly out of sorts from fatigue . . . this solution is rather viscous, somewhat opalescent and has a strange aromatic smell. At first it has a bitter taste, which yields afterwards to a series of very pleasant aromatic flavors. Dry cocaine salt has the same smell and taste, but to a more concentrated degree . . ."[2]

The paper was called "Ueber Coca." The date of publication was July 1, 1884, as announced by 29-year-old Sigmund in an exhilarated letter to his fiancée. He writes: "Coca appeared today, but I haven't seen it yet."[3] Indeed, as it happened, it was slated to disappear faster than even we could catch sight of it.

In the "Dream of the Botanical Monograph" (March 1898) that he documents in the *Interpretation of Dreams* (1900), Freud recalls that he "really *had* written something in the nature of a monograph on a plant, namely a dissertation on the *coca-plant* [1884], which had drawn Carl Koller's attention to the anaesthetic properties of cocaine. I had myself indicated this application of the alkaloid in my published paper, but I had not been thorough enough to pursue the matter further."[4] The significance of the dream sequence came to light as "a plea on behalf of my own rights." What it meant was: "After all, I'm the man who wrote the valuable and memorable paper (on cocaine)."[5]

---

*See note 2 on page 225.

The dream of "Irma's Injection" (July 1895) surreptitiously *condenses* this "plea" into a dirty needle story that was to inaugurate Freud's monumental *Interpretation of Dreams,* the official harbinger of psychoanalysis.[6] A dream about a woman who suffered from hysterical choking (there were white patches and turbinal bones with scabs on them in her throat) and ostensibly recalling a worry about his own state of health, reveals significantly more about Freud's suppressed interest in cocaine: "I was making frequent use of cocaine at that time to reduce some troublesome nasal swellings, and I heard a few days earlier that one of my women patients who had followed my example had developed an extensive necrosis of the nasal mucous membrane. I had been the first to recommend the use of cocaine, in 1895, and this recommendation had brought serious reproaches down on me. The misuse of that drug had hastened the death of a dear friend of mine. This had been before 1895 [the date of the dream]."[7] Was Freud fudging his dates?

According to his own official English language translator, James Strachey, "1885" in this context is "a slip for '1884,'" the date of Freud's first paper on cocaine.[8] Freud's lecture before the meeting of psychiatrists in 1885, "On the General Effect of Cocaine" (March 1885), does not appear in his own list of writings, nor could a reprint of this publication be found among his papers. Bernfeld's article[9] is the only authoritative history we have of Freud's involvement with cocaine and constitutes the source from which Jones's own chapter "The Cocaine Episode" in *The Life and Work of Sigmund Freud* is drawn.[10] However, Bernfeld died before its completion and the original errors, particularly in translation, have proliferated the confusion about some of Freud's writings on cocaine, subjecting Freud to unjust criticism about his enthusiasm for the drug.[11]

THE COCAINE PAPERS

Freud, of course, is best remembered for his foundational contribution to psychological and psychoanalytic theory. Nevertheless, in 1884, some time after the introduction of cocaine into both the United States and Europe (alkaloid cocaine was first isolated from the coca leaf in 1855), he became interested in its properties and effects.[12] As psychopharmacologist Robert Byck, who has put together a new collection, points out in his "Introduction" to the 1974 edited anthology, *The Cocaine Papers by Sigmund Freud:*

He [Freud] reviewed the published literature to discover all that was known about the drug and then proceeded to undertake a series of experimental investigations into its effects in man. He became an enthusiast and user (defending it vigorously against the allegations by A. Erlenmeyer that it was 'the third scourge of mankind'), and attempted to employ cocaine in halting the morphine addiction of a friend, Ernst von Fleischl-Marxow. The disastrous consequences of this experiment and the later controversies—both over the use of cocaine in such treatment and over attribution for the discovery of cocaine as a local anaesthetic—prompted him to discontinue further investigation into its central actions, although we know from *The Interpretation of Dreams* that Freud was still using the drug in 1895.[13]

While the existence of Freud's writing on cocaine is known, few modern scholars have had the opportunity to study his papers (published and unpublished) on the topic. For those who have read Jones's biography of Freud, or better, Byck's now out-of-print collection, Freud's cocaine corpus constitutes its own conundrum: none of the essays devoted to the study of cocaine, upon which Freud staked his early career, is included as part of either the original German or English editions of Freud's *Collected Works,* nor do they appear in James Strachey's *Standard Edition of the Complete Psychological Works of Sigmund Freud.*

With the exception of an abstracted translation of his infamous 1884 monograph (originally entitled "Ueber Coca," it appeared in English as "Coca" in *The St. Louis Medical and Surgical Journal* in December 1884), the papers[14] were for a long time unavailable in English, and as Byck points out "lay scattered in the prolix German literature of the 1880s" before James Hillman and A. K. Donaghue put them together for the very first time in any language.[15] They were then published once in English, in Vienna, by an obscure press in 1963, but were again "fated to disappear."[16] As they have curiously done once more: with the current unavailability of Byck's own anthology in either French or English editions.[17]

According to Byck, Freud's "mistaken" advocacy of the cocaine as a catholicon or panacea, coupled with Carl Koller's "discovery" of the uses of cocaine as a local anaesthetic—a discovery based on, but not credited to Freud's own research[18]—go a long way toward explaining that "disappearance." Nevertheless, their reappearance as part of a hidden tradition is another, even more interesting, story and sheds new light on the relationship between Freud's use of cocaine and the development of psychoanalysis.

These "papers" not only establish Freud as one of the founders of psychopharmacology,[19] a field carved out of the space between the discovery of alkaloid cocaine in 1855 and the end of the nineteenth century when cocaine, as a centrally-active (i.e., "psychotropic") drug, passes into the realm of law, sociology, and drug abuse. They also place the Freudian corpus within a tradition of drug narratives—"psychotropic writing"—that has itself been left in the shade.[20]

At the outer limits of a cure, in a pharmacy where language, psychoanalysis, and the self are the agents of a treatment—an insolent and spectacular self-medication—Freud's studies on cocaine haunt the concealed doorways of "our narcotic modernity." Indeed, they shine as mirrors, with the remarkable value of a treatment of the subject of drugs that opens onto at least three registeral labyrinths: (1) a social history of medicine; (2) a history of psychoanalysis; and (3) a biography of its founder, Sigmund Freud, that incorporates those aspects of his writing that have been suppressed by official, canonical interpretations of his work.

From inside this pharmacy we know that Freud was using cocaine throughout the time of his documented dreams and dream interpretations. In the experiments conducted primarily upon himself and scrupulously recorded (and published), in much the same way, and in the "high"-style, that De Quincey recorded his dreams, Freud came to study the "effects" of a drug upon the human body that gave upon a whole new theory of unconsciousness: one that (like the pharmacy) "keeps itself forever in reserve even though it has no fundamental profundity nor ultimate locality."[21]

ON *ÜBER COCA*

Freud worked with a purified form of cocaine and made careful recordings of his experiments on himself. He found the method of introduction into the body of little importance although there was no other substance that had so many different modes of application. It could be injected subcutaneously, drunk as a beverage in the form of coca wine, cocaine wine, or champagne, smoked in cigarettes, thrust into the nose with a brush, or employed as snuff, rubbed into the gums or inserted into the rectum. Every method had its followers. Nevertheless the greatest number preferred the nasal cavity as the place of application.[22]

In applying cocaine, Freud used "the most sophisticated measuring instruments available in order to obtain the most accurate possible psychophysiologic measures, and then correlated these simultaneously with carefully-described changes in mood and perception during the course of action of the drug. These experiments established appropriate dosage and a time course of the drug's action—a critical relationship in human experimentation."[23]

In the famous 1884 "botanical monograph," Freud's discussion moves from the structure of the coca plant, its cultivation procedure and lucrative trade, its history and uses in South America, its places of origin (Peru and Bolivia), and its accumulated myths and legends, through to its introduction into Europe in 1749 as "cocaine," first classified in 1786 in Lamark's *Encyclopédie Méthodique Botanique* under the name of *Erythroxylon Coca,* to the classification of its effects on animals. Regarding the latter he makes the remarkable observation that "we would . . . not expect to find that the effect of coca on animals in any way resembled the effects in which it has been described (in myths and legends) in man" since "we know that animals of different species—and even individuals of the same species—differ most markedly from one another in those chemical characteristics which determine the organism's receptivity to foreign substances."[24] With these variances in mind, Freud summarizes "the results" of his inquiry to the extent that "we can," in his own words: "comprehend the way cocaine affects both man and animal *'from a unified standpoint.'*"[25]

This "unified" perspective is further explored, paradoxically enough, in a fifth section, where he turns to the effects of coca on the healthy human body: his own. With his studies on cocaine, then, Freud was deeply concerned with the "human organism" as a body, which he studied by carrying out experiments on himself, that he then faithfully recorded. He measured the plant's "effects" against the findings of his contemporaries both in Europe and the United States, confirming their views and "unifying" their perspectives under the title of his own emergent corpus.

The "characteristic regard for the singular fact" that, according to Bernfeld and subsequently Jones, lay the groundwork for psychoanalysis, made Freud equally hesitant and sceptical in recognizing that his own reaction to the drug was not the general and not the most significant one.[26] For Freud:

> The rare fact, even the singular fact, always commanded respect, and impelled as much scientific thinking as the conspicuous, statistical sample based on impressive numbers. Since he himself had experienced aversion, rather than a craving for cocaine, habit formation could not—at least not automatically—be, in his view, the effect of the chemical properties of the drug.[27]

Although Bernfeld and Jones agree that "he would never have originated psychoanalysis without it,"[28] it is a curious feature of Freud's achievement that it was due precisely to this "attitude" that his work was so long stigmatized (and continues to be in some circles) as "nonscientific."[29]

FREUD ON COCAINE

Against the view that "the effect of coca is an imaginary one," or that as the Spaniards (and later all of Europe) believed, it is "the work of the devil," Freud set out to investigate the history, properties, effects, and therapeutic value of "this divine plant which satiates the hungry, strengthens the weak, and causes them to forget their misfortune."[30] He also investigated its application as a treatment for addiction: a treatment that, based on his own experiences, was to inaugurate a whole new theory of the human subject.[31]

Following Marvaud, whose Les aliments d'épargne (1873) he had at his disposal,[32] Freud became interested in the value of cocaine as a source of "nourishment" and used this as the perspective from which to explore its use as a therapeutic treatment: the treatment of dietetic disorders as well as of what were known as the disorders of the nervous system.[33] From its value in combatting hunger and fatigue to its value as "food" for another body, Freud's investigation of "the substances contained in coca leaves"[34] brought "the plant" to a theory of the unconscious mind and its psychotropic move toward language.

From his own assumed "unified perspective," Freud noted that: "in small doses, coca has a stimulating, and in larger doses a paralyzing, effect on the nervous system."[35] On the strength of his own experience, blended with the literature of the time,[36] Freud made the suggestion as to the theory of its action, since confirmed, that "cocaine acts not through direct stimulation of the brain but through abolishing the effects of agencies that depress one's bodily feelings [Gemeingefühl (coenesthesia)]."[37] "On Coca" not only confirmed Mantegazza's conclusions about the double action of cocaine, its stimulant yet numbing action on the stomach,[38] it was also to suggest to Freud its usefulness in treating melancholia and neurasthenia.

Since it now seems likely that both psychological and biological theories of mental illness and addiction will coexist,[39] consideration of Freud's studies on cocaine is particularly prescient. In testing for the biological antidepressant effects of cocaine as a stimulant and euphoriant agent,[40] Freud was unquestionably ahead of his time. According to Byck, Freud was correct in his early classification of cocaine as both a central nervous stimulant and a euphoriant. In contrast to Freud, Schroff in the 1880s and Louis Lewin in Phantastica as of 1924 (German edition),[41] had classed cocaine exclusively among the euphorica, "sedatives of mental activity . . . substances [which] diminish or even suspend the functions of emotion and perception in their widest sense. . . ."[42]

Unlike Lewin, who viewed cocaine as a narcotic, or Koller, who used it as an anaesthetic, Freud's classification of cocaine as a euphoriant as well as a stimulant, a substance that "feeds" the organism was unique. Yet no one has engaged with the significance of this nourishing "effect" for the development of psychoanalysis as we know it.

Freud's perspective on the "indirect" or double action of cocaine "unifies" the organism's production of a subject without a substance, a body without organs or gender. This brings Freud face to face with the pharmaceutical operations of a new corporeality, one in which the subject of drugs, and later the subject of psychoanalysis, takes on its own therapeutic agency. However, although this is an agency that has passed through a certain loss, it is not the loss of objects that is at stake.

THE CORPOREAL UNCONSCIOUS

Moving from descriptions of the effects of the external properties of the substance to descriptions of its internal ones, Freud devises a rhetoric of "feeling" that dissolves the boundaries between self and other, mind and body, in order to engage with unconsciousness in corporeal terms, with the narcotic effects or feelings of a corporeal interiority—a psychical space of surfaces and surface-effects—that was to give to the unconscious what in *A Thousand Plateaus* Deleuze and Guattari call the "plane of immanence that psychoanalysis has consistently botched."[43]

Consider, for example, Freud's language when in section V, "The Effect of Coca on the Healthy Human Body," he writes: "A few minutes after taking cocaine, one experiences a sudden exhilaration and *feeling* of lightness. One *feels* a certain furriness on the lips and palate, followed by a *feeling* of warmth in the lips and cold in the throat. On other occasions the predominant *feeling* is a rather pleasant coolness in the mouth and throat." Continuing with biographical descriptions of its "toxic effects," he adds: "breathing became slower and deeper . . . I noticed a slight slackening of the pulse. . . . This is often accompanied by a rumbling which must originate from high up in the intestine; two of the people I observed . . . said they were able to recognize movements of their stomachs . . ."[44]

From this and other observations, documented in a pre-analytic language of the body, Freud concludes: "The *psychic effect* of *cocaïnum muriaticum* in doses of 0.05 g–0.10 g consists of exhilaration and lasting euphoria, which does not differ in any way from the normal euphoria of the healthy person. . . . One *senses* an increase of self-control and *feels* more vigorous and more capable of work."[45]

Scrupulously outlining its effect on our "feeling" from the inside, Freud marks those narcotic or psychotropic effects not registered on the outside of the body, but on the inside: *an inside not yet constituted through language (as happens with his elaboration of the dream-work) but through the drug-work:* the organic pulsing, beating, sighing, and moving of seemingly almost detached body parts.

In this his first published paper—the "famous monograph on cocaine"—written in a language of sense that has no content, we find the first trace of the great Freudian "unconscious"—a corporeal unconscious that is not the site of energic and neuronic stasis,[46] or the passive repository of cultural images and myths that it was to become as of his and Breuer's studies on hysteria.[47] Freud, already duly cognizant of the subjective variance of these astutely and technologically measured "effects," continues his self-examination:

> During this stage of the cocaine condition, which is not otherwise distinguished, appear those symptoms which have been described as the wonderful stimulating effect of coca. Long-lasting, intensive mental or physical work can be performed without fatigue; it is as though the need for food and sleep, which otherwise makes itself felt peremptorily at certain times of the day, were completely banished. While the effects of cocaine last one can, if urged to do so, eat copiously and without revulsion; but one has the clear feeling that the meal was superfluous. Similarly, as the effect of coca declines it is possible to sleep on going to bed, but sleep can just as easily be omitted with no unpleasant consequences. During the first hours of the coca effect one cannot sleep, but this sleeplessness is in no way distressing. . . . I have tested this effect of coca, which wards off hunger, sleep, and fatigue and steels one to intellectual effort, some dozen times on myself; I had no opportunity to engage in physical work.[48]

A feature of the curious ambivalence of drugs, the relative nature of normality and good health could be nowhere better established than in the use of scientific instruments.[49] Although dependent upon the device of the dynamometer for the careful calculation of his results, Freud's treatment of the subject of drugs went well beyond this man-made instrument: into the treatment of a body without a substance and a subject without Truth, Freud discovered the making of another body and another health.[50]

It was precisely cocaine's anaesthetic suppression of bodily needs that culminated in Freud's most profound insight, a most radical idea, one that has structured the published documents of his pre-analytic works and inspired his later metapsychological ones: the appeal to cerebral anatomy as the seat of a psychotropic body that is not driven by biology. Introducing for the very first time the idea that was to claim his place in history, he writes the body in the language of unconsciousness. "One may perhaps assume," he contends in a key passage for the birth of psycho-analysis, "that the euphoria resulting from good health is also nothing more than the normal condition of a well-nourished cerebral cortex which *'is not conscious'* of the organs of the body to which it belongs."[51]

The corporeal unconscious, mapped onto the structure of the living organism, is not bound to the rhetoric of a metaphysics of substance. Rather, it behaves as though anatomy did not exist or as though it had no knowledge of it; it is *as ignorant* "of the science of the nervous system as we ourselves have learnt it."[52] In Freud's language of sense, a body without "the organs to which it belongs," is wrought out of the relation between space, deferral, and *"a newly figured language of the body."*[53]

Not cut in the cloth of culture per se, this is an internal body that "knows" how to "ward off hunger, sleep, and fatigue" because it "knows" nothing of anatomy or the reproduction of gender according to evolutionary divisions between needs and wants. The emergence of a body that knows how to nourish its "cerebral cortex" because it *knows nothing,* is unconscious, of its biology (its basic organic needs of hunger, sleep, fatigue)—is the first indication of a supplementary biology that drives psychoanalytic theory into a theory of addiction. With these words is texted a preliminary *"unconscious"* that holds in reserve what is to become Freud's theory of the drives without locking them into the ideology of objects and object-choices, its myths and representations through constructs like the Oedipus complex, castration complex, etc. It also forms the ground for much of what was to constitute Freud's pre-analytic work.

THE USES OF UNCONSCIOUSNESS

Freud's monograph on cocaine ends with a section on the therapeutic uses of cocaine. He lists altogether seven therapeutic uses of the drug: as a stimulant, in digestive disorders of the stomach, in cachexia, in the treatment of morphine and alcohol addiction, in the treatment of asthma, as an aphrodisiac, and local applications.

According to Hillman and Donaghue, none of these has been medically retained by 1963. "Despite his hopes that cocaine would be of value in internal medicine, in psychiatry and in surgery, today, cocaine as Freud used it, is generally considered medically useless."[54] However, my point here is that Freud had been far more subtle in his treatment of the subject of drugs.

Concealing the watershed between Freud's neurological and psychological writings, the disappearing papers on cocaine show that Freud's theory of the unconscious was already occupied with the instincts, "those periodically appearing imperative needs that originate in our body,"[55] and that he was searching for means toward the gratification of "certain tension producing (inner) needs, which, once they have gained mental representation, may be called instinctual drives."[56] Already Freud had conceived, "though somewhat vaguely," of a central agent interfering with normal well-being and of its restoration by the removal of the disturber.[57]

Freud's concern was—as in his first encounters with the unconscious—not so much with the external uses of cocaine, but with the internal ones. The possibility of a suppression of—a numbing, a being "not conscious" of—the requirements of the anatomical body (or indeed of the impingements of perception, reality, civilization, and so forth) by the well nourished cerebral cortex both *funds and founds* a pharmacy that places psychoanalysis outside the purview of the Platonic realm of the fixed, bounded, and inert body: the object of representation in religion, art, science, or the law.

Freud's cocaine studies gave him the sense of an internal landscape that, due to the drug, speaks the language of a body that has no history or prehistory. This is a body that is not constructed through symbol and myth; a body that has no language to be deciphered other than the machinic murmurs of its own workings. One can perceive, feel, and hear its internal organs at work. Through careful attention to the drug machine Freud could discover its secrets. What he found was the power of a toxic body, a "substance" whose effects were not the result of any *direct* stimulation but of the psychotropic operations of a very powerful urge.

To what extent is this carried over into psychoanalysis or obliterated by it? A post-analytic theory of addiction, latent in Freud's discoveries about the "functional reactions" of the organism to cocaine, acted as a blueprint for his treatment of the neuroses. Addiction was, throughout his later works, likened by Freud to the neurasthenia and the neuroses; similarly, drugs, in the Freudian-work, were also always part of the prescription.[58]

THE DRUG-WORK

If knowledge of Freud's cocaine studies is rare, inquiry into their value in exploring psychoanalysis as a theory of addiction is even rarer.[59]

Jones's official biography, which includes a chapter on "The Cocaine Episode," supports the view that, for Freud as much as for us, Freud's cocaine episode—a study which began in 1884 and ended three years later—was a failure and a mistake.

At best, Freud's studies on cocaine are understood to constitute his first scientific encounter with the neuroses, "those various forms and degrees of the impairment of happiness and capacity to work, that plagued his friends as well as himself."[60] According to Bernfeld, "the cocaine episode is therefore not only of interest to the biographical consideration of Freud, but also bears directly on the developments of psychoanalysis. For both reasons it is now also understood to deserve a thorough and detailed presentation, although it rates only a few lines in the history of pharmacology and medicine."[61]

Although Freud felt that one of the most important uses of cocaine would be by psychiatrists treating melancholia or neurasthenia,[62] he ostensibly abandoned it in favor of a different method of cure: psychoanalysis. However, if we return to the early narco-Freud, to what he discovered about the toxic drive and which broke ground for not only a study of hysterical neurosis, but also for a "narcoanalysis" of addiction "that could not obtain immediate clearance,"[63] we might arrive at a different conclusion.

I have argued that Freud's "suppressed" essays bring to light the theoretical implications of his antecedent experiments with cocaine, documented in complete minute detail throughout his vanishing (for reasons to be outlined) cocaine papers: a body of writing that puts into discourse, for the very first time in the Freudian work, the pharmaceutical operations of what cannot but be the makings of a corporeal "unconscious."

Without "being anything in itself," this is an emergent and radically other "unconscious" than that which makes itself manifest in his writings on hysteria. A network of intensities, zones, and fluxes, it is a plane of desire that is texted not in the representations, symbols, and myths of our culture, but in the language of feelings, sensations, and excitations *that come into being through the materiality of drugs*. This is also, I maintain, a plane upon which his theory of the unconscious as we know it (the unconscious of the dreamwork) becomes grafted.

In this way, Freud's cocaine studies also anticipate "the unconscious" as conceived in the later dual instinctual drive theory and in the concept of a "stimulus barrier," and prefigure its double status throughout his later works. Somewhere between the death drive and the cortical structure of the brain, it is the unconscious that renders the bioenergetic and neurological aspect of his contribution to the theory of addiction so rich and complex as an instrument of treatment, in both the therapeutic and the analytic mode.

It is the cocaine papers that yield the theory of a death instinct and the concept of the repetition compulsion as a superordinated regulatory (i.e., self-medicating) mechanism of mental functioning, the hypotheses, which according to his biographer Max Schur, "have been haunting psychoanalytic theory since 1920."[64] These works reflect the luminous idea that the death drive is not simply a "new discovery" made by Freud in his later writings, but rather, that it is already inscribed in his understanding of the corporeal unconscious that is stored in his earliest prepsychoanalytic texts where his promethean struggle for insight into the uncharted region of the mind begins.

Thus, Freud's study of the effect of coca in his infamous "On Coca" was to inaugurate his entire theoretical corpus, but with a certain twist. The dual action of cocaine reflects the dual structure of the "living vesicle" in Section IV of *Beyond the Pleasure Principle* (1920), the emergence of a prosthetic need, an appetite that lives in the internal psychotropic effects of the organism's response to pain.

AN ALTERED TREATMENT OF ADDICTION

Freud's dream, both literal and metaphorical, about "a drug from the dispensary which removes *hunger*: cocaine,"[65] expresses the antinomies of cocaine as the elixir of health. In German *"lateinische Küche"* literally means "Latin kitchen,"[66] and conveys the corporeal fashioning of a new need to be answered: the need to eliminate need. Hunger is not the only nutritional index of the body. Privations exist that call up another body, another need. The "food" in the kitchen dispenses with an unconscious that craves the drug. The understanding that this drug-craving was not organically determined, as we know today, was Freud's colossal achievement.

According to Bernfeld, "Freud speaks of addicts with overtones of pity and contempt; but he never stands in awe of these chemical poisons, which were considered by contemporary—and especially German—literature to possess the devilish property of undermining the power of moral responsibility. In his first acquaintance with the 'functional phenomenon' he oscillates, so it seems, between moral judgment and objective explanation in neurophysiological terms; between lack of will power or lability of centers. He is, in other words, a contemporary. Yet *he refuses to think of habit formation as a direct effect of the poison.*"[67]

In contrast to what was then supposed, Freud understood drug craving as a "functional" problem (not a purely "psychological problem") early on. However, it was not because of this that he relinquished coke for psychoanalysis; rather, it is because of coke that he could fashion psychoanalysis. It is not, as Hillman believes, that "in error and defeat he turned away from a physical, organic approach to the therapy of mental difficulties which led eventually to the discovery of the unconscious and psychoanalysis."[68] Rather, it was, inversely: a direct, "functional" approach to the unconscious that led eventually to the discovery of psychoanalysis as a form of therapy for mental difficulties.

Freud's theory of addiction, resulting from his own compulsive "need" to use cocaine against neurasthenia, is only articulated much later and runs alongside his theory of repression. It makes of the unconscious the form and process of a drive for a spectacular self-medication without recourse to a rhetoric of "master molecules" of addiction. He writes: "Alcoholic intoxication, which belongs to the same class of states [as mania], may (insofar as it is an elated one) be explained in the same way; here there is probably a suspension, produced by toxins, of expenditures of energy in repression."[69] The transformative pleasures of this kind of disconnection or "uncoupling" occur in the state of Dionysian-musical enchantment in which there is "an emotional dissociation or detachment of affective states from specific object relations."[70]

Already fascinated in his young mind with the uses and healing powers of unconsciousness, it was not until the *Interpretation,* and the deferral of his interest in drugs onto that of dreams, that the road would become clear for Freud. The "great cocaine excitement of the nineteenth century" that swept through Europe and especially the United States, did not, as others have supposed,[71] lead Freud astray; rather, it gave him the instruments and the method that was to become his subject for the remaining years of his life. Hillman and Donaghue hold that Freud had relied greatly upon American authorities to back his claim that the drug was harmless, and that a side effect of the cocaine episode on Freud was his subsequent embitterment with America, especially as found in his arguments against American psychiatry and medicine in favor of lay analysis.[72]

FREUD'S PHARMACY

In a letter to Fliess on June 12, 1900, Freud describes a visit to the house where he had his dream of "Irma's Injection." "Do you suppose," he writes, "that some day a marble tablet will be placed on the house, inscribed with these words?—In This House, on July 24th, 1895, the Secret of Dreams was Revealed to Dr. Sigm. Freud."[73] My argument is that, as this letter suggests, Freud's studies on the *internal* application of cocaine (its analgesic properties) anticipate the theory that was to fund/found one of modernity's greatest pharmacies: the legacy of psychoanalysis itself.

In his experiments with cocaine, Freud describes the workings of a *corporeal unconscious* that anticipates at the same time as it challenges the "unconscious" as we know it. Freud's cocaine papers enable a rhetoric and a vocabulary of sense—a language of "feelings" and sensory experiences—that dissolve the boundaries between the psychical and the physical domains, *the inside and the outside,* to radically challenge the hegemony of the (social scientific) subject of addiction, and expose the dependency of this subject (of addiction) on the binary and hierarchical model of the hallucinated, masculine subject of desire that drives psychoanalytic theory forward.

Tracing a subject without a substance, cocaine's preliminary "unconscious" extends across the smooth spaces of the Freudian drug-work. Sketched in the margins of a modern science of drugs, this "unconscious" presents us with an altogether new thought: one "proper" to a psychoanalysis of addiction. Texted not in the representations, symbols, and myths of familialism that make up our language, but in the rhythms of the body, its intensities, sensations, and excitations, this corporeal "unconscious" that finds expression in Freud's cocaine pharmacy performs the *mise-en-abyme* (evacuation and destruction) of the walled-in subject of bounded and phallomorphic desire that has hitherto occupied psychoanalysis.

Freud's cocaine experience, opening the space between the psychical and the physical body, gives way to a new horizon. Against the conventional belief in the "demonic" power of the substance,[74] Freud found, at the very heart of addiction, the agenced internal production of an other interiority, the bottomless fund of an altogether other will.

Through the drug-work emerges full-blown, and in Freud's own words, a psychotropic body; a body moved by toxicity, euphoria and the organicity of its desires. A "supplementary interiority,"[75] a cerebral tissue not yet constituted through the operations of language (as happens with his elaboration of the dream-work), but not hidden from us either (as is the unconscious), this new toxic body is one that both supplements the "unconscious" of the dream-work and supplants it.

In Freud's cocaine *pharmacy*—a space "that simultaneously holds and separates"[76]—a preliminary and subcutaneous unconscious opens to the analytic study of a drive hollowed out of the traces of a new corporeal surface. In the altered states of desire's narcotic structure, the subject of drugs takes its place at the same time as it recedes and disappears.

The "entropic" principle of mental functioning opens to another doorway: to what I term the "psychotropic principle," after Freud's studies on cocaine and what they have to show us about cravings without an end,[77] drives that exist but which the suppression of his discovery of the drug drive[78] has brought the tradition of psychoanalysis to evacuate.

NOTES

1. The "thrall" of addiction is today explained via recourse to a "master molecule" called dopamine—a mind-bending chemical secreted by the brain. Drug treatments of mental illness and studies in the neurobiology of the brain explore the biological base for drug dependence and challenge us to think in terms of a new corporeality. Is the brain a biological organ? If so, what connects it to learning and memory? Given the mutism of psychoanalysis on the subject of drugs the reader should not be surprised that consideration of Freud's cocaine papers should be key to the creation of new strategies in the treatment of addiction. The Canadian Psychoanalytic Society (Québec English Branch) and the Addictions Unit, Department of Psychiatry, Montreal General Hospital in Montreal recently held a conference "Treating Addictions: Contemporary Perspectives from Psychoanalysis and Neurobiology" (May 4, 2002), that opened with a presentation on "Historical Background: Freud's Cocaine Papers" (Richard Karmel, Ph.D.). The conference featured papers on "A Psychoanalytic Look at the Heart of Addiction and the Relationship of Addiction to Compulsion" (Lance Dodes, M.D.), and "A Neuro-psychoanalytic Perspective on Drug Addiction and the Psychology of Dreams" (Brian Johnson, M.D.).

In the following I give substance to Freud's debt to the plant without whose action the world of psychoanalysis would not have opened itself to him and I advance arguments regarding cocaine as the "secret" of his theory of dreams. Freud's "monograph on a plant," his "dissertation on the *coca-plant*" which had drawn Carl Koller's attention to the value of the external application of cocaine (its anaesthetic properties), is recalled in the first dream Freud ever submitted to an interpretation, his dream of "Irma's Injection" that opens the extraordinary tract on language and the unconscious, *The Interpretation of Dreams*.

The implications of Freud's "preliminary unconscious" for the study of gender in psychoanalytic and neuro-psychoanalytic perspectives on drug addiction will be explored in my study *Freud's Pharmacy: Sexuality and Narcotic Desire in an Altered Treatment of Addiction*. For an altered strategy in the treatment of women's addictions, see my articles "Sexuality and Narcotic Desire: Toward an Altered Strategy for Treating Women's Addictions," *Symposium: Journal of the Society for Hermeneutics and Postmodern Thought*, 2 (fall 1998): pp. 123–137; "From Care to Cure: Toward an Altered Strategy for Treating Women's Addictions. *Simone de Beauvoir Institute Review* 17 (1997): pp. 23–31. My work here and elsewhere draws on the lexicon on the addicted body produced by Avital Ronell's *Crack Wars* (1992) and by Sylvie Le Poulichet's monograph on Freud, *Toxicomanies et Psychanalyse: Les narcoses du désir* (Paris: PUF, 1987).

2. Sigmund Freud, "On Coca," translated by Steven A. Edminster, *The Cocaine Papers*, A. K. Donaghue and J. Hillman, eds. (Vienna, Zurich: Dunquin Press, 1963) p. 9. This is a translation of "Ueber Coca" (July 1884), Freud's first essay on cocaine that was reprinted in 1885, with minor corrections and an "Addenda," as *Über Coca* (February 1885). The translation has been approved by James Strachey. Freud's essay on cocaine first appears in America as "Coca" (December 1884), a translation by S. Pollak, M.D., for *The St. Louis Medical and Surgical Journal*. However, because this is both an abstract of the original and a compendium of other sources, it is not a translation in the usual sense and is not to be confused with "On Coca," although it appears alongside it in both the Dunquin Press edition by Hillman (above) and in Robert Byck's subsequent annotated anthology of *The Cocaine Papers by Sigmund Freud* (New York: Stonehill, 1974).

3. *The Letters of Sigmund Freud*, Ernst L. Freud, ed., translated by Tania and James Stern; cited in Byck, op. cit., p. 45.

4. Sigmund Freud, *The Interpretation of Dreams*, translated by James Strachey (New York: Penguin) 255; see also Byck, op. cit., p. 225.

5. Ibid., p. 259; also cited in Byck, op. cit., p. 229.

6. This dream is actually the "dream specimen" that Freud first analyzed and launches chapter II of the *Interpretation* on "The Method of Interpreting Dreams: An Analysis of a Dream Specimen," ibid., pp. 182–199.

7. Ibid., p. 187; Byck, p. 211.

8. See Strachey's editorial comment on Freud's text, ibid., note 1, p. 187; also cited in Byck, p. 211. This "slip" is also a "misprint" which occurs in every German edition of the *Interpretation;* see Byck, p. 211.

9. See Siegfried Bernfeld, "Freud's Studies on Cocaine," *Journal of the American Psychoanalytic Association*, No. 4, Vol. I, October, 1953; reprinted in Byck, 348ff; cf. also Donaghue and Hillman, p. iii.

10. Ernst Jones, *The Life and Works of Sigmund Freud*, Vol. I (New York: Basic Books, 1953).

11. See Byck, p. 323. Basing himself on a more contextual reading of Bernfeld, Byck's anthology brings to light some of the less known historical, cultural, and biographical documents surrounding Freud's cocaine studies. The subcutaneous injections of cocaine that Freud had been recommending to Ernst von Fleischl-Marxow, Freud's "dear friend" suffering from morphine withdrawal, caused Fleischl to become known as Europe's first cocaine addict. Freud's prescription of cocaine as treatment against Fleischl's addiction has been held responsible for Fleischl's untimely death in that same year, bringing Freud to renounce, although possibly (as is our version here) only cleverly *displace,* his anterior three-year interest in cocaine. The *St. Louis Medical Journal* version of Freud's paper "On Coca," which appears in Freud's *Cocaine Papers* as "Coca," is not a direct translation but a synopsis of the original and is alone to propose the absolute value of

subcutaneous injections of cocaine in the treatment of morphinism. These recommendations on the use of cocaine are not at all in his original 1884 paper. The comments attributed to Freud on the treatment of morphinism in this version are Fleischl's own; see Byck, p. 85. Indeed, in his third paper, published from the lecture, "On the General Effect of Cocaine" in March of 1885, Freud stipulates the difference between subcutaneous and other applications of cocaine in the treatment of morphinism; see Freud, *Cocaine Papers*, p. 31.

12. Byck gives the historical and cultural background to this; see op. cit., p. xvii. See David F. Musto's "Sherlock Holmes and Sigmund Freud: A Study in Cocaine," *The Journal of the American Medical Association* (April, 1968) for the cocaine addiction of another analytic hero.

13. Ibid., p. xvii.

14. Byck has collected all seven of Freud's articles on cocaine, including other documents (letters) revealing the progression of Freud's thoughts on the subject between 1884–1887. They are "Ueber Coca," July 1884; "Coca," December 1884; "Contribution to the Knowledge of the Effect of Cocaine," January 1885; "Addenda to *Über Coca*," February 1885; "On the General Effect of Cocaine," March 1885; "Parke's Universal Panacea," August 1885; and "Remarks on Craving For and Fear of Cocaine," July 1887.

15. In 1963, Freud's papers on cocaine were translated into English, read through by Freud's translator, Mr. James Strachey, edited by A.K. Donaghue and James Hillman, and published in Vienna by the Dunquin Press. Because of the obscurity of the edition, however, Freud's cocaine papers were again fated to disappear—even the historical library at the Yale University School of Medicine did not list the Dunquin Press edition, *The Cocaine Papers*, in its catalog (Byck, p. xvii).

16. Ibid., p. xvii.

17. The McGill Library, where I do much of my research, has in its collection one copy of the slim Dunquin edition by Hillman. I will spare the reader an account of my trials and tribulations in attempting to copy any portions of this work that was not only completely hidden on the shelves, in a row outside the usual traffic of call nos. and their series, but also falling, in pieces, out of my hands onto the copier, floor, and world around me as I thought how naive of me, under the circumstances, not to have anticipated and not braced myself for the frustration in advance.

18. For different discussions of the Freud-Koller appropriation story, see the biographical accounts of Freud's cocaine episode by Jones, op. cit., Bernfeld, op. cit., and Byck, op. cit. See also the article by Hortense Koller Becker, "Coca Koller," from *The Psychoanalytic Quarterly* Vol. XXXII, 1963; reprinted in Byck. See also Paul Roazen's very brief account in *Brother Animal: The Story of Freud and Tausk* (New Brunswick, New Jersey: Transaction Publishers, 1990), p. 88.

19. Ibid., p. xvii. According to Byck, Freud's papers on cocaine can be said to be not only thorough in their review and accurate in their physiological and

psychological experimentation, but they are also "almost prescient in their consideration of points that have become major issues in modern psychopharmacology," ibid., p. xxvi.

20. Freud both established a tradition in the reporting of substances with psychoactive properties (cf. Abbey Hofmann, who, in 1943, discovered the central effects of lysergic acid diethylamide or LSD), and also fell within one. This is a "tradition" that would include the likes of De Quincey, Benjamin, Artaud, Michaux, James, Cocteau, Huxley, Burroughs, and others (see Derrida's, "The Rhetoric of Drugs" in this volume and *all* the pieces in Part I).

21. Derrida, "Plato's Pharmacy," op. cit.

22. Louis Lewin, *Phantastica: A Classic Survey of Mind-Altering Plants* (Rochester: Park Street Press, 1998), p. 68. The intense action of cocaine when introduced in this way may be explained by the existence of several arterial and venous systems uniting the nasal cavity with the cavities of the cranium and the corresponding lymphatic channels; see Byck, op. cit., p. 246.

23. Byck, op. cit., p. xx.

24. Freud, *Cocaine Papers,* 7. The more experiences with cocaine Freud accumulated, the more evident it became to him that the *subjective* effects of the drug—ranging from euphoria to uneasiness and toxicity—differed vastly in different persons. See Bernfeld, op. cit., p. 333.

25. Ibid.

26. Bernfeld, op. cit., p. 346.

27. Bernfeld, op. cit., p. 346

28. Bernfeld, op. cit., p. 346.

29. Bernfeld, op. cit., p. 346.

30. "On Coca," op. cit., p. 2.

31. In the climate of reception of "new remedies" that was typical of the new American therapeutics, it was generally believed that "a harmless remedy for the blues is imperial" whether one is or is not addicted to something. The American journal *The Therapeutic Gazette,* June 15, 1880, reviewed an article "Erythroxylon Coca as an Antidote to the Opium Habit" published in the *Louisville Medical News* by Professor E. R. Palmer who found coca an efficient means for "relief from the thraldom of opium" (cited in Byck, op. cit., p. 19). The author closes with the idea, drawn from other reviews, that "one feels like trying coca, with or without the opium habit" (Palmer, op. cit., cited in Byck, op. cit., p. 21). Of all Freud's sources, however, it was Dr. Theodor Aschenbrandt's report on the effect of coca on exhausted soldiers that was his greatest inspiration ("On Coca," op. cit., p. 6). It introduced him to Mantegazza's reports of cocaine as a stimulant, whose effects impart a form of "nourishment" of the nervous system. Aschenbrandt's essay, "The

Physiological Effects and Significance of Cocaine Muriate on the Human Organism: Clinical Observations during the 1883 Fall Manoeuvres of the Second Battalion" (*Deutsche Medizinische Wochenscrift*, No. 50, December 12, 1883, pp. 730–732, translated by Therese Byck; cited in Byck, op. cit., p. 388, note 3) integrated the presence of Mantegazza's idea of "a beneficial effect on digestion, the heart, and respiration" with "a feeling of general well-being, pleasure in intellectual accomplishment" (Aschenbrandt op. cit., cited in Byck, op. cit., p. 22). See Paolo Mantegazza *"Sulle virtu igieniche e medicinale della coca, e sugli alimenti nervosa in generale,"* Milano 1859; cited in Byck, op. cit., p. 388, note 5). Mantegazza was an Italian physician and anthropologist as well as a Professor of Anthropology in Florence (Byck, op. cit., p. 402).

32. "On Coca," op. cit., p. 6.

33. Ibid., p. 7.

34. Ibid., p. 5.

35. "On Coca," op. cit., p. 7.

36. Anticipating Freud's monumental body of work on the treatment of nervous disorders Aschenbrandt writes, paraphrasing Mantegazza, "Cocaine must be regarded as nourishment of benefit to the nerves" (Mantegazza, cited in Byck, op. cit., p. 23), "a means of nourishing the nervous system" (Ibid., p. 22). For Aschenbrandt, "the alkaloid of the coca leaf, cocaine, is the substance that possesses the 'miraculous' quality described by Mantegazza" (Ibid., p. 23); for Freud, this effect was secreted by the unconscious: a subject curiously without a substance, although not one "hidden" as we have hitherto thought.

37. Jones, op. cit., p. 83; also in Byck, op. cit., p. 9, my emphasis.

38. In his discussion of the use of coca for digestive disorders of the stomach, Freud, following Mantegazza, argues that the effect of cocaine on the stomach "is twofold: stimulation of movement and reduction of the organ's sensitivity" ("On Coca," op. cit., p. 17; also cited in Byck, op. cit., p. 67, my emphasis).

39. For example, it is believed that certain depressions/addictions are biologically determined, the result of a biochemical abnormality, which is characterized by a deficiency of the hormonal neurotransmitters, ibid., p. xxvi.

40. Ibid., p. xxvi.

41. Lewis Lewin, *Der Kokainismus in Phantastica: Die Betäubenden und Erregenden Genussmittel für Ärzte und Nichtärzte* (Berlin: Verlag von Georg Stilke, 1924). The curious unavailability in English for over 30 years of Lewin's *Phantastica*—by now a "collector's item"—is another story. The edition cited in this chapter is *Phantastica: A Classic Survey of Mind-Altering Plants* (Rochester: Park Street Press, 1998). It is a reprinted version of the disappearing *Phantastica, Narcotic and Stimulating Drugs, Their Use and Abuse* (New York: E. P. Dutton, 1931).

42. Ibid., p. xxiv. Interestingly, although Lewin's inclusion of morphine, codeine and cocaine in this group, furthered a classification of psychoactive drugs which was used in the original formulation of American narcotic laws. In the modern classification of psychoactive drugs, cocaine is grouped with both amphetamine and caffeine, ibid.

43. Gilles Deleuze and Félix Guattari, *A Thousand Plateaus: Capitalism and Schizophrenia,* translated by Brian Massumi (Minneapolis: University of Minnesota Press, 1987), p. 284.

44. "On Coca," op. cit., p. 9; also in Byck, pp. 58–59; my emphasis.

45. Ibid., p. 10; also in Byck, op. cit., p. 60; my emphasis.

46. The corporeal unconscious that is stored in Freud's writing on cocaine and that functions as the organism's response to pain through a dual action, does not assimilate the notion that a body will seek to stay unchanged (keep its motion constant) with the notion that it will seek to divest itself of quantity or motion; see Teresa Brennan, *The Interpretation of the Flesh: Freud and Feminity* (New York: Routledge, 1992), p. 109. In terms of Newton's first and second laws, the principle of inertia is the principle of constancy. While the concept's history in the late nineteenth century was varied, inertia was not about lack of motion. According to Teresa Brennan, the (masculine) subject is born when it "constructs an inert point, in the common sense of inert . . . gives it a fixed 'subject-centered' point of reference . . . establishes the beginning of memory . . . the 'exigencies of life,' the biological rome of attention, etc." (ibid., p. 109). This "imaginary unity" (ibid., p. 115) subtends the identification of the death drive with a masculine subject of desire: the "link between orgasm and detumescence," the "entropic principle." For a discussion of this principle in Freud, see Elizabeth Grosz, *Space, Time, and Perversion* (New York: Routledge, 1995), 201 ff.

47. For a state-of-the-art discussion of the unconscious in Freud's writings on hysteria, see David. B. Allison and Mark S. Roberts, "On Constructing the Disorder of Hysteria," *The Journal of Medicine and Philosophy* 19 (1994): pp. 239–259. For a discussion of the unconscious as repository of ideas, see ibid., p. 255.

48. "On Coca," op. cit., p. 11; also cited in Byck, op. cit., p. 60.

49. Freud wished to find a method by which the physiological effects—increased strength and endurance—could be measured and expressed in *objective language;* from such a "testing method I expected that a real uniformity of the effect of cocaine would be divulged to me" (Bernfeld, op. cit., p. 336).

50. Freud's extensive use of the dynamometer to calculate the changes in muscle strength and motor power founds the thesis of his second paper on cocaine, "Contribution to the Knowledge of the Effect of Cocaine," (January 1885). For Freud's charts see, *Cocaine Papers;* also in Byck, op. cit., p. 97. The

Byck edition of the paper comes with an introduction by Anna Freud. See Bernfeld, op. cit., p. 336–338, for a discussion of Freud's thesis in this paper. According to Jones, "Freud had begun some tests with a dynamometer to ascertain whether the apparent increase in muscular strength obtained by the use of cocaine was a subjective illusion or was objectifiably verifiable, and in these he cooperated with Koller. They both swallowed some cocaine and, like everyone else, noticed the numbing of the mouth and lips. This meant more to Koller than to Freud" (Jones, op. cit., p. 86; also in Byck, op. cit., p. 31).

51. "On Coca," op. cit., p. 11; my emphasis.

52. This corporeal "unconscious" that animates Freud's thesis on the effects of the coca-plant filters its way through the watershed between his cocaine papers and his legitimate pre-analytic works, to shore itself up in a brilliant little study—"Some Points for a Comparative Study of Organic and Hysterical Motor Paralyses" (1893 [1888–1893], *The Standard Edition of the Complete Psychological Works of Sigmund Freud*, translated from the German by James Strachey, Volume I (1886–1899); *Pre-Psycho-Analytic Publications: Dutton and Unpublished Drafts* (London: Hogarth Press, 1966). There, he writes: "I, on the contrary, assert that the lesion in hysterical paralyses must be completely independent of the anatomy of the nervous system, since *in its paralyses and other manifestations hysteria behaves as though anatomy did not exist or as though it had no knowledge of it*" (ibid., p. 169). In "Hysteria" (1888), ibid., Freud writes: "It may be said that *hysteria is as ignorant* of the science of the structure of the nervous system as we ourselves before we learnt it" (ibid., p. 49; my emphasis). This is almost a literal replica of the well-known sentence in the French paper that we first find in Freud's "On Coca."

53. Cf. Teresa Brennan, *The Interpretation of the Flesh: Freud and Femininity* (New York: Routledge, 1992), p. xi.

54. Donaghue and Hillman, op. cit., p. iv.

55. Schur, op. cit., p. 341.

56. Ibid., p. 321, my emphasis.

57. Ibid., p. 341.

58. In *Civilization and Its Discontents* (1929), he stipulates that: "The service rendered by intoxicating media in the struggle for happiness and in keeping misery at a distance is so highly prized as a benefit that individuals and peoples alike have given them an established place in the economies of their libido. We owe to such media not merely the immediate yield of pleasure, but also a greatly desired degree of independence from the external world" (London: Hogarth, 1969), p. 15. And, "No discussion of the possibilities of human happiness should omit to take into consideration the relation between narcissism and object-libido. We require to know what being essentially self-dependent signifies

for the economies of the libido" (ibid., p. 21). Cf. this "libidinal autonomy" and "narcissistic withdrawal" in Freud's "On Narcissism," Section II and the "second degree of solitude" in Guattari, this volume.

59. Jürgen Vom Scheidt, in "Sigmund Freud und das Kokain," *Psyche,* Vol. 27 (1973): pp. 385–429, does explore the relation of Freud's cocaine studies to the development of his ego psychology, though not to addiction, and Sylvie Le Poulichet's recusive and arch-recondite study *Toxicomanies et psychanalyse: Les narcoses du désir* (Paris: PUF, 1987) touches on Freud's potential theory of addiction without regard for feminist positions on Freud's notorious and controversial psychoanalytic theory of gender. Avital Ronell, whose *Crack Wars: Literature, Addiction, Mania* (Nebraska: University of Nebraska Press, 1992) borrows from Le Poulichet, as well as Deleuze and Guattari, in *A Thousand Plateaus: Capitalism and Schizophrenia* (Minneapolis: University of Minnesota Press, 1987), having themselves borrowed heavily from Freud's cocaine corpus, elliptically comment on the cocaine studies.

60. Bernfeld, op. cit., p. 323.

61. Ibid., p. 324.

62. Bernfeld, op. cit., p. 366.

63. Ronell, op. cit., p. 53.

64. Max Schur, *Freud: Living and Dying* (New York: International Universities Press, 1972), p. 321.

65. *Interpretation,* p. 297.

66. Ibid., p. 297, Editor's note 3.

67. Bernfeld, op. cit., p. 347; my emphasis.

68. Donaghue and Hillman, op. cit., p. vi.

69. "Mourning and Melancholy" (1917), PFL 11, *On Metapsychology: The Theory of Psychoanalysis* (New York: Penguin, 1984), p. 264.

70. David Allison, "Nietzsche's Dionysian High: Morphin' with the Endorphins," p. 48.

71. Donaghue and Hillman, op. cit., p. iv.

72. Ibid., p. v.

73. *Interpretation,* p. 199, note 1.

74. Cf. attribution of "demonic power" of the substance to possess and weaken the will, which was Lewin's and others' theory of addiction. For more on these, see Eve Kosofsky Sedgwick's famous article, "Epidemics of the Will," in *Zone 6: Incorporations,* Jonathan Crary and Stanford Kwinter, eds. (Cambridge, MA: MIT Press, 1992).

75. See Ernst Jünger, *Approches, drogues et ivresse* (Paris: Gallimard, 1973). For a discussion of this "supplementary interiority" of drugs in political terms, see Ronell, op. cit., p. 33 and Sylvie Le Poulichet, op. cit., for a discussion in psychoanalytic ones.

76. Michel Foucault, "Maurice Blanchot: The Thought from Outside." In *Foucault/Blanchot,* translated by Brian Massumi and Jeffrey Mehlam (New York: Zone Books, 1987).

77. Instead, the drive as constitutive (of the body, its objects) is in this respect "constituted as a threat to the integrity of the self," Leo Bersani, *The Freudian Body: Psychoanalysis and Art* (New York: Columbia University Press, 1986), p. 60. "The identity between pleasure and pain, and the profound link between sexuality and destruction (as well as creation) are hidden . . . by an analogy with an opposition (between pleasure and death), an analogy which reduces sexuality to yet another manifestation of stasis" (ibid., p. 63). Rather, it becomes manifest in our "susceptibility to being affected, altered, sustained, and wounded, exposed to the other, exposed to pain," as writes Alphonso Lingis in "The Sensuality and the Sensitivity," in *Face to Face with Levinas,* Richard A. Cohen, ed. (Albany: State University of New York Press Press, 1980), p. 229. This is pleasure *without an end:* "pleasure in exudations, excretions, exhalations as voluptuous pleasure engulfs and obliterates purposes and directions and any sense of where it is itself going," (ibid., p. 102).

78. One must note that Freud's material on the drug drive is not only suppressed, it is also re-assigned, infinitely promising itself in the procedure of psychoanalysis itself. As Avital Ronell suggests: "If Freud was right about the apparent libidinal autonomy of the drug addict, then drugs are *libidinally invested.* To get off drugs, or alcohol (major narcissistic crisis), the addict has to shift dependency to a person, an ideal, or to the procedure itself of the cure" (op. cit., 25). According to Deleuze and Guattari: "Psychoanalysis can be taken as a model of reference because it was able, with respect to essentially affective phenomena, to construct the schema of a specific causality divorced from ordinary social or psychological generalities. But this schema still relies on a plane of organization that can never be apprehended in itself, that is always concluded from something else, that is always inferred, concealed from the system of perception: it is called the Unconscious" (Deleuze and Guattari, op. cit., p. 283). However, in Freud's cocaine studies there is "no longer a conscious-unconscious dualism machine, because the unconscious is, or rather *is produced, there where consciousness goes,* carried by the plane" (ibid., p. 284; my emphasis). It is, I argue, to this plane of the Freudian corporeal unconscious that any future "pharmacoanalysis" (ibid., 283) or "narcoanalysis" (Ronell, op. cit.) of the addicted self must go.

Chapter Eleven

SCHREBER'S ECSTASIES, OR WHO EVER LISTENED TO DANIEL PAUL?

ZVI LOTHANE

Hands, that the rod of empire might have sway'd,
Or waked to ecstasy the living lyre.

—Thomas Gray, *The Bard,* xii

To burn always with this hard, gemlike flame, to maintain
this ecstasy, is success in life.

—Walter Horatio Pater, *The Renaissance*

O we can wait no longer,
We take to ship, O soul,
Joyous we too launch out on trackless seas,
Fearless for unknown shores on waves of ecstasy to sail,
Amid the wafting winds (thou pressing me to thee,
   I thee to me, O soul),
Caroling free, singing our song of God,
Chanting our chant of pleasant exploration.

—Walt Whitman, *Passage to India,* 8

That noble and most sovereign reason,
Like sweet bells jangled out of tune and harsh:
That unmatched form and feature of blown youth,
Blasted with ecstasy.

—William Shakespeare, *Hamlet III,* i

Paul Schreber (1842–1911) left a mark on the intellectual history of Europe[1] with his immortal *Denkwürdigkeiten eines Nervenkranken*. The correct translation is: "Reflections of a nervous patient," but the English mistranslation by Macalpine and Hunter as *Memoirs of My Nervous Illness* (1903;[2] henceforth abbreviated as S) has died hard. But Schreber was at heart a *Dichter,* a poet, with a tendency to philosophize. Let me emphasize that "memoirs" in the title is not a synonym for memories, although Schreber was into remembering and recollecting a great deal. Rather, the term is closer to the now obsolete sense of "learned treatise," as in eighteenth century French: "memoires" *servir*. Professionally Schreber was miscast as Richter, judge, and even to a greater degree when, in 1893, he rose to the position of President of a *Zivilsenat* at the Superior Court of Appeals of the Kingdom of Saxony. Paradoxically wrecked by his own success, he lived through a personal odyssey of fall and redemption, during which he experienced a number of various ecstasies. As expressed by Pater above, he considered his ecstatic experiences far more important to him than his entire legal career. Like Gray, he understood the power of poetry to rise above the earthly power that declared him legally insane, reducing him to the legal level of a seven-year-old child and to imprisonment in an asylum for life. That is why he used the by then obsolete legal term, not a schizophrenic neologism, *Seelenmord* (soul murder), to proclaim that he had been a victim of *Justizmord,* a judicial murder, perpetrated on an innocent victim by the conjoined power of psychiatry and the law. This was expressed in the usually omitted subtitle of his book: "under what premises can a person considered insane be held in a mental hospital against his declared will." Like Whitman, he sailed on the wings of ecstasy to both explore and wrestle with God. Since in Shakespeare's quotation ecstasy means insanity, let us examine some poetical and pathological definitions of ecstasy and their relation to emotional illness.

THE MEANINGS OF ECSTASY

The Greek word ecstasy has two fundamental meanings. Literally, "ecstasy" means to stand or to be out of place; metaphorically, it means to be psychologically out of place, to be displaced or transported from the ordinary place of living and working to a place of astonishment, rapture, and trance. When applied to mystical experiences, it refers to a state in which the mind set free from the body contemplates a supernatural or religious phenomenon or object. But invoking the supernatural immediately creates an abyss between optical and mental vision. For what did St. John of the Cross mean when he had a vision of the Virgin? What did Joan of Arc mean when she claimed she spoke with the Archangel Michael? Did they really see and hear what they said they saw and heard, or did they merely imagine, or dream, or hallucinate their visions and voices?

When the term "vision" refers to a state of mind, it means giving oneself over to an overpowering emotion, or exaltation, in which the mind is transfixed upon, or fascinated by, some idea or some intense feeling; a state implying the transient suspension of normal psychological functions of perception, ratiocination, and goal directness. In a looser sense, one may speak of the ecstasies of mirth and joy as against those of grief and fear. Where emotions exist there is flow of energy, a flow as scientifically elusive as the feelings and the emotions themselves. For whereas it is easy to demonstrate and measure kinetic and heat energy, it has not been possible to either show or measure the energy of sexuality: Wilhelm Reich tried, and look where it got him.[3] Can you measure pleasure? No, you can only feel it and compare it to memories of past pleasures. Can you demonstrate the energy of some desire? No, but you can attest to the intensity of the awareness of desire, whether it occurs in the waking state or in dreams. The scientific criteria of measurement and quantification are inadequate as far as ecstasy is concerned. Conventionally, we can and usually do refer to something universally sharable in the common emotional experiences of mankind, such as pleasure and pain, or mirth and mourning, and we call such extrapolations into other minds feats of intuition, identification, sympathy, and empathy. But we are forever unable to know how and what the other really feels. We can only share in the other's experience by evocation through gesture, word, and tone, which, in turn, produces in us a vicarious participation in the other's experience or ecstasy.[4] We also attribute such sharing to emotional contagion, or induction of emotion.

Paul Schreber referred to both kinds of ecstasy, the religious and the emotional. It was the religious kind that got him in trouble with the powers that be. Professor Emil Flechsig, representing official science in Leipzig, and Asylum Director Guido Weber, representing forensic authority in Dresden, *a priori* defined Schreber not only as infirm but also as insane. Had he only opened himself to the emotional ecstasies of grief and despair, Schreber would have been classified—in keeping with his self-diagnosis—as merely suffering from a mood disorder, i.e., a nerve disorder, or *Nervenkrankheit,* thus temporarily infirm and capable of being restored to his previous normal state. But as he chose to allow himself to be transported into the realm of the supernatural and the religious and to tell about it, when he elected to speak of his divine

visions and divine miracles in *Flammenworte,* or words of fire, he
landed himself in serious trouble: he was diagnosed as suffering from
Geisteskrankheit, i.e., insanity, with far reaching forensic consequences.
But his insanity was harmless: he never hurt anyone, nor were his suicide attempts serious. He fled from work and marriage because he could
not handle them any longer. He screamed and roared and bellowed and
frightened his wife. But above all, like Salman Rushdie and other
heretics, he spoke words that irritated his audience: the psychiatrists and
their helpers. His symptoms were unacceptable speeches.[5]

OF SEEING AND HEARING, OF VISIONS AND VOICES

The notion of vision and miracle, as staples of the supernatural, draw
our immediate attention. We have already noted that the term "vision"
refers to the normal processes of seeing things and people in the world,
to "seeing" objects and persons not usually seen. It is not as immediately
evident that "miracle" derives from the basic Latin word *mirari,* to look,
as in the Spanish *mirar,* which is close to *admirar,* look in wonderment,
consider the thing or person seen as wondrous and wonderful, or marvelous. The same idea is expressed in the German *wunderbar* and *wun-
dervoll* and in the French *merveilleux.* However, as with "vision," these
words are used in two very different contexts. For example, such natural
phenomena as the rain forest, or even the less spectacular northern forest, are naturally wonderful, with their ecstasy of colors, sounds, and
scents. But they would be described as marvelous, not as miraculous.
The latter adjective is reserved for something that astonishes and sur-
prises us as being unexpectedly beyond nature, as being supernatural.
Naturally, winged horses and chariots do not fly in the skies, the sun
does not stop at midday, men do not walk on water, and flesh blisters
when it comes in contact with intense heat. Physical objects behave in
accordance with natural laws. We only enter the realm of the miraculous, either as mystics or as madmen, when we claim to see a painted
Virgin Mary weeping with real tears, or when we hear the sun talk to us
in a human voice.

Miracle is related to another word derived from *mirari:* mirage, or
illusion. Is then seeing a weeping painting a true miracle or just a mirage,
due to a peculiar physical effect, like the mirage in the desert? Or is the
peculiar sense-perception created by a special physiological effect—e.g.,
a metabolic condition of the body—or is it a psychological effect of the
mind and emotions, such that a particular mirage, or illusion, easily
changes into a mirage-belief, or a delusion? And by a remarkable coin-

cidence, the words miracle and admiration belong to the family of words that also contains the word" smile," whereas illusion and delusion are derived from *ludere,* to play and to laugh.

But we need not go far to find visions: they occur to everyone every night in the form of technicolor, three-dimensional kaleidoscopic scenarios, at times accompanied by speeches, in darkness, during sleep, with eyes shut to the outside world. These experiences called dreams are not perceptions but hallucinations.[6] But whereas they are considered harmless when limited to the nocturnal conditions of sleep, their occurrence as diurnal events, in wakefulness and with the eyes wide open, has traditionally and even more so today, produced a spectrum of responses ranging from amazement to awe-stricken terror. At times the psychiatrists have appeared more terrified by hallucinations than their patients, as in the case of Schreber. Just try to imagine the expression on Flechsig's face when Schreber knocked on his door in early March of 1894 to tell him excitedly about his visions, the morning after: Herr Professor, last night I had my "very first vision in which God, if I may express it so, revealed Himself to me" (S: footnote #103). Further, imagine Flechsig's "professorial arrogance" (S:113) and dishonesty, which, no doubt, the patient keenly perceived. We can only surmise what recommendation Flechsig sent up to the Ministry of Justice regarding Schreber's condition based on the result, for around that time an announcement appeared in the newspaper that Schreber's post at the *Oberlandesgericht* (Supreme Court) had been filled by another judge.[7] From that point on, Schreber's fate was doubly sealed: by the prognosis of incurability and the declaration of mental incompetence.

The major clinical fact of the case was that by March or April of 1894, as the psychotic process unraveled, the clinical picture first observed in November of 1893—agitated and suicidal depression with intractable sleeplessness—now underwent a "supernatural" switch, a major development that has eluded all Schreber commentators but one.[8] As of March 1894, the depression was transformed into cosmic delusions and ecstatic hallucinations, the prose of a humdrum tale of failure, turned into poetry and prophecy in the manner of the Bible and Goethe.[9]

What, then, are the preconditions of prophecy and pathology? "I spoke to the prophets," says the Lord, "it was I who multiplied visions, and through the prophets gave parables" (Hosea, 12:16). In the same book the people of Israel respond: "The prophet is a fool, the man of the spirit is mad." The prophet replies: "because of your iniquity and great hatred" (Hosea, 9:7). We can echo the Israelites and ask: Are supernatural phenomena and supernatural delusions one and the same thing? Are heavenly visions and prophecies genuine phenomena, or are they

merely epiphenomena of a superheated brain, in an altered metabolic
state, e.g., a state of delirium? Are they elemental, not further explain-
able originary manifestations of a dark continent called madness, as
Karl Jaspers suggests? Or are they intelligible and interpretable psychic
formations as claimed by Sigmund Freud? From clinical experience, we
know that descent into psychosis creates those preconditions that
weaken a person's contact with reality, suspend goal-oriented pursuits,
undo the critical functions and repressing forces of the mind, promote
introversion, and facilitate the emergence of repressed strivings and
dream images, that comprise a state of altered consciousness called
trance, rapture, or ecstasy. The question is how to differentiate one
product from the other. The answers that came from protagonist Schreber and antagonist Weber are illuminating.

Schreber argued before the court and against his psychiatrists,
including the great authority of the time, Emil Kraepelin, that his hallucinations were not a mark of insanity, *Geisteskrankheit,* with its dire
forensic implications for his life and fate, but a result of his *Nervenkrankheit,* a disease of the nerves, a neural disease. Was not Flechsig
originally a famous neuroanatomist turned nerve-specialist *(Nerve-
narzt),* a common name for psychiatrist in Germany? Weren't "asylums
for the mentally ill," such as Flechsig's University Hospital, at first offi-
cially designated as an *Irrenklinik* (lunatic asylum), called in the basic
language "God's Nerve-Institutes" (S:25)? Were not mental disorders
declared by Flechsig to be brain disorders? This was not mere verbal
acrobatics on Schreber's part. For, in addition, he put forward his own
theory of causation, as he explains:

> I will try to describe more closely the auditory and visual impression I
> receive as "voices," "visions," etc. But I wish to stress again as in other
> places . . . that I do not object in the least to considering a morbidly
> excited nervous system a necessary condition for the development of all
> such phenomena. Human beings who are fortunate enough to enjoy
> healthy nerves cannot (as a rule anyway: [added in footnote #112:] as
> a possible exception I would instance the cases of vision-like experi-
> ences related in the Bible) have "illusions," "hallucinations,"
> "visions," or whatever expression one wants to use for these phenom-
> ena; it would therefore certainly be desirable if all human beings
> remained free from such experiences; they would then subjectively feel
> very much better. But this does not imply that the events resulting from
> a diseased nervous system are altogether unfounded in objective exter-
> nal reality or have to be regarded as nervous excitations lacking all
> external cause. I can therefore not share Kraepelin's astonishment
> which he expresses repeatedly that the "voices" [reference omitted]

etc., seem to have a far greater power of conviction for hallucinated patients than "anything said by those around them." A person with sound nerves is, so to speak, mentally blind compared with him who receives supernatural impressions by virtue of his diseased nerves; he is therefore as little likely to persuade the visionary of the unreality of his visions as a person who can see will be persuaded by a really blind person that there are no colours, that blue is not blue, red not red, etc. (S:307–308)

Schreber makes an important observation: in altered metabolic states, such as delirium induced by fever or drugs, people are more prone to see images than under normal conditions. He would have conceded this also happens in trance induced by psychosis, were he not concerned that people like himself, classified as psychotics, even when harmless as he was, were all too easily locked up for life. Not having read Freud, Schreber could not say that his visions had psychic reality for him. "I am and, for as long as I can remember," writes Aldous Huxley in connection with his LSD experiment, "have been a poor visualizer. Words, even the pregnant words of poets, do not evoke pictures in my mind. . . . Only when I have a high temperature do my mental images come to independent life."[10]

But are these images revelations or mad ravings? Let us suspend this question for a while; but let us not repudiate Schreber's argument that merely to dismiss such visions as pathological, rather than to give them their due, would be required by anyone who lays claim to scientific impartiality. It is in this spirit that Schreber defends himself against the strictly organic model of Kraepelin and of Asylum Director Weber, who argued to the court as follows:

> Considered scientifically, . . . the appellant's mental illness . . . clearly belongs to a well known and well characterized form, . . . paranoia, . . . certainly not a usual commonplace one, just as little as the patient himself is the usual average individual. [B]ut on the whole in the formation and systematization of the delusional ideas, the disease will show the same character as that of another person whose range of ideas does not rise above the most trivial events of daily life. . . . Paranoia is a distinctly chronic illness . . . and after the stormy symptoms have run their course the slowly progressive course starts . . . and delusions, frequently in connection with hallucinations and false memories, . . . soon become fixed into a persistent, uncorrected and unassailable delusional system (Weber, S:456–457). . . . It can hardly be denied that some cases of paranoia never reach the orbit of medical experience, but remain outside it, recognized perhaps only by their closest associates, and lead the ordinary life of a citizen without any marked disturbance (458). . . .

[It is not that] . . . the medical expert [i.e., Weber] and the Judge
saw in his "belief in miracles" and the complex ideas around them only
the basis for the assumption of mental illness, and that this cannot be
so, as very many people believe in miracles without anybody thinking
or declaring them mentally ill. What is usually called belief in miracles,
the naive theoretical belief intentionally or unintentionally exempted
from every criticism, that through His almighty will God sometimes
causes events beyond or even against the laws of nature, does not apply
in the present case. His ideas, as the appellant himself repeatedly stated
and as their content clearly shows, do not emanate from a pious child's
belief, but are contrary to his earlier opinions and undoubtedly due to
pathological processes of the brain; they are evidenced by disturbances
of common sensation and hallucinations and so belong to a category
very different from the harmless "belief in miracles." It cannot be
expected that the appellant will gain the insight that these hallucinatory events (in the widest sense the muscular sensations described by
the patient belong to them also) are entirely subjective; his expositions
(reference omitted) are aimed particularly at showing that his hallucinations are something very special, and at vindicating them by finding
a basis in reality for them. It is their characteristic that they are taken
for factual and real and have the same acuity as other sensations . . . it
only remains to add briefly that in hallucinations [due to] the inner
abnormal state of excitation of the apperceiving brain apparatus . . .
the hallucinating person does not apperceive the world, but himself,
i.e., events in his own central nervous system. (Weber, S:460–461)

Clearly, Schreber's and Weber's ways of looking at individual
experience, as well as their discourse about it, are separated by an
unbridgeable gulf. Schreber's conception is functional and dynamic,
and Weber's is anatomical and static, let alone narrow-minded.
Weber's "scientific" rhetoric is, moreover, a thin disguise of his long-
standing and now weakening politics to keep Schreber incarcerated
because of his odd ideas and beliefs. On the other hand, if Weber's
cerebral organicism is accepted at face value, and if one accepts Spinoza's idea that God means nature, one might well conclude that Schreber is not merely spouting grandiose and paranoid ideas. Rather, he is
relating a theory that God does indeed reside in the brain's apperceiving apparatus, thus making perception of both natural and supernatural possible. What is sorely missing from Weber's account is the cultural, social, and ethical context for claiming truth and validity for
visions, whether ancient or modern.

Such a cultural, social, and ethical perspective has been suggested by
Pierre Quercy[11] in his analysis of St. Theresa of Avila (1515—1582). Her
spiritual life was filled with extraordinary happenings: ecstasies, visions,

and chronic depressive and hysterical symptoms such as paralysis, catalepsy, sleep walking, anesthesia, fainting. She was also the founder of convents and a reformed order called the Barefoot or Discalced Carmelites, and was later canonized. She wrote many religious and mystical tracts that are considered classics. She had visions of the blessed, of the living and dying, of angels and demons, of the Virgin, of Jesus Christ, of the Trinity, of various objects such as crosses, rings, flowers, a dove, a saber, and blood. Were her visions merely manifestations of her hysteria, including her repressed sexuality? Or were they genuine God-sent visions? The crux of the question lies in the meaning of the phrase "to touch, hear or see God": are there people who can so perceive God, directly, or are they merely speaking in metaphors animated by faith and love, by complex emotional surges, and by all kinds of mirages, illusions, and imaginings. It might be helpful to invoke St. Theresa's contemporary, her student and later confessor, St. John of the Cross (1542—1591), who, perhaps under the influence of Theresa herself, divides visions into three kinds: ordinary or sensory, of the world around us; and supersensory or imaginary, that can be either of divine and diabolical inspiration; intellectual, i.e., spiritual, or without images. Consider some of his words taken from Stanzas of the Soul:

1. Oh, living flame of love that tenderly woundest my soul in its
     deepest centre,
   Since thou art no longer oppressive, perfect me now, if it be
     thy will,
   Break the web of this sweet encounter.

2. Oh, sweet burn! Oh, delectable wound! Oh, soft hand! Oh,
     delicate touch,
   That savours of eternal life and pays every debt.
   In slaying, thou hast changed death into life.

3. Oh lamps of fire,
   In whose splendors the deep caverns of sense which were dark
     and blind
   With strange brightness Give heat and light together to their
     Beloved![12]

Quercy resolves the problem by a declaration: St. Theresa's imaginative visions are neither the run of the mill sensory nor psychical hallucinations:[13] "Ce sont les hallucinations théresiennes [these hallucinations are St. Theresa's]."[14] Let us declare with equal force: Schreber's are also no ordinary hallucinations: *ce sont les hallucinations schreberiennes*, and like in St. Theresa's case, his visions came in three varieties: sensory, imaginary, and intellectual. St. Theresa had one important advantage over Schreber: her visions were supported by a community of like-minded people who shared her experiences, while Schreber was a lonely voice in the Sonnenstein (asylum) wilderness. It was only posthumously that Schreber was able to find some credence for his claim:

> [Heretofore] I used to consider it possible and indeed advisable to exclude every discussion of my supposed hallucinations and delusions from the points at issue in the cases, the purpose of which is contesting my tutelage; I could not ignore the fear . . . that the attention of the Court would be diverted from the decisive and only question in their competence, namely, whether I possesses the capacity for reasonable action in practical life. More recently, however, I have not been able to ignore the fact that it would be impossible for me to do so without a certain appreciation of my so-called delusions or my religious beliefs and not only on the formal side of their logical sequence and orderly arrangement, but to a certain degree also regarding the question whether it is within the bounds of possibility that my delusional system, as one is pleased to call it, is founded on some truth. I have to make the attempt as regards other people, the judges in particular, not really to convert them to my miraculous belief—naturally I could do this at present to a very moderate degree—but at least to furnish the general impression that the experiences and considerations laid down in my "Memoirs" cannot simply be regarded as a *quantit negligeable*, as an empty fantasy of muddled head . . . I will mention a number of points [which] although they cannot exactly prove the reality of the state miracles, will I hope at least make the so far credible that one will hesitate to condemn the whole presentation as pure nonsense from the start but rather admit that the scientific world could make them the starting point of further researches. (Schreber,1901; S:412; emphasis Schreber's)

I fully accept Schreber's reading, as did the Court, which saw through Weber's arguments and sided with Schreber's view on the matter:

> it is possible that . . . whatever one may think of his belief in miracles, no one is entitled to see in it a mental defect which makes plaintiff require State care. One does not usually and without further reason declare the adherents of spiritualism [e.g., table rappers, believers in clairvoyance and telepathy] mentally ill and put them under a guardian, although their way of looking at things supernaturally is also neither shared not comprehended by the vast majority of their fellow men. (Judgment of the Royal Superior Country Court Dresden, S:481)

OF MARVELS AND MIRACLES

We speak openly of the marvels of modern science and technology, e.g., the brain and the computer, and we speak of miracles to describe unusual or unexpected successes in curing illness. "No doubt," Freud is quick to note, "it is an essential attribute of God to perform miracles; but a physician performs miracles too; he effects miraculous cures, as his enthusiastic clients proclaim."[15] We thus tend to speak unceremoniously of "miracles" occurring both in the natural and supernatural orders of the world. But while Freud thought that Schreber's "miracles" were "incredible, absurd, and to some extent positively silly,"[16] Schreber was of a different opinion. In fact, as I argued elsewhere contra Freud, for Schreber, his fantastic/hallucinatory/delusional miracles were bearers of deep religious truths and mystical insights[17] and a vehicle for a serious moral debate with God.[18]

In the two opening cosmological-religious chapters of the *Memoirs,* filled with fantastic and delusional scenarios, the first of which is entitled "God and Immortality," Schreber speaks of the entire "Order of the World" as a "wundervoller Aufbau" and "eine wundervolle Organisation," which Macalpine and Hunter mistranslate as "miraculous" structure and organization, tilting the expression in the direction of the delusional. Here the correct translation should have been "marvelous," for in these quotations the adjective "marvelous" still refers to marvels of nature, perhaps in conscious imitation of his father Moritz's title of an 1859 biologico-anthropological monograph: *Anthropos: Der Wunderbau des menschlichen Organismus, sein Leben und seine Gesundheitsgesetze: ein allgemein fassliches Gesammtbild dermenschlichen Natur für Lehrer, Schüler sowie für Jedermann, der nach gründlicher Bildung und kasrperlich geistiger Gesundheit strebt* ("Man, or the marvelous structure of the human organism, its life and its health laws: a generally intelligible overview of human nature for teachers, students, and everyone who aspires to a thorough education and bodily and mental health"). It should also be emphasized that it was his father's writings, and not Flechsig's numerous tracts on neuroanatomy, that would have been Paul Schreber's source of knowledge about the brain and its nerves.

Although these opening chapters are filled with scenarios that are highly fantastic, so fantastic in instances as to earn the characterization of frankly delusional, Schreber's speech, even when his references remain obscure, cannot be characterized as schizophrenic, in the sense used by Eugen Bleuler. For his definitions are precise and expressed with a pithiness rarely seen today. I hold that, among other things, Schreber wrote his book in the style of magical realism, not unlike Salmon Rushdie. Thus he makes a distinction between the usual state of affairs:

> God left the world which He had created and the organic life upon it
> (plants, animals, human beings) to their own devices . . . [and] as a rule
> did not interfere directly in the fate of peoples or individuals, . . . in
> accordance with the Order of the World," as compared to times when"
> a particularly fervent prayer might in a special case induce God to give
> help by intervening with a miracle or to shape the fate of whole nations
> (in war, etc.) by means of miracles. He was also able to get into con-
> tact ("to form nerve contact with them") with highly gifted people
> (poets, etc.), in order to bless them (particularly in dreams) with some
> fertilizing thoughts and ideas about the beyond. (Schreber:10–11;
> hence abbreviated as S)

Perhaps Schreber was like one of the above-mentioned poets blessed
with such "fertilizing thoughts" when God sent him that dream of how
nice it would be to feel what a woman feels in intercourse. Otherwise,

> such nerve contact [with God] was not allowed to be the rule,
> because . . . the nerves of living human beings particularly when in a
> state of high grade excitation, have such power of attraction for God's
> nerves that He would not be able to free Himself from them again, and
> would thus endanger his own existence. (S:11)

Note that Schreber speaks of God's nerves and human nerves in
Chapter One:

> the human soul is contained in the nerves of the body and God to start
> with is only nerve, not body, and akin therefore to human soul. But unlike
> the human body, . . . the nerves of God are infinite and eternal. They pos-
> sess the same qualities as human nerves but to a degree surpassing all
> understanding. They have in particular the faculty of transforming them-
> selves into all things of the created world; and in this capacity they are
> called rays; and herein lies the essence of divine creation. (S:6,8)

Note the equation nerves = rays = soul and an affinity between God
as the cosmic soul of the world and the individual soul, an affinity that
is the basis of reciprocal nervous influxes, influences and inspirations
from God and man and between God and man. While Schreber's terminology is fanciful and idiosyncratic, the ideas expressed are drawn from
ancient Gnostic and cabalistic theories of creation and pantheistic con-
ceptions of the divine and human soul. They also bear similarity to the
notion of the flow of nervous energy (interchangeable with soul energy)
as suggested by Anton Mesmer's theories of animal magnetism.

As a result of his illness, a miracle of a direct divine influence did
indeed happen to Schreber himself, and it threw him into a state of high-

grade excitation. Toward the end of Chapter Two, entitled "Crisis in God's realms? Soul murder," Macalpine and Hunter have Schreber remark on the "marvelous [wunderbaren] concatenation of events." The proper translation at this point, however, should be "miraculous," seeing that in conditions that were not according to the Order of the World, an extraordinary "clash of interests . . . arose in [his] case because of supposed soul murder" (S:31). Through this miraculous concatenation, Schreber, an innocent man, became a victim of double soul murder, also known as "soul theft," or the cosmic and conspiratorial "surrender of a soul to another person," in the following manner: "Since the beginning of my contact with God (mid-March 1894)," claims Schreber, "the crisis that broke upon the realms of God was caused by somebody having committed soul murder; at first Flechsig was named as the instigator of soul murder" (S:23). Like Satan in the Book of Job and in Goethe's Faust, God, at the instigation of soul-murderer Flechsig, "God Himself must have been or be in a precarious position, [he] could be enticed to a kind of conspiracy against human beings who are fundamentally innocent" (S:29–30). Indeed, God, who severely tested the innocent man Schreber by means of the fantasized soul murder, was in reality aided and abetted by unnamed co-conspirators: his boss Judge Werner at the Ministry of Justice, his wife Sabine, acting hand in hand with psychiatrists Flechsig and Weber, and the courts.[19]

The dual soul murder, human and divine, that caused him considerable nervousness compounded the already existing stress caused by the return of his first illness and a repeated failure in life: his collapse on the new job as judge presiding of a *Civilsenat* in the capital Dresden, just six weeks after it started. After Schreber became excited, hallucinating, and delusional, he transformed his prosaic personal disaster into the high poetry of a cataclysm of cosmic proportions that occurred as a result of his nervousness: "for about two years I believed [he] had to assume and was forced by [his] experiences to assume, that if God were permanently tied to [his] person, all creation on earth would have to perish" (S:31). In addition, and especially during the traumatic "early part of [his] stay at Sonnestein" (S:147), following his banishment from Flechsig's University Hospital to the public madhouse, God plagued Schreber with all kinds of divine miracles, a euphemism for divinely caused maladies, copiously described in Chapter 11 entitled "Bodily integrity damaged by miracles." These miracles of damage or destruction caused to organs by "impure rays" (also called "searing" rays) were always temporary and completely undone by "pure rays," also called "blessing" rays, thus not dangerous in themselves, just fanciful descriptions of suffering from varieties of "very painful conditions" (S:149; footnote #48).

It is of utmost importance to note that it is in this context that Schre-ber first mentions a central interest of his, the "sensation of volup-tuousness" (*Wollustgefühl*, S:153): one of the "miracles which were enacted against me" (S:147) was targeted at his seminal cord, "against which very painful miracles were directed, with the particular purpose of suppressing the sensation of voluptuousness arising in my body" (S:153). The full meaning of voluptuousness, i.e., luxuriating in any sen-sual or sensuous pleasure, but most prominently sexual pleasure, should be noted. Clearly, the above is a miracle in reverse, a euphemistic and sarcastic usage not unlike saying blessed when we mean cursed, as this blessed city traffic. Paul Schreber may perhaps be alluding, through a persecutory delusion, to conflict over and rebellion against his father's or his society's antisexual prejudice, or to his wife's lack of sexual response; or, perhaps, to the sexual deprivation and the cruelties imposed upon him by the God-like decrees of his psychiatrists, who con-demned him to nearly nine years of incarceration.

Whether the idea to test Schreber was part of God's grand cosmic scheme remains debatable. It is beyond doubt, however, that the poor devil was subjected to many forms of unwelcome stimulation. For exam-ple, while in Flechsig's asylum he was yanked out of his sleep and hauled off to an isolation cell, where, clad only in his nightshirt, he was thrown on a billiard table and overcome by burly attendants. He also reported, "a period during which I was continually kept in bed" (S:88). What role did that play in causing nightly pollutions? What did years of keeping him completely sex-starved contribute to being assailed by voluptuous sensations? He was also exposed in the Sonnenstein asylum to unbear-able barrages of stimulation by the agitated and screaming madmen—a condition not uncommon in the dark ages of psychiatry without tran-quilizers. In addition, rough attendants who had the run of the place inflicted on him such indignities as "having his ears boxed," his cigars and writing materials were doled out in niggardly fashion, and moved almost nightly "from his own bedroom to sleep in the cells fitted out for dements" (S:147), for a period of two-and-a-half years. When he was finally out of the asylum and beyond the reach of judge and jailer, he wrote a preface for his book using the term soul murder retroactively to brand Flechsig's professional conduct as medical malpractice, thus avoiding being sued for libel.

In the end, luckily for God and His creation, "even in such an extra-ordinary case, the Order of the World carries its own remedies for heal-ing the wounds inflicted upon it; the remedy is Eternity" (S:31). Schre-ber was lucky, too, for he resolved his problem before he died. After four years in the asylum, he woke up from his long religious dream ecstasy, won his trial, left the asylum, and lived happily with his wife and adopted daughter until his final and terminal psychotic journey, from 1907 till his death in 1911.

Schreber claimed for himself the status of a genuine *Geisterseher*, a seer, a mystic. But how do you certify a true prophet, mystic, or visionary, and the visions they attest to? What are the criteria by which St. Theresa is declared to be the real thing and Schreber the fake?

OF ECSTASIES HUMAN AND DIVINE

In the first two chapters of the *Memoirs*, Schreber treats of pleasures human and divine. The latter is defined by Schreber as:

> . . . souls completely cleansed by the process of purification ascended to heaven and so gained the state of Blessedness [only *Seligkeit*, in the original]. This [blessedness omitted in the translation by Macalpine and Hunter], consisted [in a state of, omitted by M. and H.] of uninterrupted enjoyment combined with the contemplation of God. (S:16; emphasis Schreber's)

This topic mightily preoccupies Freud in the first section of his essay that made Schreber immortal. He quotes copiously from Schreber's "theologico-psychological system"[20] as set forth in the aforementioned first two chapters of the *Memoirs*, freely mixing Schreber's words (without even bothering to put quotations marks around them) with his own. A central focus for Freud is expressed in Schreber's sentence: "souls that have passed through the process of purification enter into the enjoyment of a state of bliss."[21] Now "bliss" and "blessedness" are reasonably good synonyms for sensual and spiritual ecstasy and are often used in the latter sense in religious texts. It is not surprising that Freud immediately added this gloss on "bliss" in his footnote: "this consists essentially in a feeling of voluptuousness" [*Wollustgefühl*, S:153, Z.L.] (see below)."[22] (Incidentally, the quotes from Schreber in his 1911 essay appear in Strachey's 1925 translation, thus different from Macalpine and Hunter.)

To give a good account of earthly delights of sensual pleasure, Schreber invokes another divinely inspired poet: "Richard Wagner, as if with some insight into these things, makes Tannhäuser say [in the opening scene of the opera, in the cave of Venus, where the tragic hero seeks to flee the enticing Sirens and the amorous entreaties of Venus, Z. L.] in the ecstasy of love [Schreber's words are: *im hschsten Genuss der Liebeswonne*: at the height of enjoyment of love's bliss, Z. L.]: Alas your love overwhelms me; perpetual enjoyment is only for Gods, I as a mortal am subject to change" (S:17, footnote #10). According to the libretto, Tannhäuser begins by saying to Venus: "Praises to love! Its radiant wonders fire me, / Love is the joy, the power which fills my days! . . . / Only the gods such happiness can render, / Only your grace could bless a mortal man." And now the words quoted by Schreber: "But man should not win such a guerdon, / And I am tired, tired of its burden. / The gods can live in endless bliss [in the original: *wenn stets ein Gott geniessen kann*], / No mortal man can suffer this" (translation from Wagner's (1845) libretto; emphasis Schreber's). (S:17, footnote #10).

While Macalpine's and Hunter's word ecstasy serves our purpose, "bliss" is better than "enjoyment" to depict earthly delights, because it works better as a foil to the "blessedness" of the souls. Since enjoyment can also mean simply use, it misses the strong meaning of the German word *Wonne,* usually also rendered as bliss, but suggesting a high degree of sensual delight. The opening of the opera pointedly portrays the sexual exuberance of the goddess of love and the scruples and inhibitions of the earthling Tannhäuser as well as the hero's constant conflict—characteristic of Western civilization—between love sacred and profane, between the naturalness as against the religiously defined sinfulness of sexual love and sexual happiness, between heavenly blessedness and earthly bliss. And yet, the two kinds of ecstasy retain a common affinity: the mystics have often described religious transports in orgastic terms, voluptuaries have often crowed about their lusts as divine. As already suggested, and judging by the quotations from Schreber he selected, Freud is in full agreement with Wagner:

> I will now turn to another subject, which is closely related to the God, namely, this state of Bliss. This is also spoken of by Schreber as "the life beyond" to which the human soul is raised after death by the process of purification. He describes it as a state of uninterrupted enjoyment, bound up with the contemplation of God. This is not very original: . . . the coincidence between the state of bliss and voluptuousness is expressed in plainer language. . . . Thus, for instance: "The nature of the nerves of God, is such that the state of bliss . . . is accompanied by a very intense sensation of voluptuousness, even though it does not consist exclusively of it" (51). And again: "Voluptuousness may be regarded as a fragment of the state of bliss given in advance, as it were, to men and other living creatures" (281). So the state of heavenly bliss is to be understood as being in its essence an intensified continuation of sensual pleasure upon earth! (The numbers in Freud's brackets refer to the original page numbers in Schreber).[23]

Freud's exclamation mark reveals a kinship and identification with
Schreber because, like Schreber, he championed a libertarian attitude
toward the varieties of sexual experience and sexual pleasure. Unlike
Schreber, he refused to grant legitimacy and autonomy to religious experience, and as a rationalist, he reduced them to sexuality, as he says in
the continuation of the aforementioned "below":

> This surprising sexualization of the state of heavenly bliss suggests the
> possibility that Schreber's concept of the state of bliss is derived from a
> condensation of the two principal meanings of the German word
> "selig"—namely, "dead" and "sensually happy" [quoting in his foot-
> note the word "selig" from the famous "La ci darem la mano" duet in
> Mozart's *Don Giovanni*]. But this instance of sexualization will also
> give us occasion to examine the patient's general attitude to the erotic
> side of life and questions of sexual indulgence. For we psychoanalysts
> have hitherto supported the view that the roots of every nervous and
> mental disorder are chiefly to be found in the patient's sexual life.
> . . . Schreber himself speaks again and again as though he shared
> our prejudice. He is constantly talking in the same breath of "nervous
> disorder" and erotic lapses, as though the two things were inseparable.
> [In the footnote to the above Freud quotes Schreber's seminal words:]
> "Thus it seems probable that by a 'Prince of Hell' the souls meant the
> uncanny Power that was able to develop in a sense hostile to God as a
> result of moral depravity among men or of a general state of excessive
> nervous excitement following upon over-civilization."[24] (163)

Indeed, Schreber speaks of many "erotic lapses," not just sexual
ones, but also of the pleasures of pissing and shitting (words included in
Webster's Third New International Dictionary that still excludes f**k
because it is legally obscene and thus not fit to print), an innocent
delight in childhood but derogated in adulthood. And who better than
Freud showed how such dams of repression are set up as a result of over-
civilization, and who better than Freud, before Otto Gross and well
before Wilhelm Reich, inveighed against societal hypocrisy in matters of
the body and its erotic needs. As if he were rewriting his own thoughts
on anal eroticism, Freud relishes reproducing Schreber's disquisition on
shit at some length:

> Although it will necessitate my touching upon an unsavoury subject, I
> must devote a few more words to the question that I have just quoted
> ("Why don't you s—?") on account of the typical character of the
> whole business. The need for evacuation, like all else that has to do
> with my body, is evoked by a miracle. It is brought about by my shit
> being forced forwards (and sometimes backwards again) in my

intestines; and if, owing to there having already been an evacuation, enough material is not present, then such small remains as there may still be of the contents of my intestines are smeared over my anal orifice. This occurrence is a miracle performed by the upper God, and it is repeated several dozens of times at the least every day. It is associated with an idea which is utterly incomprehensible to human beings and can only be accounted for by God's complete ignorance of living man as an organism. According to this idea "s—ing" is in a certain sense the final act; that is to say, when once the urge to "s—" has been miracled up, the aim of destroying the understanding is achieved and a final withdrawal of the rays becomes possible. To get to the bottom of the origin of this idea, we must suppose, as it seems to me, that there is a misapprehension in connection with the symbolic meaning of the act of evacuation, a notion, in fact, that any one who has been in such a relation as I have been with divine rays is to some extent entitled to s— upon the whole world. But now what follows reveals the full perfidy of the policy that has been pursued toward me. Almost every time the need for evacuation was miracled up in me, some other person in my vicinity was sent (by having his nerves stimulated for the purpose) to the lavatory, in order to prevent my evacuating. This is a phenomenon which I have observed for years and upon such countless occasions—thousands of them—and with such regularity, as to exclude any possibility of its being attributable to chance. And thereupon comes the question: "Why don't you s—?" to which the brilliant repartee is made that I am "so stupid or something." The pen wellnigh shrinks from recording so monumental a piece of absurdity as that God, blinded by His ignorance of human nature, can positively go to such lengths as to suppose that there can exist a man too stupid to do what every animal can do—to stupid to be able to s—. When, upon the occasion of such an urge, I actually succeed in evacuating, and use a pail for that purpose—the process is always accompanied by the generation of an exceedingly strong feeling of spiritual voluptuousness. For the relief from the pressure caused by the presence of shit in the intestine produces a sense of intense well-being in the nerves of voluptuousness; and the same is equally true of making water. For this reason, even down to the present day, while I am passing stool or making water, all the rays' [= God, Z. L., "voices proceed from God, that is, from the divine rays," Freud:26] are always without exception united; for this very reason, whenever I address myself to these natural functions, an attempt is invariably made, though as a rule in vain, to miracle backwards the urge to pass stool and to make water. (225–7.)" [added by Freud in his footnote]: This confession to a pleasure in the excretory processes, which we have learnt to recognize as one of the auto-erotic components of infantile sexuality, may be compared with the remarks made by little Hans in "Analysis of a Phobia in a Five-year-old Boy."[25] (1909b)

Not since Rabelais have such paeans been sung to the physical and spiritual ecstasies provided by the *boyau rectum*. The text becomes more comprehensible if we substitute marvel for miracle. Either way, the language of miracles is Schreber's way to speak of matters instinctual and unconscious. Not since Freud has anal eroticism been so well described. It is as if Schreber fully shared Freud's prejudice. Indeed, Freud's anal triad of "orderly, parsimonious, and obstinate" fairly applies to Schreber's own character: it was his fight with his wife over money that catapulted him into a chain reaction that included a hostile response from his boss at the Ministry of Justice and his mental incompetence status, at the cost of the long-term loss of personal and civil liberties.[26] By the way, in the end it was Karl Abraham, not Freud, who fully realized the symbolic meaning of shitting as aggression: of shitting on the whole world. But Schreber understood that perfectly when he says that "any one who has been in such a relation as I have been with divine rays is to some extent entitled to s— upon the whole world." If we substitute "divine rays = God" as a code word for the powers that be, i.e., doctors acting as gods and the court's legal power of incarceration, if we read the above paragraphs as a parody of those power relations, then we can understand Schreber's wish to want to shit on the whole world, in the same symbolic manner as we can read Jung's famous dream of shitting on the Cologne cathedral.

But at that time Freud had a blind spot concerning aggression: indeed, in the case history of "Little Hans" Freud ridiculed Adler's 1908 paper "The aggressive drive in life and neurosis."[27] Freud, however, contradicted himself: for whereas he sought to explain Schreber's adult experiences by links to infantile oedipal libidinal-instinctual conflicts, he still managed to invoke aggression when he traced Schreber's "mixture of reverence and rebelliousness in his attitude toward [God]"[28] to the "perfectly familiar . . . infantile attitude of boys toward their father—[which] is composed of the same mixture of reverent submission and mutinous insubordination that we have found in Schreber's relation to God, and is the unmistakable prototype of that relation . . . [and which] explains [Schreber's] bitter scorn shown for such a physician [i.e., his father] . . . when declaring that he understands nothing about living men and only knows how to deal with corpses."[29] Freud missed the fact that the last time Moritz Schreber had anything to do with corpses was when he studied anatomy as a medical student. The physician who dealt with corpses was Flechsig: he miraculously cured Schreber's first depressive bout of 1884–1885, earning the encomiums of both Schreber and his wife:

> I was eventually cured and therefore I had at that time no reason to be other than most grateful to Professor Flechsig: I gave this special

expression by a subsequent visit and in my opinion an adequate hono-
rarium. My wife felt even more sincere gratitude and worshipped Professor Flechsig who has restored her husband to her; for this reason she
kept his picture on her desk for many years. (S:35–36)

Flechsig was a different man in1893—1894: this time all he wanted
was to get Schreber's brain at autopsy, to make the definitive diagnosis,
and to add the formalin-preserved specimen to the brain museum next
to his office. And that is why Schreber poured derision and scorn on his
doctor as "little Flechsig" (S:154, 158; Weber, S:383).
    What is more meaningful is Freud's awareness that Paul Schreber's
seliger (= of blessed memory) father Moritz brought his son up both
anally and genitally repressed (or was it his mother Pauline?), as shown
in the quotation that follows:

> Before his illness Senatspräsident Schreber had been a man of strict
> morals: "Few people," he declares, and I see no reason to doubt his
> assertion, can have been brought up upon such strict moral principles
> as I was, and few people, all through their lives, can have exercised
> (especially in sexual matter) a self-restraint conforming so closely to
> those principles as I may say of myself that I have done. ([S:]281)

After the severe spiritual struggle, of which the phenomena of his illness were the outward sign, his attitude toward the erotic side of life was
altered. He had come to see that the cultivation of voluptuousness was
incumbent upon him as a duty, and that it was only by discharging this
duty that he could end the grave conflict that had broken out within
him—or, as he thought, about him. Voluptuousness, so the voices
assured him, had become "God-fearing" and he could only regret that
he was not able to devote himself to its cultivation the whole day
long."[30] [And Freud quotes further in the footnote: "This attraction [of
the nerves of God to him] however, lost its terrors for the nerves in question, if, and in so far as, upon entering my body, they encountered a feeling of spiritual voluptuousness in which they themselves shared. For, if
this happened, they found an equivalent or approximately equivalent
substitute in my body for the state of heavenly bliss which they had lost,
and which consisted in a kind of voluptuous enjoyment" (179–80).[31]
    It is amazing how many dynamic themes Freud was able to encom-
pass or hint at in his essay. But his omissions are also significant. For all
his eloquence about Schreber's unresolved transference to his dead
father and older brother, he missed that it was Weber who was a more
natural candidate for such a transference than Paul Flechsig. Yet it is
remarkable that the paranoiac Schreber did not pour any scorn on

Weber, who was hostile to Schreber until he was forced to yield to the better judgment of the court that finally gave him his freedom. As might be expected, Weber reacted to these outpourings with extreme bourgeois revulsion. It was Weber who hounded Schreber in the real sense, by actively opposing his release from Sonnenstein in his reports to the court and by having this to say against the publication of the *Memoirs:*

> It is understandable that the patient felt the urge to describe the history of his latter years, to lay down his observations and sufferings in writing and to them before those who have in this or that matter a lawful interest in the shape of his fate. But the patient harbours the urgent desire to have his "Memoirs" (as presented here) printed and made available to the widest circles and he is therefore negotiating with a publisher—until now of course without success. When one looks at the content of his writings, and takes into consideration the abundance of indiscretions relating to himself and others contained in them, the unembarrassed detailing of the doubtful and aesthetically impossible situations and events, and the use of most offensive and vulgar words, etc., one finds it quite incomprehensible that a man otherwise tactful and of fine feeling could propose an action which would compromise him so severely in the eyes of the public, were not his whole attitude pathological, and he unable to see things in their proper perspective, and if the tremendous over-valuation of his own person caused by lack of insight into his illness had not clouded his appreciation of the limitations imposed on man by society (Weber, S:402). The appellant's oft repeated firm intention of publishing his "Memoirs" must also be regarded as pathologically determined and lacking sensible consideration. . . . His efforts to get his Memoirs published [can] be regarded as a harmful action [i.e., one still requiring a legal guardian]. (Weber, S:469)

Luckily, the judges on the court of appeals were more far-sighted than Weber and saved an immortal book from being lost forever. As I have argued repeatedly,[32] Freud made a serious error in narrowly interpreting Schreber's conflicts as caused by covert and overt homosexual desires. Rather, one must listen to Schreber on his own terms, consider all his libidinal manifestations in an attempt to understand as much as possible the full scope of the repressed erotic side of Schreber's life; and one must also understand how the repression came undone as a result of the psychotic process that lays the repressed bare and presents a most telling spectacle of the return of the repressed. In Schreber's case, as I have argued, it is his heterosexual conflicts, his sexual habits accumulated over a lifetime, and his identifications with women, with their unknowable roots in childhood, that returned, as a result of the facilitating processes of psychosis, at first to hound him and eventually to heal him.

CONCLUSION: OF THE ETHICS OF ECSTASIES PRIVATE AND PUBLIC

It was Freud's great achievement to have built a bridge, a continuum, between the abnormal and the normal, between the pathology of psychosis and the regressions engendered by various dynamisms, or mechanisms. Not the least of these being the regression in the psychoanalytic situation that facilitates the emergence of dreams, images, emotions, and memories that are not accessible during ordinary waking conditions.[33] One might fairly argue that ecstasy—a trance-like state combined with intense emotional excitement—is a common denominator of behavior in individuals and groups under the sway of any of the following conditions and states: deprivation (fasting, isolation chambers), drives (sexual and aggressive), dream-state (altered mental state, including hypnosis), drugs, delirium (altered bodily state, fever), and demos (people, or crowd intoxication, or as Huxley put it, herd intoxication). In all these conditions and states people may experience, or believe they experience, visions, revelations, miracles, prophecies, and the like.

   Do visions merely reveal the state of the mind or body of the visionary, or do they show us something out there? Or, to use Hippolyte Taine's expressions, are these *hallucinations vraies,* in the added sense of truth hallucinations, perceptions of something out there? The question might be considered as scientific or religious, depending on the beliefs of the questioner, but we cannot avoid Freud's insight that obsessions and their close relative, delusions, are a sort of private religion, and religion is a form of shared delusion. Aldous Huxley chose the path of the impartial, naturalistic observer:

> Like the earth of a hundred years ago, our mind still has its darkest Africas. . . . Like the giraffe and the duckbilled platypus, the creatures inhabiting these remoter regions of the mind are exceedingly improbable. Nevertheless they exist, they are facts of observation; and as such they cannot be ignored by anyone who is honestly trying to understand the world in which he lives. . . . It is difficult, it is all but impossible, to speak of mental events except in similes drawn from the more familiar universe of material things. If I have made use of geographical and zoological metaphors, it is not wantonly, out of mere addiction to picturesque language. It is because such metaphors express very forcibly the essential otherness of the mind's far continents, the complete autonomy and self-sufficiency of their inhabitants . . . at the antipodes of everyday consciousness, [in] the world of visionary experience.[34]

Schreber argued similarly:

> To make myself at least somewhat comprehensible I shall have to speak much in images and similes, which may at times perhaps be only approx-

imately correct; for the only way a human being can make supernatural matters, which in their essence must always remain incomprehensible, understandable to a certain degree is by comparing them with known facts of human experience. Where intellectual understanding ends, the domain of belief begins; man must reconcile himself to the fact that things exist which are true although he cannot understand them. (S:2)

With these words Schreber harks back to Kant's *Ding an sich* and the like. Even as there is much in his text that is psychotic, we cannot deny Schreber the cogency of some of his deeper philosophical and spiritual insights. Some people might still find Huxley less impartial than he claims—rather borrowing respectable and emotionally-loaded labels to conceal preconceived opinions. We might still want to apply the Scotch verdict about visions as perceptions of something out there: *non liquet*, not proved. On the other hand, we would not quarrel with the power of the intellectual visions of the mystics and thinkers Huxley[35] grouped under the aegis of perennial philosophy. Let us quote one of those quoted by Huxley, mystical thinker Meister Eckhart, whose ideas may be seen in Schreber's fancies about God's *Grundsprache*, ground or basic language:

To gauge the soul we must gauge it with God, for the Ground of God and Ground of the Soul are one and the same. The knower and the known are one. Simple people imagine that they should see God, as if he stood there and they here. This is not so. God and I, we are one in knowledge.[36] Thou must love God as not-God, not-spirit, not-person, not-image, but as He is, a sheer, pure absolute One, sundered from all two-ness, and in whom we must eternally sink from nothingness to nothingness.[37]

Here is a Schreber moment, mixing the fantastic and the spiritual:

The reader may have gained some idea of what I wish to express with the term "the distant God." One must not think of God as a being limited in space by the confines of a body like a human being, but one has to think of Him as Many in One or One in Many. These are not unfounded figments of my brain, but I have definite factual evidence for all these assumptions (that is to say for the expression "a distant God"), for instance at the time when the genuine basic language *[Grundsprache]* was current, every anterior leader of rays used to speak of the divine rays of the representatives of the Divinity of his trains as "I Who am distant." (S:197, footnote #83)

There was one more gnawing concern that caused Dr. Weber sleepless nights: that such beliefs are inherently dangerous to a well-run (bourgeois) society. Weber's apprehensions came only 12 years before the First World War, and 21 years before the ascension of Hitler to power, in a country that came under the sway of beliefs far more irrational and crowd ecstasies far more dangerous than the miracles and visions that inhabited the brain of Paul Schreber.[38]

Elias Canetti was dead wrong and unethical when he plagiarized Arnold Zweig in order to claim that Schreber's delusions were a prelude to the paranoia of Nazi ideology, politics, and criminal behavior. The Nazis made Adolf Hitler into a false God, or idol, and the delusional parts of his *Mein Kampf* into their Bible: theirs was an idolatry enthroned as a state religion, in imitation of the other perverters of Hegel's philosophy, the fascism of Mussolini, and the communism of Lenin and Stalin. And in this context it is essential to recall the orgiastic mass ecstasies orchestrated by the genius of Nazi mass propaganda in those fabled Nuremberg rallies,[39] as captured in the films of Leni von Riefenstahl.

In agreement with Huxley I submit that Schreber advocated a personal, mystical contemplative religion as against the official Evangelical Lutheranism in which he was raised. The difference between the two religions is fundamental:

> The religion of direct experience of the divine has been regarded as the privilege of very few people. I personally don't think this is necessarily true at all. I think that practically everyone is capable of immediate experience, provided he sets about it in the right way. We have simply taken for granted that the mystics represent a very small minority among a huge majority who must be content with the religion of creeds and symbols and sacred books and liturgies and organizations. Belief is a matter of very great importance. It has power for the believer himself and permits the believing person to exercise power over others. It does in a sense move mountains. Belief, like any other source or power, can be used for both evil and good, and just as well for evil as for good. We have seen in our very own time the terrifying spectacle of Hitler very nearly conquering the entire world through the power of belief in something which was not only manifestly untrue but profoundly evil. This tremendous fact of belief, which is so constantly cultivated within the symbol-manipulating religions, is essentially ambivalent. The consequence is that religion as a system of beliefs has always been an ambivalent force. It gives birth simultaneously to humility and to what the medieval poets called the "proud prelate," the ecclesiastical tyrant. It gives birth to the highest form of art and to the lowest form of superstition, It lights the fires of charity, and it also lights the fires of the Inquisition and the fire that burned Servetus in the Geneva of Calvin.[40]

Is mankind ready to listen to Schreber and learn from the lessons of Schreber and the likes of him?

NOTES

Even though this chapter focuses primarily on Schreber's ecstatic visions, drugs played an important role in his life. In 1884, upon his transfer from the Sonnenberg Spa to the Psychiatric Hospital of Leipzig University, Flechsig made the admission diagnosis of "bromide intoxication," since as part of the 'water cure' at the spa Schreber was given plenty of bromides. This compound, freely given in those days as a tranquilizer, was known for its side effects, such as an awful taste in the mouth, and sometimes hallucinations, and delusions. Flechsig also used bromides in combination with opiates, his discredited "Flechsig's epilepsy treatment," to induce in Schreber a kind of chemical shock treatment in the belief that all Schreber needed was drugs. The patient branded this as a white lie and lost faith in his doctor. In the language of delusions Schreber distorted the name of the opiate he was given, Narcein, as "Necrin" (from the Greek, nekros, dead) perhaps to show that these drugs were killing him. Another drug he was fed was chloral hydrate. Ultimately, all these were to no avail in curing him of his tormenting sleeplessness and the agitated depression: bliss and peace of mind came from his own ecstatic fantasies about God, God's rays, cultivation of femininity, the eventual reconciliation with the real world, and winning back his freedom from the clutches of Weber at Sonnestein.

1. See Eric Satner, *My Own Private Germany: Daniel Paul Schreber's Secret History of Modernity* (Princeton, N.J.: Princeton University Press, 1996)

2. Daniel Paul Schreber, *Memoirs of My Nervous Illness,* translated by Ida Macalpine and R. Hunter (New York: New York Review of Books, 2000). (All citations will be referred to in the text as "S.")

3. See Zvi Lothane, "The deal with the devil to 'save' psychoanalysis in Nazi Germany," *The Psychohistory Press,* 1999, 27: pp. 101–121.

4. See Zvi Lothane, Listening with the third ear as an instrument in psychoanalysis," *The Psychoanalytic Review,* 68:487–503, 1981.

5. See Zvi Lothane, "Zur Verteidigung Paul Schrebers," *Selbstbiographie und Seelenbehandlung. psychosozial,* 23: 105–117, 2000.

6. See Zvi Lothane, The psychopathology of hallucinations—a methodological analysis, *British Journal of Medical Psychology,* 55:335–348, 1982.

7. See W. Ver Ecke, "Schreber and Hölderlin: the concept of "father" or the psychological origin of mental breakdown," *Journal of the American Academy of Psychoanalysis,* 23:449–460, 1993.

8. See Zvi Lothane, "Schreber, Freud, Flechsig and Weber revisited: an inquiry into methods of interpretation," *Psychoanalytic Review,* 79:203–262, 1989.

9. See Zvi Lothane, "Goethe, Freud and Schreber: Themes in metamorphosis," In *Divano L'Immaginario e la Cura* (Bolzano: Richerche "Imago" Forschung, pp. 67–86), 1998.

10. Aldous Huxley, *The Doors of Perception and Heaven and Hell* (New York: Harper and Row, 1954), p. 15.

11. Pierre Quercy, *Etudes sur l'hallucination* (Paris: Alcan, 1930).

12. St. John of the Cross, *The Complete Works of St. John of the Cross, The Doctor of the Church,* Vol III (Westminster, MD: The Newman Bookshop, 1946), p. 18.

13. See Lothane, op. cit., 1982.

14. Quercy, op. cit., p. 290.

15. Sigmund Freud, "Psycho-anlytic notes on an autobiographical account of a case of paranoia (dementia paranoides)," *S. E.,* 12, p. 82.

16. Ibid., p. 52.

17. See Lothane, "Schreber's feminine identification: Paranoid illness or profound insight?" *International Forum Psychonalysis,* 3: pp. 61–82, 1993; "Pour la défense de Schreber: meurtre d'âme et psychiatrie: Postsciptum 1993," In *Schreber Revisité* (Louvain: Louvain University Press, 1998), pp. 11–29; "Paul Schreber's sexual desires and imaginings: Cause or consequence of his psychosis?" In *Sexual Deviations: Theory and Therapy* (Madison, CT: International Universities Press, forthcoming).

18. Zvi Lothane, *In Defense of Schreber: Soul Murder and Psychiatry* (Hillsdale, N.J.: The Analytic Press, 1992).

19. Ibid.

20. Freud, op. cit., 1911, p. 21.

21. Ibid. p. 23.

22. Ibid.

23. Ibid., p. 29.

24. Ibid., p. 30.

25. Ibid., pp. 26–27.

26. See Lothane, op. cit., 1992.

27. Sigmund Freud, "Analysis of a phobia of a five-year-old boy," *S.E.,* 10, pp. 140–141.

28. Freud, op. cit., 1911, p. 29.

29. Ibid., p. 52.

30. Ibid., p. 285.

31. Ibid., p. 31.

32. Lothane, op. cit., forthcoming.

33. See Lothane, op. cit., 1981, 1984.

34. Huxley, op. cit., pp. 83–85.

35. See Aldous Huxley, *The Perennial Philosophy* (New York: Harper, 1944).

36. Ibid., p. 12.

37. Ibid., p. 32.

38. See Zvi Lothane, "Omnipotence, or the delusional aspect of ideology in relation to love, power, and group dynamics," *American Journal of Psychoanalysis,* 57:25–46, 1997.

39. See Lothane, op. cit., 1997.

40. Aldous Huxley, *The Human Situation* (New York: Harper and Row, 1977), pp. 204–205.

Chapter Twelve

SMOKE SCREEN

The Cultural Meaning of Women's Smoking

LORRAINE GREAVES

This chapter is about women's smoking, identity, and social reactions to women's smoking. To truly understand women's smoking it is necessary to ask women what meaning it has for them. Even so, this meaning is often complicated by the astute strategies of the tobacco industry, a strong political economy surrounding tobacco and ever changing social and cultural norms and regulations regarding smoking.

I believe that women's smoking is socially adaptive and is often implicitly socially approved. Women smokers, when asked, often offer insights into how smoking helps them adapt to and comply with their life circumstances. It seems that smoking frequently acts as a buffer or screen, between women's individual, internal, lived experience and external social realities.

Central to understanding women's smoking is the recognition that smoking cigarettes also functions to maintain elements of social and economic life. High levels of consumption of tobacco, unlike alcohol and drugs, do not interfere with women's abilities to carry out their social roles and obligations. Therefore, while tobacco is a drug used for self-medication, there is no level of "overuse" that attracts attention and social sanction from society. Indeed, since tobacco use, for women at least, can temper negative emotions and contribute to compliance, women's smoking can function as a form of social control. Pregnant smokers represent the only exemption to this maxim, explaining the considerable amount of negative attention given to smoking and pregnancy over the years.

Yet despite groundbreaking studies such as Richard Klein's *Cigarettes Are Sublime* (1993), women's smoking has escaped serious analysis. Long considered secondary to men's smoking, medical research on the effects of smoking on women has lagged behind. Only recently, with the advent of more sex-differentiated research, have key differences in the effects of tobacco use on women and men been understood. In general, prevalence data on women's smoking are collected in industrial countries, but are much less available for Third World countries. The available information is inconsistent and difficult to compare as no standard methods are used to collect it.

It is clear that there are wide variations in smoking rates across countries, between urban and rural women and between various age and ethnic/racial groups. The World Health Organization,[1] in response to the lack of comparable data, has suggested improved methods of data gathering on women's smoking to facilitate the urgent action required to curtail or prevent the global female smoking epidemic.

Although there are exceptions, women's smoking tends to become established and peak first in industrial countries, in urban areas, and among those with higher formal education. As the century turns, approximately 30 percent of women in industrial countries smoke but, within and between countries, there remain vast differences in rates by age, socioeconomic status, region, and ethnic and racial group.

In Third World countries, women's smoking is less well documented but ranges between 2 and 10 percent. The World Health Organization offers some partial comparisons. About 10 percent of African women, between 10 and 40 percent of Latin American women, about 5 percent of Southeast Asian women, 8 percent of Eastern Mediterranean women, and less than 10 percent of Western Pacific women smoke. However, there are, again, vast variations between regions and subgroups of women. Sometimes women's smoking is culturally prohibited, while chewing or other more traditional modes of tobacco use are more approved. In all countries, negative attitudes toward women's and girls' smoking can distort attempts to collect accurate data. Sociological and cultural analyses of women's smoking are only now being made.

Women experience the world as a series of gendered social and economic circumstances, and smoking must be understood in this context.

However, since women occupy some very different locations across such categories as class, race, age, and sexual orientation, it is not to be assumed that all women do or will have a unitary common experience. Therefore, listening to women's own interpretations of smoking is crucial to understanding the complex contradictions involved in initiating and maintaining smoking in an era of increasing regulation and awareness of its negative effects.

Explaining the advent and continuing popularity of women's smoking cannot be limited to a singular theme. It is not solely a result of ongoing targeted advertising campaigns promising freedom. Nor is it a result of women's liberation, even though both of these explanations are often proffered. Even some tobacco control or health promotion workers hold these views, revealing a rather ironic uncritical absorption of one tobacco company's famous message, "You've come a long way baby." If this is the cause of smoking, then anyone interested in the status of women would see the cure as more worrisome.

But more seriously, this equation makes women seem passive. It is too simple to assume that women who smoke are pathetically duped by smoking culture, stupidly antihealth or servants of tobacco advertisements. Female smokers may be passive recipients of external influences, active resisters to aspects of society, or both, from time to time. However, even as overall rates of women's (and men's) smoking decline in Canada and several other developed countries, young girls' smoking is surpassing boys' smoking for the first time in history. Trends such as this raise many questions, but must certainly acknowledge female agency.

The complex and ambivalent views on women's smoking that have emerged over the centuries tend to be embedded in the Western collective consciousness for feminists and nonfeminists alike. These ambivalences continue to infect not just the explanations for women's smoking, but also the suggestions for ending it. Not surprisingly, these contradictions are also embedded in the testimony of female smokers regarding their smoking patterns.

Much of the work being done to solve the problem of women's smoking is undertaken in isolation from the women who smoke. This is often protective, as it allows advocates and policymakers to create policy and programming according to their own agenda, exempt from the realities of smokers' lives and thoughts. It also allows any unintended consequences of various interventions to go unread. It is essential to break through this divide by continuing to seek insights from female smokers, framed in the context of the history, culture, costs, benefits, and values associated with smoking. These must be the key elements in planning future actions on women and smoking.

This approach will increase the general understanding of women, as well as smoking, and will uncover insights that will enhance the future health and welfare of women. It will also inform a collective response to women's smoking. While this analysis is focused mainly on women smokers in industrial countries, and is far from generalizable, I hope that its conclusions will contribute to deterrent effect on the current globalization of the women's smoking epidemic.

HISTORICAL AND CULTURAL INFLUENCES
ON WOMEN'S SMOKING IN INDUSTRIAL COUNTRIES

Smoking has had a history fraught with conflict ever since its introduction into Europe by explorers importing it from North America. Over the centuries, tobacco smoking has evoked intense reactions and considerable moral and legal regulation. During the 1500s "tobacco-houses" were established for smokers in Europe and pharmacies sold tobacco on prescription only.[2] It is ironic that almost five centuries later in North America, smokers are once again limited to marginal social locations.

In sixteenth-century Europe, smoking was described variously as morally depraved, corrupt, a sign of "Indian Barbarianism," and a cure for cancer, asthma, headache, worms, and the "diseases of women."[3] Ever since the advent of tobacco use in Europe, the issue of women's smoking has been a contentious issue. Women's smoking, like most of women's activities, has always been commented upon. Cultural changes, social pressures, laws, and attitudes have influenced women's smoking practices for centuries.

The invention of manufactured cigarettes in the late 1800s forced the question of women's smoking to the forefront, just as it caused men's smoking to become both more widespread and a public issue. Prior to this, tobacco had been smoked mainly in pipes and cigars and had been restricted to men and some working-class women, at least in the European context. At this point, arguments against women's tobacco use centred on it being unfeminine. However, the idea that women should have an equal right to smoke had grown over the course of two centuries and, by the early 1900s, had taken a firm hold in industrial countries, especially Canada and the United States.

The origins of smoking are unclear. It may have first been established in the Americas among First Nations peoples and spread from there, or it may have arisen independently in Asia.[4] Either way, early tobacco use was considerably different and did not present the health problems that smoking gives rise to today. Among First Nations peoples, tobacco had (and continues to have) a sacred and medicinal use. Tobacco is used as an offering to the spirit world to give thanks to the Creator, protect travelers, console the bereaved, welcome guests, induce peace or prayer, cure illness and establish bonds. There is no evidence that these practices led to habituation or were even recreational. Indeed, only relatively recently has the conversion to smoking cigarettes become a serious health issue among indigenous peoples across North America and elsewhere.

FOCUSING ON WOMEN

The first cigarette advertisements explicitly directed at women in North America, the United Kingdom, and other industrial countries appeared in the late 1920s. In conjunction with other key social changes this deliberate targeting of the female market effectively launched the widespread use of cigarettes by women in these countries. The social acceptability of women's smoking continued to increase during the 1930s and by the end of the Second World War had gained wide acceptance.

During the Second World War, women were required to enter the paid labor force to replace male labor while men were in the forces. This shift in roles proved women's strength and adaptability to varied types of work. Prejudices about women's place and role were temporarily suspended. Previously "masculine" behaviors, such as smoking, became more easily adopted by women.

At this point, it served the interests of both capitalism and patriotism to have women take on the roles of men. For the tobacco companies, a large untapped market of women awaited its advertising and product development. Tobacco companies emerged as patriotic supporters of the men in the services and often ran advertising campaigns exhorting those at home to show their support for the soldiers by sending them cartons of cigarettes. Prior to the first medical links between health problems and smoking being made in the 1940s, and before the advent of widespread medical research into smoking, tobacco advertising directly appealing to women only increased.[5]

Not until 1950 did any organized lobbying against tobacco by health groups begin again in the United States, Canada, and the United Kingdom to pick up where some effective antitobacco lobbyists had left off in the pre–First World War years. At this point is was still thought that smoking-related diseases were male-specific, but the increased exposure of women to long-term tobacco use began to reveal smoking-related morbidity and mortality in women as well. Even so, prior to the 1980s, the major focus of the medical research on smoking-related diseases was on men.

FROM IMMORALITY TO FREEDOM

Manufactured cigarettes have been available for little more than a century. From the late 1800s to the 1920s, smoking by women was associated with rebelliousness and marginalization and was the occupational symbol of prostitution.[6] The number of women using cigarettes has been significant in industrial countries only since the Second World War.

While the antitobacco crusaders of this century concern themselves with both health and environmental issues, their principal concern in the early decades was the drift away from virtue that smoking represented. Women smokers were fallen women; they were "sluts," "whores," and "sinners." So well entrenched was this equation that smoking in public was considered a brazen act. As early as 1908, a woman in New York was arrested for smoking a cigarette.[7]

Despite the hint of freedom occasioned by women's experiences during the First World War, the 1920s brought a return to the image of women as domestic and maternal.[8] Homemakers and mothers did not smoke. The apparent conflict between increasing freedom for women and the anticigarette lobby was exploited with steadfast resolve by the marketers of cigarettes. Beginning in the 1920s, the Great American Tobacco Company made a concerted effort to erase the taboo against women smoking in public. Feminism was used as a marketing ploy and entered the "jargon of consumerism."[9]

A. A. Brill, hired by the company to consult on strategy, was unequivocal:

> Some women regard cigarettes as symbols of freedom. . . . Smoking is a sublimation of oral eroticism; holding a cigarette in the mouth excites the oral zone. It is perfectly normal for women to want to smoke cigarettes. Further, the first women who smoked probably had an excess of masculine components and adopted the habit as a masculine act. But today the emancipation of women has suppressed many of the feminine desires. More women now do the same work as men do. . . . Cigarettes, which are equated with men, become torches of freedom.[10]

As a result, the 1929 Easter parade in New York City included a company-organized and much publicized group of cigarette-smoking women, lighting "torches of freedom" as a protest against women's inequality. This marketing coup was accomplished with the cooperation of leading feminists in the United States. Ewen calls this "commercialized feminism" and, while not limited to tobacco, its derivatives remain a dominant approach in cigarette marketing today.

Lacking evidence confirming the effects of smoking on health, the opponents of tobacco in the 1920s had little to work with other than hygiene and morality arguments. It was easy to perceive anticigarette lobbying as antiwoman, antifeminist, and antichoice. From being a badge of prostitution prior to the First World War, cigarette smoking in the 1920s became a symbol of women's freedom in the dominant culture and a challenge to Victorian mores. Smoking became firmly aligned with dress reform, bobbed hair, nightclubbing, and suffrage.

It took over six decades for this link between smoking and women's freedom to be explicitly countered by health and social commentators. The strength of tobacco's addictive qualities only gradually became clear as smokers became aware of the difficulty of quitting. Even so, the more profound "loss of freedom" attached to smoking cigarettes was (and is) a difficult concept to transmit in light of the continued use of the freedom motif in tobacco advertising.

MASCULINE TO FEMININE

The *masculinity* implied by smoking was a key part of the cultural symbolism challenged by women smokers during the 1920s in industrial countries. Smoking tobacco had almost always been a man's domain, particularly due to the preponderance of pipe and cigar smoking prior to the advent of the manufactured cigarette. If equality was understood as being "equal to" men, then it followed that women should be allowed to do whatever men could.

Smoking cigarettes for women clearly fit in this domain. In her analysis of the cultural meaning of cross-dressing in the West, Marjorie Garber discusses the role of smoking in blurring gender lines. She notes that in the early decades of the twentieth century, smoking was generally acknowledged as a "male" taste, and lesbians in particular were seen to have an affinity for smoking as part of their adoption of male attire and attitude. Women such as Romaine Brooks, Una Troubridge, Radclyffe Hall, and Colette were illustrative of this connection between "social and sexual liberation."[11] "Liberation" was understood by the dominant culture to mean the ability and opportunity to act (and smoke) like men.

By the 1930s, an increasingly unisex trend emerged in this culture, which included cigarettes as an item of consumption for women and matched the lessening of differences between male and female dress. Since then, along with the development of more sophisticated definitions of sexual equality, there have been seven decades of elastic cultural definitions of women's smoking. Even so, the link between smoking and representations of maleness remains in some tobacco advertising and in popular culture. Garber sees this as clearly illustrated in movies featuring a gender-blurring component. *Victor/Victoria* and *Boy, What a Girl!* are two such movies where smoking a cigar is critical to the gender twists in the plot.[12]

(HETERO) SEXUALITY

By the 1940s and 1950s, cigarettes became a crucial erotic prop and a way of increasing one's attractiveness to men. This shift from masculine representations not only allowed the marketers of tobacco to access the large heterosexual women's market, but it also reinforced the North American cultural links between smoking, power, and sexual challenge.

The association of women's smoking with lesbianism was shifted to portraying it as a glamorous activity of heterosexual women. Garber suggests that this was really a way of obfuscating questions of sexual orientation and shifting the focus to questions of class.[13] Indeed, from the 1940s until the 1980s, tobacco marketers explicitly concentrated on associating cigarettes with classy sophistication and upward mobility.

A contemporary example of promoting (and exploiting) heterosexuality was the (thwarted) R. J. Reynolds' *Dakota* campaign in 1990. A new brand of cigarettes, *Dakota,* was in development, and the associated campaign was premised on targeting the "virile" female in her twenties "who liked to do what her boyfriend was doing." This was an attempt to secure the blue-collar women's market and was one of many segmented marketing strategies of the tobacco companies that has emerged as the overall North American market has shrunk. Some of these were directed at elite young women, such as the campaigns launched through fashion magazines that include images of women smoking on the runways of fashion shows.[14]

Such marketing strategies clearly reflect the values of patriarchy and capitalism in that they support the institution of heterosexuality and enhance profits. It was strategic and profitable several decades ago for the tobacco companies to override any lingering association of women's smoking with lesbianism (or even "mannishness"), just as it was strategic and profitable in the 1920s to override the association with prostitution.

On a more fundamental level, the contemporary marketing strategies also reinforce patriarchal and capitalist definitions of heterosexual women's smoking through brand development and the use of the media to display appropriate imagery and cultural symbolism. Thus, smoking has become part of the "cultural propaganda of heterosexuality" described by Adrienne Rich in her critical essay on "compulsory heterosexuality."[15] Only recently, as target markets have changed, have tobacco companies developed brands and advertising campaigns in the United States to focus on Blacks, Latinos, and gay and lesbian populations.

Over the last century, then, in industrial countries the cultural meaning of women's smoking as it relates to gender relations has moved from a symbol of being *bought* by men (prostitute), to being *like* men (lesbian/mannish/androgynous), to being *able to attract* men (glamourous/heterosexual). Sexual liberals may argue that this reflects historical differences in the power and control of a woman over her sexual existence. However, some sexual radicals would see this as evidence of further entrenchment of the institution of heterosexuality, an erasure of sexual orientation issues and a manipulation of the concept of women's power. The tobacco companies cover all this ground by simultaneously appealing to both the equality-seeking, *freedom-loving, challenging woman* (*"You've come a long way, baby"* of *Virginia* Slims), as well as to the heterosexually-defined, male-identified woman (the virile female of the *Dakota* campaign).

PATRIOTISM AND WAR

The androgynous portrayal of smoking reappeared in Europe and North America with the Second World War as women were once again drawn into the labor force, often to do nontraditional (male) work. The links between cigarettes and patriotism, established during the First World War, were more fully developed during the Second World War. Women were featured in nontraditional work roles (with cigarettes present in the images) and in active service roles as well.[16] In addition, in both the United Kingdom and the United States, cigarettes were declared as essential as food and were rationed in a similar manner. In 1941, Roosevelt declared tobacco an essential crop and even relieved U.S. tobacco farmers of military service.

The links between smoking, equality, masculinity, and patriotism were strengthened in these Western countries and overshadowed any remaining moral objections to women smoking cigarettes. The manufacturers of tobacco again made sure to connect the comfort of the "boys" abroad with the availability of cigarettes, a practice begun during the First World War. In Canada, for example, newspapers listed the names of donors to the tobacco fund with the amount of their donations. One such campaign, run by the Overseas League Tobacco and Hamper Fund, solicited donations to keep the "boys and girls overseas, including prisoners of war, well-supplied."[17] In the same paper, the C. C. MacDonald Tobacco Company advertised for members of the public to "Send the Boys the Best" by remitting three dollars for 900 cigarettes to be sent to members of the Canadian Active Services. Patriotism and support for the troops was thereby linked to the purchase of cigarettes, potentially even by nonsmokers.

Immediately after the Second World War when large numbers of women were being ushered back into traditional roles, cigarette advertisers introduced a different set of images. Women—usually young, white, and middle-class—were represented as wives and lovers expecting reunions or as brides taking cartons of cigarettes on their honeymoons.[18] During the 1940s, smoking was increasingly promoted as a companionable leisure activity to be shared by men and women, a theme still dominant in current cigarette promotions.

WORK AND LEISURE

Between 1950 and 1970, tobacco advertisements less frequently showed women as workers, housewives, or mothers. Instead, prevailing values encouraged middle-class domesticity. Possibly the emerging evidence about the health costs of smoking forced the advertisers to move away from picturing women in active poses, and toward more social and decorative representations of women's smoking. The portrayal of smoking as a leisure activity to be enjoyed in group situations became a more frequent theme of cigarette advertisements featuring women.[19] Even so, the women featured in cigarette ads were rarely shown with cigarettes in their mouths; most often they were pictured completely disconnected from the cigarette or the act of smoking. The exception to this pattern was imagery of men helping women light cigarettes.[20]

Women's smoking has become increasingly defined by marketers as a leisure activity and a source of relaxation. In the last two decades, as women's labor force participation has increased significantly, women have been viewed by those in tobacco marketing as suffering stress and needing relaxation aids. Cigarettes have been promoted as such and tobacco trade journals have particularly targeted stressed women in the labor force as an "untapped market" in the West.[21]

The marketers of cigarettes have managed to promote the idea that women are overstressed workers without picturing them in their work roles. Only during the 1930s and 1940s were women portrayed in occupational roles in cigarette advertisements, as the marketers created the image of smoking as a mark of independence and action in women.

More recently, women have been shown as "deserving" (needing) the pleasure, leisure, satisfaction, and self-indulgence represented by smoking their own cigarette, their own way, on their own time.

This marketing approach carries a more complex cultural message. It appears to promote women's independence while it subtly fosters and features women's dependence. The contradiction is artfully contained in the promotion of cigarettes as a prop through which to achieve equality or as a social symbol of pleasure and reward rather than addiction.

Contributing to this pattern, some analysts have superficially correlated the recent increase in smoking among women with the experience of and desire for increased equality felt by many women in the West and elsewhere. Howe, for example, suggests that young women in the United States may see cigarette smoking as signifying equality with males, and implies that this will attract them to the habit.[22]

This idea has been nurtured by the effective *Virginia Slims* campaign. The slogan "You've come a long way, baby" underscores images of key points and accomplishments in women's equality as a basis for selling cigarettes to women. Even health workers, analysts, and researchers promoting nonsmoking have often uncritically absorbed this linking of women's liberation with increased smoking. This interpretation of equality, used to explain and justify women's increasing smoking rates in the 1920s and 1930s, seems rather simplistic now when much more is known about the effects of smoking and when women's (and girls') occupational and social identities are considerably more complicated.

These aspects of cultural and historical shifts of meaning of smoking and women shed light on the persistent images and values that underpin women's smoking. These values and images undoubtedly affect girls and women, both in industrial countries as well as abroad, in countries with a declining rate of smoking, as well as those where the rates are on the rise. How do these factors and forces resonate in the voices of women smokers? This approach has often allowed the continued emphasis in prevention, cessation, and research activity to be on individual women's smoking behaviors, including their "choice" to smoke. Comparatively little attention has been paid to the social structural features that foster the patterns of women's attraction and attachment to cigarette smoking in contemporary Western culture.

SYMBOL AND SOLACE: WOMEN SMOKERS' VOICES

Women speak of both symbol and solace when discussing smoking. Contradictions emerge that are reflective of the cultural and historical

ambivalence surrounding smoking. Women smokers raise several major
themes such as the use of smoking to organize social relationships, create an image, control emotions, express dependence, and form identity.
Women use smoking to bond, equalize, distance, defuse, or end relationships with others. Smoking can increase independence, difference,
style, and acceptance. Women use smoking to control emotions, particularly in the reduction of negative ones. Women see smoking as a support, a source of predictability and a site of controllability. And finally,
in forming identity, smoking operates as a site of contradiction for
women, and an instigator of guilt, tension, or self-castigation.

Once addicted, what was once enhancing and empowering becomes a
dependency, a drain, and a stigma. What was once desirable about smoking may no longer be, and sometimes women who smoke are no longer
culturally desirable either. But the anchorage that cigarettes represent is
clear. While many women may begin to smoke in anticipation of feeling
independent and free, the eventual result is dependency and limitation.
The support offered by smoking cigarettes comes with conflict and a price.

> "They're (cigarettes) like a partner. They're the most dependable part-
> ner I've had. Cigarettes are my best friend. . . ." (Barb)

> "My cigarettes have been more consistent than any people in my life."
> (Carla)

When women suppress negative emotions, there is a clear benefit to society. By internalizing anger, those around the woman can remain comfort-
able and complacent. They can remain without responsibility and remain
that way as long as the woman "sucks back her anger" through smoking.
Similarly, when women control micro interactions through smoking there
are clear social benefits. Functional relationships facilitated by smoking
begin to fill needs that should be filled by adequate social structures and
policies. This illustrates one of the most solid reasons for the ongoing cultural ambivalence regarding smoking and helps explain the many contradictory messages promoted to women regarding smoking—that this control is for *others'* benefit is not articulated. In essence, the implicit
encouragement of women's smoking is a form of social control.

WOMEN, SMOKING, AND IDENTITY

> "Cigarettes do control me, I guess, but I control them." (Barb)

Smoking and female identity are wrapped around a contradiction. While
women may often start smoking in order to appear in control, the even-

tual irony is that smoking controls them. Is it traditional role behavior or breaking free? Answering this question is complicated by the changing cultural meanings over time and space and changing personal meanings as addiction takes deeper root. Can one feel both autonomous *and* dependent? In claiming the addict label self-control can be given up to the power of the addiction. In claiming the rebel label, the wilfullness of flying in the face of scientific evidence and health advice is highlighted, posing another site of internal and external critique. Is it any wonder that individual women are forced to live with profound and contradictory identities surrounding smoking when the global culture cannot itself decide?

Across the globe, women continue to have less power than most men in their society in defining social reality. Women derive the meaning of femaleness from systems and values not of their making, manifested in society's institutions such as family, church, state, school, and the media. The need for control *and* adaptation through smoking reflect two sides of the same prism of response to being female. Mediation of social life is accomplished through smoking. Smoking assists in reforming reality into a manageable form.

That women have agency in these processes is obvious. Women in even the most oppressive circumstances resist, regroup and persevere. However, when definitions of woman are consistently created externally, then buffers, mediators, and screens separate inner emotions from the outer life. Women smokers experience first hand the inconsistency between the female script and their own reality. Women often feel betrayed by the very script that they absorbed on discovering that it contains images of femaleness that do not materialize. This underlies many of the tensions and contradictions described by women when asked to consider the meaning of smoking to them.

Uta Enders-Dragaesser terms this division a "paradoxical social reality" which feels like both a contradiction and a burden.[23] Further, she says:

> dealing with these paradoxes uses up a lot of energy which is then unavailable for other things. This is particularly true for experiences of abuse and violence which we now know occur frequently and often leave traumata which last a lifetime.[24]

Consequently, women must spend considerable energy and time "getting used to it," "toeing the line," "playing along," or being a "good sport" in face of the stark reality of inequality.[25] I suggest that smoking is an aid in this process.

At times, this contradiction is lived out through the female body in its deportment, accessorizing and presentation. Assessing women's smoking from this point of view involves exploring the role of smoking from the "inside" of the body as well as the outside. But the definition of women's smoking is constantly being redefined over time and between places. As has been noted, women's smoking has, over several decades, gone from immoral to glamorous to liberated to unhealthy to stupid and marginalized, just in the developed countries! It is not surprising, then, that identity issues are so central and troublesome for the female smokers quoted above. Women's self-definitions in relation to smoking and the meaning of smoking with respect to women's selves are continually pushed to change.

The meaning(s) of smoking for women from both internal and external sources are multi-layered and variable. In developing a theory of women's smoking, therefore, the interaction between inner and outer life must be acknowledged. It is useful to apply Sandra Bartky's concept of "disciplinary practices" to women's smoking behavior. She suggests that there are three practices carried out on women to create femininity and the female identity. These are:

> ... those that aim to produce a body of a certain size and general configuration; those that bring forth from this body a specific repertoire of gestures, postures, and movements; and those that are directed toward the display of this body as an ornamented surface.[26]

Aspects of these practices that encourage certain kinds of deportment or emotional style in women are linked to the themes female smokers discuss. For example, Bartky suggests that expressions of women's true emotional states are actively discouraged. Such measures as "wearing a fixed smile" despite one's inner state or eliminating facial wrinkles despite their indication of past emotional experiences are two examples of this type of "disciplinary practice." The use of smoking to suppress negative emotions is another. Such a use of smoking by women can also be seen as a *benefit* to society; for if women actually gave vent to the emotions suppressed by smoking, those around them would be forced to react.

While smoking is eventually disempowering, in the interim it is useful for women in solidifying identity and enhancing power. From this point of view, quitting is not simply a difficult process but becomes a serious loss of part of the equipment of being female. While women may describe smoking as a burden, it is also a key part of a woman's repertoire. Looked at this way, women demonstrate agency through smoking and, as clearly expressed, would suffer a void in their identity and ability to negotiate social life if they were to give it up. Quitting smoking, then, would constitute what Bartky calls "de-skilling."[27] Recognizing this consequence is essential to understanding the possibility (or possible limitation) of a nonsmoking identity.

Rapidly changing cultural definitions of smoking and increasing regulation of public smoking contribute to contradictions and confusion around the meaning of smoking. These external shifts add to the turmoil of understanding the self in relation to smoking, or smoking in relation to self, by continually changing the rules. So for women, the questions "What does smoking say about me?" and "What can I say about my smoking?" may never be answered conclusively.

The material roots of femininity are also important to understanding the testimony of the women smokers. Dorothy Smith sees the media as key transmitters of the practices, activities and products crucial to being female.[28] Women actively engage with this process as creative players and consumers. Reading women's magazines and buying fashions and cosmetics are examples of this process.

Women use smoking to organize social relationships or to create and project images. These "disciplinary practices" are quite specific and, upon reflection, apparent to them. The deliberateness of using smoking to control behavior or circumstances or to adapt to external influences is clear. Even under the influence of the political economy of tobacco and powerful cultural messages regarding femininity, the agency of women smokers is very much apparent.

Defining the self in this way can be problematic. If identity is derived from commodities and images provided by the media, attention is deflected "from a more valuable source of identity, namely the historical precedents and the immediate politics of our circumstances."[29]

In exactly this sense, smoking functions as a screen between the women and the meaning of their lives. Experience is pushed through a sieve, reforming reality into a manageable form. Identity develops but is not grounded in pure, clear, unmediated experience. The control and adaptation facilitated by smoking has intervened. Cigarettes offer momentary resolution of the conflicts in women's experiences, and a screen of cultural and social reality.

NOTES

1. See C. Chollat-Traquet, *Women and Tobacco* (Geneva: World Health Organization, 1992), chapter 1.

2. See E. Corti, *A History of Smoking* (London: George Harrup, 1931), chapters 5 and 6.

3. Ibid., pp. 58, 75, 79.

4. See F. Robicsek, *The Smoking Gods* (Oklahoma City: University of Oklahoma Press, 1978).

5. See V. Ernster, "Mixed Messages for Women: A Social History of Cigarette Smoking and Advertising," *New York State Journal of Medicine* (July, 1985), pp. 335–340, and H. Howe, "A Historical Review of Women, Smoking and Advertising," *Health Education* (May/June 1984), p. 4

6. L. Banner, *American Beauty* (New York: Alfred Knopf, 1983), p. 76.

7. L. Cook and J. Milner, "Smoking Symbols: Gender, Tobacco Use, and the Archaeological Record." Paper presented at the Society for Historical Archaeology annual meetings, Richmond, Virginia, January 1991, p. 12.

8. See B. Ehrenrich and D. English, *For Her Own Good: 150 Years of Experts' Advice to Women* (Garden City: Anchor Books, 1979), chapter 5.

9. S. Ewen, *Captains of Consciousness: Advertising and the Social Roots of the Consumer Culture* (London: McGraw-Hill, 1976), p. 160.

10. Ibid.

11. M. Garber, *Vested Interests: Cross Dressing and Cultural Anxiety* (London: Routledge, 1992), p. 156.

12. Ibid.

13. Ibid., p. 157.

14. See A. Amos, "Women's Magazines and Tobacco—Preliminary Findings of a Survey of the Top Women's Magazines in Europe," in B. Durston and K. Jamrozik, eds., *The Global War, Proceedings of the Seventh World Conference on Tobacco and Health* (Western Australia: Health Department of Western Australia, 1990).

15. A. Rich, "Compulsory Heterosexuality and Lesbian Existence," *Signs: A Journal of Women in Culture and Society,* 5:4 (1980), pp. 631–660.

16. B. Jacobson, *Beating the Lady Killers* (London: Pluto Press, 1986), p. 44.

17. *The Star Weekly,* "Tobacco Fund Needs Donations Right Now," *The Star Weekly* (Nov. 25, 1944).

18. V. Ernster, op. cit., p. 337.

19. D. Sexton and P. Haberman, "Women in Magazine Advertisements," *Journal of Advertising Research,* 14:4 (August 1974), p. 44.

20. Ibid., p. 45.

21. B. Jacobson, op. cit., p. 48.

22. H. Howe, op. cit., p. 8.

23. U. Enders-Draegaesser, "Women's Identity and Development within a Paradoxical Reality," *Women's Studies International Forum,* 11:6 (1988), p. 585.

24. Ibid., p. 587.

25. Ibid., pp. 585–587.

26. S. L. Bartky, "Foucault, Feminity and the Modernization of Patriarchal Power," in I. Diamond and L. Lee Quimby, eds., *Feminism and Foucault: Reflections on Resistance* (Boston: Northeast University Press, 1988), p. 64.

27. Ibid., p. 27.

28. D. Smith, "Feminity as Discourse," in L. Roman and L. Christian-Smith, eds., *Becoming Feminine: The Politics of Popular Culture* (London: The Falmer Press, 1988), p. 37.

29. J. Finkelstein, *The Fashioned Self* (Philadelphia: Temple University Press, 1991), p. 190.

Wayne and Cheryl at Long Bay Gaol. Credit: Alphonso Lingis.

Chapter Thirteen

LOVE JUNKIES

ALPHONSO LINGIS

WAYNE: I hate lies. I would not tolerate lies from anybody. I've always been like that.

WILLIAM BURROUGHS: And always cops: smooth, college-trained state cops, practiced, apologetic patter, electronic eyes weigh your car and luggage, clothes and face; snarling big city dicks, soft-spoken country sheriffs with something black and menacing in old eyes color of a faded grey flannel shirt . . .

CHERYL: The nurses from the clinic would stare at Wayne and me. They had a perfect view of where I worked, because I was doing the laundry for the whole place. They had a perfect view, and could see what Wayne and I did. There was one particular nurse who had a fancy for Wayne. And as our relationship grew, her anger grew. Where she did not take it out on Wayne, she took it out on me. She was very abrupt and very rude and very against anything that I wanted.

W: Every day I was copping lectures from all the nurses: Oh but you've got to be careful with Cheryl! Don't have too much to do with her!

C: I had my drug couriers among the mailmen.

W: She has a very fast bad temper. Obviously, the nurses would upset her and she'd really run off at the mouth. Very abusive.

W: They used to warn me all the time. Of course, from all that warning, I guess—

C: He got his back up.

This was 10 years ago. But they had known one another 23 years before, having met in 1976.

At once they spoke of their passion. We keep each other alive, they said.

W: Sometimes I'm around with Cheryl 23 hours one day; the other hour I might be away on the job on a computer—and as strange as it seems to people, I miss her for that hour! I hate it. I hate it.

Wayne Jones is of medium height, strong arms, flat stomach. He is very tanned. He wears a loose, moss-green, long-sleeved light sweatshirt, light sweatpants, both very worn and patched, and new good-quality sneakers. On his wrist is a black digital watch. His head is round, with a thick black–brown walrus mustache. His thick hair is bristle black–grey, well groomed. He has clear blue eyes, luminous and direct. He says that he learned that as a child he had brown eyes. His parents had a photo of a brown-eyed youth whom he had always thought was a brother. He has two small silver rings in his left ear. His mouth is small, with sensual lips. Later, he mentions that all his teeth had to be pulled. He wears a silver chain with a masonic cross. He wears four rings on his left hand, one on his right. His hands and arms are covered with tattoos. On the base fingers of his left hand: the letters L O V E.

W: I've had a lot of fights in my time. I've never been stabbed. I got iron-barred once. The person that did that did live to regret it. Most people that know me know not to push me. The first time is accidental; the second time is coincidental; the third time is enemy action. I'll cop a lot of shit before I'll explode, but when I explode, I really explode. I'll cop shit on me; I won't cop shit for Cheryl. If someone upsets Cheryl, then that's it; there's no second chances. No chances at all. Most people here know I'll live and die for Cheryl.

Cheryl gets up at 5:00 A.M. She savors each day she is alive. She has amazing energy. She is high on washing and folding their laundry. Laundry is always happening. She offers to darn socks, to mend and alter the clothes of the men. She makes small alterations that eliminate a cloying discomfort in a garment, small alterations that make the most threadbare garment fit and even flatter its wearer. She is very ingenious.

C: Then I was pulled aside by another nurse that I get on quite well with, and she said, Cheryl, you should get access to your medical file, there's some horrendous things in there about you by a certain nurse. So I put the application in, and I got permission to have a look at my medical file. And I'm reading through the admissions; the first line of this nurse, who had come out and tried to stop it, was: I had not been informed about the patient being admitted to B ward. But there is a letter attached from Dr. Peter Paisley saying that she must be admitted to B ward. Then she said the only reason that I had come back to B Ward was to have connubial visits with Wayne. So she was actually saying that I was a sexual deviant.

Cheryl Gysin-Jones is a little taller than Wayne, quite thin, with big-boned legs, big hands somewhat discolored with bleached pink, fingernails clean and a little long. She wears a moss green t-shirt and shorts, much faded, much patched. Her face is long with high cheek bones, her cheeks sunken, her lips thin; she has very fine regular slightly yellowed teeth. She has very big brown eyes. She has a thick head of fine hair, brunette turning to blond, cut short, combed to one side. Her eyebrows are thin, plucked. In the office Cheryl has two mirrors and her makeup. So she can touch herself up at any moment. Around her neck is a long string of small beads, the kind Filipino kids sell on the beaches. She has a gold watch with a very big face, man's watch, loose on her wrist. At the first opportunity, she says she is 52.

W: I used to be 14 stone. When I was out, I ran the marathon a couple of times. Now I look fit because I get pumped with steroids. Every Friday I get an injection of 100 g of one of the best steroids you can get.

C: I'm on steroids too. I'm on Thenclol, that is made out of female horse urine, Premarin, the 0.625 micrograms—so you can imagine how strong one of them is if they're that concentrated. And I'm also on a steroid called Meclastret, which is to help me sustain my weight, and also to help me put weight on.

W: But we have an agreement that I will never allow myself to . . .

C: . . . become a burden.

W: I'll never allow myself to turn into a vegetable, or become a burden on anybody.

C: I believe that when you have got to get somebody to wipe your bottom, and to wash you and do things like that—I think that's humiliating, degrading, and I could not and would not go through that. I would pull the plug before that, before I would let that happen.

W: But there are so many stories. You tell people—I often speak to the staff, the professional staff, and they say, Oh that can't be right. And I believe that if I ever wrote a book about the facts that I'd be dead. There is no doubt in my mind whatsoever that before the book ever got to be published, they would kill me.

There are long scars on both of Wayne's arms—from knife cuts. Later, he indicates they were self-inflicted.

W: I was a bastard of a kid, you know. I was placed in a boys' home at the age of seven because my parents were divorced. My father took me, and my mother took my brother. My father started dating someone else, and I got in the way. One day I was sent to the shops to buy my father a newspaper, and when I come back there was 5 cents missing in the change. My father flogged me for almost an hour and a half, trying to get me to admit that I had spent that 5 cents on lollies. I never touched the fuckin' money! I don't know what happened to it, I dunno if I lost it, or whether the person at the shop ripped me off, or what—I was a fuckin' kid, you know what I mean? I was charged with being uncontrollable—I had to be charged with something to be taken off his hands—and put in a boys' home at the age of 7. In the end I didn't want to go home. Then once I came home from school with a black eye, and my father said "What happened?" I told him the truth, because that's all I've ever known is to tell the truth. And the truth was that I'd had a fight with a kid at school and he punched the shit out of me. So my father took me out in the back yard, and put punching gloves on, and he punched the living shit out of me. Then one day I had come home with a cut in my head. What happened? Had a fight. I won the fight. When I told him I won, he didn't take me out in the back yard and punch the cracket out of me; he patted me on the back, put his arm around me, hugged me, and said "Good on you, son, that's my boy!"

Cheryl was born and abandoned. She was adopted by a Swiss couple who lived in Cornelia, a town south of Sydney with a fine beach. Her foster parents called her Paul. She has a brother, whom she never sees. He cannot accept me, because of my sexuality, she says. She became a woman at the age of 15. During the last visit of her foster parents, 12 months ago—they have moved to Queensland, and are quite old, so everyone understood it was their last visit—she insisted they call her Cheryl. They do, however, approve of Wayne. They love him.

> C: And then on another piece of paper that I happened to notice in my medical file was an entry by a doctor. He goes through all my medication. And his last words, before closing off—this is on the discharge summary: To take Cheryl off her medication would be like trying to take a bone away from the Doberman.

> W: Cheryl was going through a real hard time. She was copping a lot of flak and discrimination from some of the nursing staff. Really having a hard time. She was not dealing with it well. Cheryl has never dealt with stress well. The only way Cheryl's ever known how to deal with those sorts of issues is with drugs. Over the past 10 years I've been able to get through to Cheryl that she can talk to people. But occasionally she still does need assistance. So this time she went to see the doctor to ask the doctor for an increase in her evening Valium just to help her go through that period of time. And he notes that he's giving her the increase to shut her up, and that the only cure that he could come up with for Cheryl is chemical lobotomy.

On his left hand Wayne has tattooed the blazon of his favorite football team. On his right hand, a large cross with the words *In Memory*.

> W: It's of my uncle. He was a biker, finally crashed and smashed both his knees. When I got out of the boys' home, I worked on my uncle's carnival, with the ferris wheels, racing cars, roller-coasters. We traveled all over Australia. It was very hard work. One had to work 48 hours without sleeping to set it all up. Carnival is especially for kids, and I was of course mainly after the girls. Carnivals have a bad reputation: people think everybody will be in fights and they have to lock up their daughters. One does have to use force: when a couple of blokes come up for a ride, they are not inclined to put down their cigarettes and beer bottles. So I got into fights.

—Where did you get hepatitis C?

> C: Shortly after we got together.

> W: We're pretty sure Cheryl got the hepatitis from me.

> C: We're not sure, though.

W: We're reasonably sure. Because she was hep negative when we first got together . . .

C: I became hep C-positive, when I wasn't using any needles.

There was no note taken of Mardi Gras this year. Three years ago the Correctional Service had a banner in the parade as did the police; there are lots of gay officers. But the last 2 years they did not.

In the past decade Mardi Gras has become the biggest tourist attraction in Sydney, more than a million people come to watch the parade of revelers. Whole planes arrive from Japan, Singapore, and Hong Kong. Up against a wall on the parade route where the floats of the outrageous and the exhibitionist pass, 7 Christians stand under a banner reading "God forgive Sydney."

Morality is the principle that happiness, which is welfare, prosperity, satisfaction of wants and needs; is something to be pursued, that is acquired through a procedure, that is earned. That happiness is acquired by fulfilling obligations. Morality is the principle that one has to suffer for one's transgressions. Suffering is something that is owed. Pangs of conscience, guilt is something one owes, a debt.

C: I trained to be a registered nurse. I was caught stealing drugs and dismissed, but no charges were filed against me. I went to King's Cross; I found gigs as a female impersonator in the cabarets—Les Girls, Simone, Candy. Carlotta, who now acts in the weekly show on TV called *Beauty and the Beast,* was a close friend. Carlotta still writes me, twice a year; she sends me the programs of shows. Another close friend was Diane Darling, who died in 1993, of AIDS. Back then with the showgirls I had toured the jails.

W: HIV came into the New South Wales prisons in 1985. When the prison services discovered that they had three HIV-positive inmates, they segregated them. You didn't have a choice; you got put in the AIDS unit. The discrimination was outrageous, horrendous—from inmates, officers, everybody. In the first 6 months of the first opening, there was a transsexual that went in there called Diane Darling, who was a very good friend of mine. I'd known Diane for a lot of years. So when I heard that Diane was in the AIDS unit, I saw the high ranker in the jail and asked if I could go in there and talk to her. At first they said "No," that they wouldn't have people going back and forth. And then they said, "Well, it's up to them: if they want to see you, you can go in." So I went in. When I come out of there, people'd say, "Wayne what are you doing down in there, you'll be catching AIDS!" I found myself all the time having to justify why I'd go in there to see them: They're friends of mine. Well, I was doing that for my own bat for maybe 6 months when Head Office started what they called the AIDS Task Force, which was a group of civilians who went around to a couple of the selected jails to educate inmates about HIV. They had already heard about me going in and out of the unit all of the time, so they approached me and said, "Well look, we know you're already educating people; would you like to be a peer educator?" And I said Yes. And that's how I did their course. Cheryl and I ran the HIV-AIDS and Hep C committee for 5 1/2, almost 6 years. Every year we put on a different event for World AIDS day—put on some really big events a couple of times. We've printed up our own pamphlets, our own posters, and things like that. We printed up one poster that said: "HIV-AIDS doesn't just mean a death sentence; it means a life of hell." A lot of people took offense to that. They made me take it down.

There is nothing sly about Wayne. He is very direct and enterprising; he would do anything for you. Cheryl can put in a word for your parole in the right ears.

W: It's a big thing with me—honesty. The only things I've ever done I've done honestly. See, I believe that a real relationship—not just a relationship like ours, but even a relationship between two good friends—can't last if there's not total honesty at all times. Honesty has always been a thing for me all my life. It's something I never got from my family, so it's something I've always demanded from my friends and the people around me.

At King's Cross part of joining the scene was drugs. Cheryl has been addicted to heroin now for 36 years, She also did cocaine and bennies, but not marijuana. Being a showgirl was hard work, doing four or five shows a night, but it did pay well. Not well enough, though, to sustain her habit. She supplemented her income with prostitution, then with armed robbery.

Long Bay Gaol is the men's maximum security prison of New South Wales. Built outside Sydney on a rocky coast, it contains some 1,200 prisoners. They are murderers, rapists, child molesters. And men convicted of armed robbery. The cells are 6 by 10 feet, containing a bed bolted to the wall, a toilet, a sink. You are allowed to have—if you pay for them—a jug, a TV, a walkman. One wing of isolation cells without windows was closed in 1992 under pressure from Amnesty Internal. The authorities have opened one room to the public; it displays ingenious weapons that were found during cell searches.

W: So for many years I was an asshole, and then I reached a stage
in my life where I couldn't handle what I used to see in the mirror
each morning. When you look in the mirror you either see your best
friend or your worst enemy. I was sick of seeing my worst enemy. So
I said to myself, from now on I either see my best friend or I won't
see anybody. That's when I started to make a lot of changes in my
life. I made promises to myself that I was going to stop being a bastard of a kid and start trying to do things to help other people. I got
help from a magical, magical lady called Loretto Kane who was running the Drug and Alcohol Abuse Program at the time. She got me
involved in Drug and Alcohol, and we ran Drug and Alcohol
together. We used to run groups together; I used to run groups. For
a long time I was doing really good. I did a soul search, really started
to change, I was 13 months out of jail, and for 13 months my life
was perfect. Then my life just went haywire, and I come back to jail.
When I was in the police cells, I saw my reflection again and I was
back to that stage of seeing my worst enemy. It was when I tried to
kill myself. This was in 1989. When I woke up in hospital, I realized
obviously that I hadn't died. They put me down in D Ward, which
is the psychiatric ward for the self-harming people. I spent about 5
or 6 weeks down there. While I was down in D ward, in D ward
there's no way you could harm yourself down there—seriously,
because you're under 24-hour observation.

C: You walk around there pretending . . .

W: There's nurses and officers everywhere that watch you all day
and all night. So, for the 6 weeks that I was in there, I sort of played
the game to get out of there. I said I'm alright now, and I'd rather
live now, and I don't want to die now. So I got out. But the whole
time it was in the back of my head that the day I was going to go to
court, I was going to plead guilty to everything. And the day I got
sentenced, I was going to die. I had already written a lot of things,
and the media was going to know all those things about our relationship. Because before that day came, Cheryl and I had built this
relationship. I had been honest with Cheryl and told her, I said to
Cheryl right to the word go: Don't get emotionally attached to me!
Because I'm not going to be there. I didn't tell her straight away why
I wasn't going to be there. I just told her that I wasn't always going
to be there. Once the relationship had got to the stage that I knew I
could talk to her about anything, then I was honest with her telling
her why I wasn't going to be there. Never once did Cheryl say
"Don't do it!" or, "I won't allow you to do it"—or anything like

that. She never tried to talk me out of it. But see, it didn't happen, because Cheryl got me back to the stage of looking in the mirror and liking what I saw and seeing my best friend there. And for a while I was sort of postponing it and saying I'll just take it for 3 months, or take it for 6 months, and see how it goes. And then it got close to Cheryl's time to go home on parole, and I thought "Well I'll wait till Cheryl goes home, and then I'll do it," but she came back.

Wayne has spent 23 years in prison, Cheryl a few years more than that. An estimated 65% of the prisoners at Long Bay Gaol have Hepatitis C.

W: As far as a lot of them are concerned, because we're criminals, we're supermen! We're supposed to be able to put up with pain, we don't feel pain like normal people.

When his uncle died, recently, Wayne was not allowed to go to the funeral. He did this tattoo with the big cross and *In Memory,* and went to the warden and told him to cite him. In prison, doing a tattoo on someone is cited as bodily assault; doing a tattoo on oneself is self-mutilation. Wayne has covered his hands and arms with tattoos. He improvised a tattoo machine, using the motor taken from a Walkman, the handle of a toothbrush, and an ordinary sewing needle. He uses lampblack for ink.

W: People say to us: you have our sympathy. I don't want your sympathy. If I want sympathy, I'll look it up in the dictionary—it comes between shit and syphilis.

Wayne was in Kumer prison. This is the place where they put corrupt politicians and police—and trannies. Corrupt politicians and especially police would be in real danger being put among ordinary convicts. The trannies are considered harmless to them. At the time Wayne was in a relationship with the transsexual cabaret performer Diane Darling.

Wayne and Cheryl have used their clout with the staff to get in disinfectants strong enough to kill the HIV virus, for use with needles. For there is heroin enough for all in the prison, supplied, of course, by the screws for those $11 or $13 a week the prisoners can earn. Wayne and Cheryl have also insisted that a condom dispenser get installed, but which they then mounted on the wall next to the officer's quarters. So blokes have to expose their intentions to the officers, and expose themselves to their shouts and jeers.

C: At this stage I was the first transsexual ever to be put in the main jail of a maximum security institution of New South Wales. It had never been done before.

W: I'd like to think that in many ways we've proven that if two people really love each other, they can conquer anything, because the hurdles and obstacles that we've had to overcome in the last 10 years , I mean, it's . . .

C: astronomical.

W: This place, this environment is not conducive to a relationship like ours. It doesn't happen, because there's just too many people in jail: but the prison regulations state, and they have never been rewritten, that inmates should not be placed two out in any circumstances: they are to be one out, or three out. Because to be two out was seen to be allowing homosexuality. Because if someone was three out, that would reduce the chance of homosexuality. In many ways Cheryl and I have tested the water for the Department of Corrective Services in that area. In many ways we have set the precedents that have allowed things to happen. Now there are other relationships going on in the system—not quite the same as ours, but they are happening.

C: They're being allowed to happen, instead of being judged and screwed up.

A Brazilian bloke name of Xavier had made his way to Australia, as a mule for some drug smugglers. They caught him. He was very mechanical. Out of bits of wire, discarded tin cans he would pick up, he made clocks. Big extravagant, hallucinating clocks, covered with glitter, with photos of cheesecake women, mug shots of criminals, car crashes from magazines. His whole cell, all the walls, were eventually covered with them. He was terrified of being transferred. One day, they did transfer him to another prison. The following day he was found murdered.

At the main entrance of Long Bay Gaol, there is a small shop, where visitors can buy artifacts made by the prisoners. The prices are fixed by the prison staff. The most popular items are Aboriginal dot paintings. Galleries in Sydney fix very high prices for Aboriginal dot paintings, much sought after in the world art market. After Xavier's death, the shop put on an exhibition of Xavier's clocks.

W: In my time I've probably met 10,000 to 15,000 people in jail these many years that I've been here. Out of those there's probably 100 that would say that I'm their friend; out of that hundred, there's probably 60 that I would call my friends; out of that 60, 20 that I would say that I know they're honest and up front with me and I trust them implicitly, and out of that 20 there are 5 that I would die for or kill for.

Your crime also determines how much respect you get. There was bloke there had done a $6 million drug deal. He was a big man in Long Bay.

> C: This happened many years ago. A guy came in doing 17 days. For traffic offenses. As a joke, the sweepers changed it to 17 years on the card. But when he walked out of the cell the next morning, he saw 17 years on the card. He couldn't understand English, but he could read numbers. And when he walked out of the cell, he said to some-body, called them over and said: How long? How long? And they said, 17 years. He said What? They said, 17 years.

> W: To shake him up, they said the screws put it there. And because he believed the screws put it there—you know to him the screws were like the police, so it must be true . . .

> C: He had never been to jail . . .

> W: So he freaked, I mean he just freaked . . .

> C: He went downstairs onto the mall, sat there with a plastic knife and cut his penis off. And then, after they sewed it back on, he woke up and he ripped it off again.

Shit happens. While working as a sweeper in the clinic, Wayne was stabbed by a patient. A few weeks later Cheryl was in the hospital with anorexia; in the middle of the night two men who were HIV-positive raped her. Shit happens.

> C: They're both dead, now, so it doesn't matter. May they rest in peace.

Forgive and forget. Just forget, she says. One would have to remember and forgive everything, from the day you were born and abandoned.

> W: Cheryl cannot change who she is. It's one of the things I love so much about her. I get mad at people, people who do wrong by me, and I find it extremely hard to forgive them. Cheryl—she can not only forgive, but she can forget 5 minutes after it's happened. She's a person that was raped by two people and given AIDS, and is dying of that virus—yet the day when one of those people was dying them-selves she was able to go to a service that they were holding and pray for the guy! You know what I mean?

When he was transferred to Long Bay Gaol, Wayne met again Cheryl, whom he had known at that time for 13 years. She was always viva-cious, good-humored, hot-tempered, outrageous. Now he noticed she was withdrawn and silent.

C: I had gone from being a very flamboyant, happy-go-lucky person, so that you could get two or three words out of me and then I'd say "Please go away, I'm busy."

W: Then I overheard nurses and the doctor saying she was HIV-positive—something they should not have said where it could be overheard. I went up to her and said I had heard that. I told her that if she ever needed to talk, or cry, to scream, I would be there. At the time I was in a relationship, and I had always been faithful in relationships.

W: We were friends, we'd been working on building this relationship. I hadn't committed to it 100%, but I was aware that the relationship was going to get to that stage. But what got my back up was—I think it was two weeks after they put us two out—they wanted to move me to Lithcough. So they'd thrown us together, knowing that we were friends, knowing that there was the start of a relationship there already. So they threw us together, put us in a situation where that relationship was able to take off and flourish, and then wanted to split us up. And sent me to Lithcough jail, which was miles and miles and miles away in the country. And it was then while I was at Lithcough that I came back with a positive diagnosis.

So I wrote to an officer I met years before called Ron Robson, who was the head of the classification branch at the time. I said, Look, you people put Cheryl and I in a position to allow our relationship to flourish. Don't take that away from us. We're both HIV-positive. The only way we're going to survive our jail terms with this virus is to be able to continue to give each other the support and affection that we've been doing. If you take that away from us, then you're condemning us to death.

An old trooper Ashleigh from the King's Cross cabarets got herself arrested and with Cheryl organized the Long Bay Cowgirls. Out of scraps of fabric found and saved Cheryl sewed up a frock for herself, very extravagant, very theatrical.

C: But the one thing that we have in difference: there's only one other cited case in the world that has been found, and that was in America, in the States—that my AIDS virus is not to any great extent replicating in my blood: it's replicating in my bone marrow. So all those little critters that get in there are in my bone marrow, eating away at my bones.

W: It's actually by chance, really, that they even got on to it. It's that we had an extraordinarily good nurse working here for awhile as part of the HIV Health and Information Unit—Semantha Richardson. She was an extraordinary good nurse, a very professional nurse. Incredible good woman, beautiful person. She left here because of the—she just got fed up. Cheryl kept coming back with good T-cell readings and viral load readings, but she kept having all these secondary infections. No one could work out why. Semantha knew about this other case in America, the virus replicating in the bone marrow. She said, Well maybe it could be happening to Cheryl. So she arranged with the immunologist for Cheryl to get the bone biopsy done.

Wayne has a great knack for anything electrical, anything involving engineering. He can fix anything. He has earned 28 certificates in computer programming. Screws bring their computers from home for him to repair, or to fix some programming glitch. For 10 years, Wayne worked in the clinic, as a sweeper and cleaner. Cheryl ran the laundry. In 1992, he and Cheryl began to work in the education department. They do the clerical work. In the education department, they earn $24 a week. The ordinary prisoner can earn $11 or $13 a week.

W: It's only because we fight for it; we don't sit back and wait for everything to land in our hands. Because if we did, we'd never have a goddamn thing. If we sat back and just waited, we wouldn't even be together. They would have had us split up 10 years ago. But we fight every inch of the way. And the only way that we've been able to do that is as a couple. Because of the love that we have for each other, we give each other the strength. So many times, as I've said to you, I could just lay down and just turn off the lights. But Cheryl gives me that motivation to keep going, to keep fighting. And I'd like to think that I do the same thing for Cheryl.

C: Wayne doesn't control my thoughts. I control my thoughts. I say what I think. If I think he's wrong, the same as if he thinks I'm wrong—he won't say it then. He'll wait until we walk away from the conversation and we pull each other aside and he'll say, Hey I think you were wrong there. And I think you should have, you know, looked at it a little bit differently.

W: I can't stand it if she wanders off somewhere without telling me where she's going. Because I really worry about her, you know. That's not a possessive thing at all. Cheryl knows she can go anywhere she wants to go, talk to anyone she wants to talk to. As long as I know where she is and where I can find her. If I hear a scream, I know where the scream's coming from, I know where to go.

Because she's a transsexual, she's a woman in a men's maximum security jail—it's not always safe for the one that's wandering around. So that's why I need to know where she is at all times. Cheryl doesn't have to worry about me. But she still gets upset if I, like the other day, had to go and give a call to the ophthalmologist over at the clinic, and Cheryl didn't know where I'd been called to, why I'd been called, or anything, so she sort of felt the same thing, you know.

C: I went and found out. I went and made inquiries and found out. But it's a very—you got to remember, it's a very vicious place, and we've seen murders here and stabbings, bashings.

W: All the victims are all people who are deemed to be an easy mark.

Outside, in the city, we speak of couples a lot. As though two people in lawful or natural law marriage are coupled together. The central part of the day, at least 9 hours, they are in different places, at work. It is mostly when we come to visit them that they sit together, complete one another's sentences, coupled before a third party. Perhaps it is in coupling up for an hour or so before us that their partnership feels like love, to us and to them.

For ten years Wayne and Cheryl have been locked in a 6 by 10 foot cell all night and most of the day.

Cheryl gives a lot of support to transsexuals who end up in the jail. One who was sinking rapidly had a great fear of dying alone. Cheryl accompanied her all the way while she was going nowhere, she was there, with her, when she died.

W: There's some days when I could just say quietly say, That's it. I don't, for Cheryl's benefit. You know for a long time I wouldn't go with any of their therapies. I believe that they should be available for those people that want them. If that's the way someone wants to handle their virus, then, good: let them do that. The side effects of most of those tablets are horrendous. And really all I'm doing—I mean the chances of me surviving this jail sentence are a million to one. I'm just not prepared to take their drugs any more. I'll take the steroids still, because that's the only way I can get out of bed. But they're just using us as guinea pigs. It's absolutely ludicrous that a person with my health status has to wait 5 weeks to see a doctor. I've got a bad chest infection: that in itself could be life-threatening. If I get PCP, it could be life-threatening to me. We have both written out our wills and testament, because neither of us feels confident that we'll survive to the end of this year. Cheryl could very easily survive this year physically, but everybody knows, I think, that the moment one of us dies, we'll both die.

Prisoners are strip-searched before and after any transfer from one jail to another. They are also strip searched before and after meeting with any visitor they may be allowed. A strip search freaks out Cheryl. She would be mocked by the screws for not having testicles. By regulation, female prisoners should be strip searched by female guards.

C: They took all my clothes off and they put me in a shroud. A paper shroud. And in a dry cell, with nothing. And they put: Not to associate with anybody.

W: Those paper shrouds are lime-impregnated. And they make you really itch. They're horrible things. They're for dead people!

C: Since we've been together, we've not attempted, or threatened, in any way self harm. Alls we've said to them is that if you choose to split us up, you will have two corpses on your hands. That is all we have said.

Cheryl keeps up an intense level of energy. When she has vacuumed all the education floor, she vacuums the apartment. She calls the cell the apartment. She keeps everything impeccably clean. Psychotherapists may be tempted to see something to analyze in that. But perhaps Cheryl is a perfectionist. When a screw asks Wayne to type out his resume for him, or brings in his own home computer for Wayne to fix, he concedes that Wayne is a perfectionist.

W: I see Cheryl there, and I—When she went home recently, although she was only gone 36 hours, this feeling that you just can't explain: To be with someone for 24 hours a day for 10 years and then all of a sudden that person's not even there for 24 minutes in the day! It's devastating, it's really devastating.

W: But at the end of the day it comes down to what is going to make us live a little bit longer and little bit more of a quality life.

C: Even 24 hours. Even an hour.

W: As long as it's quality, you see.

W: When I get things like this, I expect to be able to walk over and say, "Well OK, what is this? What can you do to stop me scratching at these things?"

C: Oh, it's a hair follicle—that's what he's told! A hair follicle. Turn around and it'll go away.

W: They itch like hell, they hurt like hell. The ones that's on my back side, it's like sitting on boils. It's really painful. And how about treating all the things that I've got over my testicles? They put me in agony when I take off my underpants for the night, and they're stuck to my testicles because of the scabs. I take them off and it rips the scabs off. It's excruciating. It fuckin' kills me!

C: They'll say, I'll put your name down on the doctor's list. Now that's a 5-week wait. It takes 5 weeks to see the normal doctor! I am scheduled to see him every 3 months.

W: My toilet is the scene of torture. You know it's like 20 or 30 minutes to get a 10-second crap.

C: It takes a half an hour, at a minimum. Some nights, 2 hours later he's still there.

W: I used to say this to the immunologist all the time, if you give me some sort of guarantee that these things are going to keep me alive long enough to live to see the sentence out and for Cheryl and I to have some time together outside at the end of it, I'll take them with a passion. The chances of my living until this sentence is finished is the impossible dream. So by me agreeing to take their therapies, their combination therapies, all I'm doing in doing that is keeping myself alive a little bit longer to do a bit more jail. And I used to say to him, to the doctor, Listen, I will keep myself alive while Cheryl needs me. I will not allow myself to die whilever Cheryl needs me. I don't need your drugs to do that. I have the will in me, the love that I have for Cheryl in me, to keep myself alive while Cheryl needs me.

W: A lot of people think that no one'll touch Cheryl, no one'll rape Cheryl because she's got AIDS. But that's a fallacy. People in here think, one, they can't get AIDS from forcing Cheryl to give oral sex to 'em. Then, there is this condom thing, this safe sex thing.

C: Some of them believe that unless they ejaculate inside me, that's the only way . . .

W: And then of course some of them don't give a damn anyway! You would be absolutely amazed at the amount of people that have actually approached us over the months and actually asked us for our blood! You would be amazed! All for different reasons: some people want our blood because they believe if they get AIDS it can help them get out of jail a little bit earlier. Some people believe that if they get AIDS that it can help them get some other privileges. Some people want our blood because they want to commit suicide but they don't have what it takes to commit suicide, so this is a way of doing it. Other people want to square up on somebody they don't like—there is many, many reasons. Most times it's easy: I could take him apart and say, "Fuck off, never ask me that again!" But when it's someone who you classify as a really good friend, it's not that simple. You can't just say, "Fuck off!" And our friendship ended up hanging. He starts off saying: "Come off, Wayne, you're playing God with my life."

Cancers, putrescent infections, blindness, madness, agonizing pain await people dying of AIDS. Those who care for them, those who love them leave their bedside, to go to the other room to get food, to answer the telephone, to receive visitors, they go out to buy groceries, and do the laundry. They can, when they can no longer endure to keep watch, slip out of the room. They are not locked in a 6 by 10 foot cement cell all the weeks and hours, all the days and the nights of the infections, the despair, the agony, the delirium, the dying.

The numbers drag queens do depend entirely on surprise, their effects momentary. Surprising the aggressor with a put-down so witty he finds himself unable not to laugh at himself. At the moment of laughter, there is a transparency among individuals. They are no more separate then are two waves, though their unity is as undefined, as precarious as that of the agitation of the waters.

To hide this transparency, the drag queen is strip-searched and then covered with a white lime-impregnated paper shroud, while the police are covered with heavy dark blue uniforms. To hide this transparency, photographs are not allowed in Long Bay Gaol, nor allowed to photograph its high outer walls topped with razor-wire coils.

The sense of good luck is joyous. Happiness is *fortuna*. The proof of being lucky that comes in the lucky find makes one's happiness a joy of existing. Makes existing, makes one's birth, makes being abandoned at birth a stroke of luck. The happiness of good luck is realized, is real, is released in laughter. Laughter is a release out of oneself, an onrush of vibrant energy that breaks out of oneself and bounds forth across the distances, laughter is a release out of oneself, liberation.

C: How lucky I am! How lucky I have been! How lucky to have met Wayne. How lucky not to die alone, like other transsexuals. How lucky to have quality life. Even 24 hours. Even an hour.

And then one day the prison authorities summoned Cheryl and presented her with her release. She was led back to the cell, she packed her clean green prison clothes and the Long Bay Cowgirls frock. They gave her a small sum of money. The gates of Long Bay Gaol closed behind her. Within 24 hours Wayne's condition deterioriated and he was hospitalized.

> C: Of course I did not know that. I scored some coke. I called the parole officer, asking how long it takes to get one's parole revoked for noncompliance. He said, "two or three weeks." I had spent the money they gave me on cocaine, I could not buy a real gun. I took a perfume bottle, practiced holding it in my hand wrapped in a scarf. Went to the McDonald's; it was a little after midday. I went up to the cashier and handed her a piece of paper on which I had written: This is a holdup. Give me $200. On the back of the paper I had written: my name, my address, and my phone number. And: PS. Don't call until 9:30; I won't be ready.

> —Did they wait until 9:30?

> C: Yes, they came at 9:30.

The gale of wild laughter rocked Long Bay Gaol.

Chapter Fourteen

POSSESSION, ADDICTION, FRAGMENTATION

Is a Healing Community Possible?

BRUCE WILSHIRE

The nonaddictive body-self viscerally acknowledges and makes its own its primal needs and urges as an ecstatic being-in-the-world. It possesses itself. When I ran with Buppie in the fields and swam with the salmon I was coherent ecstatically. Their awareness of me felt by me strengthened my alertness and individuation within the Whole. The experience was valuable and satisfying in a way that unutterably vouched for itself.

But what exactly is this ecstatic coherence, this oneness? Any individual, no matter how fractured in addictions, is called one individual. Indeed, each is one being, but only as understood for our everyday—even scientific—purposes of classification and control. When we try to grasp human identity as we actually experience it through time, we find that the assumed oneness often papers over and conceals addictive cravings experienced mockingly as "both me and not me." What remains is numbed repetition and baneful trance.

Thinking of the person as an individual, as one, the thinker easily slides into thinking of him or her as like the number one: a unit homogeneous through and through and simply identical to itself. As 1 = 1, so "I" = "I," Ego = Ego! As if identity of self were merely an abstract one like a number's!

The danger of oversimplifying human identity by naively contrasting self and other ("I'm one, you're another, that makes two"), inheres in all mathematical approaches, particularly in all that are also dualistic. The mind is supposed to be one mind, and essentially reflective of its "mental contents," as if it were a mirror-lined container. We might define the self as that which says "mine" of itself. It is then tempting to infer that since the mind does this, *it* therefore *is* the self, or the core of it.

But once "the mind" is exposed as a verbalism parading as concrete reality, the impression evaporates that anything important about self has been learned. Defining self in this way is no better than saying I am who I am, identical to myself, because there's a little man inside my body—me—who is identical with himself. But what makes the little man identical with himself? There's a still smaller man inside him who is identical with himself. And smaller and smaller men inside men—homunculi—are supposed, ad infinitum. This gets us nowhere.

I think that the self is in fact a body, the inside of which directly experiences itself resonating to the rest of the world, and which as a being that moves itself contrasts itself frequently to everything else in the environment. Without this frequent contrasting there could be no personal mineness, no sense of myself. The inner body's primal sense of mineness is what ought never to be violated or infested with otherness that cannot be made one's own. When we possess continuously a visceral sense of "my own body-self," mocking "me and not me" cravings are impossible, crazy-making cravings cannot happen.

Even when we are bogged in addiction and guilt, however, the call to the self of maturity and freedom is seldom completely silenced. We may at least be free to remonstrate with ourselves, to persist in a state of dissatisfaction that might yet prompt a leap of abandonment in some greater matrix of energies. A wild bird may flash into a life, or a dog, or a fish, or a dawning day may awaken one to startling possibilities . . .

REDRAWING THE CONCEPTUAL MAP

The initial strokes of a new conceptual map have already been laid out. . . . The body-self is primally individual because it distinguishes its movements from the rest of the world's. But this is to be understood within James's idea of pure experience, at a level more fundamental than that of the simple oppositional distinction between self and other (or mind and matter).

We must now better grasp the envelope of the body not just as skin that moves relative to other things in the environment, perhaps touching them, but as that which encloses and locates its own innards—dark inner cavities, organs, fluids, subvocal speech—and provides much of the basis for the sense of "my inner self." We must grasp this envelope well enough to understand the loss of self in demonic possession, and its impairment in demonic infestations, addictions—impairment captured in these overheard words, "You couldn't have called her that, after all she has done for you. It must be the booze or the drugs talking."

I argue that addiction is a function of vulnerability of body-self, of our inability to trust the world to respect and nourish the integrity of our "inner self." I mean our inner self as an individual body immediately experiencing itself from within itself, experiencing basic periodic needs: for ingestion, digestion, excretion, exploratory initiatives; for sexual activity; for centeredness and poise that can found initiative; for this innerness to be recognized by all as that which makes each self fully human. Above all there is the need to feel one's life to be significant, to be fully one's own, the need to which other needs may be sacrificed.

RITUALS

Addiction is the failure to stand trustingly open to circular power returning periodically and regeneratively into itself through ourselves— body both suffused by the environment yet able normally to contrast itself to it.

How does the self achieve integrity as an integral member of the ongoing regenerative world? Only through rituals, I think, such as initiatory ones at crucial stages of development, that weave a moment of our life into the abiding and timeless ground of our being in the world. Ritual interweaves the two temporal dimensions of our lives: the linear on the one hand, and the eternal present, or cyclical, on the other. Like all events, any particular performance or performing of a ritual happens at an unrepeatable point in time. But what is performed is the very same event reactivated: that which established and repeatedly reestablishes identity in individual and group. (An archetypal example, "At thirteen all Jews have been, and will always be, inducted into adulthood.")

Such rituals operate at the level of origin myth. By "myth" I mean just the opposite of "false" or "fantastic." For only by the means of myth can we be true persons, solid and coherent. . . . Myth is the unquestioned sense of the unconditional power and value of the Sources that have generated and do regenerate us and cannot be effaced by time, that have names that should be capitalized. This sense of our Sources is sustained in ecstatic ground moods that stabilize us.

Only rituals based in origin myth secure the intrinsic value and genuine self-regard of the person. They affirm us as most individuated when
most in tune with the Whole. This is an obvious corollary of the general
principle of value. Ritual is the deliberate intensification and clarifica-
tion of ourselves.

It is impossible to mark sharply where ritual begins in everyday life.
Is brushing one's teeth a ritual? If it were merely a repeated behavior that
could be understood in completely utilitarian terms—brushing deposits
off the teeth—then perhaps not. But this is probably never altogether the
case. For nearly always some statement is being made in repeated behaviors, even if only to oneself—in the tooth-brushing case it might be, "I
am a conscientious and cleanly person"; and the behavior tends to reinforce these character traits through time.

Every performance of origin myth is obviously ritualistic. When one
reaffirms one's place as a member of the World-whole, the deepest need
is satisfied—to *be* vitally.

Given the use of drugs in our scientistic and secular society, it is easy
to think that all use of drugs is addictive and degenerative. When, however, we turn to an indigenous group such as the Yanomamma of
Venezuela, we may think differently, for everything these people do is
done within the context of origin myth, of the "spirits" that generate
and maintain their World. Anthropologist Kenneth Good writes,

> The purpose of drug taking . . . was to put them in contact with the
> spirit world. The shamans took the drug for that specific reason and
> for that reason only. Other men could also take it, and they did, but
> only by way of participating in the shamanistic chant. Drugs were not
> taken just to get high. Without a ritual context and purpose, drug tak-
> ing would seem a foolish activity.[1]

Moreover, these people recognize excessive or deviant use of drugs:

> Taromi is intoxicated with yakoana drug, as he is every day . . . Ebrewe
> looks at him with a contemptuous pout and delivers the following
> judgment: "He inhales only the yakoana drug, which ages you before
> your time when taken to excess. Look at his buttocks, already fur-
> rowed and slack."[2]

DEMONIC POSSESSION AND ADDICTION

Only when we grasp the absolute importance for the integrity of body-
self of regenerative rituals can we grasp how their breakdown may

entail demonic possession—and its seemingly milder but more insidious form, demonic infestation, addictions. For body-self is not a homogeneous unit over against the otherness of the world, but an ecstatic body with a crucial kinesthetic sense of its own insides as they resonate with the wide world. If this wider reality is untrustworthy, is disrespectful of the inner-person–inner-body as the self tries to maintain itself, it can become a part of the self that is incompatible, that is also "not myself." It lies outside my approval and agency, uncontrollable. The takeover can be abrupt and total—demonic possession—or creeping and insidious, as when one speaks of an addiction, "That can't be you talking, it must be the booze." Even our own bodily urges can be experienced as thing-y, incompatible, if we cannot appropriate them whole-heartedly as our own.

Any uninvited incursion into the body, threatened or realized, is not just a violation of the body, but a violation of the self. Even one's own body's urges may be experienced as incursions. To repeatedly serve them is to become servile, polluted. Addictions can be understood as degenerate rituals that not only fail to prevent pollution or infestation, but also constitute forms of them.

Here Mary Douglas's monumental *Purity and Danger* should be consulted. She analyzes ancient Hebrew purification practices integral to their origin myth. These embody the belief that clean things live and move properly in their environments, while dirty things do not. Eels, for instance, have no fins and move improperly in the water and hence are unclean according to Hebrew law.[3] It is particularly the eating of these creatures that is polluting, for a disordered thing that enters the body tends to disorder the self. What is disordered must be kept outside the body.

Likewise, what is inestimably valuable if kept inside—saliva or blood, for example—will be polluting if ejected improperly, particularly if recontacted or reincorporated. Pollution involves mixing what ought to be kept separate, especially mixing materials inside the body with those that are outside. Such mixing threatens our survival as the beings we are.

Body-self's course is ecstatic, serpentine, vulnerable, and so can be thrown off-balance. In some situations engulfment in intimate otherness is thrillingly joyful, in others a terrifying pollution or possession. For persons of sound identity, engulfment in compatible and respectful others in appropriate circumstances is consummate intimacy and ecstasy, Engulfment in disrespectful others is hell. Even in joyous erotic relationships, when lovers probe each others' mouths with their tongues, it is not clear that they would happily accept each other's saliva if it passed

between them in the form of drool. It would be too public, too experi-
enceable by others—even by themselves, separated as they are in space
and capable of objectifying themselves. When persons experience themselves as objectified and vulnerable, the exchange of bodily fluids threatens their identities, and frightens and abases them.[4]

Thus, the dense wrapping of rituals in which all societies enclose
sexual activity to prevent violation of self (all societies except perhaps
segments of our own today). Thus, the very personal and neurotic rituals that some devise to somehow deny the reality of violations in early
life. Or thus just the garden variety of addictions, such as smoking in
secular settings, that force a continuity of self in the face of threatened
incursions and disruptions.

In the face of threat, addiction is concerted action to constrict the
scope and depth of alternating ecstatic fusion and differentiation, the
pulse of life. At the fully demonic stage, the alternating rhythm breaks
down completely: the possessed person is clogged with incompatible
otherness. In the case of addiction, body-self doesn't lose control immediately and completely, but loses it only of that element of self that cannot be made its own. An addictive craving is a fragment of self that
repeats itself mechanically. It simulates integrality and continuity and
tries to eliminate the possibility of demonic possession.

MORE ON DEMONIC POSSESSION

There are innumerable well-documented accounts of behavior so altered
that observers believe another being has taken control of the person's
body. From ancient to contemporary times, reports emerge of frail persons suddenly endowed with superhuman strength. One rips up saplings
by the roots while a stench emanates from her.[5] There are accounts of
once-devout persons shrieking obscenities in an unrecognizable, low,
rasping voice; and of once-devoted children estranged violently from
their parents. In such cases the ultimate pollution of self occurs, and the
person seems to be invaded by what we call a demon.

Letting in too much alien and disrespectful otherness is the worst
way in which ecstatic openness goes wrong. Recall James noting that the
other's condemnation works directly in my body to produce those
changes that both express and are my shame. We are mimetically
engulfed in others' bodies and these bodies' attitudes. If this goes far
enough, we lose the clear awareness that it is their presence as opposed
to our own; demonic possession may result. And it needn't be merely
human others that possess us.

I am supposing that we are body-selves incorporating other persons' and things' presence and regard. Our experiencing is not perfectly sealed off from others.' Mature selves, however, seldom wholly lose the distinctive immediacy and presence of their own individual bodies—the cubic mass we feel all the while, and its continuities of organic excitement.

Whenever threatened, the strong self can contrast its experiencing and experienced complexity, its articulable I-and-me, its I-myself, to the other being or person. Able to say "I" or "I-myself," the strong self expresses (with some degree of adequacy) its immediate experiencing-experienced reality that can exclude incompatible others. And, as I have tried to show, all this is done by a body, body as self.

Now, what happens when persons can no longer protect their privacy and make the simplest decisions about what is to be accepted or rejected? Suppose a young girl is raped by her father. His presence overwhelms her habitual defenses against incompatible and disrespectful otherness. She identifies with him unwittingly (if she could speak: "He's a loved part of me, how could this violation and destruction within myself and by myself be happening?") She can only try to flee, but can only flee from herself. All respectful distance between the one addressing and the one addressed breaks down; the other, commingling in her torn body-self, usurps her place as agent. The articulations and distinctions of the resonating body-self-in-the-world collapse. She speaks in a low, rasping, unrecognizable voice and exhibits startling strength. She is beside herself in a grotesquely literal sense: the other's view of her becomes an alien, moving, and viewing presence in the girl's body. With good reason we say she is possessed by a demon.

In such cases, the integrity of the bodily envelope has not been respected. One's ability to collect oneself and keep one's own counsel has been overwhelmed. In other words, the dynamism of experiencing-experienced self over against a world experienced has collapsed. The menacing other's experiencing is not just something experien*ced*—a distinction a strong self can make when necessary—but floods one's own experien*cing*. One is taken over by the other—some hideous, floating being that does not belong in this body.

ADDICTIONS CONFRONTED

Origin rituals and myths authorize basic needs and appetites. It is right that we have them, right that we be. Substitute gratifications addictively repeated violate our integrity; they amount to incompatible otherness. We fail ourselves at the heart of ourselves, and must feel guilt.

Energies of evasion and denial of guilt are practically limitless because demonically fueled. Addictive life hangs on fiercely, since for it, trapped in its wheel, the only alternative it feels is withdrawal sufferings and death. In the Biblical account, a demon asked its name replies, "My name is legion." This is atomization of body-self—will, understanding, appetite fly apart. The demon would banish Jesus from its sight, for the possibility of a coherent form of life means its death. It begs Jesus to release it into a drove of hogs. Jesus obliges, but the swine stampede into the sea and are drowned.[6]

ANGELIC POSSESSION

As engulfment in disrespectful and powerful others is demonic possession—a particularly grotesque version of its sibling, addiction—so engulfment in respectful and powerful others is angelic possession.

Saint Paul writes ecstatically, "I am crucified with Christ: Nevertheless, I live; yet not I, but Christ liveth in me."[7] But there is no doubt that this is the same person who was Saul before his conversion and who is now Paul—the same who was struck down on the road to Damascus by a blinding light. In this case, the discontinuity radically strengthens the self: it is angelic, anything but demonic. And since angelic possession is inherently expansive, it does not resist acknowledgment. The demonic variety and its addictive sibling are self-enclosing.

Margaret Prescott Montague revives a pagan-like experience of angelic involvement in Nature as a whole:

> Entirely unexpectedly (for I had never dreamed of such a thing) my eyes were opened and for the first time in my life I caught a glimpse of the ecstatic beauty of reality . . . its unspeakable joy, beauty, and importance. . . . I saw no new thing but I saw all the usual things in a miraculous new light—in what I believe is their true light . . . I saw . . . how wildly beautiful and joyous, beyond any words of mind to describe, is the whole of life. Every human being moving across that porch, every sparrow that flew, every branch tossing in the wind was caught in and was part of the whole mad ecstasy of loveliness, of joy, which was always there. . . . My heart melted out of me in a rapture of love and delight. . . . Once out of all the grey days of my life I have looked into the heart of reality; I have witnessed the truth.[8]

Magnificent. But a primal person would be equipped with rituals that would reenact periodically one's ecstatic groundedness in the generative and regenerative world. It would not be a once in a lifetime experience.

Selves of strong character employ regenerative rituals as magnificent obsessions which invoke from time immemorial authoritative others. These are mythic beings who respectfully recognize one's individual being as a member of the Whole and thereby constitute it as such. Black Elk has invoked for him in his vision the Six Grandfathers.[9]

The composer Anton Bruckner suffered repetition compulsions. But what he longed for is disclosed in his music. The entranced repetitions in the climaxes of his symphonies, and the ever-repeated cycles of stress and relaxation throughout, evoke the regenerative repetitions of Nature herself. The sterile repetitions of Bruckner's addiction—his numbering mania—aimed at something far beyond itself: the regenerative climaxes of Nature. At least in his music he discovers this. Sonic climaxes give way to silences: awe in response to the cycling world feeding back into itself, reclaiming itself.

If integrated some way ritualistically into daily living, awe evoked in the music might undermine addiction by satisfying the needs to belong to the World-whole that drive the music and ourselves. Addictions are powered by a hysterical hunger for ecstatic enlargement, for relief from nattering fears and frustrations. The hunger easily trips itself up, probably more dangerously today, when rituals have been eroded for so many people.

In periods of lucidity and industry between heavy bouts of drug addiction, William Burroughs recounts in wretching detail the course his hunger took. At first glance his story is utterly different from that of Bruckner, for there is the composer's numbering mania, but also his nearly continual creativity and devout Catholicism.

But we detect some common ground. Burroughs shows how the addict guiltily conceals from himself the hunger for heroin behind endless rationalizations. He makes rules for ingestion ("only every other day") but these allow numerous exceptions. He says, "I can quit any time," but in the agonies of actual withdrawal the will is powerless. Why the guilt, unless the addict dimly realizes he is cheating himself of real freedom, and denying the world his ecstatic involvement with it as a responsible being.

The hunger for ecstatic enlargement through drugs entangles itself. Burroughs: "As a habit takes hold, other interests lose importance to the user. Life telescopes down to junk, one fix and looking forward to the next, 'stashes' and 'scripts,' 'spikes' and 'droppers.'"[10]

One must fix what is fractured. In periods of lucidity he glimpses deeper motivations nearly hidden behind his rage for the next fix to deliver from "junk sickness." Note: "a mild degree of junk sickness always brought me the magic of childhood. 'It never fails,' I thought. 'Just like the shot. I wonder if all junkies score for this wonderful stuff.'"

But after making the injection, "The junk spread through my body, an injection of death. The dream was gone. I looked down at the blood that ran from elbow to wrist. I felt a sudden pity for the violated veins and tissue."[11]

What is this magic of childhood that he finds fleetingly? Burroughs is short on description.

The last lines of *Junky:*

> I decided to go down to Colombia and score for yage . . . I am ready to move on south and look for the uncut kick that opens out instead of narrowing down like junk. . . . Kick is seeing things from a special angle. Kick is momentary freedom from the claims of the aging, cautious, nagging, frightened flesh. Maybe I will find in yage what I was looking for in junk and weed and coke. Yage may be the final fix.

But his whole framework has shrunk and he within it. He remains in a drug user's world—only a better *fix* could "open out instead of narrowing down." He is trapped in infantilism.

Of course, Burroughs is writing about all this, which suggests there must have sometimes been the ecstasy of writing. Perhaps not unlike Bruckner's in the sonic climaxes that transcend the composer's numbering mania? But how Burroughs incorporated this in his life I do not know. Life is many days, day after day, moment by moment.

NOTES

1. Kenneth Good (with David Chernoff), *Into the Heart: One Man's Pursuit of Love and Knowledge among the Yanomamma* (London: Penguin, 1992), p. 74.

2. Jacques Lizot, *Tales of the Yanomami,* Cambridge Studies in Social Anthropology (Cambridge: Cambridge University Press, 1991), p. 30.

3. Ibid., pp. 55–56.

4. "God . . . divided the waters which were under the firmament from the waters which were above. . . . The human body is a recapitulation of this . . . for the body itself is a firmament which divides the waters of the brain from the waters of the genitals. Because of the sacred numinosity of the waters, all fluids of the human body—saliva, sweat, semen, and blood are sacred and mysterious substances." W. I. Thompson, *The Time Falling Bodies Take to Light* (New York: Palgrave, 1996), p. 18.

5. Felicitas Goodman, *How About Demons?* (St. Louis, MN: Macalister Park Publishing Co., 1947), pp. 111, 116.

6. Mark 5:7–13.

7. Galatians 2:20.

8. "Twenty Minutes of Reality."

9. John G. Neihardt, *Black Elk Speaks* (Lincoln, NB: University of Nebraska Press, 1979). (The Grandfathers are invoked in the dedication of the account and throughout.)

10. William S. Burroughs, *Junky* (New York: Viking Press, 1985), p. 22.

11. Ibid., p. 126.

Chapter Fifteen

GAMBLING AND ADDICTION

JON ELSTER

INTRODUCTION

In this chapter, I discuss compulsive (excessive, pathological) gambling and whether it is usefully seen as an addiction. Compulsive gamblers are those who experience loss of self-control, by spending more than they intend (a within-episode phenomenon) or by quitting and then relapsing (a between-episode phenomenon). Following Dickerson (1984), an operational criterion is whether the gambler has sought help or treatment to control the gambling or to give it up altogether.

In the next section, I give a brief overview of the main varieties of gambling behavior and their quantitative aspects, both in terms of the number of persons concerned and in terms of the amount of money involved. In Section 3, I discuss the phenomenology of gambling. In subsequent sections, I survey various explanations that have been offered of compulsive gambling; the final section offers a brief conclusion.

I agree fully with the following observation:

Scientific models of compulsive or excessive gambling are relatively new. Because compulsive gambling is one of the last excesses to be included under the addictive behaviors umbrella, theories of drug and alcohol addiction provide most of the early explanations of this phenomenon. We may readily be able to generalize explanations of alcohol

and substance addiction to gambling. If so, we do not have to reinvent
the conceptual wheel. If not, explanations of gambling will have to be
framed as an excessive behavior unlike the others. We must be ready for
either outcome. (Shaffer 1989, p. 6)

Or in the words of Lea, Tarpy, and Webley (1987, p. 270), "the
issue of whether [gambling] can properly be labeled an addiction will
probably not be resolved until the nature of addiction in general is better understood." Thus, in exploring the nature of compulsive gambling,
one should try not to be misled by superficial similarities—mistaking
sharks for whales. An example of the kind of error that is important to
avoid is found in the following passage:

> The more alcoholics drink, the more shame they feel; the more shame
> they feel, the more they drink to forget the shame, or at least make it
> bearable. The more compulsive overeaters eat, the fatter they grow; the
> fatter they grow, the more disgusting they find themselves to be, and
> the more they turn to food in search of comfort in the face of that
> self-disgust. The more compulsive gamblers gamble, the deeper into
> debt they go, and the more they gamble to pay off those debts. (See-
> burger 1993, pp. 20–21)

Drinking may indeed be a self-sustaining activity, to the extent that
people drink to escape from the awareness that they are drunks. And it
has also been argued, as we shall see, that people may gamble to forget
the shame associated with their gambling. In these cases, we are dealing
with action motivated by the desire to reduce secondary withdrawal
symptoms. The mechanism mentioned in the last sentence of the quoted
paragraph, however, is entirely different. At a superficial level, it may
look like the two other phenomena identified. As with drinking and
overeating, gambling "both creates the problem and is a way of resolv-
ing that problem." (Lesieur 1984, p. 16). But in alcoholism or overeating, there is no causal mechanism even remotely similar to the need to
gamble in order to earn money to pay off gambling debts. The latter
mechanism is more similar to what happens when an embezzler steals
money from one account to put money back into another. Presumably,
nobody would refer to that phenomenon as a form of addiction.

This phenomenon of the "chase" (Lesieur 1984)—gambling to win
back money that one has lost—can also be used to illustrate another
misleading analogy. It is often argued that tolerance is a key factor in
addiction. As we shall see, it is not quite clear what tolerance implies in
the case of gambling, but one meaning of the term in that context might
be the need to play for ever higher stakes. In a discussion of addiction as

gambling, Dickerson (1984, p. 78) writes that "Loss of control, escalation of stake size and 'cold turkey' experiences following sudden cessation of high-frequency gambling have all found limited support." Presumably, escalation is taken as evidence for the presence of tolerance—the need to bet more and more in order to achieve the same level of excitement. And as we shall see, this mechanism may indeed operate. However, it is not the only mechanism that will produce escalation: The need to gamble more to repay debts will have the same effect (Lesieur 1984, p. 12 and passim). To distinguish the whales from the sharks, we need the full causal story.

It is possible to take this line of argument one step further, and ask whether the various kinds of gambling are produced by the same underlying process or processes. Thus, one objective of Dickerson "is to emphasize the difficulties in building . . . general models of the addiction by illustrating that the psychological process underlying two common forms of gambling [poker machines and off-course betting] may be very different." The zombie-like machine player and the dedicated racetrack bettor may be subject to entirely different motivations and, more generally, psychological processes. Although they may both, at various stages, experience craving and difficulties in giving up, these features may, . . . rest on a number of different mechanisms. The point will also be abundantly illustrated in the following sections.

VARIETIES OF GAMBLING BEHAVIOR

On a conceptual level, forms of gambling may be classified along several dimensions. First, there is the distinction between games of pure chance and games of mixed skill and chance. In theory, and disregarding quantum-mechanical phenomena, there can be no such thing as a game relying on pure chance. Random events have to be generated by a randomizing device, with a pattern that can in principle be detected by a skillful player. Casino players are said to observe the pattern of wins in order to detect irregularities in the wheel that might give them an edge. With regard to poker machines, "players' claim that they spot sequences of reel spin results that precede a large pay out may have some validity, if recent work on the 'errors' in the random nature of the latest generation of poker machines can be replicated" (Dickerson 1993, pp. 237–238; see also Griffith 1994, pp. 290–291). In practice, these possibilities do not matter, except in feeding the self-deceptive tendencies of many gamblers.

In mixed games, skill can be attributed either to the gambler only or to both the gambler and the object on which he is betting. A good blackjack player is one who is good at remembering which cards have been played, the element of chance being provided by the random shuffling of the cards. A good horse-race gambler is one who is good at identifying good horses. In this case, elements of chance are provided not only by accidents that may prevent the best horse from winning (according to Murray [1991, p. 106], "there are a thousand ways at least to lose a horse race that have nothing to do with skill"), but also by a very large number of factors that determine which horse, on one particular day, with one particular rider, is the best. Whereas the former elements are irreducibly random (in the epistemic sense of being unpredictable), the latter can to some extent (the larger the better the player) be eliminated, but never completely.

A second distinction is between games in which there is a "continuous action," which allows one to be carried away by a win or a loss to place another bet immediately, and those in which games occur at preset and relatively long intervals.[1] The latter games apparently carry little potential for becoming "compulsive," "excessive," "pathological," or "addictive." They include betting on sport events such as soccer or basketball matches or on state-sponsored lotteries such as Lotto. In the claim that, in lotteries "players and the states who operate the games become afflicted with exactly the same type of addiction" (Karcher 1992, p. xiv), "addiction" is obviously not used in anything like a scientific sense. Although lotteries may give rise to problems of self-control, this is not a sufficient criterion of addiction. (Procrastination, too, may be due to lack of self-control.) The idea (suggested by Karcher [1992, p. xvi]) that lotteries are subject to a tolerance effect, so that ever-higher prizes are needed to attract players, does not seem to have any empirical support. Also, whereas the vast majority of Lotto players never win anything, "the pathological gambler invariably has a history of a big win" (Peck [1986, p. 463]; see also Lesieur [1984, p. 31]; Cornish [1978, pp. 187–188]).

Frequency of playing is one choice variable for the gambler. Others include the choice of stakes and (in horse-race betting) of odds. When gamblers escalate their playing, they may do so by playing more frequently, for larger stakes, or against higher odds. With regard to the phenomenon of tolerance, the following observation may be important. A player who increases the stakes (for given odds) stands to win more *and* to lose more. By raising the odds against him (for given stakes), he stands to win more but not to lose more. If the excitement from gambling derives mainly from the hope of winning, raising the stakes and raising the odds ought to be equally preferred by players who find that the game is turning stale. If the excitement also depends on the fear of losing, raising the stakes would be the preferred method. From the literature surveyed below, the latter appears to be the case. I return to this issue in the next section.

"Today, the poker machine, the roulette wheel, and betting on horse and dog races represent the three most popular forms of gambling" (Dickerson 1984, p. 9). Other types of gambling that ought to be mentioned because of their somewhat different characteristics are blackjack (played against a dealer who behaves according to fixed rules) and card games against other competitive players. These examples suggest a distinction among games on the basis of the nature of the gambler's "opponent." In fruit-machine games, the opponent is the machine. In roulette the opponent is the relatively neutral croupier. Wins and losses among the players are entirely uncorrelated. In blackjack, the dealer is the "common enemy": If he goes bust (exceeds 21), then all the players who did not bust are automatically winners. Because of this correlation among wins, a potential is created for solidarity among the players (Ocean and Smith [1993]; see also Wagenaar [1988, p. 37]). In poker, of course, each player is opposed to the other players. Similarly, in race-track betting each gambler is opposed to the others, because their betting behavior determines the odds. If he or she believes he or she has picked the right horse, he or she wouldn't want others to pick it too.

The quantitative aspect of gambling in current societies can be assessed in various ways. (For a historical survey, see France [1902].) For the United States, "the best estimate at this time is 1.1 to 4 million compulsive gamblers" (Peck 1986, p. 462), a number that may be compared to a common estimate of 5 million alcoholics. Also, "gambling probably ranges up to $90 billion per year." The Rotschild report from 1978

> . . . gave the following in £ billion for the UK: Gambling 7.1, defence 5.6, housing 4.7, health 6.5. However, if on average across all forms of gambling almost 90 percent of this expenditure is returned in winnings, it can be seen that "turnover" figures are misleading. Despite this, the remaining 10 percent lost or spent in 1980 terms is likely to be something over a billion pounds and is the largest single component of the total leisure industry. (Dickerson 1984, p. 20)

An indication of the place of compulsive gambling within this total can be gleaned from the estimate that "1.5 per cent of the adult population accounted for more than half of the total stake on horse and dog races." Overall, Dickerson estimates that in countries with reasonable availability of at least lotteries and off-course betting, 80–90 percent of the population gamble a few times a year; about 30 percent gamble on lotteries, football pools, or poker machines most weeks; and about 5 percent gamble regularly two to three times each week. The latter are what Dickerson (1984, p. 38) refers to as high-frequency gamblers, which include as two distinctive subsets compulsive gamblers (about 350,000 in the United Kingdom) and a small number of professional gamblers.

PHENOMENOLOGY OF GAMBLING

What is it like to be a gambler? In addressing this question, I suffer from a handicap. With respect to alcohol, nicotine, and food, personal experience and introspection help me understand how one could become addicted. I am too risk-averse, however, to really understand what makes the gambler tick. Risks make me afraid, not excited. I have to rely, therefore, on other people's reports of the experience and the attractions it has for them. Especially valuable in this respect is Henri Lesieur's *The Chase,* based on in-depth interviews with 50 compulsive gamblers. I have also benefited much from three enjoyable crime novels by Walter Murray (1985, 1990, 1991) located on and around the racetrack. I did not learn much from the vastly more famous fictional accounts of gambling by Dostoyevski (1964) or Hamsun (1954). The behavior of the gamblers in these works seems as mysterious to me as it does to them.

In addressing the phenomenology of gambling I shall follow the main categories: craving, tolerance, withdrawal, and problems of self-control.

Craving

The following discussion concerns the craving associated with the primary rewards of gambling. Secondary rewards are considered in the section on learning and reinforcement theories of gambling. Also, I limit myself here to craving associated with nonmonetary rewards. Gambling for the sake of monetary gain is considered when I discuss rational-choice theories of gambling.

With regard to the motivation for gambling, there is a general dichotomy in the literature between *pull* versus *push*, excitement versus escapism, and thrill versus anesthesia (see, e.g., Rosenthal [1989, p. 123]). According to Pascal (the inventor both of roulette and of probability theory), people gamble because they seek distraction or diversion *(divertissement)* from their chronic state of *ennui* (in Pascal, a kind of anxious emptiness). Even a king, "attended with every pleasure he can feel, if he be without diversion and be left to consider and reflect on what he is, this feeble happiness will not sustain him; he will necessarily fall into forebodings of dangers, of revolutions which may happen, and, finally, of death and inevitable disease" (*Pensées* 139). People seek distraction because they cannot stand being alone with themselves, which would force them to reflect on their existence. "Thus so wretched is man that he would weary even without any cause for weariness from the peculiar state of his disposition; and so frivolous is he that, though full of a thousand reasons for weariness, the least thing, such as playing billiards or hitting a ball, is sufficient to amuse him" (ibid.).

Gambling is one of the activities that people will take up to forget about their existential or metaphysical *ennui*:

> This man spends his life without weariness in playing every day for a small stake. Give him each morning the money he can win each day, on condition he does not play; you make him miserable. It will perhaps be said that he seeks the amusement of play and not the winnings. Make him, then, play for nothing; he will not become excited over it and will feel bored. It is, then, not the amusement alone that he seeks; a languid and passionless amusement will weary him. He must get excited over it and deceive himself by the fancy that he will be happy to win what he would not have as a gift on condition of not playing; and he must make himself an object of passion, and excite over it his desire, his anger, his fear, to obtain his imagined end, as children are frightened at the face they have blackened. (Ibid.)

Along similar lines, let me reproduce two passages from Stendhal's *Le Rouge et le Noir*, the first a quotation from a sixteenth-century work describing Marguerite de Valois and the second a reflection that Stendhal imputes to her latter-day incarnation Mathilde de La Mole.

> *An itch for excitement*, such was the character of [. . .] Marguerite de Valois.[. . .] A need for hazardous sport was the whole secret of this amiable princess's character.[. . .] Now what can a young woman hazard? All that she has most precious: her honor, her lifelong reputation. (II.XII)
>
> He [Julien Sorel] has tremendous power over me, since he rules by terror and can inflict a frightful punishment on me if I try him too far. This idea was enough of itself to incline Mathilde to insult him, for courage was the prime quality of her character. Nothing could stir her in any way or cure her of an underlying feeling of boredom constantly springing to life again, except the idea that she was putting her whole existence at hazard. (II.XVII)

The gambler seeks excitement, but not for its own sake—only because of its ability to drive out other thoughts, something that the mere amusement in a game in which nothing is at stake could never do.[2]

Thus for Pascal, gambling provides both excitement and escape, but the excitement is valued only because it provides escape (in fact, nothing else can provide it). For other writers, gambling can serve as a means of escape even when it does not generate excitement. Thus Dickerson (1993, p. 239) found that poker-machine playing does not generate much excitement (as measured by heart rates and subjective reports). Rather, "for such players, the strongly habitual person—machine interaction may represent an unthinking escape from negative emotions" (ibid., p. 240).[3]

Conversely, some writers find the main benefit of gambling is excitement sought for its own sake. There are innumerable reports about the thrills and highs experienced in high-stakes gambling. "*All* compulsive gamblers (and many noncompulsive gamblers) talk of the action aspect of gambling. It is described in terms of 'getting my rocks off,' 'adrenaline flowing,' and most often compared to sexual excitement" (Lesieur 1984, p. 44). Anderson and Brown (1984, p. 408) write that "if excitement or arousal is restored to a central role in the explanation of gambling behavior, a personally experienced and objectively verifiable state of arousal, not sexual, but probably autonomic, might be seen as being sought repeatedly by the regular gambler for its own sake." Whereas it is clear enough why gambling (as any form of risk-taking) might generate arousal, it is more puzzling why the arousal would be pleasurable, especially if it is true that the fear of loss is an important condition for the excitement.

Let us return to Pascal, and his comparison among (i) genuine gambling, (ii) playing without stakes, and (iii) assurance of earning every day the maximal sum that can be won by gambling. (Remember that he refers to the gambler who plays "every day for a small stake.") To this list we might add (iv) being offered a prospect with some chance of winning but no risk of losing. (Imagine a roulette game where the players have a fixed daily number of opportunities to choose a number and on each occasion get a fixed reward if it comes up.) Pascal would claim, I believe, that the regular gambler would prefer (i), not only to (ii) and (iii), but also to (iv). I suspect he would be right—but why?

At this point, it is natural to bring up the psychoanalytical theory of gambling, according to which people gamble because they have an unconscious wish to lose (Bergler [1957]; see also Dickerson [1993, p. 239], Walters [1994, p. 176], Peck [1986, p. 463]). As gambling careers are usually triggered by an early big win rather than by an early big loss, the theory does not look very promising; yet it does at least address the apparent violation of the sure-thing principle. It does not answer, however, the important question: What's in it for the gambler? More pedantically: How can the prospect of loss of a standard reinforcer act as a reinforcer?[4] Pascal's answer would be that the feelings of hope generated by option (iv) would not be strong enough to crowd out the existential *angst.* Dr. Johnson said that nothing concentrates a man's mind so much as the knowledge that he is about to be hanged. Similarly, writers on gambling have noted that it tends to focus concentration and thereby enable the gambler to forget about his or her worries (Rosenthal and Rugle 1994, p. 34; Lesicur 1984, p. 14).[5] If he had nothing to lose, this effect might not obtain. These are obviously speculative remarks, but they address, I think, a real problem.

Tolerance

Under this heading, I shall first recapitulate various observations already made above. I referred to the idea that gambling might be subject to tolerance, in the sense that ever-larger stakes and/or ever-higher odds are needed to generate the same excitement. I also mentioned the behavioral phenomenon of *escalation,* that is, the observed tendency for heavy gamblers to raise the stakes and/or the odds. I asked whether escalation in itself is evidence for tolerance and suggested two reasons for thinking that it is not. First, escalation might be produced by an alternative mechanism, for example, the need to make larger and riskier gambles in order to repay old debts. Second, I have not seen it claimed that gamblers raise the odds to sustain the thrill. When horse-race players play long shots in the last race of the day, their motive is usually to recoup losses from earlier races (Wagenaar 1988, p. 105; Cornish 1978, p. 168).

This being said, escalation of *stakes* may be caused by the need to sustain a thrill that otherwise might become jaded. According to Lesieur (1984, p. 44), the nature of "action" in gambling has "an uncanny similarity to 'tolerance' among alcohol, barbiturate, and narcotics addicts. Once the 'high' of a $500 event has been reached, the $2 bet no longer achieves the desired effect." Cornish (1978, p. 203) similarly refers to "the possibility that habituation to certain levels of excitement may occur as a function of experience, so that it becomes necessary to raise one's stakes in order to recapture the same subjective quantity of 'thrill.'" Note the difference, though, between these two statements. Lesieur may well be right in that once the larger bets have been made, smaller bets are less satisfactory, but that does not imply that Cornish is right in that dissatisfaction with the small bets is why the gambler moves on to larger bets. The escalation might originally be caused by the need to repay debts, and then sustained by a "contrast effect" (Tversky and Griffin 1991). Before you've experienced the best, you're happy with the second best; but once you've been exposed to the best, perhaps by accident, there is little thrill to be had from the second best. Although the contrast effect and the phenomenon of tolerance are superficially similar, the underlying causal mechanisms are quite different.[6]

Withdrawal

What happens to compulsive gamblers when they stop gambling? Some report a feeling of relief (Wray and Dickerson 1981), but most report a number of psychological and (more rarely) somatic problems. The most common symptoms are irritability, anxiety, and depression, which are also observed among abstaining alcoholics. It is far from obvious, however, that these reports suffice to show the presence of (primary) withdrawal. Here is a description of gamblers who have *not* quit: "Compulsive gamblers are never relaxed, but the restlessness, irritability, paranoia, hypersensitivity at this stage [the final stage of "desperation"] increase to the point that sleep and eating are disturbed" (Peck 1986, p. 464). If they continue to feel this way after they quit, there is no need to explain the feeling by their quitting.

Moreover, it is quite possible that we are dealing with secondary rather than primary withdrawal. . . . Rosenthal (1989, p. 104) writes that "In my experience withdrawal has been relatively insignificant both in the course of treatment and as a diagnostic criterion. There may be depression when the person stops gambling. This may be an underlying depression against which the gambling had defended. Alternatively, it may be that once the individual stops gambling he realizes how destructive the behavior had been." More recently, Rosenthal and Rugle (1994, pp. 33–34) made the following important observation:

> Some gamblers will continue to be unstable, and depending on the outcome of their last gambling episode, will be plagued by feelings of shame and guilt which will send them back into action. . . . Pathological gamblers frequently believe that if they can win back what they lost, it not only erases the debt, but it also is as if they had never gambled in the first place. Guilt is dealt with by the psychological defense of undoing. . . .
>
> Shame, on the other hand, is not something that can be undone. However, gambling offers an escape from painful awareness. The intense concentration involved in gambling, which blots out all memories of everyday life, offers a kind of primitive avoidance and a hiding out from the eyes of the world. At the same time, the social acceptance of the casino or race track denies one is disapproved of or an outcast.

The emergence of these secondary symptoms may indeed send the player "back into action," just as the painful awareness that one is an alcoholic may induce more drinking. More robust evidence for primary withdrawal comes from a report by Custer (1982) that "if gamblers had just stopped betting prior to admission to hospital it was not uncommon for staff to observe 'tremulousness, headache, abdominal pain, diarrhea, cold sweats, and nightmares to occur for a few days after admission.' He suggested that these may represent withdrawal symptoms or might be due to sleep starvation" (Dickerson 1984, p. 59). This sounds more like the real thing, that is, primary withdrawal caused by the organism adjusting to the new situation. But, in the absence of any knowledge of the neurobiology of gambling, these remarks, too, remain speculative.

Problems of Self-Control

Gamblers, like drug addicts or overeaters, often want to quit but find it difficult.[7] Many of the difficulties are of their own making, caused by the primary or secondary cravings discussed early in this section. Other obstacles are deliberately created by those who stand to gain from their gambling. Thus, "casinos seem to be set up entirely to hinder self-monitoring cues. For instance, it is impossible to see outside from inside a casino (the few windows and doors are often blacked out), so that it is impossible to tell whether there is day or night. There are no clocks on the wall, and dealers are reluctant to tell players the time" (Baumeister, Heatherton, and Tice 1994, p. 218). That drinks are freely served also contributes to loss of self-control. "Slot machines are grouped together in sets of hundreds, so that the rattling of money is heard continuously" (Wagenaar 1988, p. 12), enabling players to obtain "vicarious reinforcement from the success of others" (Cornish 1978, p. 189). Because "betting and listening to race commentaries may result in gamblers experiencing difficulty in maintaining control of the frequency of betting and the amount staked . . . , the design of the off-course betting office may influence the occurrence of gambling-related . . . problems" (Dickerson 1984, p. 137). The gambling arena is rigged against self-control.

Gamblers want to quit when they accumulate an intolerable combination of financial, personal, and legal problems. In one sense it is harder to quit and then get on with their lives. Usually, they also have to clean up the mess they have created, notably by setting up a credible debt repayment scheme. (One of the compulsive gamblers interviewed by Lesieur [1984] had 22 concurrent loans.) Undoing of past wrongs is also one of the 12 steps of Alcoholics Anonymous, but in that case the purpose is to help the exalcoholic find peace with himself or herself rather than to keep victims at bay. If the gambler's life was unexciting to begin with, it is likely to be even more so when he has to live off what little income is left by creditors. This makes for an additional source of relapse.

As with alcohol or overeating, loss of self-control can take two forms. First, the gambler may decide not to gamble any more and then break his or her resolution. Second, within any given gambling session he or she may spend more than intended, notably by "chasing" or otherwise acting differently from what he or she had planned (e.g., by changing bet selections at the last moment). Both types of breakdown may be caused by the behavior itself. As noted, gambling may create guilt that can be relieved only by more gambling. Within a given episode, increased levels of arousal may lead first to higher concentration and then to "the irrational, confused, and superstitious thinking which results in carefully prepared plans and strategies being abandoned in the midst of the gambling session and the making of seriously damaging decisions which the gambler afterward cannot understand" (Brown 1986, p. 1008).[8]

The compulsive gambler has a counterpart that does not exist with any other addictive or excessive behaviors: the professional gambler. Some forms of gambling do in fact enable skilled players to gamble for a living. Blackjack has actually a winning strategy that, depending on the rules of the casino, allows a skilled player to have a positive expected value of between 0.5 percent and 2 percent of the stakes (Wagenaar 1988, p. 20). Because of the high variance of the outcome, however, the win may be quite delayed. With an expected value of 0.5 percent, the player would have to play 100 hands an hour, 8 hours a day, for 270 days in order to be assured of a 99 percent chance of profit (ibid.). This feature of the strategy, combined with the counting skills needed, may be part of the explanation why it is so rarely used. For other explanations the reader is referred to chapter 3 of Wagenaar (1988).

Although there seem to be few skilled "counters" who make a living by playing blackjack, there are probably more who make a living by betting on the outcome of horse races or sport events. (I disregard the living that can be made by rigging the games.) In addition to information and good judgment (see the next section), professional gamblers need considerable self-control. "'Loss of control' is . . . recognized by professional gamblers as an occupational hazard against which various precautions can be taken" (Dickerson 1984, p. 58). Also, it is important to avoid the various modes of superstitious thinking that characterizes most gamblers. Thus in Murray (1991, p. 105) the professional gambler Jay engages in the following dialogue with the main character, Shifty:

"I'll bet him in the place hole."

"A wimpish wager, Shifty. I'm ashamed of you. I mean, if he's good enough to be a good place bet, then he's good enough to win, isn't he?"

"Jay, I'm just coming out of a real bad streak."

"Suit yourself," the handicapper said. "But that's not a good betting style."

EXPLANATIONS OF COMPULSIVE GAMBLING

The following discussion of some candidate explanations of compulsive gambling will draw both on the literature on gambling and on the wider literature on addictive behaviors. I shall not discuss theories that explain excessive gambling by personality variables such as sensation seeking (Brown 1986, Coventry and Brown 1993), chronic hypotension or hypertension (Jacobs 1989), low self-esteem (Walters 1994, p. 163), or high self-esteem (Baumeister, Heatherton, and Tice 1994, p. 222). Dickerson (1984, pp. 40–43) reviewed many of these accounts and found them generally unpersuasive. Although I am no expert on these matters, my impression is that in these studies both the dependent variable (compulsive gambling) and the independent ones (personality traits) are subject to so many measurement problems that it is hard to see the findings as very robust. Also, some of the studies are largely speculative. In any case, it is intrinsically more satisfactory to search for explanations that embody causal mechanisms of a reasonably well-understood kind. These include rational-choice theories, theories based on hyperbolic discounting, and theories based on learning and reinforcement.

Rational Choice

It seems *a priori* implausible that compulsive gamblers behave in an entirely rational way. And I do not in fact think that view can be defended. Nevertheless, I believe the confrontation between rational-choice theory and gambling behavior is worthwhile, for several reasons. First, it may enable us to identify the precise kind or kinds of irrationality that are involved. Second, some aspects of gambling behavior, even among compulsive gamblers, may actually be rational. Third, if we find that rational choice explanation does not work for gambling, and if we decide that compulsive gambling satisfies Becker's criteria for addiction, then his general theory of rational addiction may be in some trouble.

Before I confront the rational-choice model with gambling behavior, it should be observed that the model makes sense only if the beliefs and desires are given independently of the behavior they are supposed to explain (see the blocked arrows from action to desires and beliefs). As we shall now see, this is not always the case. With regards to beliefs, we may cite Dickerson:

> Players' expectations of payouts are not consistently associated with variations in play rate. Even when play rates suddenly fall for two minutes or so after a big win, this is not associated with a lowering of expectations for future payouts. This has led us to the proposition that it is the machine reinforcement schedule that "drives" the behaviour, and that the cognitive processes are by-products that provide the player with a verbal "explanation" of the behaviour of his or her body. . . . At one time or another it would seem that players may express almost any reason for continuing to play, and it is this overall perspective to the cognitive aspects of poker machine playing that leads us to consider them as the players' attempts to understand the way in which their stereotypic habit has a "life of its own." As Walker . . . expressed it, "it is the gambling behavior that maintains the irrational thinking rather than the reverse."

With regard to reported desires, several findings suggest that these may also be ex post rationalizations of behavior rather than causally efficacious in their own right. They serve as *excuses,* not as motives. Thus

> . . . subjects who had won as many times as they had lost became more conservative in their choice of a bet, whereas those that had a high win–lose ratio and those with a low win–lose ratio became relatively more risky in their choices. The authors reasoned that the successful subjects behaved as if their former good luck would continue in the future; by contrast, the least successful appeared to behave recklessly, as if they were trying to compensate for a run of bad luck (Lea, Tarpy, and Webley [1987], citing Greenberg and Weiner [1966]).

Similarly, Tversky and Shafir found that a majority of subjects assert that they will accept a second gamble both if they have won in a prior gamble *and* if they have lost in a prior gamble; however, only a minority say they will accept a second gamble if they do not know whether they will have won or lost in the first. I suggest that in both cases what we observe is the search for excuses to gamble.

Assuming now that the desires and beliefs are in fact independently given, could gambling be a rational form of behavior? The mere fact that the expected monetary value of most forms of gambling is negative does not, of course, make it irrational to gamble. Some individuals may be risk seekers rather than risk averse: They seek the thrill rather than the monetary gains (Bromiley and Curley 1992).[9] Gambling is, indeed, part of the "entertainment industry." The more complex motivations discussed previously under the heading of "Cravings" might also find rational satisfaction through gambling. Also, for most people the marginal utility is an increasing function of money through some intervals, particularly at those points where it can transfer an individual from a lower socioeconomic status to a higher one (Friedman and Savage 1948; Cornish 1978, p. 94). An analogous argument applies to compulsive gamblers who have accumulated high debts. If gambling induces a "financial and legal crisis, a person may rationally risk losing even more money on the chance of winning sufficient to retrieve the situation" (Dickerson 1984, p. 134). It is rational to choose probable disaster over certain disaster. Needless to say, the behavior that forced this choice on the gambler may not have been equally rational.[10]

Heavy involvement in gambling, however, usually indicates that rationality has been left behind. Numerous reports of loss of self-control among gamblers indicate that gambling can be a form of weakness of will. As Gjelsvik explains, we then have to ask whether we are dealing with Davidson's or Ainslie's concept of weakness of will. Between-session loss of control is probably best explained along Ainslie's lines (see the discussion of "Hyperbolic Discounting" in the next section). Within-session loss of control might be an instance of Davidsonian weakness of will. The arousal caused by heavy gambling may plausibly cause the kind of short-circuiting of rational choice that is at the core of Davidson's theory. However, Stein's model (see the discussion of "Hyperbolic Discounting," in the next section) indicates that within-session loss of control, too, might be explained on Ainslie's lines.

Consider now the beliefs involved in gambling and their rationality. A general question is whether people who start out on a gambling career fully understand the prospect of disaster that they face. The original rational-choice model of addiction in Becker and Murphy (1988) assumes accurate beliefs in this regard. The modified probabilistic version in Orphanides and Zervos (1992) assumes unbiased beliefs. For my part, I find the following statement more plausible: "People's risk behaviors are . . . imperfect indicators of the risks that they believe themselves" to be taking. For example, investors may not realize that they are boarding an emotional rollercoaster when they assign half of their pension to an equity fund. Nor is there any guarantee that the impact of acknowledged consequences "will be perceived accurately" (Fischhoff 1992, p. 137). Note that what is questioned here is not the accuracy of people's beliefs about future chance events (this is discussed below), but the accuracy of their beliefs about how these events will affect them emotionally.

It is overwhelmingly clear from the literature that virtually all gamblers who reach the compulsive stage suffer from some kind of irrationality in belief formation. They believe their chances of winning are higher, even much higher, than what can be justified by the information they have. Even in games of pure chance, gamblers fervently believe that they are on winning or losing streaks.[11] Sometimes, belief formation operates by wishful thinking (illustrating the blocked arrow from desires to beliefs in Figure 15.1). There is evidence that "as frequency of betting increases so does the belief that one's selection involves more skill and yet the observed behaviour actually becomes less skillful, with escalating stakes, hurried bet selection and last minute changes in selection" (Dickerson 1984, p. 134).

I suspect that "hot" mechanisms of this kind operate very frequently to shape beliefs about winning.[12] Yet, in studies of gambling, "cool" varieties of irrational belief formation figure much more prominently, perhaps because they are readily connected with the large literature on statistical fallacies. In fact, the "gambler's fallacy" is the very paradigm of erroneous statistical reasoning. This fallacy and its converse can be explained in terms of two heuristics of decision making identified by Tversky and Kahneman (1974):

> When in a game there is a 50 percent chance of winning, people expect that a small number of rounds will also reflect this even chance. This is only possible when runs of gains and losses are short: A run of six losses would upset the local representativeness. This mechanism may explain the well-known gamblers' fallacy: The expectation that the probability of winning increases with the length of an ongoing run of losses. The *representativeness heuristic* predicts that players will increase their bet after a run of losses, and decrease it after a run of gains. This is indeed what about half the players at blackjack tables do. . . . But the other half show the reverse behaviour: They increase their bets after winning, and decrease them after losing, which is predicted by the *availability heuristic*. After a run of losses, losing becomes the better available outcome, which may cause an overestimation of the probability of losing. (Wagenaar 1988, p. 13; italics added)

Another important mechanism is the "psychology of the near-win." When the outcome of the gamble is in some sense "close" to that on which the gambler had put his money, this is perceived as a confirmation of his beliefs. Wagenaar (1988, p. 109) offers a graphic example:

> [An] example of confirmation bias is the roulette player who suddenly places a large single bet on number 24, completely out of his routine

betting pattern. His reason was that 12 is always followed by a 24. After he lost his bet I enquired what had gone wrong. He said: "It almost worked." The number that did come out was 15, which is adjacent to 24 on the number wheel. Probably he would have considered other outcomes like 5, 10, and 33 also confirmations, because they are nearby on the wheel. Also he could have taken the outcomes 22, 23, 25, and 26 as confirmations because their numerical value is close. Or the numbers 20, 21, 26, and 27, because they are adjacent on the tableau. Thus 13 out of 37 possible outcomes could be taken as confirmations of a rule that has no predictive value whatsoever. We can add to this number all the occasions on which 24 or another confirmatory number occurred, not immediately, but in the second round.

If the confirmation bias can operate in gambles of pure chance, it is obviously even more likely to be observed in gambles that involve a mix of chance and skill. At the roulette table, the concept of a near-win is pure magic or superstition. In games with handicapping, it has some evidential value, although less than what many gamblers believe. At the racetrack, choosing for a winner a horse that comes in second is seen both by the gambler himself and by others as proof that he was on to something.[13] According to Gilovich (1983, p. 1122), the "tendency to accept wins at face value but to transform losses into 'near wins' can produce overly optimistic assessments of one's gambling skill and the chances of future success" when betting on professional football games.

There are a number of distinct mechanisms that may be involved here. First, there is the idea that near-wins serve to confirm beliefs about one's ability to predict the outcome. Second, there is the idea that near-wins serve as reinforcers of gambling behavior, much in the same way as actual wins do. I return to this idea in the discussion of reinforcement theories. Third, several writers (Brown 1986, p. 1010; Griffiths 1991, p. 351) appeal to the views of Kahnernan and Tversky (1982) about the "cognitive regret" produced by near-wins, and they suggest that the stronger the regret, the stronger the urge to gamble again. I am somewhat puzzled by this claim. Because regret is a negative feeling, it would seem more likely to be perceived as aversive and thus to make gambling in the future less likely. (If I miss my plane by 2 minutes won't this make me more careful in the future than if I miss it by half an hour?) Nonetheless, the general idea that near-wins reinforce the propensity to gamble, by cognitive or motivational mechanisms, has strong empirical and theoretical support.

In addition to the gambler's fallacy (and its converse) and the near-win fallacy, we may cite two general sources of irrational belief formation: the illusion of control (Langer 1975) and depressive realism (Alloy and Abrahamson 1988). The first mechanism refers to the tendency of subjects to believe that they can control chance events and to overestimate their control over outcomes that are partly but not wholly under their own control. The second refers to a general tendency among non-depressed subjects to view the world in a rosier light than is justified. Depressed subjects tend to be more evenhanded in their causal attribution of credit and blame, whereas nondepressives typically attribute negative events to others and positive events to their own intervention. Nondepressive subjects see themselves more positively than they do others with the same objective characteristics, whereas the depressed are not subject to this self-serving bias, nor to the opposite, self-deprecating bias. Depressed subjects have an accurate idea of how other people perceive them, whereas nondepressives exaggerate the good impressions they make on others. Finally, nondepressives exhibit the illusion of control whereas depressed subjects judge their degree of control accurately. Moreover, nondepressives show an "illusion of no control" when the outcome is associated with failure.[14]

Let us consider, finally, the third optimality requirement of the rational choice model: optimal investment in the acquisition of new information. Whereas other forms of addiction may be characterized by a tendency to invest suboptimally in information (heavy drinkers probably do not check their liver as often as they should), some forms of gambling are characterized by an overinvestment in information. The very existence of the Monte Carlo *Revue Scientifique,* which logs successive outcomes at roulette (Cornish 1978, p. 108), is proof that gamblers are willing to spend money gathering worthless information. In games of pure chance, *any* investment in information is by definition excessive. In games of mixed skill and chance, gathering and processing of information can improve the odds. On the racetrack, "professional gambling is typified by a rational and controlled approach sustained by hours of information collection, detailed accounting and the like" (Dickerson 1984, pp. 66–67). What distinguishes the professional gambler from the compulsive gambler (and steady loser) is probably not that the former more closely approximates the optimal investment in information, but that he has better processing skills.

I take it for proven that compulsive gamblers typically—not only occasionally—behave irrationally. Does this invalidate the Becker–Murphy model of rational addiction? To answer this question, we must first ask whether compulsive gambling satisfies their properties $P\,1$ and $P\,2$. On a first approximation, this can be rephrased as a question of whether compulsive gamblers experience tolerance and withdrawal symptoms. It is possible that tolerance does evolve, although some of the alleged evidence is open to other interpretations. There is little evidence of primary withdrawal and some evidence of secondary withdrawal. Let us assume, for the sake of argument, that properties $P\,1$ and $P\,2$ are satisfied. As Skog observes, however, the model does not allow us to say that this high equilibrium is excessive or corresponds to compulsive gambling. There may well be some noncompulsive Becker–Murphy gamblers around. Compulsive gamblers, however, are likely to violate some of the other assumptions of the Becker–Murphy model. They do not stick to their plans, and they do not form rational beliefs. The behavior of these gamblers cannot be predicted by the model.

Hyperbolic Discounting

The Becker–Murphy assumptions might also be faulted on another point: because we are so constructed as to discount the future hyperbolically, as proposed by George Ainslie, rather than exponentially, as assumed by Becker and Murphy. An explanation of gambling based on Ainslie's theory would probably have to be combined with the cognitive irrationalities discussed above. If people had accurate expectations about the outcome of gambling, they might not only prefer abstention to gambling ahead of time but also continue in this preference right up to the time of choice. The preference reversal that is the key to Ainslie's theory might occur only if the short-term expected benefits are blown up (and/or the long-term costs diminished) by irrational beliefs.

In the literature on gambling, there are a few explicit references to Ainslie's work. The brief reference in Walters (1994, p. 167) involves only the contrast between the short-term and long-term effects of gambling (thrill versus loss of money), with no mention of the hyperbolic shape of the discounting function. A more sustained argument that does refer to hyperbolic discounting is found in Stein (1989, pp. 77–80). It combines a straightforward application of Ainslie's theory of impulsive behavior with a Piaget-inspired account of impulse control. Stein stipulates a within-session problem: a man who starts a night of gambling, intending to leave the casino when he has $100 left. This intention is highly motivated because he knows he has to pay a loan shark at least $100 the next day, and he could be physically hurt if he does not pay. Yet, when he is down to his last $100, the imminent thrill he would get from betting looms larger than the risk that will only materialize later. Stein then goes on to assert that the way to overcome this problem is to move from "concrete operations" to "formal operational reasoning." In a somewhat confusing manner, this shift is related not only to Piaget's theory of developmental stages but also to the Gamblers Anonymous slogan "One day at a time" and to Ainslie's theory of bunching.[15]

In a very different application of hyperbolic discounting to compulsive gambling, Rachlin (1990) makes no reference at all to preference reversal. Rather, he demonstrates that gambling can have a positive expected value for the gambler if three conditions are satisfied. First, the gambler is not motivated by the subjective value of a single gamble but by the subjective value of a string of gambles, averaged over all strings. Second, a string ends with the first win. Thus the possible strings are Win, Loss–Win, Loss–Loss–Win, Loss–Loss–Loss–Win, etc. Third, the subjective value of a string is the sum of the monetary values of the component gambles (a series of losses followed by a win) discounted hyperbolically. Summing up for all the possible strings, he finds that gambling has a positive subjective value. He also argues that neither of two frequently recommended ways of achieving self-control is of much help to the compulsive gambler. First, decreasing the degree of discounting (i.e., making the future more salient) does not necessarily reduce the value of the gamble. Second, it does not help to "organize behavior over a large span of time and to count up the benefits and subtract the losses only after very long anticipated or experienced temporal units" (Rachlin 1990, p. 297), because an identical argument would then apply to this increased time period.

This last conclusion does not directly contradict Ainslie's theory that the gambler may overcome his problem by bunching because the two theories stipulate different principles for aggregating choices into larger temporal units. Rachlin argues, however, that the mode of aggregation he stipulates is more natural because "the signal indicating the end of a unit (a win) is intrinsic to the activity itself. Count-based or time-based restructuring would require count or time signals not typically provided within the gambling situation" (ibid.). The only way gamblers may be able to quit is by running out of money. In that case, relapse should be a very common phenomenon as soon as the gambler is back on his or her feet financially. Moreover, with Rachlin's theory, it is hard to see why there are any noncompulsive gamblers. On both counts, Ainslie's theory performs better. Relapse is prevented by successful bunching. Gambling in moderation is made possible by the use of personal rules. This being said, Rachlin's theory is simple, powerful, and intriguing. It would be worthwhile following it up.

Learning and Reinforcement

The gambling setup, unlike most other addictive behaviors, is very similar to a laboratory learning experiment. The animal (the gambler) makes a response (places a bet) at freely chosen times. Rewards are made available as some function of the pattern of responses. The pattern of rewards, in turn, shapes the pattern of responses in the future, by the process known as reinforcement. In gambling, the reward pattern is a *variable-ratio* (VR) schedule, meaning that the ratio of wins to stakes is variable in the short run. Such schedules have two relevant properties. First, it is hard to establish behavior on a VR schedule. It is a big help to have a large win early on; in fact, as we saw, this appears to be a precondition for becoming a compulsive gambler.[16] As casino and racetrack managers lack the technology for sucking in novices by offering them big wins, they have to rely on chance-generated luck. (Con-man operations, however, rely on the deliberate inducement of early wins by the mark; see, e.g., Freundlich [1995, p. 28].) Second, once the behavior is established, it can be maintained on a VR schedule even if the rewards are quite skimpy or even declining.[17]

In such explanations the function of *reward* is obviously very different from its use in rational-choice explanations. In reinforcement, the link between reward and behavior does not pass through conscious choice among alternatives that are weighed against each other for the purpose of reward maximization. Actual reward, not anticipated reward is what matters. Moreover, unlike natural selection (another mechanism by which actual rewards can shape behavior) reinforcement does not mimic maximization. It produces melioration, not maximization. For these reasons, there is not full agreement on the appropriateness of using reinforcement theory to explain gambling behavior, some forms of which seem to be very much based on conscious choice and deliberation: "Human behavior will only be determined by schedules of reinforcement when people are not trying to 'solve' the problems posed by the schedule. We must therefore not expect schedules to account for the complex systems used by roulette or blackjack experts, as an example. But the repetitive, apparently mindless, paying of a simple slot machine may well yield to an analysis in terms of the schedules in operation" (Lea, Tarpy, and Webley 1987, p. 287). The description in Dickerson (1993) of poker-machine players as driven by a reinforcement schedule they do not understand also fits this picture.

Moreover, gambling differs from most reinforcement settings in one important respect:

> . . . in gambling, unlike the case of many other types of behavior, money (a general conditioned reinforcer) is being risked for more of the same—a state of affairs which both makes the experience of nonreinforcement punishing (loss of some reinforcer) and evaluations of profit and loss easier. In many forms of behaviour which operate under VR

schedules, the loss involved in making a response which is subsequently not reinforced is much more difficult to calculate (how is the effort of telling a joke set against the nonappearance of a smile?) or calculable only within wide limits. (Cornish 1978, pp. 190–191)

At the end of a day at the racetrack, you *know* that you have less money in your pocket than when you arrived. It becomes less plausible that gambling can be maintained merely by monetary reinforcers. Other, secondary rewards must take up the slack. Most obviously, the thrill of gambling may serve as a reinforcer of the behavior. Now, by all accounts the thrill is generated by betting, not by winning. This implies that the reward is forthcoming not on a VR schedule, but on a *fixed-interval* (FI) schedule (the reward is made available following a fixed interval after the response). Specifically, Dickerson (1979, 1984, p. 87 ff.) argues that stimulus events such as reels spinning or race commentaries provide intense arousal and excitement that allow them to serve as reinforcers on a FI schedule. Furthermore, it has been argued that casino betting offers reinforcement in the form of social approval by other gamblers (Ocean and Smith 1993), presumably also on a FI schedule. In addition, we have seen that near-wins may serve as reinforcers on a VR schedule. Although each of the near-wins presumably is less reinforcing than an actual win, there are more of them.[18]

CONCLUSION

I conclude by briefly addressing two questions. What explains compulsive gambling? Is compulsive gambling an addiction?

With regard to the explanatory question, I shall make two distinctions. On the one hand, different explanations may apply to different stages in a gambling career. On the other hand, different explanations might apply to different types of gambling. Although I shall sketch a stylized gambling career that is intended to apply to many different types of gambling, some forms may call for a different analysis. In particular, I agree with the writers who claim that fruit-machine or poker-machine playing stand apart from other games. For this type of gambling, reinforcement theory is the natural analytical approach. Reinforcers include, as we have seen, not only one's own wins, but also one's own near-wins and the wins of others. There is virtually no scope for the exercise of skill, even imaginary skills. The roulette player can at least choose a number.

With regard to most other forms of gambling. I suggest that a typical career unfolds as follows: In the first stage, moderate, occasional gambling is triggered by a desire for entertainment and a hope for monetary gain. In a second stage, often following an early big win, the gambler begins to play more frequently and for higher stakes. Secondary rewards from near-wins and social approval also begin to appear at this stage. At the third stage, an interaction between arousal, irrational belief formation, hyperbolic discounting, and manipulation by the gambling establishment eggs the player to go on. In a fourth stage, subjective tolerance and the objective need to repay debts conspire to make the players gamble for ever-higher stakes and/or on longer odds. More or less at the same time, secondary withdrawal symptoms appear that make it even more difficult to stay away from the gambling scene. In this sequence, the crucial step is the passage to the third stage. Irrational belief formation, in particular, seems to be an essential ingredient in the making of a compulsive gambler. "In order for a person to continue gambling at a regular pace, the losses must be rationalized in some fashion or other" (Lesieur 1984, p. 49).

Are compulsive gamblers addicts? A full answer must await more knowledge about the neurophysiology of addiction. We do not know whether gambling exhibits anything like the patterns of neuroadaptation described by Gardner and David. If gambling turns out to exhibit primary as well as secondary withdrawal symptoms, there is a strong case for classifying it as an addiction. If not, there will nevertheless remain a number of features that gambling has in common with the core addictions.

NOTES

1. For an early recognition of this distinction and its importance, see an observation from 1799 by a Paris judge quoted in Freundlich (1995, p. 33).

2. This observation is echoed in a study of young fruit-machine players:

Money, paradoxically, seemed to be a fundamental factor in producing high arousal levels because none of the group said they would enjoy playing a fruit machine if they had one in their bedroom that gave free plays at the push of a button. This seems strange, considering the object of playing in these addicted players, which was to stay on the machines as long as possible using the least amount of money, that is, playing *with* money rather than *for* it. (Griffith, 1991, p. 125)

3. This seems to contradict Dickerson (1984, p. 93):

An anxiety reduction concept (analogous to that used in the explanation of compulsive behavior) does not seem to fit with the other empirical data or with the proposal in the previous section that the very process of gambling may be exciting or arousing particularly for those who bet frequently and persist when gambling. There are few observations that a session of gambling may be calming or anesthetising.

In his earlier work, Dickerson may have been less aware of the difference between the psychological mechanisms underlying different types of gambling. The following observation may also be relevant here:

> For those who are hyperactive (and many gamblers meet the diagnosis of Attention Deficit Hyperactivity Disorder), the intensity of gambling, at least initially, has a paradoxical effect; like cocaine or amphetamines, it slows them down, allowing them to concentrate, process affects, and feel normal. (Rosenthal and Rugle, 1994, p. 30)

4. In general, I agree with Fischholf (1992, p. 137) in that:

> When making risky choices, people may consider more than the uncertain and negative consequences of their actions. Indeed, they presumably would not voluntarily expose themselves to a risk if there were not some compensating benefit. That benefit may "just" be avoiding a more serious risk (or a certain negative consequence). Or, it may be bundled with the risk itself, such as the exhilaration of driving fast.

I am suggesting, however, that some people may have a preference for risky driving for its own sake.

5. Later in this section I discuss the possibility that some of these worries might be caused by gambling.

6. One might also ask whether tolerance could not also lead to evermore frequent play, without increasing stakes and odds. In that case, compulsive gambling would be more like smoking than like heroin addiction. I do not know any discussions of this question. My impression is that when people go from occasional gambling to regular gambling it is simply because they find the experience pleasant and want to have more of it. If tolerance to gambling exists, it sets in later and takes the form of gambling for higher stakes.

7. As I mentioned initially, Dickerson (1984, p. 38) defines compulsive gamblers as those who have sought treatment for help. In Dickerson (1993), he explicitly deals with the causes of impaired self-control, defining that concept operationally as "persistence when losing." He is aware that this measure, although reliable, might not be entirely valid. Whereas the former criterion is underinclusive (it misses gamblers who lose control but do not seek help), the latter is overinclusive (it covers those who are happy to lose their money in exchange for the fun).

8. Thus, we have seen that gambling may cause loss of control over gambling, drinking may cause loss of control over drinking, and drinking may cause loss of control over gambling. Could gambling cause loss of control over drinking?

9. Note that a person may be a risk-seeker and yet have decreasing marginal utility of money throughout the relevant interval. See Bromiley and Curley (1992, p. 103 ff.) for a discussion of how to "decontaminate" utility-based measures of risk-seeking by removing the contribution of the marginal utility of money.

10. Gambling with a negative expected monetary value may actually tend to increase the gambler's wealth by the following nonintentional mechanism. Because of the gambler's system of mental accounting (Thaler 1985), "spending money on lottery tickets can be expected to replace other small expenditures, while large wins may not always be returned to the spending stream, but be saved instead" (Cornish, 1978, p. 43). Hence, it may be that "the betting-shops' imposition of payout limits on combination bets stems not only from their desire to maximize their profits on this form of betting but also to prevent the potential 'win' from becoming large enough to tempt the winner to use it for purposes other than re-betting" (ibid., p. 178).

11. Even casino owners may be prone to such thinking. Dealers who have lost badly may be replaced (Wagenaar 1988, p. 109) or even dismissed (Dickerson 1984, p. 31).

12. A study of gamblers who root for particular teams concludes that "If bettors were able to overcome their emotional wishes for the sake of financial gain, the bets played by all groups of fans, nonfans, and neutral respondents should not have differed from each other. The findings clearly showed that paid bets reflected wishful thinking" (Babad and Katz, 1991, p. 1934). Although an instance of hot cognition, this finding differs from the mechanism discussed in the text, namely wishful thinking *induced* by the desire for financial gain.

13. A gambler might exploit this mechanism to make money by selling "inside information." He or she might, for instance,

> . . . tell nine different people about the inside information on nine different horses. In this way he or she would have at least one, and possibly two or three people come to him or her the next time he touted. He or she would have more than one person because the people who received the second and third horse that came in would think that the tout was close and 'if only' they had put the money to place or show it would have paid off. (Lesieur, 1984, p. 180)

14. There is at least a *prima facie* tension between these findings and the suggestion by Rosenthal (1989, p. 105) that gambling is caused by depression.

15. Stein's discussion is also complicated by opaque references to the gambler's beliefs about the chances of winning. Perhaps what she has in mind is the idea mentioned in the text: As the time of betting approaches, the prospect of imminent gain looms larger both because of the hyperbolic discounting and because of irrational belief formation.

16. It is not clear from the literature whether this is a within-episode mechanism or a between-episode mechanism. Most plausibly, it is both.

17. Lea, Tarpy, and Webley (1987, pp. 287–288) refer to experiments by Lewis and Duncan (1957, 1958) that "permitted university students to play a slot machine that was programmed to present reward on 0, 11, 33, 67, or 100 percent of the plays. Except for the zero condition, the smaller the percentage of reward, the greater the persistence later when reward was discontinued." On reflection, this is not surprising. If the response has been fixed on a very low reward schedule, it *must* take longer to find out that the reward is no longer forthcoming. I cannot agree, therefore, when Lea, Tarpy, and Webley (1987, p. 288) draw the conclusion that "it is the rarity of success of gambling that induces the gambler to return to the game, not the profitable run of good luck." The laboratory setup in which rewards are first provided on a VR schedule and then withheld altogether has no analogue in real-life gambling.

18. Lea, Tarpy, and Webley ([1987, p. 287], citing Strickland and Grote [1967]) similarly report that

> . . . subjects who saw more winning symbols on the drums that stopped spinning first or second were more likely to continue to play. . . . One explanation of this finding comes from traditional learning research. It is well known that the sooner a reward is delivered, the stronger the response. . . . Delayed rewards lead to lower rates of behavior. There seems little doubt that the winning symbol is a reward for playing the machine. If this is the case, then it makes good sense for the strength of the response, measured by the willingness to play beyond the first 100 games, to be lower when the winning symbol is consistently in the third position. This effect, that responses closest to the onset of reward are the most strongly reinforced, would also predict that, for regular gamblers, late bets should increase and earlier bets decay.

Dickerson (1979, p. 321) confirms this prediction, but explains it by the FI schedule discussed in the text.

WORKS CITED

Alloy, L. and L. Abrahamson (1988). "Depressive realism " in L. B. Alloy, ed., *Cognitive Processes in Depression*. New York: Guilford Press, pp. 441–485.

Anderson, G. and R. I. F. Brown (1984). "Real and laboratory gambling, sensation-seeking and arousal." *British Journal of Psychology* 75: 401–410.

Babad, E. and Y. Katz (1991). "Wishful thinking—against all odds." *Journal of Applied Social Psychology* 21: 1921–1938.

Baumeister, R. F., T. F. Heatherton, and D. M. Tice (1994). *Losing Control: How and Why People Fail at Self-Regulation*. San Diego: Academic Press.

Becker, G. and K. Murphy (1988). "A theory of rational addiction." *Journal of Political Economy* 96: 675–700.

Bergler, E. (1957). *The Psychology of Gambling.* International Universities Press.

Bromiley, P. and S. P. Curley (1992). "Individual differences in risk-taking." In J. F. Yates, ed., *Risk-Taking Behavior.* New York: Wiley, pp. 87–132.

Brown, R. I. F. (1986). "Arousal and sensation-seeking components in the general explanation of gambling and gambling addictions." *International Journal of the Addictions* 21: 1001–1016.

Cornish, D. B. (1978). *Gambling: A Review of the Literature and Its Implications for Policy and Research.* London: Her Majesty's Stationery Office.

Coventry, K. R. and R. I. F. Brown (1993). "Sensation seeking, gambling and gambling addictions." *Addiction* 88: 541–554.

Custer, R. L. (1982). "Pathological gambling." In A. Whitfield, ed., *Patients with Alcoholism and Other Drug Problems.* New York: Year Book Publishers.

Dickerson, M. G. (1979). "FI schedules and persistence at gambling in the UK betting office." *Journal of Applied Behavior Analysis* 12: 315–323.

———. (1984). *Compulsive Gamblers.* London: Longman.

———. (1993). "Internal and external determinants of persistent gambling: Problems in generalising from one form of gambling to another." *Journal of Gambling Studies* 9: 225–245

Dostoyevski, F. (1964). *The Gambler.* New York: Norton.

Fischhoff, B. (1992). "Risk taking: A developmental approach." In J. F. Yates, ed., *Risk-Taking Behavior.* New York: Wiley, pp. 133–162.

France, C . J. (1902). "The gambling impulse." *American Journal of Psychology* 13: 364–407

Freundlich, F. (1995). *Le Monde du Jeu à Paris (1715–1800).* Paris: Albin Michel.

Friedman, M. and L. Savage (1948). "The utility analysis of choices involving risk." *Journal of Political Economy* 56: 279–304.

Gilovich, T. (1983). "Biased evaluation and persistence on gambling." *Journal of Personality and Social Psychology* 44: 1110–1126.

Greenberg, M. E. and B. Weiner (1966). "Effects of reinforcement history on risk-taking behavior." *Journal of Experimental Psychology* 71: 587–592.

Griffith, M. (1991). "Psychobiology of the near-miss in fruit machine gambling," *The Journal of Psychology* 125: 347–357.

———. (1994). "Beating the fruit machine." *Journal of Gambling Studies* 10: 287–292.

Hamsun, K. (1954). "Far og sønn. En spillehistorie" ("Father and son. A gambling tale"). In K. Hamsun, ed., *Samlede Verker*, vol. 4. Oslo: Gyldendal, pp. 73–91.

Jacobs, D. F. (1989). "A general theory of addictions." In H. J. Shaffer, S. Stein, and B. Gambino, eds., *Compulsive Gambling*. Lexington, MA: Lexington Books, pp. 35–64.

Kahneman, D. and A. Tversky (1982). "The simulation heuristic." In D. Kahneman, P. Slovic, and A. Tversky, eds., *Judgment Under Uncertainty*. Cambridge, UK: Cambridge University Press, pp. 201–208.

Karcher, A. J. (1992). *Lotteries*. New Brunswick, NJ: Transaction Books.

Langer, E. J. (1975). "The illusion of control." *Journal of Personality and Social Psychology* 32: 311–328.

Lea, S. E. G., R. M. Tarpy, and P. Webley (1987). *The Individual in the Economy: A Survey of Economic Psychology*. Cambridge, UK: Cambridge University Press.

Lesieur, H. R. (1984). *The Chase: The Compulsive Gambler*. Rochester, VT: Schenkman Books.

Lewis, D. J. and C. P. Duncan (1957). "Expectation and resistance to extinction of a lever pulling response as functions of percentage of reinforcement and amount of reward." *Journal of Experimental Psychology* 54: 115–120

———. (1958). "Expectation and resistance to extinction of a lever pulling response as functions of percentage of reinforcement and number of acquisition trials." *Journal of Experimental Psychology* 55: 121–128.

Murray, W. (1985). *Tip on a Dead Crab*. New York: Penguin.

———. (1990). *The King of the Nightcap*. New York: Bantam Books.

———. (1991). *The Getaway Blues*. New York: Bantam Books.

Ocean, G. J. and G. J. Smith (1993). "Social reward, conflict, and commitment: A theoretical model of gambling behavior." *Journal of Gambling Studies* 9: 321–339.

Orphanides, A. and D. Zervos (1992). "Rational addiction with learning and regret," unpublished manuscript.

Peck, C. P. (1986). "Risk-taking behavior and compulsive gambling." *American Psychologist* 41: 461–465.

Rachlin, H. (1990). "Why do people gamble and keep gambling despite heavy losses?" *Psychological Science* 1: 294–297.

Rosenthal, R.J. (1989). "Pathological gambling and problem gambling." In H. J. Shaffer, S. Stein, and B. Gambino, eds., *Compulsive Gambling*. Lexington, MA: Lexington Books, pp. 101–125.

Rosenthal, R. J. and L. J. Rugle (1994). "A psychodynamic approach to the treatment of pathological gambling: Part 1. Achieving abstinence." *Journal of Gambling Studies* 10: 21–42.

Seeburger, F. F. (1993). *Addiction and Responsibility*. New York: Cross Road.'

Shaffer, H. (1989). "Conceptual crises in the addictions: The role of models in the field of compulsive gambling." In H. J. Shaffer, S. Stein, and B. Gambino, eds., *Compulsive Gambling*. Lexington, MA: Lexington Books, pp. 3–33.

Strickland, L. H. and F. W. Grote (1967). "Temporal presentation of winning symbols and slot machine playing." *Journal of Experimental Psychology* 74: 10–13.

Thaler, R. (1985). "Mental accounting and consumer choice." *Marketing Science* 4: 199–214.

Tversky, A. and D. Griffin (1991). "Endowment and contrast in judgments of well-being." In R. J. Zeckhauser, ed., *Strategy and Choice*. Cambridge, MA: MIT Press, pp. 297–318.

Tversky, A. and D. Kahneman (1974). "Judgment under uncertainty: Heuristics and biases." *Science* 185: 1124–1131.

Tversky, A. and E. Shafir (1992). "The disjunction effect in choice under uncertainty." *Psychological Science* 3: 305–309.

Wagenaar, W. A. (1988). *Paradoxes of Gambling Behavior*. Hove and London: Lawrence Erlbaum.

Walters, G. (1994). "The gambling lifestyle: I. Theory," *Journal of Gambling Studies* 10: 159–182.

Wray, I. and M. G. Dickerson (1981). "Cessation of high frequency gambling and 'withdrawal symptoms.'" *British Journal of Addiction* 76: 401–405.

Chapter Sixteen

ADDICTS WITHOUT DRUGS

The Media Addiction

MARK S. ROBERTS

From a distinctly professional, mostly technical topic, bandied about by therapists, psychopharmacologists, various health-care providers, criminologists, politicians, and others, the problematic of drugs and addiction has, in the past few years, assumed a central place in what would seem a most unusual area: postmodern discourse. The evidence of such a shift is obvious, from Guattari's early writings on drugs, gangs, and other social marginalia to Derrida's reading of Plato's *pharmakon* and Richard Klein's sublime smokes. One might even go so far as to say that drugs and addictive behavior are to postmodernism what madness, dreams, and sexuality were to twentieth-century modernism: the ultimate alterities, the final lines of transgression, the outside.

But even this outside has conventional parameters. Much of the postmodern discourse on drugs and addiction focuses on the psychological, cultural, philosophical, and sociopolitical implications of a real dependency on real drugs and other addictive substances. Drugs may be "untheorizable," as Derrida suggests, but the postmodern reading still affirms their materiality and ubiquity within any given society or culture. They remain substances—controlled, uncontrollable, untheorizable, or in any other form. In short, some tangible substance always serves as the object of the addictive process, no matter how intangible that substance may at first seem.

In the case of a certain type of modern addiction, however, there seems to be no object at all underlying the addictive process. What I am here calling the "media addict" appears, rather, to be acting out his or her dreadful and terrifying performances with no particular thing in mind. What this sort of addict hungers for is an information high— information in the form of electronically produced images and sounds, flashing signs of the real without reality or substance. This type of addict is not a sufferer in the common sense of the term, someone who continually craves a forbidden substance to keep the body alive and moving, but is, rather, an inert "monitor" who seeks desperately to dissolve media into life, to frantically lose himself or herself in what Jean Baudrillard calls "the ecstasy of communication."[1]

A case in point is that of Charles Stuart, a Boston fur salesman, who, on one fateful night in October of 1989, issued a shrieking alarm on his car phone. Stuart, whose cry for help was being monitored by a local radio station, tuned into the police band, told a shocked radio audience that he and his wife, Carol, had been attending a childbirth class, and on their way home, were attacked and robbed by a vicious young black male. Stuart fought bravely against his attacker, but was seriously wounded. His pregnant wife, shot in the head, eventually succumbed to her wounds.

Although tragic in itself, the incident had national and international repercussions. By pure chance, the aftermath of the event, including Stuart's treatment in the emergency room and his subsequent hospitalization, was videotaped by a television crew that happened to be cruising Boston's inner city. On the following evening, the tragic video footage was aired on network television's *Rescue 911,* and a shocked America sat in disbelief at the utter inhumanity of the whole event. Even the usually circumspect national news media was thoroughly shocked by the awful fate of "nice people" when they wander into "the urban jungle."

The gravity of the event was not lost on the Boston police nor the local population either. In an emotionally wrought news conference, the then mayor of Boston, Raymond Flynn, fought off tears to memorialize these "good, decent people" who had their "lives snuffed out." Flynn's touching remarks were echoed by virtually every righteous voice in the Boston area. Impassioned pleas were made for restoring the death penalty in Massachusetts; there were calls for new legislation to wage an uncompromising war on urban ghetto criminals in Boston. Indeed, the police took it upon themselves to put a quick halt to this kind of uncon-

trolled "wilding." They fanned out patrols and spread impressive drag-
nets throughout the mostly African-American Roxbury neighborhood,
picking up and grilling any black men who even remotely resembled
Charles Stuart's gasping, emergency-room description of the assailant.
Finally, after several false starts, the police found a dead ringer for the
killer: Willie Bennett, a small-time criminal and addict who even
bragged of committing the murder and robbery.

Of course, as is now widely known, it was Stuart himself who killed
his wife, blaming the murder on an invented black assailant. Ostensibly,
Stuart was concerned to recover insurance money from his wife's death
so he could purchase a new luxury car. With his plot unraveling, Stuart
eventually killed himself. His brother was later tried and convicted of
conspiracy in the case, having served as a drop-off for the jewelry that
the "black assailant" had supposedly stolen from Stuart's wife. Interestingly—at least for our purposes—Stuart's brother told the court that the
original idea for the murder was inspired by a television movie.

A much less well known, but quite similar, crime was committed
several years later in Milwaukee, Wisconsin. In this instance, a white
couple was leaving a trendy restaurant when the husband, Jesse Anderson, claimed that two black men jumped them and repeatedly stabbed
his wife in the face and neck. When he rose to defend his wife, the men
stabbed him in the chest and ran away. Mrs. Anderson, like Mrs. Stuart,
eventually succumbed to her wounds, while Mr. Anderson, like Mr. Stuart, recovered fully. Anderson was even able to retrieve the murder
weapon—a fishing knife—and a basketball insignia cap purportedly left
at the scene by one of the murderers. This time the media, rather than
promoting Mr. Anderson's plight, contributed to his downfall. It seems
that he had purchased the insignia cap from a black man in a mall prior
to the crime, and the cap was immediately identified by this individual
when it was broadcast on local television. Anderson, quite predictably,
turned out to be the real murderer, and the two black assailants turned
out to be imaginary figures invented for this neatly copied story line. He
was eventually tried and convicted of the crime. (In an ironic twist to
this "sequel," Anderson was himself killed by an inmate, along with his
prison buddy, the infamous Jeffrey Dahmer. The killer believed he was
Jesus Christ, saving the world from evil, and was, somewhat providen-
tially, a *real* "black assailant.")

A still more bizarre, and even more obviously staged, case of media
addiction occurred a number of years ago in New York's Grand Central Station. The security police, hired by the Metro North railway to
patrol the station, decided to videotape their late evening activities—to,
in effect, simulate a night on the job. In this somewhat bizarre video

enactment, several of the police filmed themselves abusing and ridiculing the homeless people who often sought shelter in the station. There were also a number of video segments devoted to long racist diatribes and actual physical attacks on minority individuals living in the station. Several of the officers stripped and mugged in front of the camera in the nude. All considered, a strikingly real distillation of many of the "hidden" acts and desires of the security police, played out on videotape. What the "actors" actually did and felt (abuse and degrade the homeless and engage in blatant racism) was simply reenacted through the acting out on videotape of these actions. The tape was not a fiction, a recreation, or representation of certain types of behavior, but, rather, a reproduction, a sheer simulation of those images and acts carried out regularly by the security police. In short, a way for the police to see themselves *as* pure media event, *as* monitors of their own reprehensible actions.

Another nationally reported incident involved what appeared, at first, to be yet another senseless, motiveless mass murder. An apparently deranged man, who was later identified as Gian Luigi Ferri, a mortgage broker, entered the board room of a San Francisco law firm and started firing three automatic weapons randomly. After killing eight people and wounding six others, he tried to make his escape up a flight of stairs. He was later trapped in the stairwell by police, and, moments later, shot and killed himself.

Following the tragedy, police and other authorities searched for some commensurate motive for this heinous crime, but seemed to come up with only the fact that Ferri had had certain strained dealings with the law firm. However, on further investigation, they found a handwritten note in Ferri's briefcase. The note contained the names and addresses of no less than a dozen television talk shows, including the *Phil Donahue Show* and the *Oprah Winfrey Show*. A story in the *San Francisco Examiner* concluded: "Taken together, the evidence has suggested to police that Ferri intended to flee 101 California [the building] and eventually hole up with the hostages. Then he apparently hoped to go on national TV with his story. . . ."

What the above scenes, as well as numerous others (all those acts and events that are presumably staged for or absorbed by media)—the "great O.J. chase," a recent self-immolation on the L.A. Freeway, replete with a sign large enough for news helicopters to photograph—indicate, among other things, is a growing trend toward a novel form of addictive behavior, an acting out, not of some repressed unconscious content, but of the electronic hyperreality of media, an "addiction" in which the actor seeks to become an integral part of the very physical laws and body of a media event itself. In this sense, the actions of the media addict do not seem to be motivated primarily by some hidden inner compulsion, some personal dispostion toward anger, fear, hatred, or violence. The media addict does not seem to carry out his or her murderous, antisocial or depraved gestures as a direct result of reverie, imagination, denial, obsession, childhood trauma, conflict, projection, delusion, and so on. Rather, he or she is obsessed by a desire to serve as a kind of anonymous monitoring screen of the hyperreal, of vaguely remembered television movie plots, of the scenic repetition of disembodied sounds and images—in other words, a bizarre, addictive process of acting out that is located neither in the actor nor on some remote stage.

PURGATIVE ACTING OUT:
TRADITIONAL VIEWS OF DISTANCE AND EVENT

This monitoring, this total absorption of the media addict into some fully constructed event is not only bizarre but it is also peculiar to the postmodern period. Traditional views of the subject's relation to an event usually involved quite specific causal coordinates—that is, the subject was generally viewed as responding to some inner affective signal triggered by an external event. Within dramatic poetics, for example, the subject of the spectacle, the play, was commonly viewed as susceptible to certain associations and feelings induced by the artwork. The spectator never really merged with the artwork, but, rather, "felt" its message through an aesthetic connection and identification with the imitated actions presented in the play. If, according to the classical model, the play was truly tragic, then the spectator would be aroused by the unfolding plot itself, though, in a somewhat degraded sense, could also be moved by the spectacle. Either way, the emphasis was principally on the event as distinct from the spectator, as the external cause of the emergence and eventual, almost ritual, ablution of deeply rooted ideas and emotions:

> Fear and pity can be caused by the spectacle or by the plot structure itself. The story should be constructed that the events make anyone who hears the story shudder and feel pity even without seeing the play. The story of Oedipus has this effect. To arouse pity and fear by means of the spectacle requires less art and costly performance. And those plays which, by means of the spectacle, arouse not fear but amazement have nothing in common with tragedy. We should not require from tragedy every kind of pleasure, but only its own peculiar kind.[2]

As a rule, then, classical poetics hypothesized a distinct subject of tragedy, or, for that matter, of any dramatic presentation; and, in effect, argued that each dramatic genre—such as comedy, tragedy, farce—strikes this subject in a somewhat different way. The individual struck, of course, is struck at a distance, is witness to a set of techniques characteristic of the style and composition of the genre of poetic production being presented. The spectator, in this view, is thus either moved or not moved by the play's technical structures—the plot or the spectacle—which indicates that the spectator does not participate directly in the play itself, but only receives its messages. Subject and event are interconnected, relational, but are in no way fully integrated with one another, nor is it in any way desirable that they should be. Indeed, if the spectator were to get too absorbed in the play, he or she would lose the very possibility of partaking of the play's cathartic effect, since the plot's message would no longer be received but rather actually enacted through a projection onto the play's action. Maintaining the communicational binary, sender–receiver, was paramount in classical poetic theory.

Similar notions of the nonintegration of subject and event abound in psychological theory, particularly psychoanalysis. For example, in Freud's classic account of acting out, "Remembering, Repeating and Working Through," he is careful to point out that catharsis—the bringing of the first moment of symptom formation into focus—occurs at the deepest levels of the unconscious. Indeed, acting out entails a compelling urge to repeat the past, in contradistinction to remembering it. The subject resists telling his or her fantasies and thoughts to the analyst, resists the secondary process of understanding and interpreting those thoughts and fantasies. Instead, the subject tends to represent a memory or experience that has never been formulated in secondary process thinking. The main thrust of acting out, then, is toward activity, and is related generally to mastering affects pertinent to passive and dependent situations, such as childhood trauma:

> We have learnt that the patient repeats instead of remembering, and repeats under the conditions of resistance. We may now ask what is it that he in fact repeats or acts out. The answer is that he repeats everything that has already made its way from the sources of the repressed into his manifest personality—his inhibitions and unserviceable attitudes and his pathological character traits. He also repeats all his symptoms in the course of treatment.[3]

Given this view of addictive acting out, we could say that the subject, traversed by deeply repressed impulses and feelings, tends to represent that inner world by repeating the conditions that contributed to these formations. What is seen, experienced, are all repressed at the point of their actual occurrence and then repeated through a ritual of symptomatic gesturing. Like the inner response to a dramatic presentation, the subject purges himself/herself of traumatic material through some form of external stimulation—stimulation usually provided by the analytic transference. What was deeply buried and then held down by resistance, rises to the surface by reliving, by repeating ineffable impressions. In a manner of speaking, the subject is an "actor" responding—retroactively—to a previously lived "story line"—to, as it were, nonverbal "stage directions" that have been inscribed within the unconscious, and which in turn motivate his or her actions. The subject of analytic acting out is thus not directly acting out trauma, but rather purging himself of that original moment of symptom formation by responding to an intrapsychical "script," by making manifest what cannot be put into words.

This psychoanalytic definition of acting out also extends to the modern broadening of the term. Recently, the term "acting out" has been used to describe the behavior of people who externalize their conflicts in actions without connection to some therapeutic situation. This form of acting out includes the various impulsive characters, symptomatic acts of neurotics, and the deviant, often violent behavior of sociopathic personalities. These kinds of behaviors are seen as similar to those arising in the analytic relation because impulses are discharged through actions rather than through fantasies and into words. Effectively, impulses associated with anger, hatred, violence, and hostility, for instance, become catalysts for actions. But catalysts that arise from pathological sources—conflicts that remain unresolved deep within the unconscious of the "actor." In this view, much like that of the therapeutic relation, acting out consists in behavioral and gestural responses triggered by a "scenario" inscribed at some earlier time—a scenario composed largely of habitual impulses that the "actor" is forced to repeat, to make manifest through certain actions.

Thus the traditional poetic–dramatic and psychoanalytic theories of the relation between subject and event, of catharsis and acting out, posit a marked distance between event (i.e., scene) and subject. The former takes the position that purgation occurs as a result of strong reactions to a dramatic presentation. The play, structured in a certain manner, effects the responses in the spectator, evoking deeply rooted emotions. But the spectator cannot effect such emotions apart from this role as spectator, his or her particular relation to the spectacle. The relational distance between spectacle and spectator, then, is an absolutely necessary element in the transmission of the play's message.

The latter, psychoanalytic theory, is perhaps even more emphatic about this separation of scene and spectator, subject and event. Acting out is always associated with the compulsion to represent an event or trauma. The event or trauma lies dormant in the psyche of the subject, much like the a hidden scenario. The subject, in the analytic setting, and usually through a transference to the analyst, "stages," by repeated gesturing, the original moment of this event. The subject is unaware of the event as something remembered, that is, made manifest in either fantasy or word, but rather discharges directly the impulses associated with the event. Fear, anger, and anguish are all expelled through the compulsive repetition of material long ago repressed in the subject's unconscious—an unconscious that is triggered by an external event or situation and thus moved to express externally something that is already inscribed within.

ACTING OUT MEDIA ADDICTION

Clearly, the above traditional views place great stress on interiority, on immanence, and on a distinct separation of subject and event as the necessary causal conditions for cathartic acting out. However, if we recall the above crime scenes, the inner experience of the subjects seem by and large lost in these distinctly postmodern forms of acting out, of media addiction. This is also the case with the distance between subject and event. After all, the principal motivation for Charles Stuart was not the acting out of some inner compulsion, or even the desire to represent some profoundly repressed scene. Rather, these various media addicts were concerned primarily with monitoring faithfully an event *as if* it was being recorded through some medium—a concern for how one might appear within another image or screen, inspired, in most instances, by yet another image. In short, the media addict craves to *become* the medium itself. This being the case, one might seek a possible explanation for this bizarre craving in the radically different ways in which we have come to view human subjectivity vis à vis electronic and informational media, that is, our means of reproducing images of ourselves and our specific relation to these images.

Some of the earliest investigations into this odd self-view appear in Marshall McLuhan's seminal works on media. Although many of his original ideas regarding perception and media, particularly television, have been subsequently challenged, the notion of media serving as "extensions of man" is still of considerable heuristic value. The idea, briefly stated, assumes that fragmentary and mechanical technologies extended our bodies in space. The industrial machine, for example, was able to do the work that we originally did with our hands. The radio was an extension of speech, television, of sight, the computer, of thought, and so on. All this was, of course, a boon to technological progress, resulting in vastly increased industrial production and communication, which, in turn, rendered isolated communities and cultures into what McLuhan calls a "global village." But, according to McLuhan, this progress was not free of drawbacks:

> With the arrival of electronic technology, man extended, or set outside himself, a live model of the central nervous system itself. To the degree that this is so, it is a development that suggests a desperate and suicidal autoamputation, as if the central nervous system could no longer depend on the physical organs to be protective buffers against the slings and arrows of outrageous mechanism.[4]

And further:

> The principle of numbness came into play with electric technology, as with any other. We have to numb our central nervous system when it is extended and exposed, or we will die. Thus the age of anxiety and of electric media is also the age of the unconscious and of apathy. . . . With our central nervous system strategically numbed, the tasks of conscious awareness and order are transferred to the physical life of man, so that for the first time he has become aware of technology as an extension of the physical body.[5]

More recently, Mark Poster, in *The Mode of Information*, makes a similar case for our being cut off from ourselves by our own technologies and inventions. In discussing databases and informational technologies, he argues that the unprecedented spread of database technology has created a "multiplication of the individual"—a new form of subjectivity that has assumed its place alongside the Cartesian vision of the subject. As a result, the Cartesian idea of immanence, mind as superior and distinct from material substance, is no longer conceived as the central model for identity. The self, traditionally viewed as circumscribed within an inner realm, is now, in the postmodern era, grafted onto completely external, impersonal systems. And these systems are composed entirely of electronic information about individuals, databases.

The average database entry, the "additional self," contains hundreds, sometimes thousands, of bits of information composing the person's file. A credit information file, for example, might contain pertinent biographical data on a person (age, sex, educational background, etc.), but also a list of every financial transaction he or she has engaged in (including, for example, college loans), as well as, in many cases, extremely personal information, like home costs, political affiliations, present salary, criminal records, subscriptions to communist publications, unpaid parking violations, medical conditions, etc. In effect, the data-bank profile constitutes a subject that is entirely separate from the person, but which, in many instances, touches significant portions of the "real" subject's life—serves, as it were, as a surrogate for the subject. For example, the database "self," due to certain pertinent facts in the file, can be turned down for a mortgage, thus affecting how the "real" subject lives, where his or her children go to school, who the neighbors are, what kind of employment he or she is able to accept, etc. "We see databases . . . as the multiplication of the individual, the constitution of an additional self, one that may be acted upon to the detriment of the "real" self without that "real" self ever being aware of what is happening."[6]

The advent of this additional subject, one rooted in extension rather than immanence, is also accompanied by the novel possibility of shifting human agency to nonhuman or artificial entities. Perhaps no area is more indicative of this shift than the relation between humans and computers. In his book, *Technopoly*, Neil Postman, focusing directly on this shift from human to machine subjectivity, suggests that we have effectively equated man with machine by allowing the "man–machine" metaphor to run completely wild, by subordinating and amputating those characteristics thought to be most human:

> The fundamental metaphorical message of the computer, in short, is that we are machines—thinking machines, to be sure, but machines nonetheless. It is for this reason that the computer is the quintessential, incomparable, near-perfect machine for Technopoly. It subordinates the claims of our nature, our biology, our emotions, our spirituality. The computer claims sovereignty over the whole range of human experience and supports its claim by showing that it "thinks" better than we can. Indeed, in his almost hysterical enthusiasm for artificial intelligence, Marvin Minsky has been quoted as saying that the thinking power of silicon "brains" will be so formidable that "If we are lucky, they will keep us as pets." An even giddier remark, although more dangerous, was offered by John McCarthy, the inventor of the term "artificial intelligence." McCarthy claims that "even machines as simple as thermostats can be said to have beliefs."[7]

The point of Postman's argument is that those characteristics always thought to be distinctly human are simply, and conveniently, grafted onto machines, computers in this case. Even the most basic human attribute of belief is denied its origin and place within the mind itself. Rather, it is seen as merely an action, something that can be done, and thus as attributable to any machine—including a thermostat—that can simulate a human idea or action. This, in turn, extends what we ordinarily consider human subjectivity to a vast range of external systems and objects. If what is most distinctly human, limited to our conception of subjectivity, can be extended to virtually any machine, system, or medium that can simulate human thinking, or feeling, or movement (robotics), or imagery, then these external systems and media will, no doubt, profoundly affect the way in which we act and relate to ourselves. Humans are therefore not only compelled to share their own attributes with external systems and machines, but also must necessarily alter the locus and center of their own actions, thought and volition in general. In short, humans must locate themselves both in the immanence of the subject and the alterity of their extensions, their machines, systems, and media. With the advent of these sorts of extensions, the mere simulation of human thought, feeling, or action can very well count *as* thought, feeling, or action.

If computers are seen as perfect extensions of human mental capacities, if they arrogate our inner thinking processes, then television tends to project us into a space entirely disconnected from our inner lives—a space locatable neither inside nor outside our bodies and minds. This is precisely the point Baudrillard makes when discussing the television-verité experiment, *An American Family*. The show originally aired on Public Broadcasting stations, and was intended as a documentary record of 7 months in the life of a typical American family, the Louds. However, some unanticipated, remarkable events occurred as the project advanced. The family began to disintegrate, and the documentary descended into the depths of familial anguish and acrimony, finally ending with the Louds' divorce. What was fascinating about all this, Baudrillard suggests, is that life went on "as if TV wasn't there."[8] What the 20 million viewers who pried into the life of the Louds were treated to, according to Baudrillard, was not the ultimate exercise in voyeurism, but rather the thrill of "reality," a glimpse of life at its most hyperreal: "It is . . . a kind of thrill of the real, or of an aesthetics of the hyperreal, a thrill of vertiginous and phony exactitude, a thrill of alienation and of magnification, of distortion in scale, excessive transparency, all at the same time."[9] Thus, television itself, in the case of the Louds, substitutes, in the eyes of the viewer, for the Louds' truth. Television becomes the very source of the true, becomes the rendering of the truth. The emotions spent by the disintegrating family, by "real" people in real trouble, are not seen at a distance, effectively absorbed by the viewer, but are rather rendered real through an electronic transference, by the very watching of television itself. Or, perhaps more accurately, by *being* the watching itself.

> It is entirely different with the Louds: "You no longer watch TV, TV watches you (live)," or again: "You no longer listen to *Pas de Panique*, *Pas de Panique* listens to you"—switching over from the panoptic apparatus of surveillance (of *Discipline and Punish*) to a system of deterrence, were the distinction between active and passive is abolished. No longer is there any imperative to submit to the model, or the gaze. "YOU are the model!" . . . You are news, you are the social, the event is you, you are involved, you can use your voice, etc." A turnabout of affairs by which it becomes impossible to locate an instance of the model, of power, of the gaze, of the medium itself, since *you* are always already on the other side. No more subject, focal point, center or periphery: but pure flexion or circular inflection. No more violence, or surveillance; only information . . .[10]

What Baudrillard proposes here, then, is that media and the information they carry tend to implode reality, drawing us into their rarefied domain. With this implosion, the distance between subject and object is eliminated. We become the event and the event becomes us, leaving us "frozen" in a hyperreal space consisting of subjects converted into objects and events and vice versa. We no longer participate in the event, but, rather, the event participates through us. And this, to be sure, leaves the subject in an unsettled position in its relation to the "reality" of events. As frozen moments within the vast schema of electronic media and information, we can no longer move up against these events, nor can we absorb them, understand them, or react to them. Our capacity to respond to them from a deeper inner level, to respond to them in what might be considered conventional, cathartic ways, is severely restricted, if not entirely effaced. The loss of distinction between the watcher and the watched, the listener and the heard, eliminates the necessary poles for catharsis and acting out, for the very essence of addictive forms of behavior. There is no longer the possibility of delving into the inner, unconscious world of the subject, to touch a "cathartic nerve." Purgation, catharsis, become the very terms of the model, of the YOU. There is no longer anything secret, dissimulated. Everything you are and will be is already inscribed in the very act of watching, contemplating, listening to, performing, becoming media and information.

Another striking example of this total absorption of the subject into television and media in general appears in therapeutic and confessional type television programming, that is, programming that attempts to expose and discuss interior life in the minutest detail. Although there are numerous genres of this type of programming (Mimi White, in her book *Teleadvising*, lists several distinct categories, including religious programs, home-shopping shows, sex-advising shows, and others),[11] the standard talk show provides more than sufficient evidence of the aforementioned phenomenon. The most revealing of these examples are the shocking candor of the participants (including audiences, guests, and participating viewers), and their overall lack of resistance to "internal" probing.

Freud once argued that the entire art of psychotherapy hinged upon resolutely drawing out intelligible material from the most profoundly hidden and repressed regions of the unconscious, since "one hardly comes across a single patient who does not make an attempt at reserving some region or other for himself so as to prevent the treatment from having access to it."[12] This, however, never seems to be a problem on television talk shows. All Oprah, Jerry Springer, Jennie Jones, and others have to do is ask the simplest question, push the most convenient button, and each and every participant is more than willing to discuss in the minutest detail his or her battle with incest, fetishism, exhibitionism, pyromania, impotence, hallucinosis, bulimia, opioid dependence, cyclothemia, Münchausen syndrome by proxy, bingo addiction, and so on.

Why Oprah and not Freud? The answer lies, I suggest, in the fact that Freud posits an inner subjectivity, an unconscious that resists simple exposure; that dissimulates itself by virtue of its being other than the subject, but yet located at the very center of that subject. Repression maintains the interiority of subjectivity, while also legitimizing the traditional subject/object paradigm. In the case of television talk and confessional shows, no such distinction exists. As a form of pure simulation, television absorbs the private into the public, effaces the conventional barriers between the two. Mimi White, writing on couples shows, like *The Dating Game*, puts it in a similar but slightly different way:

> The very existence of all these couples programs signals a blurring of the distinction between personal and social, private and public, individual and mass. . . . These programs consolidate the couple as a social body whose circulation as simulation secures the repetition and displacement of consuming interests and passions, where the social is always personal and vice versa. This body is constructed as unstable and decentered; it is always already in division and under stress.[13]

One could say, then, that without an apparent distinction between inner and outer, without the clearly marked distance between spectator and event, mentioned earlier, both the participants and audience of these confessional/talk shows become caught up in what Paul Virilio calls the "aesthetics of disappearance." People are no longer involved in face-to-face communication, in a stable relation, but are rather sucked into the incredible, blinding speed of electronic media. The addictive obsession *becomes* the very confession on the television screen, an absorption and disappearance of the subject into the anonymous, indissoluble light of camera, sound, image, and color. Nothing is hidden, yet nothing remains. Or, as Virilio puts it: "What happens in the train window, the car windshield, in the television screen is the same kind of *cinematism*. We have gone from the aesthetics of appearance, stable forms, to the aesthetics of disappearance, unstable forms."[14] This "instability" in turn fragments, depersonalizes, and decenters the very inner, private world of the media participant/confessee: "My sickness is your sickness, and yours is mine. I have no secrets from you; you are my screen. YOU are ME. I am YOU." Here, on the screen, there is no distinction between subject and object in the conventional sense of the term. Nor is there a readily distinguishable other of the self. A *face*, which, Levinas argues, must be confronted morally. There is only a "hybrid monster" forged by the fragmented extensions of a self absorbed into the blinding speed of electronic media. A self that reveals itself only by taking on and speaking through, i.e., monitoring, the very form of the media to which it owes that existence—in short, by acting out an addiction to "speed."

All these modes of what McLuhan calls "extension," in the end, contribute, I suggest, to the decline of addiction and addictive acting out as a real, causal phenomenon, as a form of behavior, expression, or defense associated with the subject/object paradigm. Slowly, the very concept of inner/outer, private/public, has given way to a transformation of whatever was, formerly, construed as the "real," acting subject—the so-called "inner self"—into its mechanistic extensions, into media, into pure information. The subject/object centered language of dramatic poetics and psychoanalysis—defense, purgation, catharsis, response, inner, outer, event, spectator—is no longer fully operative, since, in the postmodern, electronic era, it has become virtually impossible to locate an instance of the paradigm, the model out of which the language evolves. Baudrillard states it quite succinctly: "No more subject, center or periphery: but pure flexion or circular inflection. No more violence or surveillance: only "information," secret virulence, chain reaction, slow implosion, and simulacra of spaces where the real-effect again comes into play."[15]

It is thus no great mystery as to why the Stuarts, Andersons, security guards, Ferrises, Simpsons, and others tend to addictively act out their crimes with such cold precision, such guiltless detachment. They were simply monitoring the dissolution of television and media in general into life. Seeking a high that was only attainable by virtue of an objectless and, ultimately, subjectless quest to be the perfect monitor, seeking to be a "real" participant in a hyperreal drama, an invented or remembered story line. In this respect the media–addict–murderer is always entrapped in a state emptied of the traditional modes of causality, of the distinction between active and passive, between human and machine, between media and life, between subject and object, between one's actions and their real consequences—in short, the ultimate high, the final absorption.

NOTES

1. Jean Baudrillard, *The Ecstasy of Communication* (New York: Semiotext(e), 1987.

2 Aristotle, *Poetics* (XIV, 1453b).

3. Sigmund Freud, "Remembering, Repeating, Working-Through," *Standard Edition,* V. 12, p. 151.

4. Marshall McLuhan, *Understanding Media: The Extensions of Man* (New York: Signet, 1964), p. 53.

5. Ibid., p. 56.

6. Mark Poster, *The Mode of Information: Poststructrualism and Social Context* (Chicago: University of Chicago Press, 1990), p. 56.

7. Neil Postman, *Technopoly: The Surrender of Culture to Technology* (New York: Knopf, 1992), p. 111.

8. Jean Baudrillard, *Simulations* (New York: Semiotext(e), 1983), p. 50.

9. Ibid., p. 50.

10. Ibid., pp. 53–54.

11. See Mimi White, *Tele-advising: Therapeutic Discourse in American Television* (Chapel Hill: The University of North Carolina Press, 1992).

12. Sigmund Freud, "Resistance and Repression," *Standard Edition,* 15:228.

13. Mimi White, op. cit., pp. 80–81.

14. Paul Virilio and Sylvère Lotringer, *Pure War* (New York: Semiotext(e), 1983), p. 84.

15. Baudrillard, op. cit., pp. 53–54.

Chapter Seventeen

THE DRUG ADDICT *IN ABSENTIA*

Hidden Populations of Illicit Drug Users and the Gaze of Power

JOHN FITZGERALD

How does it happen that my look, enveloping them, does not hide them, and, finally, that, veiling them, it unveils them?"[1]

—Merleau-Ponty, *The Visible and the Invisible*

I am concerned with the scopic technologies employed by public health in the way it attempts to enumerate illicit drug users. Specifically, the institutional discursive practices—the "strategies"[2] used by public health to create, enumerate, and monitor those illicit drug users who are invisible to public institutions—"hidden populations" of drug users, or in other words, drug addicts *in absentia*. In an attempt to create a parallel to the panopticism of risk discourse, I will provide some ethnographic detail to illustrate spaces where the tactics employed by a "hidden population" of ecstasy users in the rave and warehouse party scene in Melbourne, Australia, both define and undermine the gaze of public health.

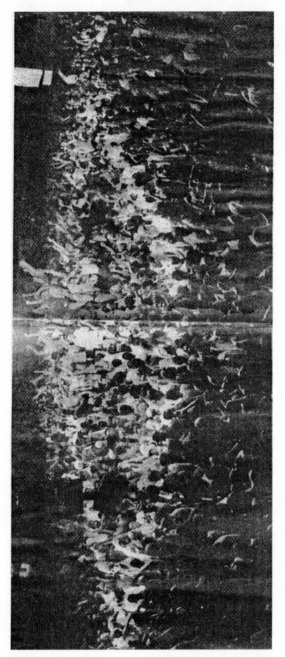

FIGURE 17.1
Hidden Populations

This story begins with a newspaper image of people dancing at a rave. I start with a visual image in order to pose a central problematic: that these people, made visible to you now, were and perhaps still are, members of a hidden population, although perhaps, through naming they have been disclosed in some way. It is how they have come to be visualized and named as part of this "hidden population," and the circular sleight of hand between scientific visibility and invisibility, which is the object of my inquiry.

DESCRIPTIONS OF THE HIDDEN POPULATION

In the early 1990s, in an environment of heightened public fear of HIV transmission related to unsafe intravenous drug use, specific attention became focused on those drug users who were hard to reach, evaded detection, or were not socially visible. These drug users, according to public health educators, were those not getting access to treatment services or risk reduction information. As Lambert and Weibel stated:

> Hidden populations euphemistically refers to those who are disadvantaged and disenfranchised: . . . These populations are often omitted from nationally representative surveys, largely because they have no fixed address or because they are less likely to be found at home or to agree to an interview. Ironically, those who belong to hidden populations are often at greater *risk* of drug abuse and drug-related morbidity than the general population.[3]

They are the absent Other, rhetorically responsible perhaps for further contributing to the HIV epidemic through unsafe drug use. They are unaccounted for, and yet somehow present—a trace in the calculations of risk. Actuarial technologies that make risk estimates possible rely fundamentally on the enumeration of public subjects.[4] These drug users are of considerable interest because through their absence they both define and undermine the risk calculations of public health.

Inspecting a piece of Swedish epidemiological research from 1985 provides an illustration of the scopic regime employed by public health that enables the movement of the abstract absence into a concrete positivist social formation.

The vertical axis denotes the percentage of a sample of Swedish students from a longitudinal study in which students, interviewed originally in 1968 were followed for a period of 15 years and interviewed about their drug use. Over that time period, the proportion of the group that reported their own drug use in interviews was compared to

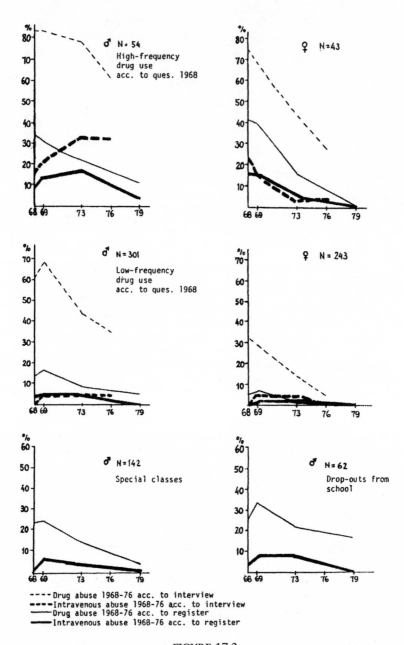

FIGURE 17.2
From Holmberg, M. B. (1985). Acta Psychitrica. Scand. 71:197–200.

the proportion who appeared in public registers of drug use. This graph is of a strata of the study sample who were high-frequency drug users.

The thin dashed line denotes the percentage of those interviewed who reported that they were high-frequency drug abusers. In the interpretation of this graph, the thin dashed line was then compared to the thin solid line, which denotes the percentage of those interviewed who appeared in public registers as high-frequency drug abusers. The space between the two lines, the difference between those registered and those "self-reporting" has been suggested by the authors of the study as representing the "hidden" population of drug abusers. I will not critique the claims of the authors, other than to suggest that the interpretations of the findings are far more complex than has been suggested. Importantly, the presence of the absence leaves a trace of that which is not visible, and that which is not visible can be named as the hidden population of drug users.

However, no one really knows what this population is like. Because the defining characteristic of the population is that the population is hidden, reliable estimates of the population cannot even be made. Superficially, the term refers to a "subset of the general population whose membership is *not readily distinguished or enumerated* based on existing knowledge and/or sampling capabilities."[5] This population has also become an important focus for HIV prevention strategies. Because they are "unreachable" they are apparently not in contact with public-health strategies, and thus are an "at risk" population.[6] Those who do not participate in public-health initiatives are not only "at risk" but also constitute risk for the rest of the community. With the prospect of an unknown, uncontrolled, and unreachable population of drug users, public health has embarked on a campaign of trying to reach the unreached and target the hidden. The unknown Other of the normative productive body in this moment of an ascendant "risk" society,[7] may not therefore be the addict, but the hidden population of addicts.

But targeting the hidden is quite a task. The very fact they are hidden precludes knowing who and what they are. Once information is obtained about a drug user, that user no longer can be said to be part of a hidden population. By definition, the population *in absentia* carries no identity and no voice. So how could this hidden population be a population in a positivist sense. The most compelling and identifiable feature is the presence of its absence.

"HIDDEN POPULATIONS" AS DISCURSIVE PRACTICE

I have chosen to use Foucault's gaze of power as an analytic strategy to help illustrate the process through which public health visualizes drug users, and subsequently constructs the "hidden population." The speaking gaze produces a language for that which was not visible. Through naming, the wholly expressible becomes wholly visible,[8] and through the production of the object of power, the augmentation of regulatory scientific regimes is guaranteed.[9] By definition however, total description is never achievable; it is an "ever-withdrawing horizon; it is much more the dream of a thought than a basic conceptual structure."[10]

Cheek and Rudge[11] explored the gaze within a metaphoric "examination" where the examination of clients by experts is a highly ritualized utilization of power. I will use the metaphor of the examination, and the rituals and rhetorics of examination to structure the analysis.

It would also be prudent of me at this stage to be clear about what aspects of the gaze I will be drawing on. The scopic regime, central to Foucault, had a number of characteristics, of which I am interested in the following:

- the gaze observes and constructs an epistemic field, constituted as much visually as it is linguistically.

- the transformation by a speaking gaze of that which was once hidden into visible truths.

- Martin Jay's reading of Foucault, namely, that perhaps for Foucault seeing was "an art of trying to see what is unthought in our seeing, and to open as yet unseen ways of seeing."[12]

- Foucault's rereading of the sites of juridical power relations as possible heterotopic sites.[13]

I will be synchronic in method and will not attempt a kind of genealogy. At other points, I will depart from Foucault's gaze into a space that I believe is parallel to the scopic regime of public health. To discuss this space I will draw on the work of Michel de Certeau and James Scott[14] to discuss some drug-using practices of everyday life, and the problematics of a totalizing gaze for understanding what the drug addict *in absentia* does when it's not being enumerated by public institutions.

RITUALS OF EXAMINATION

I will focus on two of the most commonly used types of research, or rituals of examination, used in studies of hidden populations of illicit drug users: drug indicator research and ethnographic research.

Drug Indicator Research. Drug indicator research, as its name suggests uses "secondary indicators" that refer implicitly to illicit drug use. Often the indicators include law enforcement data, arrests and seizures, drug treatment admissions, early warning networks, coroners' reports, urine drug-screen analysis, or prescription tracking systems.

Drug indicators are often used as the final arbiter of visibility. If you have been enumerated, you are visible. The scientific and medical terminology used to describe the known, privileges visual evidence gained from observations. An example of the technology of enumeration can be found in the use of the "capture-recapture" technique. The "capture-recapture" technique, initially used in ecological studies, has been a primary method of "enumerating" hidden populations. As described by Sudman in a 1988 article from the journal *Science:*

> The technique requires obtaining two or more independent *observations* on the same population. Most commonly for human populations at least one observation is based on a complete enumeration.[15]

The language of "capture-recapture" is particularly poignant. If capturing and recaptufing human populations is in effect, to enumerate members of the population, then the power of the gaze to enumerate is clearly meant to control the object of the gaze. Without a complete enumeration, the utility of the capture-recapture is severely undermined. In this sense, the very presence of an uncalculable population threatens the capacity of the gaze to obtain the evidence necessary for population estimates. The presence of the incalculable, however, also makes possible the project of capture-recapture, through the necessity for enumerating the hidden.

The attribute of not being enumerated is as much a function of how "hidden" a person is, as it is a function of the indicator, and the costs involved with constructing the indicator.[16] If the expense required to gain access to the population is high, there will often be a reduced willingness to sample that population. Thus, the deployment of the power of the gaze, as a definer of what is a hidden population, is often governed by the economics of funding and the political imperatives of the time. Sudman clarifies this point:

> Some may be surprised by the attention that has been paid to costs in this paper, but efficient use of scarce resources is at the heart of all sampling techniques and is critical for rare populations.[17]

An indicator is therefore not simply an indicator of drug use. Drug indicators more directly reflect the drug policies of the time. As a European Union scientific committee on hidden populations in 1994 suggested:

What is most known, therefore, is the nature and number of negative consequences of drug use. In most countries these data are used as the only indicators of the size and magnitude of drug use. These figures appear to represent society's reaction to the drug problem more than anything else.

The gaze of power declares what is seen and what is hidden by virtue of what are the most cost effective and productive indices available in order to validate and justify the drug policies of the time.

Ethnographic Research. The next ritual of examination—ethnographic research—is one that I am directly engaged in as a public-health researcher. Public-health ethnographies of illicit drug use in hidden populations are, more often than not, realist treatises with many of the narrative devices characteristic of the realist genre. I want to explore a suggestion that the realist ethnographic project acts, in an extension of Foucault's metaphor, as the speaking gaze. The speaking gaze provides a language for that which is not visible but then, through observing and narrating, the hidden becomes articulable and then visible. In this sense the unobtrusive observer becomes instrumental in the actuarial project of public health. Ethnography provides the contextual information so necessary for the formation of human behavior categories.[18] Ethnographic research had a role in establishing different HIV risk group categories such as gay, bisexual, and MSMs (Men who have Sex with Men). Ethnography is a technology of risk calculation and a deployment of power.

The ritual of ethnographic examination is, however, quite specific. Not any sort of ethnography is suitable. For an ethnography to have credibility and authenticity in this field, certain narrative devices and guidelines should be followed. The main object of the realist ethnography is to create a reading position such that the tale presents an accurate and believable account of a social reality. Even in recent ethnographic studies of illicit drug use, the claim for authenticity using an unproblematized voice of the other abounds:

> *From a drug user's perspective,* however, being caught with a syringe is a serious matter . . .

and

> *As they explained it,* having violations for paraphernalia on their record would make it difficult to convince a judge of their innocence . . .[19]

Realist ethnographic conventions provide reassurance to the reader that the language of the speaking gaze is familiar and can be trusted. Authenticity in realist ethnographic studies is established through the demonstration of a close proximity of the researcher to the Other. This can be performed in a number of ways: using the codified language of the subject, letting the subject speak for itself through the use of tape recordings or through the demonstration of intimate knowledges of previously hidden behaviors. More recently, the use of "indigenous interviewers" has become in vogue to establish credibility and access to the hidden Other:

> In their study of crack users in New York, the authors noted that the use of indigenous interviewers, who had themselves been drug users, increased the likelihood of *valid answers.*

This enhanced "validity" of responses was supplemented by better "access":

> Coming from *the inside,* so to speak, appears to make it easier for indigenous casual interviewers to contact other networks of drug users than it would for other research workers.[20]

The inherent collapse of logic in the argument that a close proximity to a hidden and unknown Other can be ratified through a positivist epistemology, does not appear in this type of ethnography.

THE RHETORIC OF EXAMINATION

Different rhetorics sustain the metaphoric examination of hidden populations of illicit drug users. The rationale for examining must be understood, believed, and validated in different ways for different audiences. Three groups I believe are central to the hidden populations project: those who fund the examinations, those who examine, and those who are examined.

Firstly, the rhetoric that sustains funding for the gaze of power is a rhetoric of "productivity." Productivity in the public-health arena centers on the ability to plan the use of scarce public-health resources effectively. This theme appears consistently in the literature, and is exemplified by the following:

> In order to plan facilities in agreement with needs and to evaluate effects of general intervention strategies, an effective drug use intervention policy requires reliable estimates of the *sizes* of drug-using populations.[21]

There is, however, a constant problem because the estimates are invariably undermined by the presence of the unknown absence, that which cannot by definition be described. Thus, the quest to know the size of "at risk" populations, is an interminable one, ghosted by the hidden. The rhetoric focuses, however, not on the impossibility of gaining an accurate estimate but on the need for more accurate estimates. This rhetoric based on an absent object is not unfamiliar to this audience. Risk itself, the foundation of modern public-health discourse, is in its essence an absence that constitutes a noncontact with the experience of the visible world.[22]

The second audience for which a rhetoric of examination exists is that of the examiners. For researchers there must be a language that justifies participation in the gaze. The most potent rhetoric of examination is the rhetoric of "discovery" and the application of their findings for the good of public health. Indeed van de Goor et al. noted that:

> It is intriguing that despite a continuous development of approaches
> and research methods applied in the drug use field, important aspects
> of the drug problem remain unclear.[23]

The irony of this observation from Europe's most respected forum on hidden population research should not be taken too lightly. This observation reveals a fundamental tension within the narrative of discovery characteristic of late modernity's legitimation narratives that serve to underwrite hidden population research in the face of flagging results.[24] The hidden populations of drug users continue to evade surveillance even after an intensification of public-health strategies to disclose and monitor them.

The third audience for which a rhetoric of examination exists is the hidden populations of illicit drug users. The most common rhetoric of examination posited to users is "We want to hear your side of the story." An excerpt of an information sheet to hallucinogen users in a recent ethnographic study demonstrates this:

> There was a lot of research done on hallucinogen use in the 1970s but
> very little has been done since then. We feel things have changed, and
> the best way to understand its use now is to ask the people who use it.[25]

Do users benefit from coming under the gaze of power? In the case of understanding safe needle use and restricting the spread of HIV, there would be no doubt that the community benefits from research that identifies unsafe practices and works with the illicit drug-using community to alter those behaviors.

Ruptures and Breaks in the Scopic. Martin Jay briefly notes in his "Downcast Eyes" that Foucault while most renowned for positing a monolithic gaze, also looked for absences, ruptures, and episternic breaks. These heterotopias constitute the space for that which elude or simply fall outside the scopic regimes of institutions. Similarly, I propose that resistance to the gaze can be understood in a range of practices that upset the gaze. It is to this space that I wish to devote my attention in the next section of the chapter.

For Researchers. For ethnographers, alternative research strategies that substantially alter the terms of knowledge production potentially allow for ruptures and breaks in the field of the gaze. For example, if ethnographers moved away from realist ethnographic portrayals and gave space to other forms of writing and knowing, different epistemic spaces may emerge. Researchers could continue to participate in the gaze, and thus be initiates to the closed world of words, but on altered terms. No longer providing an unproblematized language for the gaze. Bourgois[26] attempts this in his recent work on crack use in East Harlem. His reflexivity is limited to a few pages discussing the need to be reflexive and then moves to a critique of bourgeois poststructuralist political inaction. The realist ethnographer in this sense has claimed epistemic space among the academy, but clings to metaphors of groundedness and organicism for authenticity:

> Ethnographers usually live in the communities they study, and they establish long-term, *organic relationships* with the people they write about. In other words, in order to collect "accurate data," ethnographers violate the canons of positivist research; we become intimately involved with the people we study.[27]

He then states later:

> . . . postmodern debates titillate alienated, suburbanised intellectuals; they are completely out of touch with the urgent social crises of the inner-city unemployed. Scholarly self-reflection often degenerates into narcissistic celebrations of privilege.[28]

This call to arms for "intimate" ethnography exhumes the naive realism of 1950s sociology. Being an initiate into the closed world of words can perhaps allow researchers a greater capacity to alter the rhetorics of examination. For example, many researchers discontinued the use of the confessional tale in ethnographic accounts[29] after van Maanen's exposure of this realist convention.

AGENCY OF THE HIDDEN POPULATIONS
AND RESISTANCE TO EXAMINATION

Agency and resistance are problematic terms when used in the context of Foucault's gaze of power and the notion of hiddenness. Traces of the rational actor appear whenever the words "agency" and "resistance" are invoked. I do not plan to invoke the rational actor of public health[30] but rather the reflexive subject of late modernity.[31]

Public health, and in particular health promotion, uses a model of the rational unified self that consciously makes reasoned decisions about daily conduct and care of the self.[32] For example, when discussing how to change behavioral norms among the intravenous drug using community, Friedman poses the question of how to enforce new norms:

> There will be resistance to new norms. Here, the question to ask is how this resistance can be broken down. In part, simply by mobilising as much of the scene as possible behind the new norms and *letting the power of example and arguments sway others*. . . . In addition communication and watchfulness are needed. When someone learns that a peer group or network is *disobeying the norms,* friendly but *firm social pressure should be brought to bear*.[33]

Friedman clearly proposes a disseminated form of regulation that draws on not only institutional "power of example and argument" but also on a "peer group" or "network" that can exert firm social pressure. This extended form of governmentality is reminiscent of Rose's[34] theorizing of decentralised regulation through the use of community and outreach groups.

One form of agency for drug users is not to participate in research and public-health initiatives, and thus not to become subject to the gaze of power. This resistance may, however, have negative consequences that may not be in the best interests of either illicit drug users or public health. For example, the provision of needle and syringe exchange facilities, which have had a significant role to play in AIDS prevention relies heavily on a dialogue between intravenous drug users and public-health institutions.[35] A breakdown in the communication between these two groups may endanger the success of such initiatives. Alternatively, participation in these community-based interventions necessarily involves placing oneself as subject to the gaze. I do not wish to invoke a vision of people attempting to be outside discourse; however, I believe there is a range of options as to how one appears in discourse. In this case, there is an option for those subject to the gaze of power to engage in ethnographic refusal.

A second alternative is for illicit drug users to participate in the gaze of power but with altered terms of relation. Lee and Ackerman[36] reported on the growing awareness of research subjects, of the mechanisms of knowledge production and their capacity to control the ethnographic representation of their experiences, resulting in people filing for defamation if the ethnographic representation has not been acceptable to them.

All this, of course, presumes some scopic reciprocity between the institution and the subjects of the research. By definition, there is no reciprocal Other that can glance back at public health and question the activities of the gaze. The drug addict *in absentia* cannot directly engage in a reciprocal gaze. I wish to spend the rest of the chapter discussing the problematic of that which perhaps falls outside the scopic regime, which constitutes the hidden population.

OUTSIDE THE SCOPIC REGIME

One such example I wish to describe is a reading of a particular piece of public literature from the Rave/nightclub scene in Melbourne. The rave scene has an underground image as a place to use drugs; in particular, to use ecstasy, amphetamines, and LSD. In reference to James Scott, I wish to highlight a public performance of a hidden transcript in order to depict some discursive practices of this population of hidden drug users. These illustrations will suggest, as de Certeau has suggested, that the everyday has a certain strangeness that does not wholly surface, and whose surface itself outlines against the visible and remains indefinitely Other.[37]

In the flier for the Rave party called "Solid" held in Melbourrie some 15 months ago, focus your attention to the icon located at the upper left region of this advertisement. The word is THURSTEE, which is the logo of a radio DJ who was to play at the venue. One of the Es in THURSTEE has been replaced by a circle with a dove insignia in its center. The dove sign is an icon for a particular type of Ecstasy.

The Dove. It is not that a dove sign means one thing that is the most important feature of the dove icon. The dove can mean many things; the ambiguity and multiplicity of readings gives the sign a high symbolic capital in this social world. The chain of semiosis that sustains different readings such that at one point the sign is an icon for a type of ecstasy tablet, then an arbitrary symbol for a type of drug or an indexical sign pointing to a location of a type of music, and an intimate knowledge of the experience of raving, sustain the alternative and clandestine image of the Rave scene as something special, different, and distinguishable from the mainstream music and entertainment industry.

The difficulty in locating what a Rave can signify, through a proliferation of signs, a number of authors in Steve Redhead's book *Rave Off* have

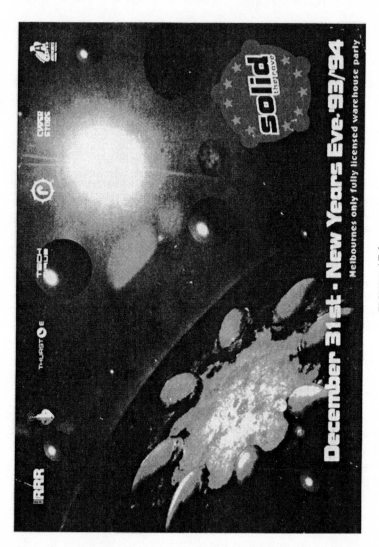

FIGURE 17.3
Solid

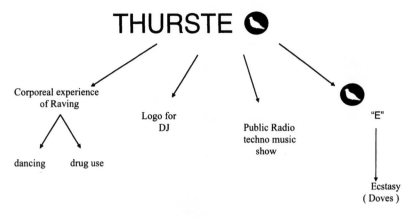

FIGURE 17.4
The Dove

interpreted as a deliberate strategy by Ravers to cause the disappearance of the signified from sight, and is thus a form of resistance and agency. I wish to draw on a second sign from the scene to explore this argument.

It is *both* the slippage between readings *and* the attempts to fix subject positions that enables certain readings to exist. I do not believe that Ravers disappear in an ecstasy of communication as Redhead would have us believe. The subject position of the Raver in itself is portrayed in the social world, as seen in this second advertisement for Euphemism.

Again, there is the highlighted location of an "E" for ecstasy in the shop name at the base of the advertisement. But importantly, the woman, as subject, is produced in a particular way. She is marked by the three elements—hair, fashion, and music. Redhead's truly hidden Raver who defies signification is as much a fiction as the determinacy they wish to undermine. She is an emblem for the store. She is marked as a Raver, when a rhetoric claims that the Raver is characterized by the impossibility of a Raver to be marked.

The subject is produced in a specific way and the form of the reading position being created is one that could almost be read as a performative. The store name *is* what the store names itself to be, a euphemism. The woman Raver depicted also, is named as a euphemism for what a Raver is meant to be. In the terms of James Scott, the euphemism is a form of hidden transcript, a scriptual space that evades domination. The speech act self-consciously says this is a euphemism, an overcoding in a self-conscious public performance of a hidden transcript, that perhaps Scott would not have anticipated.

FIGURE 17.5
Euphemism

In Ravers' naming the tactic for what it is, there is no loss of political clout. The overcoding simply adds layers to an already complex epistemic field. The linguist Halliday categorized such reversals, negations, and over-codings performed by marginal groups as characteristic of antilanguages. Drawing on a vision of Baudrillard who posited a late capitalist world in which the self is lost in an unculture of the hyperreal, resulting in a the situation where even "the protagonist of the secret would not know how to betray the secret,"[38] to propose a discrete structure such as an antilanguage would be difficult to sustain. It certainly looks, however, as though some elements of this discursive practice of incorporating drug references into public texts could be understood in this way. The feature of this discourse is that the language is transformed to discuss that which is difficult to discuss in a public forum, the language creates a polyphony of counterdiscourse, codified and self-consciously ambiguous. An essential element of the language of the Rave social world is the language of hidden illegal drug use.

How does public health cope with this social world. It is a hidden population. Ethnographers have been sent into this social world over the past three years in Australia to try and provide a language to enumerate this population. This social world, however, is not easily visualized, marked and enumerated as has been done in past rituals of examination. The constant slippage, fragmentation, and self-conscious play that characterizes the Rave scene poses quite a difficulty for public health and law enforcement. Few estimates have been made of how many people go to Raves and what quantities of illegal drugs are consumed. They are for the time being the drug users *in absentia*.

CONCLUSION

The final question concerns a problematic of what to do with an analysis that posits two objects: a regulatory discursive practice that constitutes an unattainable hidden Other, and a social drug-using practice that continually avoids examination. Both discourses speed away on independent trajectories that seem unlikely to meet, except in death or tragedy. I can only suggest that the institution of public health is on a never-ending quest to better the health of the community and will waste a great deal of public money if they continue with policies based on a hidden population they have produced through the presence of an absence.

Michel de Certeau posited in *The Practice of Everyday Life* that

> . . . the powers in our developed societies have at their disposal rather subtle and close-knit procedure for the control of all social networks: these are the administrative and "panoptic " systems of the police, the schools, health services, security, etc. But they are slowly losing all credibility. They have more power and less authority.[39]

This loss of authority, I feel public health has yet to fully experience.

I would like to conclude with a road map that gave directions to a Rave that was held in late 1994, in the mountains an hour outside of Melbourne. This map was distributed in only a couple of specialist

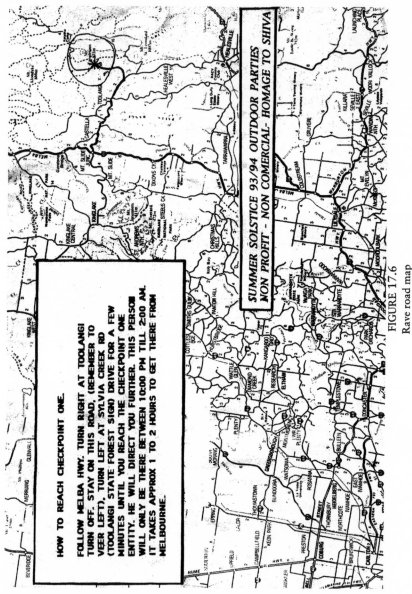

FIGURE 17.6
Rave road map

record stores and is perhaps an indication firstly, of the lengths to which people will I go to have good time, but also the impossibility of a totalizing gaze. In reference to Merleau-Ponty, the gaze envelops and produces that of which it speaks but cannot control the intimate reflections it creates.

At issue is perhaps not whether public health can access this population, for it imbues this "population" with a positivist presence. It is perhaps the problematic of public health to observe this group through their lens based on enumeration and the very nature of the practice of raving and the practice of illegal drug use. Even with the directions and the language of ravers literally mapped out, the hidden drug addict will continue to evade public health by the very fact of the scopic relationship between public health and its drug addict *in absentia.*

NOTES

1. M. Merleau-Ponty, *The Visible and the Invisible,* translated by Alphonso Lingis (Evanston: Northwestern University Press, 1968), p. 131.

2. The term "strategy" is used in the sense described by de Certeau, *The practice of everyday life* (Berkeley: University of California Press, 1984), in his discussion of statistics. A strategy is the "calculus of force relations which becomes possible when a subject of will and power (a proprietor, an enterprise, a city, a scientific institution) can be isolated from an environment." A strategy will conceal beneath objective calculations the connections between power and the institutions from which the strategy emerges. Statistical inquiry isolates and decontextualizes the subject and the inquirer, and consequently shrouds the deployment of power in the inquiry. M. de Certeau, op. cit., pp. xviii–xix.

3. E. Y. Lambert and W. W. Weibel, eds., "Introduction" in *The Collection and Interpretation of Data from Hidden Populations,* NIDA Monograph 98, National Institute on Drug Abuse, Maryland, p. 1.

4. See F. Ewald, "Insurance and Risk," in G. Burchill et al., eds., *The Foucault Effect: Studies in Governmentality* (Chicago: University of Chicago Press, 1991), pp. 197–210.

5. See W. W. Weibel, "Identifying and Gaining Access to Hidden Populations," in E. Y. Lambert, ed., *The Collection and Interpretation of Data from Hidden Populations,* NIDA Research Monograph 98, National Institute on Drug Abuse, Maryland, 1990.

6. See R. Power et al., "Drug Injecting, AIDS and Risk Behavior: Potential for Change and Intervention Strategies," *British Journal of Addiction,* 83:649–654.

7. See U. Beck, *Risk Society: Towards a New Modernity* (London: Sage, 1992).

8. M. Foucault, *The Birth of the Clinic: An Archaelogy of the Human Sciences* (New York: Vintage, 1973), p. 115.

9. J. Butler, "Sexual Inversions," in J. Caputo and M. Yount, eds., *Foucault and the Critique of Institutions* (University Park, PA: Pennsylvania State University Press, 1993), p. 82.

10. M. Foucault, op. cit., *The Birth of the Clinic*, p. 115.

11. See J. Cheek and T. Rudge, "The Power of Normalization: Foucauldian Perspectives on Contemporary Healthcare Practices," *Australian Journal of Social Issues*, 28(4): 27/1–284, 1993.

12. Jay observes a quiet hope that beyond the dangers of panopticism Foucault may have been attempting to open up other ways of seeing; see his *Downcast Eyes: The Denigration of Vision in Twentieth-Century French Thought* (Berkeley: University of California Press, 1984), p. 414. This, of course, runs contrary to other readings of Foucault, which propose that his emphasis on the hegemony of the eye resulted in a blindspot to micropractices (ibid., p. 16).

13. In *The Order of Things* (p. xviii) Foucault compares the security of utopias in language to the disturbing work of heterotopias: "Heterotopias are disturbing, probably because they secretly undermine language, because they make it impossible to name this *and* that, because they shatter or tangle common names, because they destroy syntax in advance, and not only syntax with which we construct sentences but also that less apparent syntax which causes words and things to "hold together.". . . [H]eterotopias dessicate speech, stop words in their tracks, contest the very possibility of grammar at its source; they dissolve our myths and sterilize the lyricism of our sentences." The 1986 translation of a 1967 lecture, published in *Diacritics* divides the dimensions of heterotopias into six principles. In short, the heterotopia is a real space (as opposed to the utopia that is not a real space), which enables virtual utopic spaces to manifest. The prime example being the mirror which "makes this place that I occupy at the moment when I look at myself in the glass at once absolutely real, connected with all the space that surrounds it, and absolutely unreal, since in order to be perceived it has to pass through this virtual point which is over there." The mirror acts as a sort of counteraction on the position that is occupied. Consistent across these two types of heterotopia is an emphasis on the disjunctive and indeterminacy of the heterotopia.

14. See Michel de Certeau, op. cit.; and J. C. Scott, *Domination and the Arts of Resistance: Hidden Transcripts* (New Haven: Yale University Press, 1990).

15. See S. Sudman et al., "Sampling Race and Elusive Populations," *Science*, 240 (485S), pp. 991–996, 1988.

16. Ibid., p. 991.

17. Ibid., p. 992.

18. See R. Power and S. Harkinson, "Accessing Hidden Populations: The Use of Indigenous Interviewers," in P. Aggleton et al., eds., *AIDS: Facing the Second Decade* (London: The Falmer Press, 1993), pp. 109–118.

19. See S. K. Koester, "Copping, Running, and Paraphenernalia Laws: Contextual Variables and Needle Risk Behavior Among Injection Drug Users in Denver," *Human Organization* 53: 287–295, 1994.

20. Power and Harkinson, op. cit., pp. 113–114.

21. D. J. Korf et al., "Estimating the Number of Heroin Users: A Review of Methods and Empirical Findings from the Netherlands," *The International Journal of Addictions,* 29: 1393–1417.

22. In *Domination and the Arts of Resistance,* Scott separates hidden and public transcripts. He problematizes this dichotomy, however, through locating the performance of those transcripts within contingent power relations: "The hidden transcript is a social product and hence a result of power relations among subordinates. Second, like folk culture, the hidden transcript has no reality as pure thought; it exists only to the extent it is practiced, articulated, enacted and disseminated within these offstage social sites" (p. 119). In this sense, I am interested in how hiddenness is performed within the particular, rather than (as Scott has done) in the general sense.

23. L. A. M. van de Goor et al., "Research Methods for Drug Use in Hidden Populations: Summary Report of a European Invited Expert Meeting," *Journal of Psychoactive Drugs* 26: 33–40, 1994.

24. It is the utter familiarity of public-health funding agencies with invisible entities (such as risk) that structure the public-health discourse through actuarial processes that leads me to believe that an eternally hidden Other is entirely acceptable for this audience. Beck (Risk Society) goes further to suggest that a feature of late modernity is the internalization of risk such that the evaluation of the visible world is constituted through the presence of a second invisible world of risk. The doubletake on the visible world is individualized to the extent that those who simply experience the world without taking stock of the risks, inherent (yet invisible) in their activities, are "not only naive but they also misunderstand the hazards that threaten them and thus expose themselves to such hazards with no protection. . . . [T]heir invisibility [i.e., the actual hazards] is no proof of their nonexistence; instead, since their reality takes place in the realm of the invisible anyway, it gives their suspected mischief almost unlimited space" (p. 73). According to Lyotard's *The Postmodern Condition: A Report on Knowledge* (Minneapolis: University of Minnesota Press, 1984), p. 32: The legitimation narrative makes recourse to metaphysical entities such as for the good of "humanity as the hero of liberty" and other metadiscourses for the continued commitment of resources to scientific enquiry.

25. See J. L. Fitzgerald and M. H. Hamilton, *An Exploratory Study of Hallucinogen Users in Melbourne,* Report to the Drug Rehabilitation and Research Fund, Melbourne, 1994.

26. See P. Bourgois, *In Search of Respect: Selling Crack in El Barrio* (New York: Cambridge University Press, 1995).

27. Ibid., p. 13.

28. Ibid., p. 14.

29. See J. Van Maanen, *Tales of the Field: On Writing Ethnology* (Chicago: University of Chicago Press, 1988).

30. See D. Lupton, *The Imperative of Health: Public Health and the Regulated Body* (London: Sage, 1995).

31. See S. Lash and J. Urry, *Economies of Signs and Space* (London: Sage, 1994), pp. 31–59.

32. See D. Lupton, op. cit., 1995.

33. S. R. Friedman, "Going Beyond Education to Mobilising Subcultural Change," *International Journal of Drug Policy,* 4: 92, 1993.

34. See N. Rose, "The Death of the Social? Refiguring the Territory of Government." Paper Presented to the History of the Present Seminar, University of London, 1996.

35. See M. Singer et al., "Needle Access as an AIDS Prevention Strategy for IV Drug Users: A Research Perspective," *Human Organization,* 50: 142–152, 1991; and R. S. Broadhead and D. D. Heckathorn, "AIDS Prevention Outreach Among Injection Drug Users: Agency Problems and New Approaches," *Social Problem* 41: 473–495, 1994.

36. See R. L. M. Lee and S. E. Ackerman, "Farewell to Ethnology? Global Embourgeoisement and the Disprivileging of the Narrative," *Critique of Anthropology,* 14: 339–354, 1994.

37. M. de Certeau, op. cit., p. 93.

38. See A. Melechi, "The Ecstasy of Disappearance," in *Rave Off* (London: Ashgate Publishing, 1993), pp. 29–40.

39. M. de Certeau, op. cit., p. 40.

CONTRIBUTORS

ANNA ALEXANDER has published in the areas of philosophy and cultural studies. She teaches courses in sexuality, feminist ethics, and feminist perspectives on health at the Simone de Beauvoir Institute in Montréal, and is currently working on a book on addiction entitled *Freud's Pharmacy: Sexuality and Narcotic Desire*. Her articles have appeared in (among others) *Philosophy Today, Hypatia,* and in the *Simone de Beauvoir Institute Review.*

DAVID B. ALLISON is Professor of Philosophy at the State University of New York at Stony Brook. He has published in the areas of history of philosophy, psychoanalysis, and modern European Philosophy. He is the editor of numerous books in philosophy and criticism, including *The New Nietzsche*. His most recent work is *Reading The New Nietzsche* (2001).

DAVID L. CLARK is Associate Professor in the Department of English, McMaster University, and was Visiting Professor at the Centre for the Study of Theory and Criticism at the University of Western Ontario. He is co-editor of *New Romanticism: Theory and Critical Practice* and *Intersections: Nineteenth Century Philosophy and Contemporary Theory*. His most recent publications include: "On Being the Last Kantian in Nazi Germany: Dwelling with Animals After Levinas," "Animal Acts: Configuring the Human in Western History," "God Without Ground: Marion, Schelling," and (with Catherine Myser) "'Fixing' Katie and Eilish: Medical Documentaries and the Subjection of Conjoined Twins."

ALINA CLEJ is Associate Professor of French and Comparative Literature at the University of Michigan, Ann Arbor. She is author of *A Genealogy of the Modern Self: Thomas De Quincey and the Intoxication of Writing*

(1995) and is currently completing a study on addiction and memory in nineteenth-century France. This book is entitled *Phantom Pain and Literary Memory: Remembering the Past in Nineteenth-Century French Literature*.

JACQUES DERRIDA is perhaps the best known philosopher and critical theorist at work today. He has taught at the Ecole des hautes études en sciences sociales and the Collège internationale du philosophie, and at several universities in the United States, including Yale and Johns Hopkins. His intellectual production has been enormous, and his books, translated into many languages, range from early works critical of phenomenology, like *Speech and Phenomena* (1973), to later ones involving such diverse subjects as psychoanalysis, art, addiction, and literature.

JON ELSTER is Robert K. Merton Professor of Social Science at Columbia University and the author of numerous books, including *Alchemies of the Mind: Rationality and the Emotions, Making Sense of Marx*, and *Political Psychology*.

JOHN FITZGERALD is completing a Ph.D. in the Department of English at Monash University, Australia. It is a supplement to his first Ph.D., which was on the pharmacology of ecstasy. He is currently in the Department of Criminology at the University of Melbourne doing research on visibility, spatiality, and heroin use.

LORRAINE GREAVES is a sociologist, writer, educator, and activist on women's health issues, particularly women's smoking and violence against women. She is the director of the Centre of Excellence for Women's Health at B.C. Women's Hospital in Vancouver, British Columbia. Her works include the prize-winning book *Smoke Screen: Women's Smoking and Social Control* (1996), and *Mixed Messages: Women, Tobacco and Media* (1996). She has co-authored *Dome of Silence: Sexual Harassment and Abuse in Sport* (1998).

FÉLIX GUATTARI was a major figure in the psychoanalytic movement in France. He studied with Jacques Lacan and became an analyst member of the Freudian School of Paris in 1969. He was often associated with alternative movements in psychiatry, where he worked with such important figures as David Cooper and R.D. Laing. His own works include *Psychanalyse et transversalité, La Révolution moléculaire (Molecular Revolution)* and *L'Inconscient machinque*. His very important collaborations with Gilles Deleuze include *Anti-Oedipus* and *A Thousand Plateaus*. He died in 1992.

MICHAEL ISRAEL is an Assistant Professor of English Language at the University of Maryland, College Park. His research and teaching interests focus on the relation between grammar and cognition in literature and everyday language. Recent publications include work on language acquisition, language change, lexical semantics, construction grammar, and the cognitive and functional bases of linguistic structure.

ALPHONSO LINGIS is Professor Emeritus of Philosophy at Pennsylvania State University. He has published dozens of articles in the fields of contemporary European philosophy, psychoanalysis, literary theory, philosophical anthropology, among others. Among his many books are *Abuses* (1994), *Foreign Bodies* (1994), *Deathbound Subjectivity* (1989), and *Libido: The French Existential Theories* (1986).

ZVI LOTHANE, M.D. is a psychiatrist and psychoanalyst, who also teaches at Mt. Sinai Medical Center. He has published numerous articles in the fields of history of psychoanalysis and psychiatry, with a particular emphasis on the case and figure of Daniel Paul Schreber. His work on Schreber culminated in a monumental volume entitled *In Defense of Schreber: Soul Murder and Psychiatry* (1992). His most recent projects include "The Deal With the Devil to 'Save' Psychoanalysis in Nazi Germany" (1998) and a forthcoming book on Sabina Spielrein.

ELISSA MARDER is Associate Professor of French and Comparative Literature at Emory University. She has published articles in *Diacritics, Camera Obscura, Hypatia, Yale French Studies,* and *Autrement.* She is currently completing a book entitled *Dead Time: Temporal Disorders in the Wake of Modernity.*

JEFFREY T. NEALON is Professor of English at Penn State University. He is author of *Alterity Politics: Ethics and Performative Subjectivity* (1998) and *Double Reading: Postmodernism after Deconstruction* (1993). In addition, he is co-editor of *Rethinking the Frankfurt School: Alternative Legacies of Cultural Critique* (2002).

MARK S. ROBERTS teaches philosophy at the State University of New York at Stony Brook. He has published numerous articles in the fields of continental philosophy, aesthetics, psychoanalysis, and media theory and has edited seven books in philosophy, cultural studies, and psychoanalytic theory. He has recently published a book (with David B. Allison), *Disordered Mother or Disordered Diagnosis?* (1998), critical of the bizarre psychiatric "disorder," Münchausen by Proxy Syndrome.

GARY SHAPIRO is Tucker-Boatwright Professor in the Humanities and Professor of Philosophy at the University of Richmond; his books include *Nietzschean Narratives* (1989), *Alcyone: Nietzsche on Gifts, Noise, and Women* (1991), and *Earthwards: Robert Smithson and Art After Babel (1995).*

ALLEN S. WEISS has most recently published *Perverse Desire and the Ambiguous Icon* (1994); *Mirrors of Infinity: The French Formal Garden and 17th Century Metaphysics* (1995); *Phantasmatic Radio* (1995); *Unnatural Horizons: Paradox and Contradiction in Landscape Architecture* (1998); and *Taste, Nostalgia* (1997). He is Professor of Performance Studies and Cinema Studies at New York University.

BRUCE WILSHIRE is Professor of Philosophy at Rutgers University. He has published numerous works in the field of phenomenology and existential philosophy, and has focused recently on the work of William James and John Dewey. His most recent publications are *Wild Hunger: The Primal Roots of Modern Addiction* (1998), and *The Primal Roots of American Philosophy* (2000).

INDEX

addict, the: anguish, in constant state of, 199; and assemblages of enunciation, 202–203; both free and sick, 207; collective fantasy of, 203; and desire, 207; and economic machine, 199; entrapment of, 199; filthy bum, 203; and freedom to care for self, 204; ghettoized, 199; in Levinas, 181; and pleasure, 207; and police control, 204; and responsibility, 203; as scapegoat, 207; as someone who does nothing, 181; tragic condition of, 204; vilified and eclipsed, 5. *See also* addicts; parasitism

addict-writer, the: and artificial paradise, 25–26; and artists, 33; and the city, 25 (*see also* Benjamin's hashish passages); and coffee and cigarettes, French cult of, 34; as cut off, 25; and drugs as writing, 24; and end of addiction, 25; as escapee, 25–26; and experimentation with drugs, 33; and graceful inspiration, 29; as man or woman of the simulacrum, 25–26 (*see also* Plato); productive receptivity of, 29; productivity, social value of, 26; and question of truth, 25; Sartre, 34; and the oeuvre, 30; and thinkers, 33; and trances of writing, 34; Valéry, 35. *See also* writing as drug; writing on drugs

addicted body, the, xii; addiction, extended paradigm of, 2; and Ronell, xii; space of, 2; and structure of the will, 2. *See also* narcotic desire

addiction: auto-addiction, 205; as concept, 20; and diction, 20; and drugs as institutional object, 205; institutional/instituted definition of, 20; leadership-

addiction, 205; as modern plague, 42; sports-addiction, 205; tele-addiction, 205; as transitional object, 205. *See also* drug addiction; gambling addiction; media addiction

addiction, altered treatment of, 221–222. *See also* coca

addiction and demonic possession, 300–303; and breakdown, of regenerative rituals, 300; —, of integrity of body-self, 300; and drug-substance, as the other, 301; —, as *the not-me*, 301; and ecstatic body, 301; trance and repetition, 297; and loss of self, 299. *See also* addiction and possession; drugs and demonic possession; healing community; *jouissance*

addiction, gambling. *See* gambling addiction

addiction, media. *See* media addiction

addiction and modernity, 2–5; addiction, and art, 3; —, and Continental philosophy, xi; —, creative value of, 3; —, disciplinary rhetorics of, 3; —, and discourses of digression and dissent, 3; —, disease of modernity, 5; —, and drug abuse, 15; —, and drug dependency, 15; —, as enigma, 4; —, ethical value, loaded with, 2; —, as experimental field, 4; —, and explanatory frameworks, 15; —, extended paradigm of, 2; —, in modern era, visionary excesses of, 3; —, in modern literature, 3; —, as incorporation of a foreign substance, 4; —, modern referent of, 3; —, nineteenth century isolation, 2; —, nominalist/conceptualist views of, 4; —,

202; mechanism of, 200; as microfascist, 203; as mode of expression, 202 (*see also* drug culture); as molecular assemblages of desire, 203; as molecular revolution, 203; mythology of, 201, 202; not chemical molecules, 203; as production of culture, 202 (*see also* drug culture); and repressive judiciary intrusion, 200; and repressive police intrusion, 200; and rock groups, 201; and scientific methodology, 200; and socialist societies, 203; and solitude, 202; and Stalinism, 203; and subjective individuation, 202; as system of blockage, 201; and taste for disaster, 202

drugs, knowledge of: and audiovisual intoxication, 201 (*see also* media addiction; surrealist intoxication); and demonic possession, 221–223 (*see also* addiction and demonic possession); as enfeebled phantom, 27; as enigma, 28; —, and enigma of woman in Freud, 209; history of, and literary inscription, 27; in literary modernity, 27; and modern legislation, 23; and nourishment of the nervous system, 228n36 (*see also* coca); and other health, 217; as phantasm, 28; as phantom knowledge, 28 (*see also* phantom); poststructuralist subject of, 210; subject without a substance, 210; subject without truth, 217; and use of, 199–204

drugs, language of, 4. *See also* rhetoric of drugs; writing as drug; writing on drugs

drugs, mode of consumption, 202; and addict, 199; and capitalism, 201; and distribution, 201; and microeconomy of desire, 202; physiochemical character of, 201; and soft drugs, 202; and solitude, 201. *See also* drug assemblage; hard drugs; soft drugs

drugs, mode of production, 202; collective assemblages of desire, 202; and collective assemblages of enunciation, 202; and drug environments, 202; and hard drugs, myth of, 201, 202; production of modes of culture, 202; production of specific modes of expression, 202; solitary drugs of capitalism, 202. *See also* drug assemblage; hard drugs; shamanism

drugs, in the modern sense: and feeding, model of, 24; and irresponsibility, 24; and parasitism, logic of, 25; and *pharmakon*, 24; to be "consumed," 24. *See*

also drugs as nutriment; feeding, model of; narcotic modernity

drugs, mystification of, 201; and art of the insane, 202; conveyed by addicts, 200; mythology of, 200; and rock groups, 201; and scientific methodology, 200; and theatricalization, 201. *See also* hard drugs

drugs, as nutriment, 1; and emission, 33; and expression, 33; and feeding as model of addiction, 24; and foreign body, 29; and incorporation, 29; and ingestion, 29; and inhalation, 29; and injection, 29; and inspiration, 29; and introjection, 33; and oral consumption, 33; and the other, 33 (*see also* the other); and parasitism, logic of, 24; and productive receptivity, 29; and reappropriation, 29; and spit, 33; supplement, unclassifiable, 33; and orifices, new, invention of, 33. *See also* coca; corporeal unconscious; drug consumption; feeding; healing community

drugs, phenomenon of: beyond specializations, 199; and criminalization, 199; and medicalization, 199; and proselytizing, 199; and psychiatrization, 199; and psychologization, 199; and socialization, 199

drugs, politics of. *See* politics of drugs

drugs, problem of, 35; and artificial insemination, 35; and Eastern bloc nations, 39; and echoes of the black hole, 200; collapse of old modes of enigma of, 28; impossibility of any theorem, 28; impossibility of isolating, 35; and interminable questioning, 28; and international borders, 39; and modern technology, 35; and socioethico-political problems, 35; subjective territorialization, 200

drugs, prohibition of: and addiction as experience without truth, 25–26 (*see also* experience of fiction); and citizen as legal subject, integrity of, 21; and culture, concept of, 21–22; and culture, survival of, 21; as fundamental, 21; and productivity, evaluation of, 26; and subject, mastery of, 21; as supplementary, 21

drugs, question of, 201; and AIDS, 35; and birth, 35; and the concept, 35; and death, 35; and literature, 35; and memory, 35; and reason, 35; and reterritorialization, 201; and truth, 25